Photographer's Guide to the Canon PowerShot S110

Photographer's Guide to the Canon PowerShot S110

Getting the Most from Canon's Pocketable Digital Camera

Alexander S. White

White Knight Press
Henrico, Virginia

Published by
White Knight Press
9704 Old Club Trace
Henrico, Virginia 23238
www.whiteknightpress.com
contact@whiteknightpress.com

ISBN: 978-1-937986-16-2 (paperback)
        978-1-937986-17-9 (e-book)

Printed in the United States of America

This book is dedicated to my wife, Clenise.

Contents

9

Introduction

This book is a guide for users of the Canon PowerShot S110 compact digital camera, which is one of the most capable "point-and-shoot" digital cameras on the market today. If you are reading this book, chances are you are already convinced that the PowerShot S110 is one of the best choices available today in the realm of small digital cameras. But I'll still mention some of the features that make it an outstanding choice in my opinion.

For me, the one feature of the S110 that stands out above others is its truly small size. This camera, unlike virtually any other current model with such advanced features, is not just portable but "pocketable." It will fit readily into a jacket, trousers pocket, or purse, and can be held unobtrusively in one hand when you don't want to call attention to your camera. And, in order to gain this degree of portability, the camera doesn't give up much in the way of capability. You can set the S110 to its AUTO shooting mode and get great results most of the time with no further settings. However, the camera also offers full manual control of focus and exposure, continuous shooting, focus and exposure bracketing, excellent low-light performance, and numerous special features, including a variety of ways to manipulate colors, and a built-in HDR (High Dynamic Range) shooting option. Like other cameras in this class, the S110 provides HD (high-definition) video shooting. The camera also has a built-in capability to transfer images over a wireless Wi-Fi network, and it has a very convenient touch screen that lets you control focus, take pictures, and make various settings with the touch of a finger.

The S110 is not the perfect camera, of course; no camera can serve as the ideal tool for all situations. One drawback often cited is that the camera lacks an optical viewfinder and has no system for attaching one. A related issue is that the S110 has no accessory shoe, which could be used to attach items such as a viewfinder or an external flash unit. (There are a couple of Canon flash units that can be used with the S110—the HF-DC1 and HF-DC2 High-Power Flash, which are discussed in Appendix A.) Some users are unhappy with the camera's tendency to run down the battery rather quickly. All in all, though, the S110's virtues far outweigh its negatives.

This introduction to the camera's features does not cover every detail, but it serves to illustrate that this camera has an impressive set of capabilities that should be attractive to serious photographers—those who want a camera that gives them numerous options for creative control of their images and that can be carried around at all times, so they will have a substantial photographic apparatus with them when a good picture-taking opportunity pops up.

My goal with this book is to provide a thorough and useful guide to the camera's features, explaining how they work and when you might want to use them. The book is aimed largely at beginning and intermediate photographers who are not satisfied with the technical documentation that comes with the camera and who need a more user-friendly explanation of the camera's many controls and menus. For those who are seeking more advanced information, I provide some discussion of topics that go beyond the basics, and I include in the appendices information that should help you uncover additional resources.

If you have upgraded from the PowerShot S100 to the S110 and have read my guide to the S100, you will notice that a good deal of the same information appears in both books.

That situation was inevitable because of the similarities between the two cameras. However, I examined every feature of the new camera carefully to make sure I explained it accurately, and I took all new photographs with the S110, even when photographs taken with the S100 would have looked virtually identical.

One note on the scope of this guide: I live in the United States, and I bought my camera in the U.S. market. I am not familiar with the variations for cameras sold in Europe or elsewhere, such as different batteries or chargers. The photographic functions are not different, though, so this guide should be useful to photographers in all locations, apart from that narrow range of issues. I have stated measurements of distance and weight in both the Imperial and metric systems, for the benefit of readers in various countries around the world.

If you find any problems in this book, including typographical errors or information that appears to be confusing or incorrect, please let me know through the contact form at whiteknightpress.com or by e-mail to contact@whiteknightpress.com. Also, if the images in one of the electronic versions of the book do not look good on a particular device, such as an iPad or Kindle, let me know that as well so I can take steps to remedy the situation. Feedback from readers is the best source of information for improving books such as this one. If you have general comments or feedback to provide, you also may want to post a review of the book at Amazon.com or one of the other sites that sells the book.

Finally, here is a note about the discussions of how to make settings with the PowerShot 110. Throughout this book I describe various features, with details about which button to push or dial to turn to carry out a particular procedure. Because the S110 has a strong touch-screen capability, in many cases you can touch the screen to accomplish the same result that you can by pressing a button or turning a dial. As I discuss features, I often point out the possibility of using the touch screen to accomplish these results. However, I do not make that statement every time it would apply; it seemed to me that to do so would lengthen the discussions and risk making them tedious and unwieldy. So, if I do not always mention that you can use the touch screen to carry out an action, please do not consider that omission to be a mistake. It is usually not a bad idea to try to use the touch screen to see if it will do what you are trying to do with the menus and other screens, even if I have not specifically stated that the touch screen can be used for that operation.

Chapter 1: Preliminary Setup

Setting Up the Camera

When you receive your new PowerShot S110, the box should contain the camera itself, battery, battery terminal cover, battery charger, wrist strap, USB cable, software and user's manual on a CD, and the brief "Getting Started" instruction pamphlet. There may also be a warranty card and registration card.

You might want to attach the wrist strap as soon as possible, because it can help you keep a tight grip on the camera. The strap can be attached to the mounting bar on either the left side or the right side of the camera. I will admit that I have never attached the strap myself, though, because this camera is so small that I find I can hold it firmly in my hand without much risk of dropping it, even without a strap.

Charging and Inserting the Battery

The Canon battery for the PowerShot S110 is the NB-5L. This battery has to be charged in an external charger; you can't charge it while it's in the camera, even if you connect the camera to the optional AC adapter. So it's a very good idea to have at least one extra battery if you're going to be doing a large amount of shooting with the camera, especially if you plan to use the battery-draining features such as continuous autofocus, Movie Digest mode, or transferring images over a Wi-Fi network. I'll talk about batteries and other accessories in Appendix A.

For now, let's get the battery charged. You can only insert the battery into the charger one way; look for the set of three goldish-colored metal contact strips on the battery, then look for the corresponding set of three contacts inside the battery compartment, and insert the battery so the two sets of contacts will meet up, as shown in Figure 1-1.

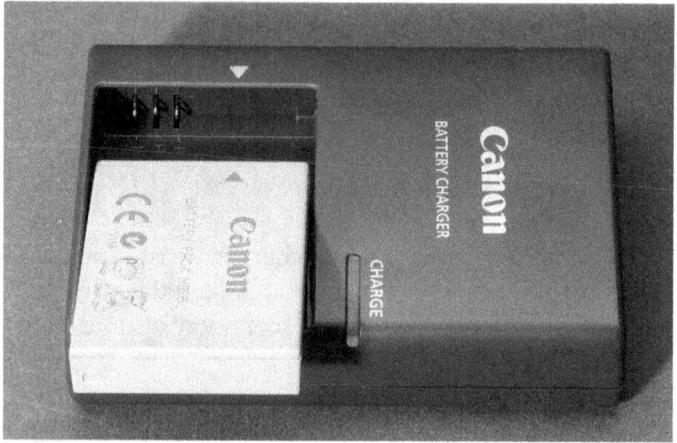

Fig. 1-1: Battery Being Inserted into Charger

With the battery inserted, plug the charger into any standard AC outlet or surge protector. The orange light comes on to indicate that the battery is charging. When the green light comes on, after about two hours, the battery is fully charged and ready to use.

Now that you have a charged battery, hold the camera upside down so the writing on the bottom is right side up. Press down on the raised area with eight dots at the far right of the camera's bottom, and slide the battery compartment door to the right until it pops open. To insert the battery, look for the sets of three metal contacts on the battery and inside the battery compartment, and guide the battery accordingly, as shown in Figure 1-2. You may need to use the right side of the battery to nudge the brown latching mechanism inside the battery compartment to the right, to allow the battery to slide in. Slide it all the way in until the brown latch catches above the battery and locks it in place, as shown in Figure 1-3.

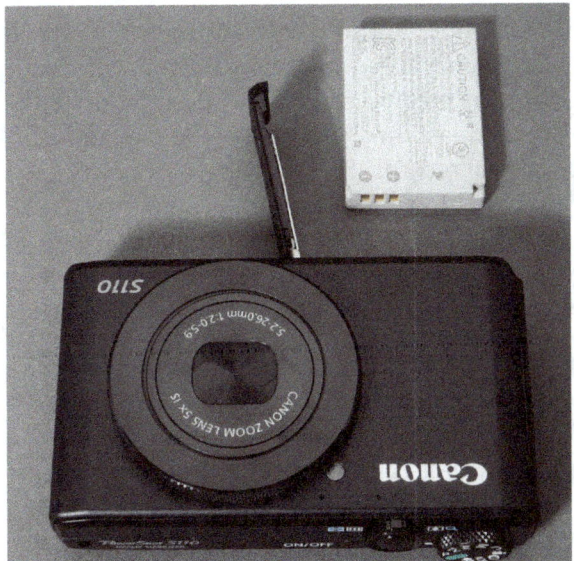

Fig. 1-2: Battery Ready to Go Into Camera

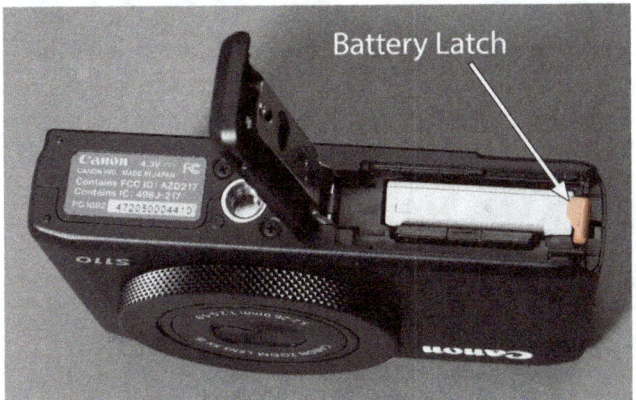

Fig. 1-3: Battery Secured by Latch

Then close the battery compartment door, slide the door back to the left until it catches, and you're done. (Or you can leave the door open if you're going to insert a memory card, as discussed next.)

Inserting the Memory Card

The PowerShot S110 does not ship with any memory card. If you turn the camera on with no card inserted, you will see the error message "No memory card," and if you then press the shutter button to take a picture, you will see the even more urgent warning "Cannot record!" So, the chances are pretty good that you will notice that your pictures are not being saved. Some other camera models have a small amount of built-in memory so you can take a few pictures even without a card, but the PowerShot S110 does not have any such safety net.

To avoid the frustration of having a great camera that can't save any images, you need to insert a memory card. The PowerShot S110 uses SD cards, which are quite small—about the size of a large postage stamp. These cards come in several varieties. The standard card, called simply SD, comes in capacities from 8 megabytes (MB) to 2 gigabytes (GB). A higher-capacity card, SDHC, comes in sizes from 4 GB to 32 GB. The newest, and highest-capacity card, SDXC (for extended capacity) comes in sizes of 48 GB, 64 GB, 128 GB, and 256 GB as of this writing; an SDXC card can have a capacity up to 2 terabytes (TB), theoretically, and SDXC cards generally have faster transfer speeds than the smaller-capacity cards. Figure 1-4 shows samples of SD cards of several different capacities.

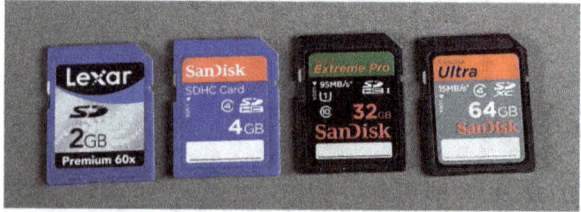

Fig. 1-4: Cards: SD 2GB, SDHC 4GB, SDHC 32GB, SDXC 64 GB

Note that the S110 cannot use another type of similar-sized memory card called a MultiMediaCard (MMC), even though an earlier model, the S95, could use them. Those cards are very similar in shape and appearance to SD cards, so be sure you are not trying to use one in your S110.

The type and size of memory card you use depends on your needs and intentions. If you're planning to record a good deal of high-definition (HD) video or large numbers of Raw photos, you should get a large-capacity card, but don't get carried away—the largest cards have such huge capacities that you may be wasting money purchasing them.

There are several variables to take into account in computing how many images or videos you can store on a particular size of card, such as which aspect ratio you're using (16:9, 3:2, 4:3, 1:1, or 4:5), picture size, and quality. Here are a few examples of what can be stored on a given card. If you're using a 16 GB SDHC card and the fairly standard 4:3 aspect ratio, you can store about 890 Raw images (the highest quality), 2747 high-quality JPEG images (Large size and Superfine quality), or more than 80,000 of the smallest size and lowest-quality images.

If you're interested in video, here are some guidelines. You can fit about 60 minutes of the highest-quality high-definition (HD) video on a 16 GB card. That same card will hold about 85 minutes of slightly lower-quality HD video or about 3 hours of video at the standard-definition setting of 640 X 480 pixels, also known as VGA quality. Note, though, that the camera is limited to recording just under 30 minutes of HD video in one sequence, or about one hour of VGA video.

One other consideration is the speed of the card, which is important for getting good results when recording still images and video with this camera. You should try to find a card that writes data at a rate of 6 MB/second or faster to record HD video. If you go by the class designation, a Class 4 card should be sufficient for shooting stills, and a Class 6 card should suffice for recording video. A fast card also will help when you set the camera for continuous shooting of still images.

Finally, if you have an older computer with a built-in card reader, or just an older external card reader, there is a chance it will not read the newer SDHC cards. In that case, you would have to either get a new reader that is compatible with SDHC cards, or transfer images from the camera to your computer using the USB cable.

Using the newest variety of card, SDXC, also can be somewhat problematic because of compatibility issues with cameras, computers, and card readers, but at this writing in the spring of 2013 those issues appear to be fading away. For example, I installed a Lexar Professional 128 GB SDXC card in my PowerShot S110 and the camera immediately recognized it and recorded images to it with no problems. When I tried a SanDisk Ultra 64 GB SDXC card (shown in Figure 1-4), it also worked as expected.

If you will have access to a wireless (Wi-Fi) network where you use your camera, you may want to consider getting an Eye-Fi card. This special type of storage device, two versions of which are shown in Figure 1-5, looks very much like an ordinary SDHC card, but it includes a tiny transmitter that lets it connect to a wireless network and send your images to your computer over that network as soon as the images have been recorded by the camera.

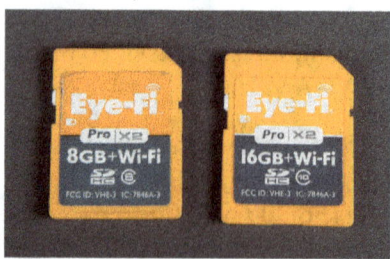

Fig. 1-5: 8 GB and 16 GB Eye-Fi Cards

I have tested the 8 GB and 16 GB Eye-Fi cards, the Pro X2 models shown here, with the S110, and they both worked well for me after some time spent configuring the cards with my wireless network. Within a few seconds after I snap a picture with either of these cards installed in the camera, a little thumbnail image appears on my computer's screen showing

22

the progress of the upload. When all images are uploaded, they are available in the Pictures/Eye-Fi folder on my computer. You also can get an app for the iPhone or Android phones that will let you upload images directly from the camera to the phone when an Eye-Fi card is used.

As of this writing, there are several alternatives to the Eye-Fi card, including the ezShare Wi-Fi card, the Transcend Information card, and the Toshiba FlashAir card, all of which advertise similar ability to transfer images wirelessly to your computer or other device. I have not tried any of them, but they appear to be worth looking into. In addition, Eye-Fi itself has released a new type of card called the Mobi that supposedly provides a simple way to transfer images directly from the card to a smartphone via the card's own Wi-Fi network. That card was released too late for me to test it for this book.

However, with the PowerShot S110, there is yet another approach you can take. You do not need to use an Eye-Fi card or similar device to transfer images wirelessly, because the camera has a built-in Wi-Fi capability that lets the S110 connect over a wireless network to a computer, smartphone, or wireless printer, or to a Canon internet portal to share and upload images. I will discuss that feature in Chapter 9.

In summary, you have quite a few options for choosing a memory card. Personally, I like to use a high-speed 16 GB SDHC card, just to have extra capacity and speed in case they are needed.

Once you have selected your card, open the same little door on the bottom of the camera that covers the battery compartment, and slide the card in until it catches, with its label facing the battery, as shown in Figure 1-6. To remove the card, push down on its edge until it releases and springs up so you can grab it. Once the card has been pushed down until it catches, close the compartment door by pushing it to the left.

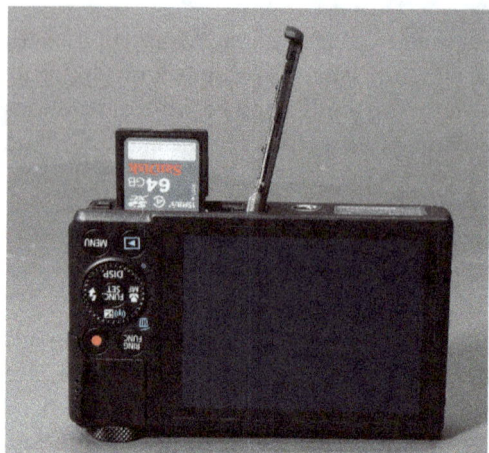

Fig. 1-6: Memory Card Being Inserted into Camera

Although the card may work fine when first inserted in the camera, it's always a good idea to format a card when first using it in a camera, so it will definitely be set up with the correct file structure and will have any bad areas blocked off from use. To do this, turn on the camera by pressing the power button, press the Menu button at the bottom right of the camera's back, then press the right direction button (right edge of the control dial on the camera's back) to highlight the tab at the top of the screen with the wrench and mallet icon. That icon indicates the Setup menu, as shown in Figure 1-7.

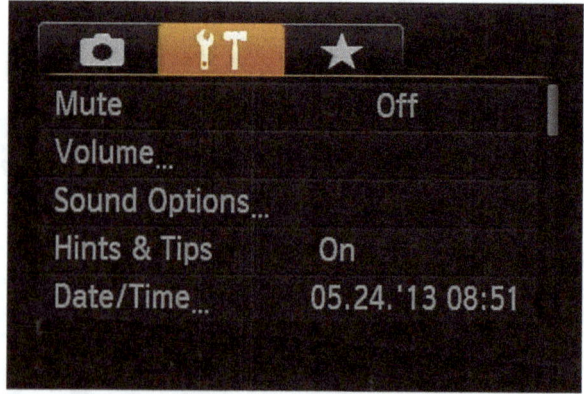

Fig. 1-7: Wrench and Mallet Icon for Setup Menu Highlighted

24

Then use the down direction button or the control dial to scroll down through the Setup menu until you reach the Format command, shown in Figure 1-8.

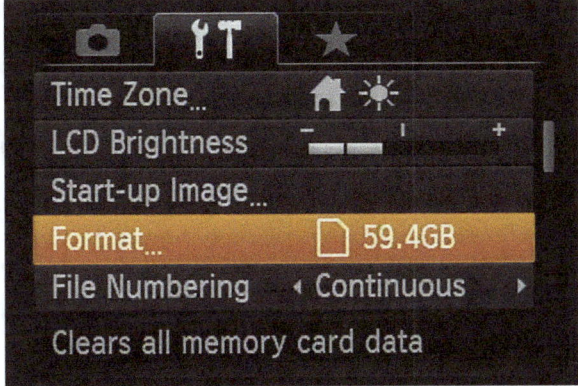

Fig. 1-8: *Format Command on Setup Menu*

Press the Func./Set button (in the center of the control dial) when that command is highlighted, then, on the next screen, shown in Figure 1-9, highlight OK, and press the Func./Set button again to carry out the command.

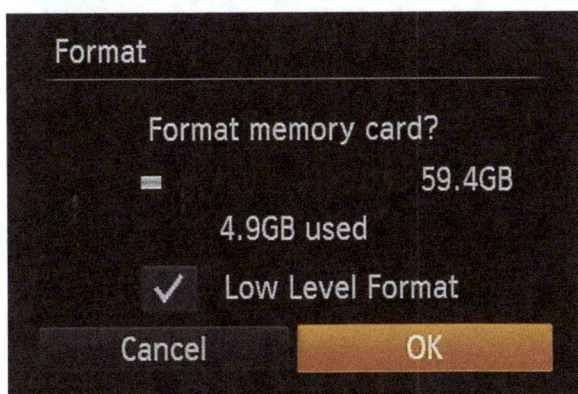

Fig. 1-9: *Confirmation Screen for Format Command*

As I noted in the Introduction, you also can use the touch screen to carry out this and many other operations. After you press the menu button, scroll the screen with your finger, then touch the desired command with a finger to select it.

One note for when you're shooting pictures with the camera: When it's recording to an SD card, the little green light on the back of the camera, just above the Playback button, blinks. When that indicator is blinking, it's important not to turn off the camera or otherwise interrupt its functioning, such as by taking out the battery or disconnecting an AC power adapter. You need to let the card complete its recording process.

Setting the Language, Date, and Time

The S110 records date and time information (sometimes known as "metadata," meaning data beyond the information in the picture itself) invisibly with each image and displays it later if you want. Someday you may be very glad to have the date (and even the time of day) correctly recorded with your archives of digital images. Also, if you are going to use a smartphone to send GPS location information to your images, as discussed in Chapter 9, it's important to have the date and time set accurately in the camera.

To get these basic items set correctly, go to the Setup menu, as discussed above, but this time move the highlight down to the Date/Time line on the menu, shown in Figure 1-10, and press the Func./Set button to activate the date and time settings.

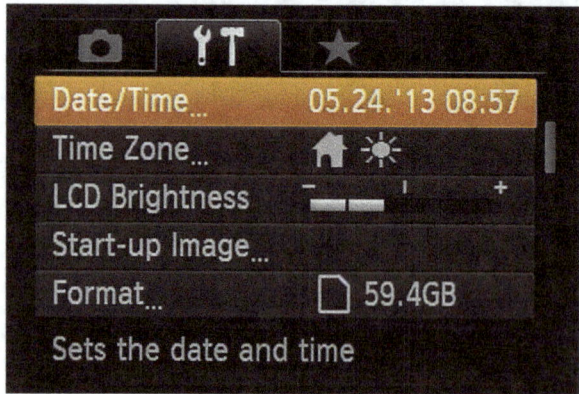

Fig. 1-10: Date/Time Option on Setup Menu

Move left and right through the date, year, and time settings, as shown in Figure 1-11, and change the settings with up and down movements of the cursor.

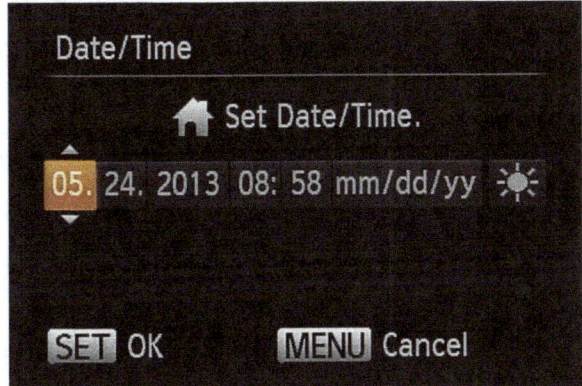

Fig. 1-11: Date/Time Settings Screen

When everything is set correctly, press the center Func./Set button to confirm.

If you need to change the language that the camera uses for the menus and other messages, navigate on the Setup menu to the next-to-bottom line, and press the Func./Set button to select the Language menu item, shown in Figure 1-12.

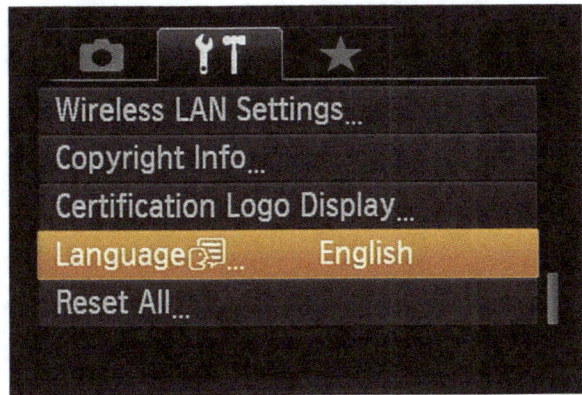

Fig. 1-12: Language Option on Setup Menu

Then navigate with the direction buttons to the language of your choice, and press the Func./Set button to select it. If you want to bypass the menu, here is a shortcut: You can press the Playback button to put the camera into playback mode, then press the Menu button while holding down the Func./Set button, to take you directly to the Language screen.

Chapter 2: Basic Operations

Taking Pictures

Now that the PowerShot S110 has the correct time and date set and has a fully charged battery inserted along with a memory card, I'll discuss some scenarios for basic picture-taking. For now, I won't get into discussions of what the various options are and why you might choose one over another. I'll just describe a reasonable set of steps that will get you and your camera into action and will record a clear image or video on your memory card.

Introduction to Main Controls

Before I discuss some of the basic options for setting up the camera using the menu system and controls, it may be helpful to introduce the main controls, so you'll have a better idea of which button or dial is which. I won't discuss all of the controls here; they will all be covered in some detail in Chapter 5. For now, here is a series of images that show the major controls. As I come to each item for the first time in the text, I will describe its position and function; you may want to refer back to these images for a reminder about each control.

Top of Camera

On top of the camera are some of the more important controls and dials, shown in Figure 2-1. The mode dial is used to select one of the camera's numerous shooting modes. For basic shooting with the camera making most of the decisions, turn this dial so the green AUTO label is next to the white selection marker. The large, black shutter button is used to take pictures;

press it halfway down to lock focus and exposure, and press it all the way down to record the image.

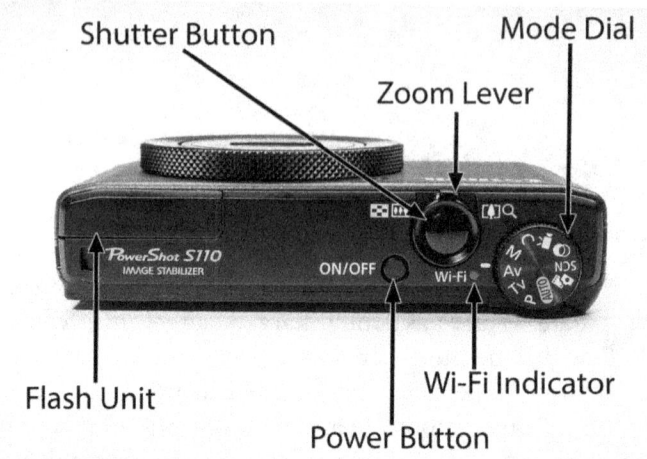

Fig. 2-1: Controls on Top of Camera

The zoom lever, surrounding the shutter button, is used to zoom the lens in for telephoto shots and out for wide-angle ones; it also is used to change the view of images in playback mode. The power button is used to turn the camera on and off. The Wi-Fi light is illuminated in blue when the camera is connected to a wireless network to transfer images.

Back of Camera

Figure 2-2 shows the major controls on the camera's back. The Display button selects various screens for viewing information about shooting settings when images are being recorded and about the images themselves when they are being played back. The red Movie button starts and stops the recording of a video sequence. The Ring Function button is used to set the function of the camera's control ring (the ring around the lens) and can be assigned other functions as well. The Playback button places the camera into playback mode so you can view your recorded images. The Menu button calls up the camera's system of menu screens with various settings for shooting and other values, such as control button functions, audio features, and others.

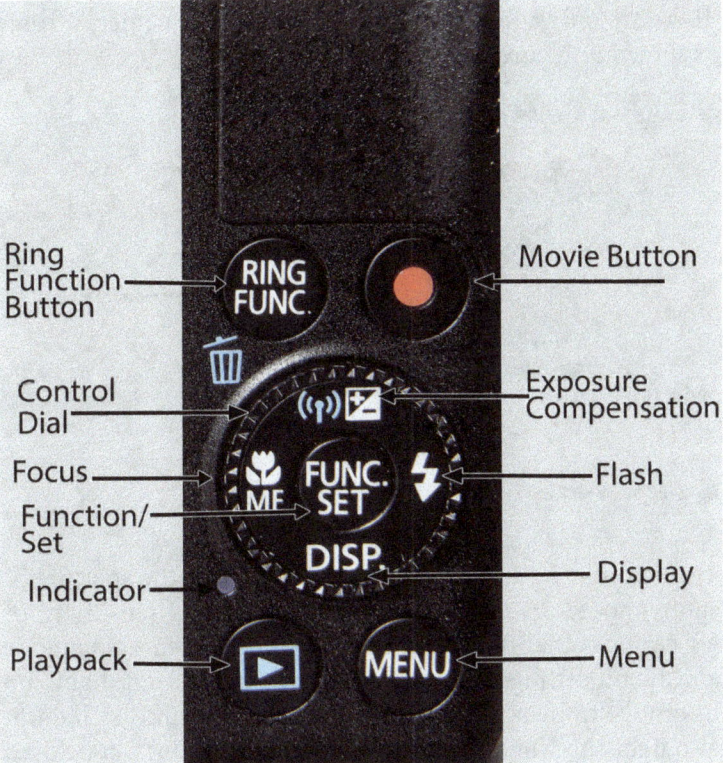

Fig. 2-2: Controls on Back of Camera

The control dial acts as a wheel for setting values such as exposure compensation and for navigating through menu screens. In addition, each of its four edges acts as a button when you press it in, for selecting items including flash mode, exposure compensation, focus mode, and the display screen. The Func./ Set button in the center of the dial is used to confirm selections and for some miscellaneous operations. The Indicator lamp lights up green to remind you that the camera is turned on when the LCD screen is dark and to show that the camera is busy recording or transferring images.

Front of Camera

There are only a few items to point out on the camera's front, as shown in Figure 2-3.

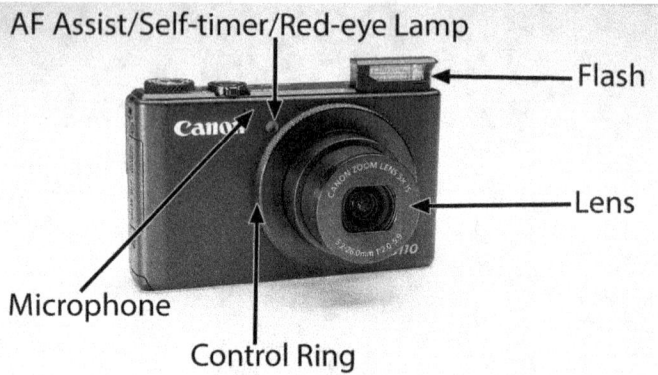

Fig. 2-3: Items on Front of Camera

The control ring around the lens is used to set the aperture or shutter speed, to zoom the lens, to set the ISO sensitivity, or for various other functions, depending on the shooting mode and menu settings. The AF Assist/Self-timer lamp lights up in orange to help the camera with autofocus in dim light; it also lights up when the self-timer operates and it can be used to help prevent "red-eye" in flash pictures. The microphone, marked by two tiny holes just above that lamp, receives sounds to be recorded along with videos. And, of course, the camera's zoom lens itself is located here; it has an actual focal length of 5.2mm to 26.0mm, but, because of the small size of the camera's sensor, the zoom range is usually described in terms of its "35mm-equivalent," meaning the focal length the lens would have to have in order to produce a similar angle of view on a traditional 35mm film camera. In those terms, the zoom range of the PowerShot S110's lens is reported as 24mm to 120mm.

Right Side of Camera

Inside the door on the right side of the camera are the ports for connecting to a computer, a printer, a standard TV set, or an HDTV, as seen in Figure 2-4.

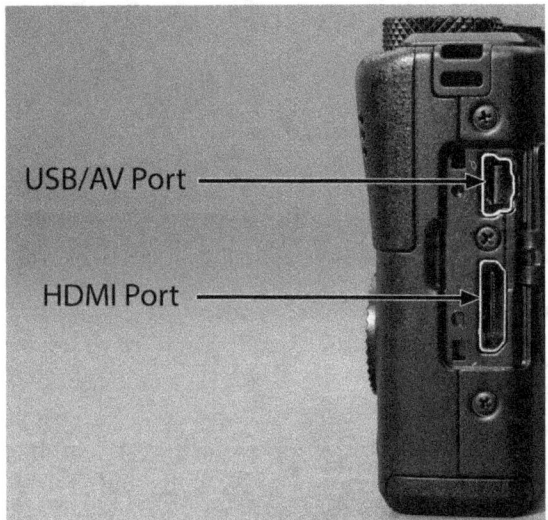

Fig. 2-4: Ports on Right Side of Camera

The upper port is where you connect the USB cable that comes with the camera, when you want to transfer images to a computer or printer. That port also is where you connect an optional audio-video cable for connecting the camera to a standard-definition TV set. The lower port is for an optional HDMI cable to connect the camera to an HDTV set for viewing your images and videos.

Bottom of Camera

On the bottom of the S110, shown in Figure 2-5, you will find the tripod socket for attaching the camera to a tripod, as well as the door that covers the battery/memory card compartment. The door contains a flexible flap that must be pulled up when you install the AC adapter in the camera, as discussed in Appendix A.

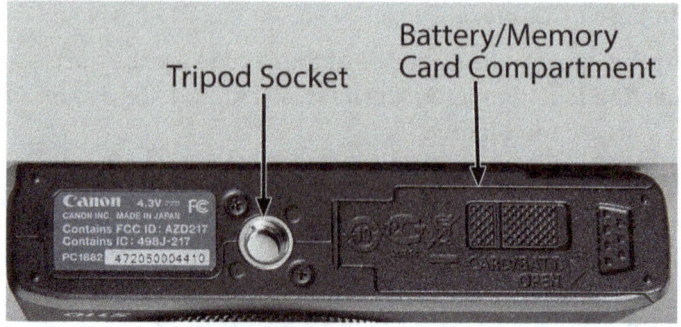

Fig. 2-5: Items on Bottom of Camera

Fully Automatic: AUTO Mode

Now let's talk about how to use these controls to start taking pictures and videos. Here's the procedure if you want to set the camera to its most automatic mode and let it make (almost) all of the decisions for you. This is a good procedure to use if you're in a hurry and need to take some quick shots without fiddling with settings, or if you're new at this and would rather let the camera take control of most functions without much input from you.

1. Find the mode dial on top of the camera at the right, and turn it so the word "AUTO" is next to the white indicator line, as shown in Figure 2-6.

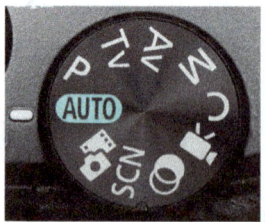

Fig. 2-6: AUTO Mode

2. Turn on the power by pressing the power button. The LCD screen will illuminate to show that the camera has turned on.

34

3. Press the Func./Set button in the center of the control dial on the back of the camera. This brings up a line of numbers at the bottom of the screen and a line of icons along the left side of the screen, as shown in Figure 2-7.

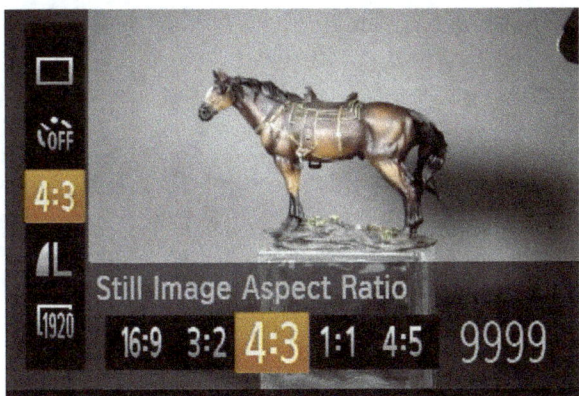

Fig. 2-7:   Function Menu in AUTO Mode

Press the lower edge of the control dial (the part marked by the DISP. label) enough times to move the orange highlight block to the next-to-bottom entry on the left side of the screen. This entry will be either L, M1, M2, or S. Highlight the L, to select Large for your image size.

4. If the menu has not disappeared, press the up direction button (marked by a symbol with plus and minus signs) to highlight the numbers above the L. These numbers will be either 16:9, 3:2, 4:3, 1:1, or 4:5. They represent the aspect ratio of the image—that is, the ratio of the width of the image to its height. For example, with 4:3, the image is 4 units wide for 3 units high. I recommend that you select 4:3 at this point.

5. Press the Func./Set button again to make the menu disappear, if it hasn't done so already.

6. Aim the camera toward the subject and look at the LCD screen to compose the picture. Locate the zoom lever on the ring that surrounds the shutter button on the top right of the

camera. Push that lever to the left, toward the icon showing a group of three trees, to get a wider-angle shot (including more of the scene in the picture), or to the right, toward the icon showing a single tree, to get a telephoto, zoomed-in shot.

7. If you're indoors or in an area with low light, be careful not to hold your finger on top of the flash at the top left of the camera. The camera may try to pop the flash up, but it can't if your finger is blocking it.

8. Once the picture looks good on the LCD screen, push the shutter button halfway down and hold it in that position. You should hear a little beep and see one or more green focus frames at some location on the LCD screen, indicating that the picture will be in focus, using the area inside those frames as the focus points. If you hear a beep but don't see any green frames, the camera was unable to focus; you can try to re-aim and see if the autofocus system can do better from a different distance or angle.

9. After you have made sure the focus was properly set in the previous step, push the shutter button all the way down to take the picture.

Basic Variations from Fully Automatic

At this point I won't go into a discussion of all of the various still-picture shooting modes, except to name them. Besides AUTO, which I just discussed, there are Program (P), Shutter Priority (Tv), Aperture Priority (Av), Manual (M), Scene (SCN), and Creative Filters (Icon of interlocking circles). There is also one custom mode (C), which you can set up yourself. I'll talk about all of the still-shooting modes in Chapter 3, and the Movie mode and Movie Digest mode in Chapter 8. For now, I'm going to discuss some of the main functions and features of the PowerShot S110 that you can adjust to suit whatever picture-taking situation you may be faced with. Not all of the settings can be adjusted in AUTO mode, so we'll set the camera down to a lower level of automation, to the Program mode. In that mode, you'll be able to control most of the camera's functions for taking still pictures.

I'm not going to repeat the basic steps for taking a picture, because those are quite simple. If you need a refresher on those steps, see the list in the above discussion of AUTO mode.

First, set the mode dial to P, for Program, as seen in Figure 2-8.

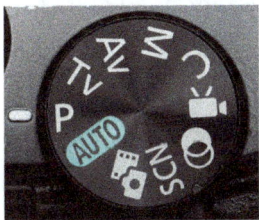

Fig. 2-8: Program Mode

You will immediately see some different items on the LCD screen, indicating that some of the settings that were present in AUTO mode are gone, and that some settings have newly become available, because you now have more control over matters such as image quality, ISO, exposure compensation, and others. Using the Program setting, the camera will determine the proper exposure, both the aperture (size of opening to let in light) and the shutter speed (how long the shutter is open to let in light). So in this mode you won't be making any decisions about those settings; those adjustments can be made in other modes, which I'll discuss later, in Chapter 3. That still leaves lots of decisions you can make, though, so let's talk about the various settings you can adjust in Program mode.

Focus

Now that the camera is not in AUTO mode, you have more control over focus. Your first choice is between manual focus and autofocus. In other words, you have the option of using the MF setting, for manual focus. You also have the ability to select which of several types of autofocus operation you want the camera to use, if you opt for autofocus instead.

37

Autofocus

I'll discuss autofocus modes in more detail in Chapter 4. Here we'll just make sure a standard autofocus mode is selected. First, press the left direction button on the control dial (marked by a flower icon and the letters MF). This action puts a small menu on the LCD screen with three options: the flower icon, for macro (closeup) autofocus; an icon showing mountains and a person, for normal autofocus; and the letters MF, for manual focus, as shown in Figure 2-9.

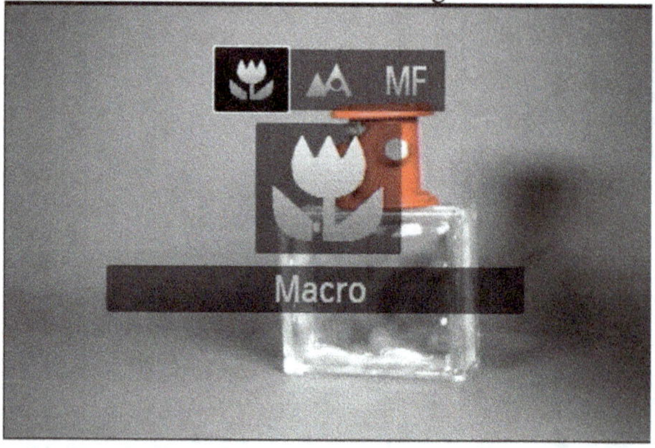

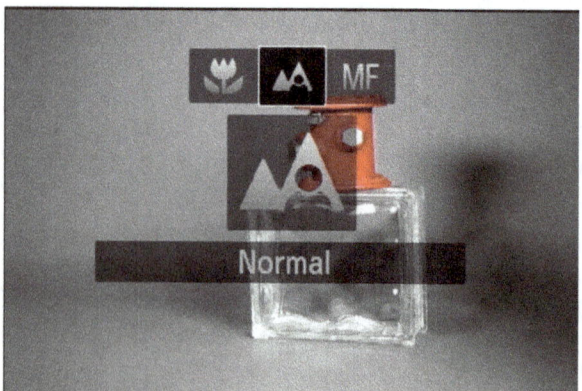

Fig. 2-9: Focus Mode Menu

For now, use the direction buttons to select the center icon, for normal autofocus, as shown in Figure 2-10.

Fig. 2-10: Normal Autofocus Mode Selected

(You have to be quick; the three choices disappear within a few seconds.) You can press the Func./Set button to confirm your choice, or just let it go and the choice will confirm itself.

There are some other focus-related options you can set, but for now let's just use one of them. Press the Menu button at the lower right of the camera's back to bring up the menu screen. Then press the down direction button, labeled DISP., to move the orange highlight bar to the AF Frame item on the menu. The setting for that menu item, either 1-point or Face AiAF, will appear in a block to the right, as shown in Figure 2-11.

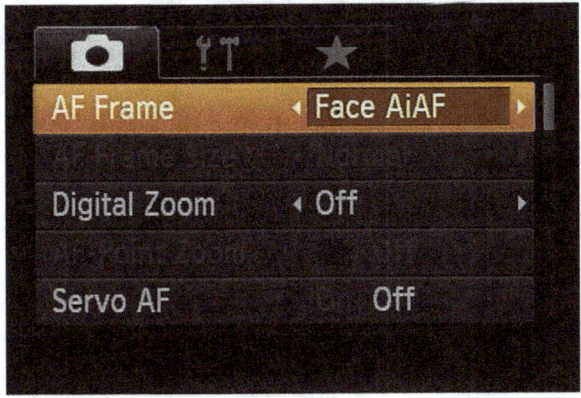

Fig. 2-11: AF Frame Menu Item

(The letters AiAF stand for artificial intelligence autofocus.)

Press the right or left direction button, if necessary, to bring the Face AiAF option into the selection block. With this option, the camera will not display any permanent focus frame on the display. However, if it detects one or more human faces, it will place a white frame around the face that appears to be the main subject, and up to 2 gray frames on other faces, as shown in Figure 2-12.

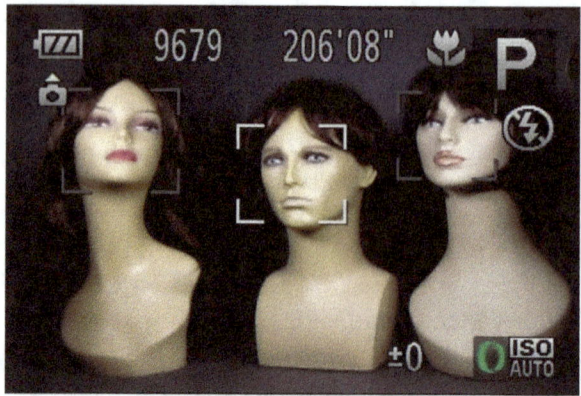

Fig. 2-12: Multiple Faces Detected with Face AiAF Setting

When you press the shutter button down halfway to evaluate focus and exposure, the camera will display up to nine green rectangular frames at various parts of the screen, as shown in Figure 2-13, indicating the areas that the camera's artificial intelligence believes to be the most important areas to focus on.

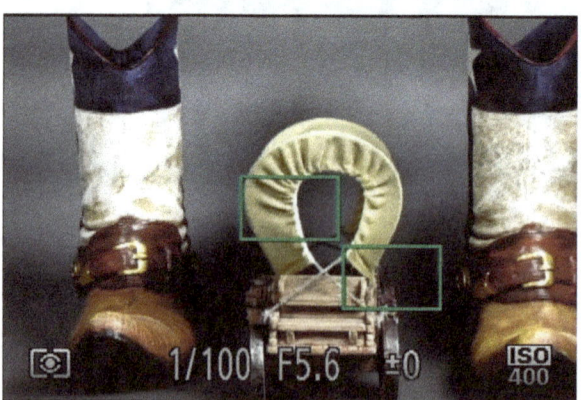

Fig. 2-13: Multiple Focus Points with Face AiAF Setting

If the camera detects human faces, it will concentrate on those. The Face AiAF option is discussed further in Chapter 4, in the discussion of Shooting menu options.

If you see a flashing orange icon of a camera with curved lines below it, as shown in Figure 2-14, the camera is warning you that the shutter speed is so slow that the picture may be blurred from camera shake.

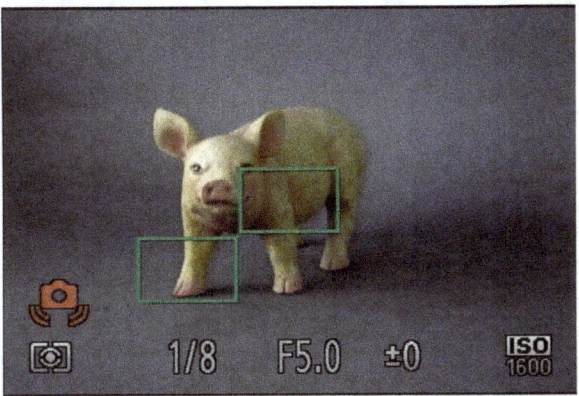

Fig. 2-14: Flashing Camera Icon in Lower Left Corner of Screen

If that happens, press the right direction button, marked by a lightning bolt, and then use the direction buttons to select the icon of an A next to a lightning bolt, which turns on Auto Flash mode and pops up the flash unit. If everything looks okay to you, press the shutter button all the way down to take the picture.

Suppose you want to take a picture in which your main subject is not located where your focus frame is. Maybe your shot is set up so that a person is standing off to the right of center, and there is some attractive scenery to the left of the scene.

Here is one way to set the focus in this situation. Aim the camera so the most important subject—in this example, the person at the right—is centered in the frame. Then press the shutter button halfway down until the camera focuses and beeps. A green focus frame should appear over the person. Keep the button pressed halfway to lock in the focus (and exposure) while you move the camera back to create your desired composition, with the person off to the right. Then take the picture, and the area you originally focused on will be in focus.

41

Another way to focus on an off-center subject is to use the 1-point selection for the AF Frame menu option. With that setting, you can move the focus frame around the screen and change its size. That process is discussed in Chapter 4.

Manual Focus

There are other autofocus options, but I won't discuss those now. For now, I will talk about manual focus, the other major option for focusing. Why would you want to use manual focus when the camera will focus for you automatically? Many photographers like the amount of control that comes from being able to set the focus exactly how they want it. And, in some cases, such as focusing in dark areas or areas behind glass, taking extreme closeups, or where there are objects at various distances from the camera, it can be useful for you to be able to control exactly where the point of sharpest focus lies.

To take advantage of this capability, go back to the left direction button, with the letters MF, and press it; then press the same button quickly twice again to navigate over to the rightmost option and select the MF icon on the screen, as shown in Figure 2-15.

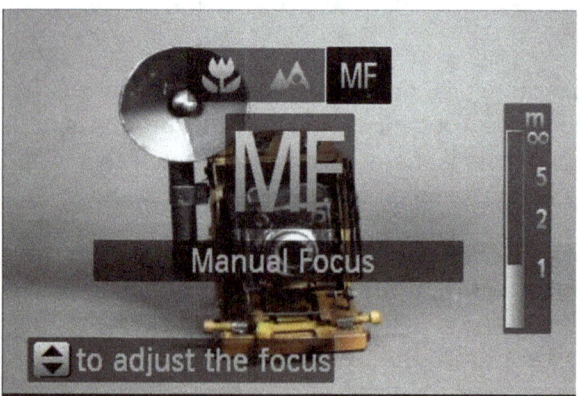

Fig. 2-15: Manual Focus Selected

This action places the camera in manual focus mode. At this point, all you need to do is adjust the focus by turning the control dial, the ridged wheel on the back of the camera, or by pressing the up and down direction buttons. As you do so, you will see a white bar go up and down inside a scale on the right side of the LCD screen, indicating the approximate focusing distance, as shown in Figure 2-16.

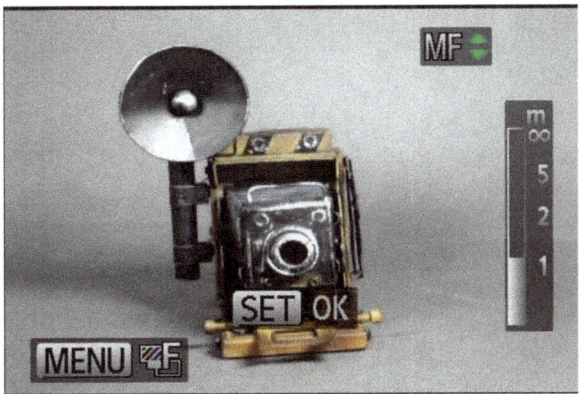

Fig. 2-16: Manual Focus Scale Ready to Adjust

You also may see an enlarged area in the center of the screen, depending on the menu options that are in effect.

Continue moving the control dial back and forth or pressing the up and down buttons until you achieve the sharpest possible focus for whatever part of the picture you want to focus on.

If you would like to take advantage of the camera's autofocus capability but then fine-tune the focus manually, here is a different approach: Start out in normal autofocus mode, and press the shutter button down halfway to let the camera focus automatically. Then, while the shutter button is still halfway down, press the MF (left) button. This action places the camera into manual focus mode, with a starting focus point already set by the autofocus mechanism. You can then adjust the focus using the control dial or the up and down buttons, as needed. Press the Func./Set button to finish the focusing process and return to the shooting screen.

Exposure

Next, I'll discuss some ways to control exposure, rather than letting the camera make all the decisions. The S110's Auto mode is very good at choosing the right exposure, and so is the Program mode. But there are going to be some situations in which you want to override the camera's automation.

Exposure Compensation

First, let's take a look at the procedure for adjusting exposure to account for an unusual, or non-optimal, lighting situation. For example, consider Figure 2-17, in which I photographed a decorative cowboy boot against a white background.

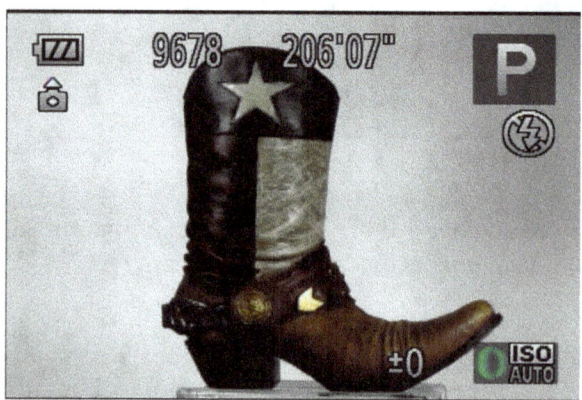

Fig. 2-17: *Image Needing Exposure Compensation Adjustment*

The boot was considerably darker than the bright background. In this image, the camera exposed for the larger white area, leaving the boot underexposed.

One solution for this situation is to use the S110's exposure compensation control. Look closely at the top direction button on the control dial. That button is labeled with a little plus and minus sign, with the plus on a black background and the minus on white, as shown in Figure 2-18. This control activates the exposure compensation system, which will override the automatic exposure as much as you tell it to, within limits.

Fig. 2-18: Exposure Compensation Button

(You don't always need to use this button when you want to activate exposure compensation, but it's good to know about it for the times when you do need it, as I'll explain in a minute.)

Go ahead and set up your camera in Program mode and aim at your subject. Now press that top button, and you will see a scale show up on the screen, reading from -3 to +3 EV in increments of one-third EV, as shown in Figure 2-19.

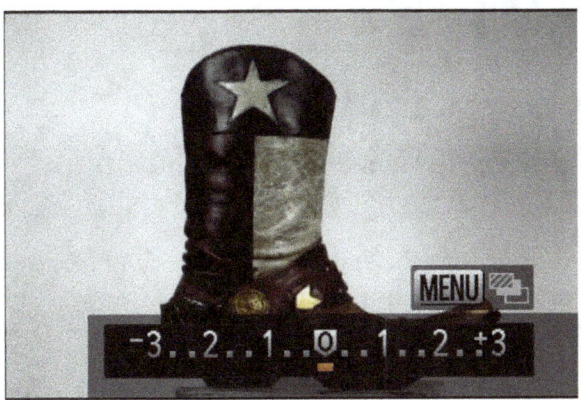

Fig. 2-19: Exposure Compensation Scale on Screen

The EV stands for Exposure Value, a standard measure of brightness. Once this scale has appeared, you turn the control dial clockwise or counter-clockwise or press the right and left direction buttons to move the values higher or lower, as indicated by an orange dot that moves beneath the value that is being set. (You also can use the touch screen for this process.)

If you move the orange dot all the way left to -3, the picture will be considerably darker than the automatic exposure would produce. If you move it in the other direction to +3, the picture will be noticeably brighter. The camera's screen will brighten or darken to show you how the exposure is changing, before you take the picture.

With exposure compensation adjusted upward by 1 1/3 EV, as seen in Figure 2-20, the boot becomes brighter and is no longer underexposed.

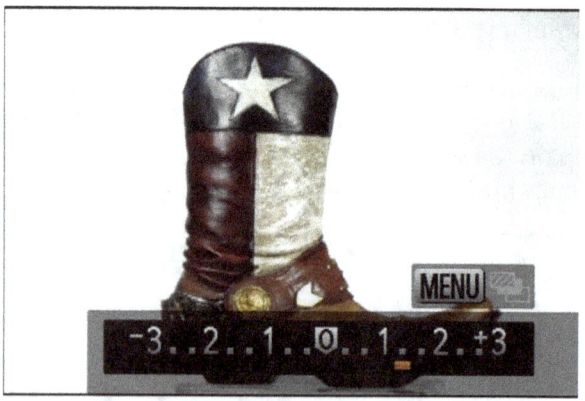

Fig. 2-20: Exposure Compensation Adjustment Made

This example shows how the exposure compensation control works to adjust the brightness of your images when you are faced with an unusual or uneven lighting situation.

When you're using exposure compensation, don't settle for just one adjustment. If you have the time and want to really fine-tune your exposure, try this technique: Shoot, then check the result on the LCD; if it's too bright or too dark, adjust the exposure compensation again; repeat shooting and adjusting until the exposure looks just right.

Once you've taken the picture, you should reset the EV compensation back to zero, in the middle of the scale, so you don't unintentionally affect the pictures you take later. You need to be careful about this, because the camera will maintain any EV value you set, even when it's turned off and then on again.

Now I will explain what I meant earlier when I said you don't always need to press the exposure compensation button to activate exposure compensation. You can set the control ring (the large ring around the lens) to control that value, using the Ring Function button, as discussed in Chapter 5. If you do so, you can just turn the ring; you don't have to press the exposure compensation button first.

Finally, when you are adjusting exposure compensation, if you press the Menu button, the camera switches into Auto Exposure Bracketing mode, and presents you with the screen for setting the bracketing interval. (Bracketing is discussed in Chapter 4.)

Flash

In Chapters 3 and 4, I'll discuss other topics dealing with exposure, such as Manual exposure mode, Aperture Priority and Shutter Priority modes, i-Contrast, and others. For now I'm going to discuss the basics of using the PowerShot S110's built-in flash unit, because that is something you may need to do on a regular basis. In Chapter 9 I'll discuss other options for using the flash, such as controlling its output and preventing "red-eye," and in Appendix A, I'll discuss using external flash units.

The built-in flash on the S110 is not especially powerful, but it can provide enough illumination to let you take pictures in dark places and to brighten up areas that would otherwise be lost in shadows, even outdoors on a sunny day. The flash unit will pop up on its own in certain situations, or you can cause it to pop up yourself. The key to controlling the behavior of the flash is the right direction button at the right edge of the control dial on the back of the camera; as shown in Figure 2-21, it has a lightning bolt icon on it to announce its identity as the Flash button.

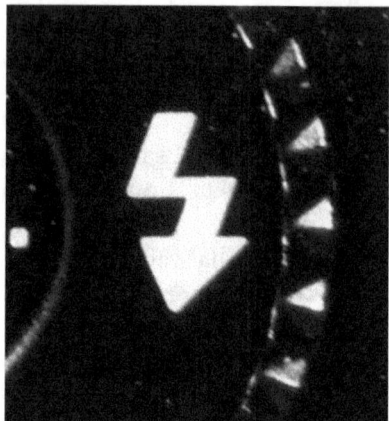

Fig. 2-21: Flash Button

In any shooting mode for still pictures, press this button once to summon the flash mode icons, and then press it again one or more times to select the icon you want.

Depending on the shooting mode the camera is in, the options may be Auto Flash, Forced Flash, Slow Synchro, and Flash Off. When the camera is set for certain types of shooting, such as HDR (in the Creative Filters shooting mode), the Fireworks and High-Speed Burst HQ settings in Scene mode, or Movie mode, the flash is forced off and cannot be turned on.

Let's explore a common scenario to see how the flash works. Make sure the camera is turned on and the mode dial on top of the camera is set to the AUTO shooting mode.

Go ahead and press the Flash button. As illustrated in Figure 2-22, you will see just two options on the pop-up menu—a lightning bolt with an A, for Auto flash, and a lightning bolt with the universal "no" sign crossing it out, for flash forced off. You can press the Flash button again to select either of these choices.

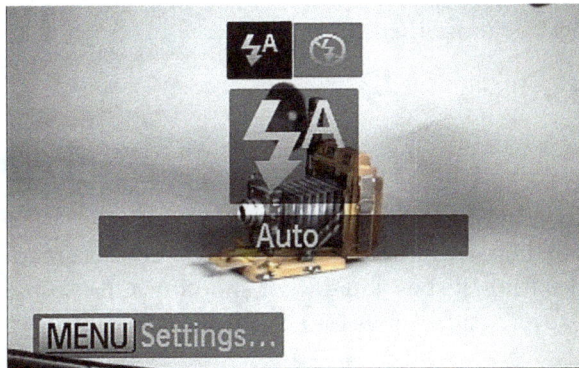

Fig. 2-22: Flash Mode Menu in AUTO Mode

Next, try setting the mode dial to P, for Program mode, and then press the Flash button to select a flash mode. You will find that more options are now available for the flash mode. You will be able to select from Auto Flash, Forced Flash, Slow Synchro, and Flash Off, as seen in Figure 2-23.

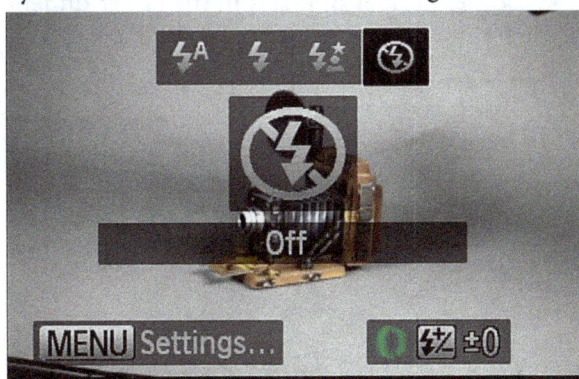

Fig. 2-23: Flash Mode Menu in Program Mode

You can move through this list in various ways—keep pressing the Flash button, use both the left and right buttons, or turn the control dial to move from option to option. (You also can use the touch screen and just touch the icon you want to select.) I find that the easiest method is just to press the Flash button repeatedly until the icon you want is highlighted. Later on, in Chapters 4 and 9, I'll talk more about the various flash options, such as Slow Synchro, and how they work. For now, you know how to choose them.

Movie Recording

Let's take a look at recording a short video sequence with the PowerShot S110. In Chapter 8, I'll discuss other options for video recording, but for now I'll stick to the basics. Once the camera is turned on, turn the mode dial on top of the camera to the AUTO setting, just as you did for shooting stills, so the camera will use its basic settings for exposure, focus, and other values.

Next, press the Func./Set button in the center of the control dial to pop up the Function menu at the left side and bottom of the screen. Use the up and down direction buttons to navigate to the bottom entry on the left side of the screen, as shown in Figure 2-24, which is a number inside a half-rectangle—either 640, 1280, or 1920, the number of pixels in the larger dimension of the movie frame.

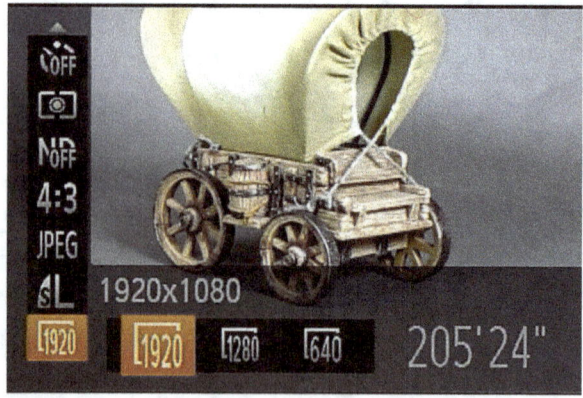

Fig. 2-24: 1920 Option Selected for Movie Format

Use the direction buttons or control dial to choose 1920, which sets the camera to record with its maximum quality of high-definition (HD) video at a size of 1920 X 1080 pixels. Press the Func./Set button again to dismiss the Function menu.

Now compose the shot the way you want it, and, when you're

ready, press the red Movie button on the right side of the camera's back. You don't need to hold the button down; just press and release. The camera will automatically adjust the exposure and focus.

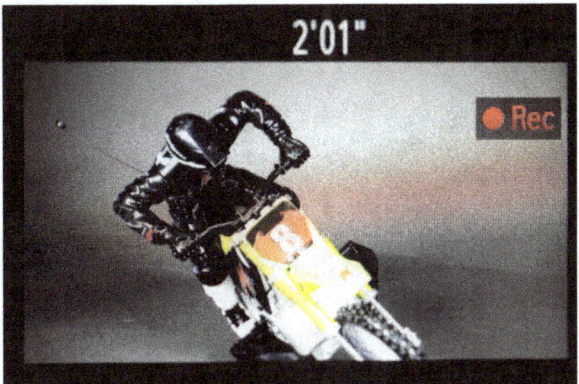

Fig. 2-25: Movie Recording Screen

The LCD screen will show a REC indicator as shown in Figure 2-25, and the camera will keep recording until it reaches a recording limit, or until you press the Movie button again (or the shutter button) to stop the recording. Don't be concerned about the level of the sound that is being recorded, because you have no control over the audio volume while recording.

While the camera is recording, it will continue to adjust focus and exposure as the distance from the subject and the lighting conditions change. You also can zoom in and out using the zoom lever on the ring around the shutter button.

This ability to zoom while recording movies brings up a point that's not specific to the PowerShot S110: Unless you have a good reason to do otherwise, try to hold the camera as steady as possible, and don't zoom unnecessarily or move the camera except in very smooth, slow motions, such as a pan (side-to-side motion) to take in a wide scene gradually. Video from a jerkily moving camera can be very disconcerting to the viewer. You should note, also, that the sounds the zoom mechanism

51

makes will be recorded along with the video.

Viewing Pictures

Before I discuss more advanced settings for taking still pictures and movies, as well as other matters of interest, I will discuss the basics of viewing your images and videos in the camera.

Review While in Shooting Mode

First, every time you take a still picture, the recorded image will show up on the screen for a brief (or not so brief) amount of time, if you have the Shooting menu's Review option set for that function. I'll discuss the details of that setting in Chapter 4. By default, your image will stay on the screen for 2 seconds after you take a new picture.

Reviewing Images in Playback Mode

If you want to review images that were taken previously, you enter playback mode by pressing the Playback button, which is marked with a small blue triangle on the right side of the camera's back.

You can then scroll through the recorded images using the left and right direction buttons or the control dial. If you turn the control dial quickly, the images will rush by in a continuous stream, as they can on an iPod. (This Scroll Display function can be turned off through the Playback menu.) You also can touch the screen and drag left or right with your fingers to scroll through the images.

You can enlarge the view of any image by moving the zoom lever to the right, and you can scroll around in the enlarged image using the direction buttons. If you press the zoom lever in the other direction, toward the wide-angle setting, you will see index screens with increasing numbers of thumbnail images; you can select any image from those screens by pressing the Func./Set button. I'll discuss more of your playback options in Chapter 6.

Playing Movies

To play back motion pictures, move through the recorded images by the methods described above until you find an image for which the screen shows the movie camera icon at the upper left next to the word SET, as shown in Figure 2-26.

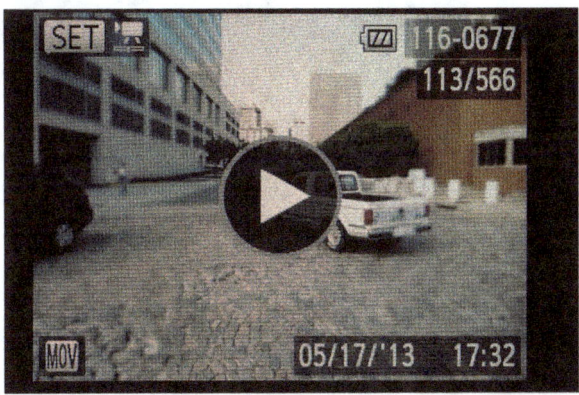

Fig. 2-26: Movie Ready to Play in Camera

With the still frame from the motion picture displayed on the camera's LCD, press the Func./Set button (the button in the center of the control dial) to bring up a menu of VCR-like controls, as seen in Figure 2-27.

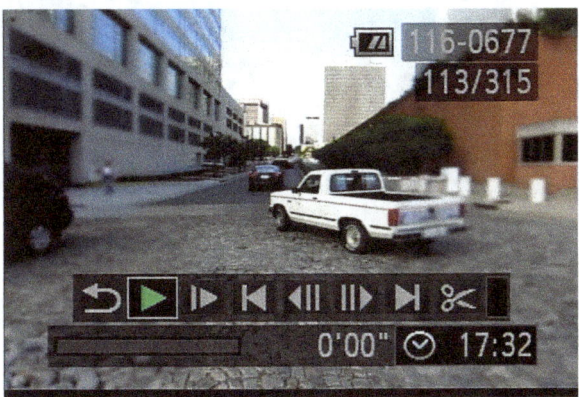

Fig. 2-27: Movie Playback Controls on Screen

Scroll through the line of controls using the direction buttons or the control dial, and press the Func./Set button to activate the control you want to use. To pause the movie, press the Func./Set button to bring up the control menu again. You can then raise or lower the volume of the audio by pressing the up and down direction buttons. You will see an orange volume bar raise and lower at the end of the line of on-screen controls when you adjust the volume in this way.

You also can play a movie using the touch-screen features of the camera; I will discuss the use of the touch screen for playback in Chapter 6.

If you want to play the movies on a computer or edit them with video-editing software, they will import nicely into software such as iMovie for the Macintosh, or any other program for Mac or Windows that can deal with video files with the extension .mov. This is the extension for Apple Computer's QuickTime video playback software; QuickTime itself can be downloaded from Apple's web site. For some Windows-based video editing software, you may need to convert the Power-Shot's movie files to the .avi format before importing them into the software. You can do so with a program such as mp-4cam2avi, which can be downloaded from http://mp4cam2a-vi.sourceforge.net/.

Chapter 3: The Shooting Modes

Until now I have discussed the basics of setting up the camera for quick shots, relying heavily on features such as AUTO mode to take pictures whose settings are controlled mostly by the camera's automation. As with other sophisticated digital cameras, though, with the Power-Shot S110 there is a large range of options available for setting the camera, particularly for taking still images. One of the main goals of this book is to explain the broad range of features available. To do this, I will turn my attention to two subjects—shooting modes and the Shooting menu options. In this chapter, I'll discuss the shooting modes.

Whenever you set out to record still images, you need to select one of the available shooting modes: AUTO, Program, Shutter Priority, Aperture Priority, Manual, Scene, Creative Filters, or Custom. (The other two shooting modes are for movies and movie digests, as discussed in Chapter 8.) So far, I have discussed the AUTO and Program modes. Now I will talk about the others, after some review of the first two.

AUTO Mode

This shooting mode is the one you probably should select if you need to have the camera ready for a quick shot, maybe in an environment with fast-paced events when you won't have much time to fuss with settings of things such as ISO, white balance, aperture, or shutter speed.

To set this mode, turn the mode dial, on top of the camera to the right of the shutter button, to the green label with the word "AUTO" in it, as shown in Figure 3-1.

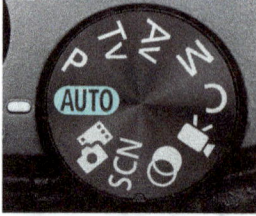

Fig. 3-1: AUTO Mode

When you select this mode, the camera makes quite a few decisions for you and limits your options in several ways. For example, you can't change the focus mode, set ISO or white balance to any value other than Auto, choose the metering method, or use exposure bracketing.

Perhaps most important, in AUTO mode you cannot select Raw for the image quality setting, which is set automatically to JPEG. I'll discuss Raw further in Chapters 4 and 9, but if you want to have the highest possible quality of images or intend to process them using one of the more sophisticated photo editing programs, like Adobe Photoshop, you won't like having to do without the Raw quality setting.

One interesting aspect of AUTO mode is that, in this mode, the camera uses its built-in programming to attempt to figure out what sort of subject or scene you are shooting. (See the chart of icons displayed and what they mean at page 101 of Canon's Camera User Guide for the S110.) So, if you see different icons, or the AUTO icon with different-colored backgrounds, that means that the camera is evaluating the scene for factors such as brightness, backlighting, the presence of human subjects, and the like, so it can use the best possible settings for the situation.

For the image in Figure 3-2, the camera used its generic AUTO setting, while, for the one in Figure 3-3, where the subject was closer to the lens, the camera interpreted the scene as a macro, or closeup shot, and switched automatically into Macro mode, indicated by the flower icon. (The AUTO icon is not shown in Figure 3-2, because that figure shows the final image rather than the view from the camera. The scene-detection icons appear only before the image is captured, as in Figures 3-3 and 3-4, not in the final image.)

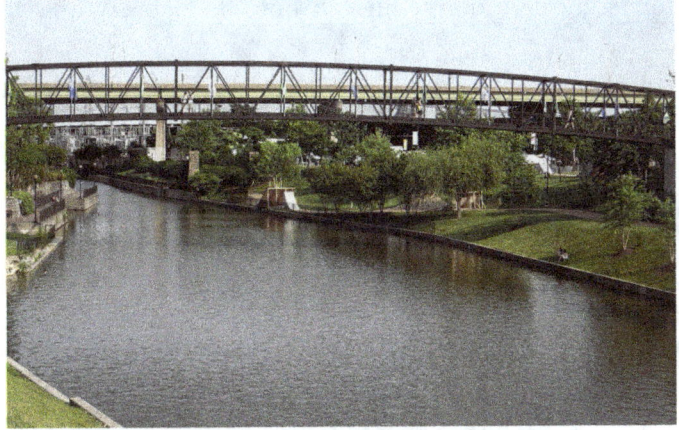

Fig. 3-2: Image Shot in AUTO Mode - Scenery Example

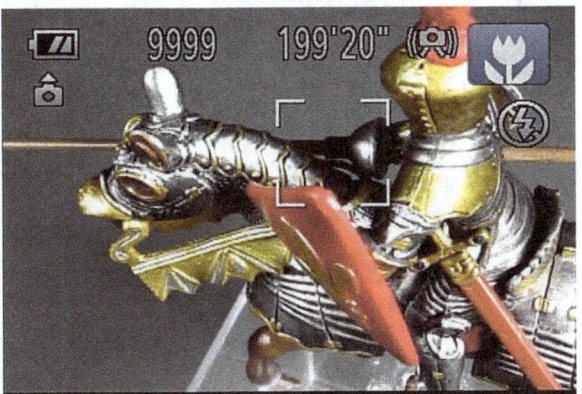

Fig. 3-3: Macro Scene Detection Icon in AUTO Mode

At other times, the camera may decide that the subject is a backlit human, a human in a spotlight, or a sunset. It's interesting to note that the camera does not have a dedicated "sunset" setting as a Scene type that you can select; but, if you want the camera to use good settings for a sunset scene, you can try using AUTO mode, and the camera presumably will attempt to set itself so as to optimize the scene, by emphasizing reddish hues, for example. Similarly, the camera has no special setting for pets or sports, as many other compact cameras do; in AUTO mode, the camera may display an icon for its "In Motion" scene detection setting, as shown in Figure 3-4.

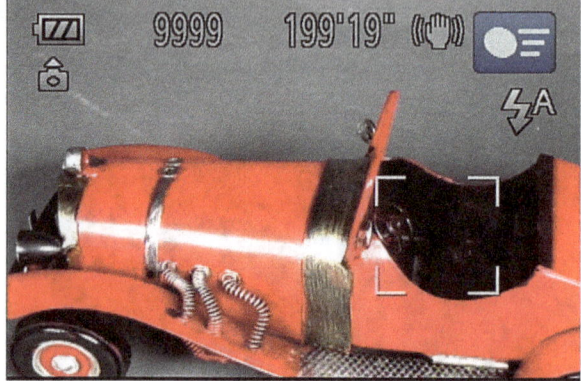

Fig. 3-4: In Motion Scene Detection Icon in AUTO Mode

One other setting that you can adjust in AUTO mode is the Auto Drive setting. To get access to it, you need to use the Function menu. To do that, press the Func./Set button in the center of the control dial, which will bring up a menu of icons at the left of the screen, as shown in Figure 3-5.

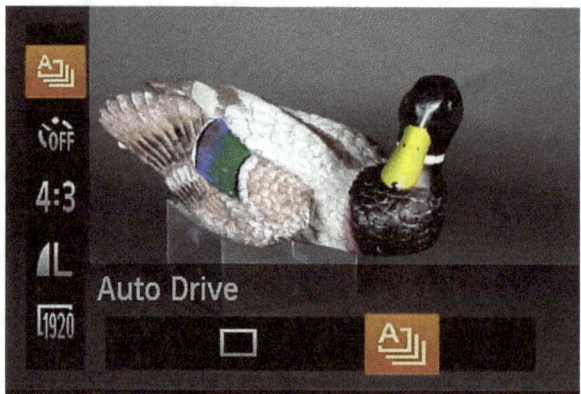

Fig. 3-5: Auto Drive Setting in AUTO Mode

Using the direction buttons, make sure the top icon is high-lighted, then press the right button. The orange highlight will then move across the two icons at the bottom of the screen. By default, the camera is set to use Auto Drive; with that setting, the highlight rests on the icon that looks like a stack of frames with the letter A on top.

With that setting in place, the camera will try to detect smiling faces, sleeping faces, or children. If it does detect any of these, it will use its programming to take multiple shots in an ef-fort to improve the results of your shooting. For smiles, it will take multiple shots and then make its own determination as to which one of those shots is the "best" and should be kept. For sleeping faces, it will take multiple shots and combine them internally into a single composite shot that avoids the visual noise that can result from shots in low light. For children, it will take three consecutive shots and save all of them so you can decide which one(s) to keep.

If you would prefer not to have the camera take so much control of your decisions about which shots to keep, you can use the Function menu to select the icon of the single frame, which will set the camera to take single shots in all cases. If you want to take continuous shots but exercise more control over how those shots are taken and saved, you can switch to another shooting mode, such as Program, in which you can set the camera's continuous-shooting options according to your needs, as discussed in Chapter 4.

Program Mode

Choose this mode by turning the mode dial to the P setting, as seen in Figure 3-6. With this mode, the camera will automati-cally gauge the lighting and set both the aperture and the shut-ter speed. In addition, Program mode lets you control many of the settings available with the camera, apart from those two values. (You still can override the camera's automatic exposure to a fair extent by using exposure compensation, as discussed in Chapter 2, as well as exposure bracketing, discussed in

59

Chapter 4, and Program Shift, discussed in Chapter 5.)

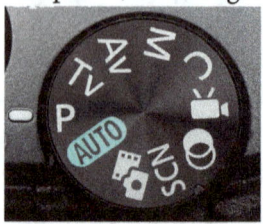

Fig. 3-6: Program Mode

You don't have to make a lot of decisions if you don't want to, because the camera will make reasonable choices for you as defaults. However, you should note that, even though shutter speeds as slow as 15 seconds are available in Shutter Priority and Manual exposure mode, the camera will never choose a shutter speed longer than one second in Program mode.

One way to look at Program mode is that it greatly expands the choices available through the Shooting menu and the Function menu. You will be able to make choices involving picture quality, image stabilization, ISO sensitivity, metering method, and others. I won't discuss all of those choices here; if you want to explore that topic, go to the discussions of the Function menu and the Shooting menu in Chapter 4 and check out all of the different selections that are available.

It is important to note that Program mode has the great advantage of letting you choose Raw quality for your still images.

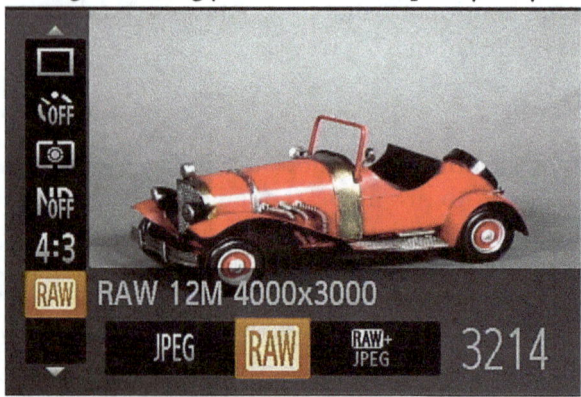

Fig. 3-7: Raw Image Type Selected on Function Menu

60

To do that, activate the Function menu by pressing the Func./ Set button in the center of the control dial. Using the up and down direction buttons, navigate down to the third-to-bottom item on the list of icons on the left side of the screen. Then use the right button or the control dial to select Raw from the list on the bottom of the screen, as shown in Figure 3-7, as opposed to JPEG. (JPEG stands for Joint Photographic Experts Group, an industry group that sets standards for photographic file formats.)

Or, if you prefer, select Raw+JPEG. With that setting, the camera actually records two images as noted, so you will have both the Raw and the non-Raw (JPEG) image available. This choice can be useful if you won't have immediate access to software for editing the Raw images, and want to be able to use the lesser-quality images quickly.

Aperture Priority Mode

You set the camera to the Aperture Priority shooting mode by turning the mode dial to the Av setting, shown in Figure 3-8.

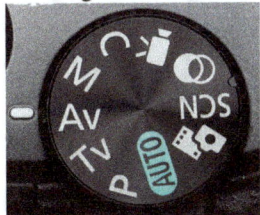

Fig. 3-8: Aperture Priority

Av stands for Aperture value. With this mode, you select the aperture, and the camera will set a corresponding shutter speed that should result in a good exposure.

Before discussing the nuts and bolts of the settings for this mode, I'll discuss what aperture is and why you would want to control it. The camera's aperture is a measure of the width of its opening that lets in light. The aperture's width is measured numerically in f-stops. For the PowerShot S110, the range of f-stops is from f/2.0 (wide open) to f/8.0 (most narrow). The amount of light that is let into the camera to create an image on the camera's sensor is controlled by the combination of aperture (how wide open the lens is) and shutter speed (how long the shutter remains open to let in the light).

For some purposes, you may want to control the width of the aperture but still let the camera choose the corresponding shutter speed. Here are a couple of examples involving depth of field. Depth of field is a measure of how well a camera is able to keep multiple objects or subjects in focus at different distances. For example, say you have three friends lined up at different distances—five, seven, and nine feet (1.5, 2.1, and 2.7 meters) from the camera. If the camera's depth of field is quite shallow at a particular focusing distance, such as five feet (1.5 meters), then, in this case, if you focus on the friend at that distance, the other two will be out of focus and blurry. But if the camera's depth of field when focused at five feet is broad, then it may be possible for all three friends to be in sharp focus in your photograph, even if the focus is set for the friend at five feet.

What does all of that have to do with aperture? One of the rules of photographic optics is that the wider open the camera's aperture is, the shallower its depth of field is at a given focal length. So in our example above, if you have the camera's aperture set to its widest opening, f/2.0, the depth of field will be relatively shallow, and it will be possible to keep fewer items in focus at varying distances from the camera. If the aperture is set to the narrowest opening, f/8.0, the depth of field will be greater, and it will be possible to have more items in focus at varying distances.

With a camera like the PowerShot S110, with its relatively small sensor and wide-angle lens, the effects of aperture on depth of field are not as pronounced as with some other cameras. However, Figures 3-9 and 3-10 generally illustrate the effects of aperture settings on depth of field, using an owl figurine as the foreground subject.

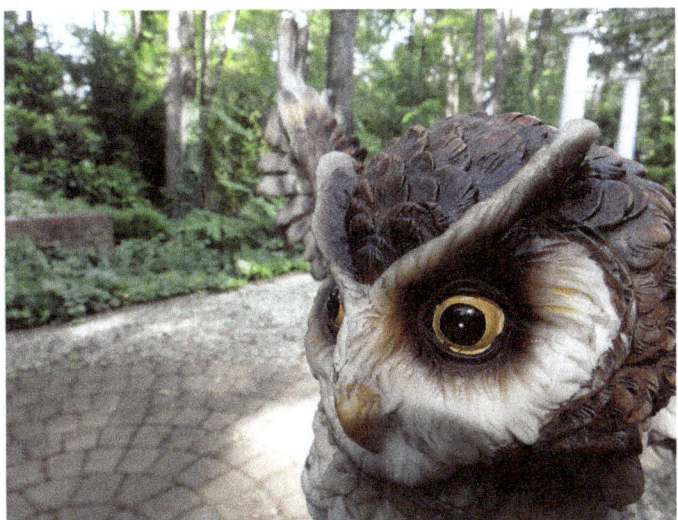

Fig. 3-9:   Fairly Sharp Background with Aperture at f/8.0

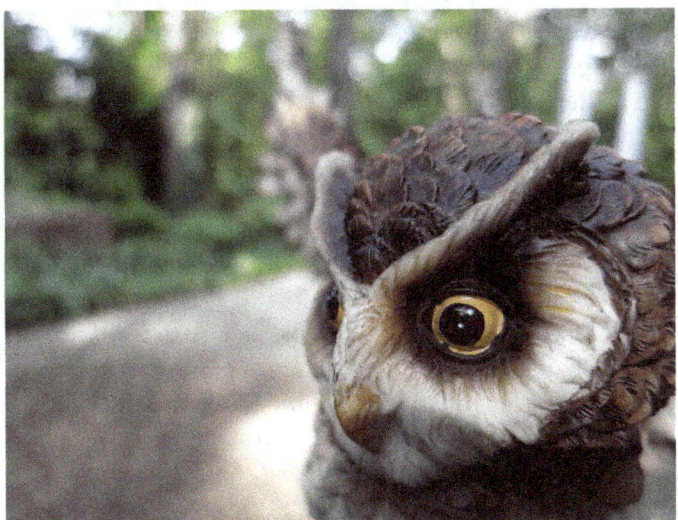

Fig. 3-10:   Blurry Background with Aperture at f/2.0

Both images were taken with the S110 set to Aperture Priority mode under identical circumstances. The only difference is that, in Figure 3-9, the aperture was set to f/8.0 and in Figure 3-10 it was set to f/2.0. As you can see, in Figure 3-9, with

63

the aperture set to its most narrow setting, the background of trees and other foliage appears quite sharp. This is because, when the aperture is narrow, the depth of field is quite extensive, so both the background and foreground can be in focus.

In Figure 3-10, however, with the aperture at its most wide-open setting of f/2.0, the depth of field is relatively shallow. As a result, the background is considerably more blurred than in the other image. The blurriness of the background creates a pleasing backdrop for the sharply focused owl, and reduces the distraction caused by the trees and other items in the background.

These photos illustrate fairly clearly the advantage of "stopping down" to a narrow aperture such as f/5.6 or even f/8.0 when you want to enjoy a broad depth of field and keep as many subjects as possible in sharp focus.

In practical terms, if you want to have the sharpest picture possible, especially when you have subjects at varying distances from the lens and you want them to be in focus to the greatest extent possible, then you may want to control the aperture, and make sure it is set to the highest number (narrowest opening) possible.

On the other hand, there are occasions when photographers prize a narrow depth of field. This situation arises often in the case of outdoor portraits. For example, you may want to take a photo of a subject outdoors with a background of trees and bushes, and possibly some other, more distracting objects, such as a swing set or a tool shed. If you can achieve a narrow depth of field, you can keep your subject in sharp focus, but leave the background quite blurry and indistinct. This effect is sometimes called "bokeh," a Japanese term describing an aesthetically pleasing blurriness of the background. In this situation, the blurriness of the background can be a great asset, reducing the distraction from unwanted objects and highlighting the sharply focused portrait of your subject. For example, in Figure 3-11, I took a closeup photo of an orchid.

64

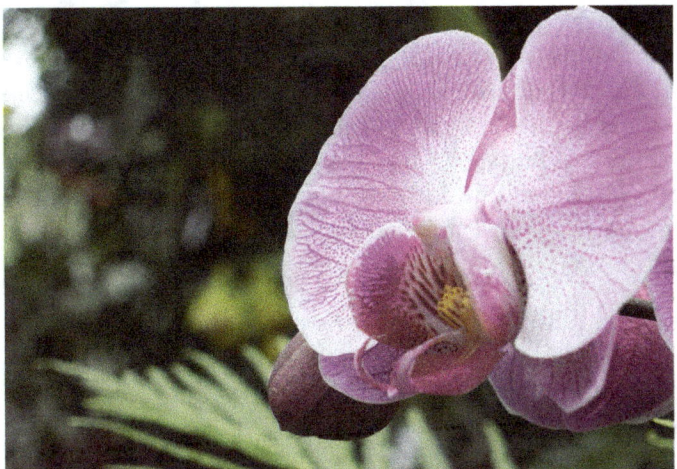

Fig. 3-11: Example of Bokeh Effect

Because the depth of field was shallow, the background was blurred, creating a non-distracting field of green against which the colorful orchid is highlighted.

So with an awareness of the virtues of selecting an aperture, here are the technical steps involved. Once you have moved the mode dial to the Av setting, use the control ring (the large, ridged ring around the lens) to change the aperture. (If the control ring does not work this way, check the setting for the Set Control Ring Func. item on the Shooting menu; it should be set to STD.)

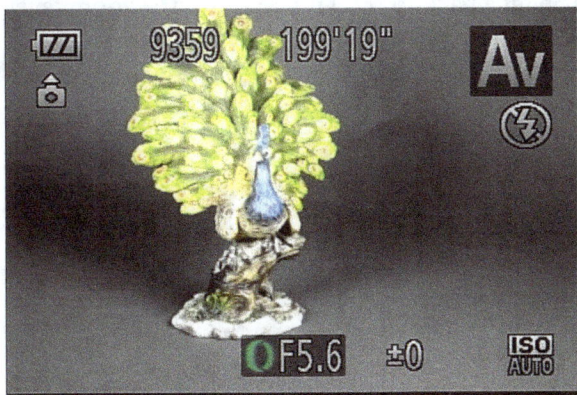

Fig. 3-12: Aperture Setting of f/5.6 Displayed on Screen

The number of the f-stop (in the case shown here, f/5.6) will appear in the bottom center of the screen, as shown in Figure 3-12. The aperture number appears next to a circular green icon showing that you can use the control ring to change the aperture. The shutter speed will show up also, to the left of the aperture number, but not until you have pressed the shutter button halfway down to let the camera evaluate the lighting conditions.

One more note on Aperture Priority mode that might not be immediately obvious and could easily lead to confusion: Not all apertures are available at all times. In particular, the widest-open aperture, f/2.0, is available only when the lens is zoomed out to its wide-angle setting (moved toward the icon of a group of trees). At the highest zoom levels, the widest aperture available is f/5.9.

To see an illustration of this point, here is a quick test. Zoom the lens out by moving the zoom lever all the way to the left, toward the group-of-trees icon. Then select Aperture Priority mode and select an aperture of f/2.0 by turning the control ring all the way in the direction for lower numbers. Now zoom the lens in by moving the zoom lever to the right, toward the single-tree icon. After the zoom action is finished, you will see that the aperture has been changed to f/5.9, because that is the limit for the aperture at the telephoto zoom level. (The aperture will change back to f/2.0 if you move the zoom lever back to the wide-angle setting.) Also, as with Program mode, the camera will never choose a shutter speed longer than one second in Aperture Priority mode.

Shutter Priority Mode

In Shutter Priority mode, you choose whatever shutter speed you want, and the camera will set the corresponding aperture in order to achieve a proper exposure of the image. In this mode, you can set the shutter to be open for a variety of intervals ranging from 15 full seconds to 1/2000 of a second. If you are photographing fast action, such as a baseball swing or a

66

hurdles event at a track meet, and you want to stop the motion with a minimum of blur, you will want to select a fast shutter speed, such as 1/1000 of a second. For example, in Figure 3-13, with a shutter speed of 1/1250 second, the camera was able to freeze the motion of a trick bike rider as he seemed to levitate over the ramp.

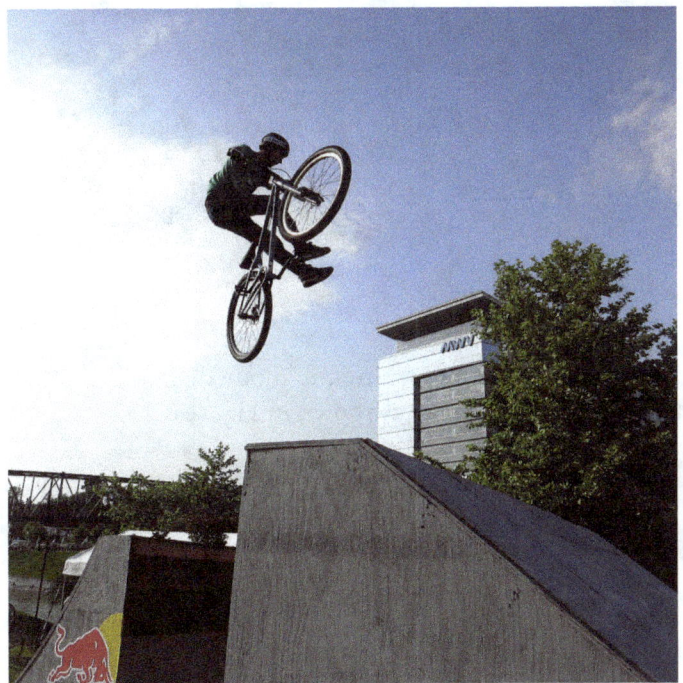

Fig. 3-13: Shutter Speed 1/1250 Second

In other cases, for creative purposes, you may want to select a slow shutter speed to achieve a certain effect, such as leaving the shutter open to capture a trail of automobiles' taillights at night. In Figure 3-14, I purposely used a slow shutter speed of 0.4 second to convey a sense of motion among the people browsing through an indoor exhibition of butterflies.

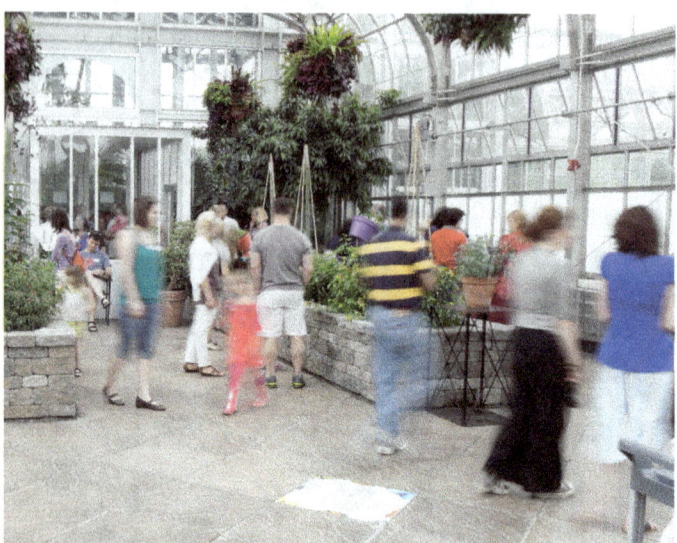

Fig. 3-14: Shutter Speed Set to 0.4 Second

You select this mode by turning the mode dial on top of the camera to the Tv indicator, as shown in Figure 3-15.

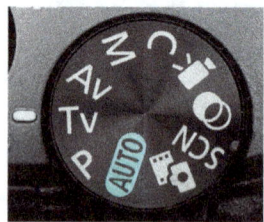

Fig. 3-15: Shutter Priority

Tv stands for "Time value," but this mode is more commonly called "Shutter Priority." You select the shutter speed by turning the control ring—the large, ridged ring that surrounds the lens. (Again, as with Aperture Priority mode, the Control Ring function must be set to STD for this procedure to work this way.) The LCD will display a scale showing the changing shutter speeds, and the selected speed (here, 1/320 second) will then appear on the left side of the screen, next to a green circular icon that indicates that the control ring is used to change the shutter speed, as shown in Figure 3-16.

68

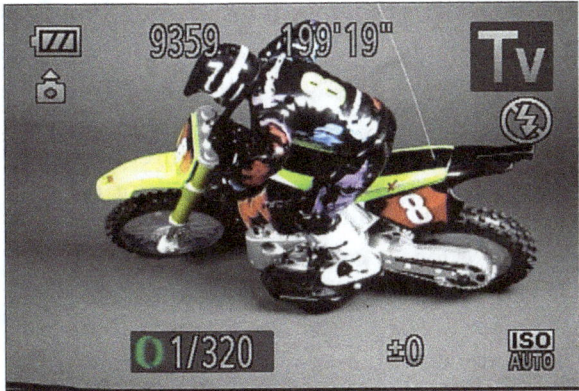

Fig. 3-16: *Shutter Speed Setting of 1/320 Second Displayed on Screen*

When you press the shutter button halfway down to evaluate the exposure, the camera will select the aperture for a good exposure and display the f-stop to the right of the shutter speed.

Once the shutter button is halfway down, watch the color of the aperture (f-stop number) on the screen. If that number turns orange, that means that proper exposure at that shutter speed is not possible at any available aperture, according to the camera's calculations. For example, if you set the shutter speed to 1/320 of a second in a fairly dark indoor environment, the aperture number (such as f/4.5, the widest setting when the lens is zoomed to a certain point) may turn orange, indicating that proper exposure is not possible, as shown in Figure 3-17.

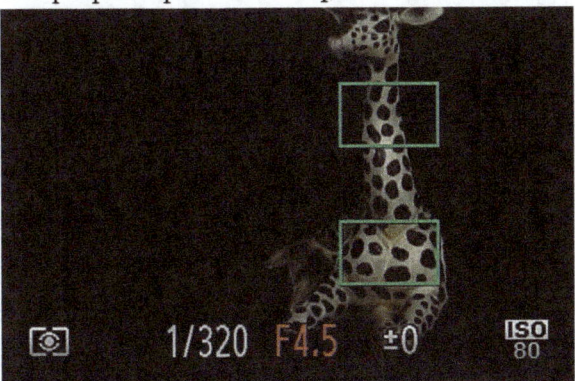

Fig. 3-17: *Aperture Number Orange When Light Not Sufficient*

One good thing in this situation is that the camera will still let you take the picture, despite having turned the number orange to warn you. The camera is saying, in effect, "Look, maybe you shouldn't do this, but that's your business. If you want a dark picture for some reason, help yourself." (This situation is less likely to take place when you're using Aperture Priority mode, because, unlike the situation with f-stops, there is a fairly wide range of shutter speeds for the camera to choose from: a range from 1 second to 1/2000 second.) If you want to reduce the risk of a badly exposed image in either Aperture Priority or Shutter Priority mode, you can use the Safety Shift feature, discussed in Chapter 4, which will override your setting of aperture or shutter speed if necessary to expose the image properly.

There is one somewhat unusual aspect to setting shutter speed on the S110: Whenever you set the shutter speed to any time longer than one second, the ISO setting automatically switches to ISO 80, the lowest possible setting. This behavior limits your options a bit, but, as long as you're aware of it, it should not interfere with your ability to capture good images.

When setting the shutter speed, note that the fractions of a second are easy to read, because they are displayed as standard fractions, such as 1/5 or 1/200. Some of the longer times are a bit harder to read; the camera displays them using quotation marks. So, for example, 0.3 second is displayed as 0"3, and 2.5 seconds is displayed as 2"5.

Manual Exposure Mode

The PowerShot S110 has a fully manual mode for control of exposure, which is one of the great features of this camera. Not all compact cameras have a manual exposure mode, which is a tremendous boon for serious photographers who want to exert full creative control over exposure decisions.

The technique for using this mode is not too far removed from what I discussed in connection with the Aperture Priority and Shutter Priority modes. To control exposure manually, set the mode dial to the M indicator, as shown in Figure 3-18.

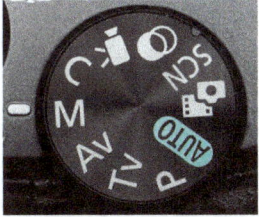

Fig. 3-18: Manual Mode

You now have to control both shutter speed and aperture by setting them yourself. With some other cameras, this process is confusing, because you have to use the same button or knob for both settings and switch its function back and forth between them. With the S110, there is no such problem because of the existence of both the control ring and the control dial.

To set the aperture, turn the control ring around the lens (assuming the control ring is set for this function); to set the shutter speed, turn the control dial on the back of the camera. You will see green icons to the left of the two values, indicating the use of the control dial for shutter speed and the control ring for aperture, as shown in Figure 3-19.

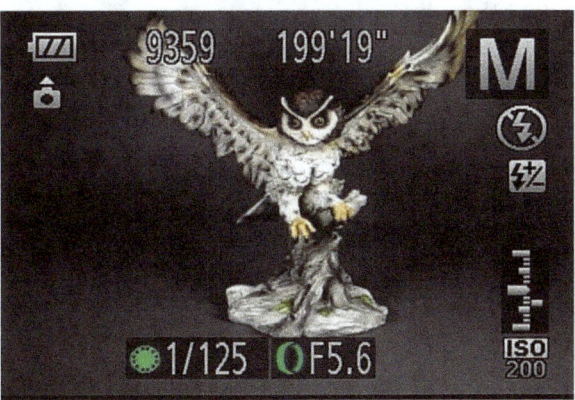

Fig. 3-19: Shutter Speed and Aperture Values Displayed on Screen

As you adjust those values, watch the vertical scale in the lower right corner of the screen, as also shown in Figure 3-19. You

71

will see a small white indicator that moves up and down along the right side of the scale as the values change. When the exposure is set so the camera's meter judges it to be normal, the white indicator is centered halfway up the scale. If the indicator is below the center, the exposure is too dark; if it is above the center, it is too bright. If the setting becomes more extreme than the scale can indicate, the indicator turns orange.

Of course, you don't have to center the indicator; it is there only to give you an idea of how the camera would meter the scene. You very well may want parts of the scene to be darker or lighter than the metering would indicate to be "correct."

If you would like to start out by setting the exposure manually but then let the camera take over, once you have set the aperture and shutter speed, press the shutter button down halfway, and, while holding it there, press the up direction button (exposure compensation button). At that point, the camera will display a scale of aperture and shutter speed settings and will adjust the exposure to the "correct" metered exposure, if it is possible to do so under the existing lighting conditions. You can then press the shutter button down the rest of the way to take the picture at the adjusted exposure, or you can continue to adjust the shutter speed and aperture manually.

As with Aperture Priority mode, you cannot set the aperture to f/2.0 when the lens is zoomed in.

With Manual exposure mode, the settings for aperture and shutter speed are independent of each other. When you change one, the other one stays unchanged until you adjust it manually. The camera is leaving the creative decision about exposure entirely up to you, even if the resulting photograph would be washed out by excessive exposure or underexposed to the point of near-blackness.

Finally, you should be aware of the procedure for setting the camera's ISO in Manual mode. In Chapter 4, I'll talk more about the ISO setting, which controls how sensitive the camera's sensor is to light. With a higher ISO number, the image is exposed more quickly, so the shutter speed can be faster or the aperture more narrow, or both, depending on conditions. In other shooting modes, the camera can set ISO automatically, but in Manual mode you have to set the ISO value yourself.

To do so, press the Func./Set button in the center of the control dial, highlight the ISO icon near the top of the menu on the left, and scroll across the menu at the bottom of the screen, as shown in Figure 3-20; use a low number like 80 or 100 to emphasize image quality when there is plenty of light; use a higher number in dimmer light.

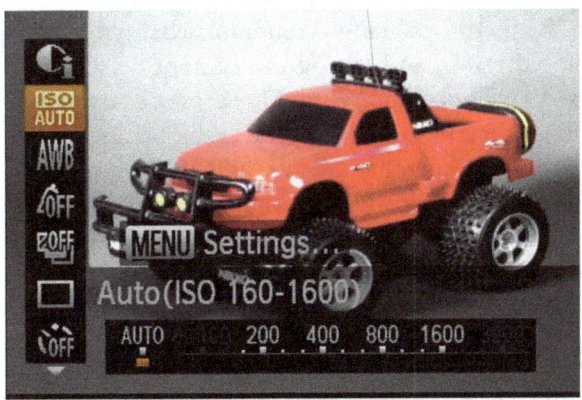

Fig. 3-20:   ISO Item Highlighted on Function Menu

You also need to realize that higher ISO settings are likely to cause visual "noise," or graininess, in your images, so you need to weigh the advantages of being able to take pictures in dim light against the risk of having images that are excessively grainy in appearance. Generally speaking, you should try to set the ISO no higher than 400 if you need to ensure the highest quality for your images. You can still get quite acceptable results with ISO 800 or 1600, though, unless you need to make very large prints.

As noted above, you cannot set ISO to Auto in Manual exposure mode as you can in other modes; you must set it to a numerical value. If you had it set to Auto before selecting Manual mode, the camera will reset it to ISO 80. And, as with Shutter Priority mode, if you set a shutter speed longer than one second, the ISO value will automatically be reset to 80.

Scene Mode

Scene mode is considerably different from the other shooting modes I have discussed so far in this chapter. This mode does not have a single defining feature, such as permitting control over one or more aspects of exposure. Instead, when you select Scene mode and then choose a particular scene type within that mode, you are in effect telling the camera what sort of environment the picture is being taken in or what type of image you are looking for, and letting the camera decide what settings to use to produce that result. One aspect of using this shooting mode is that, in most cases, you are not able to select many of the menu options that are available in Program, Aperture Priority, Shutter Priority, and Manual exposure mode, such as Raw quality, My Colors, white balance, and ISO. (There are some exceptions to these limitations, which I will discuss later in this chapter.)

One thing that struck me when I first got my PowerShot S110 is that it actually has relatively few settings within Scene mode that are meant for specific subjects or environments. Its predecessor models, the S100 and S95, had settings for Landscape, Kids & Pets, Beach, and Foliage, which the S110 does not have. Many other compact cameras have a specific setting for sunset shots. With the S110, there are relatively few types of scene that the camera provides settings for in Scene mode. Perhaps this situation reflects the fact that the camera does an excellent job with a wide variety of scenes when you use AUTO mode or Program mode.

You select Scene mode by turning the mode dial to the SCN indicator, as shown in Figure 3-21. Now, unless you want to settle for whatever type of scene setting is already in place, you need to pick one from the list of 9 choices.

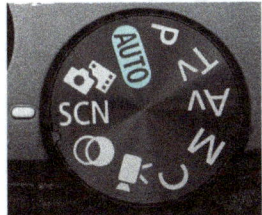

Fig. 3-21: Scene Mode

To make this further choice, use the Function menu by pressing the Func./Set button in the center of the control dial. The icon for the current Scene mode setting is at the top of the string of icons at the left of the screen, as shown in Figure 3-22.

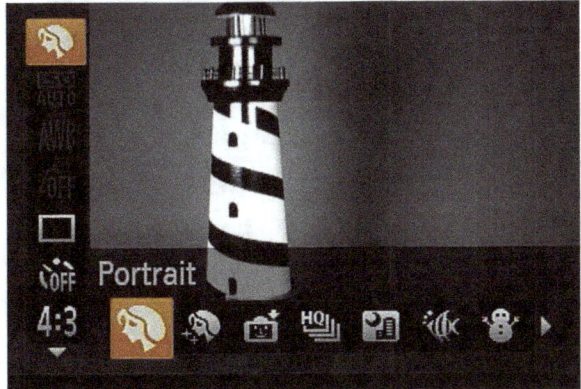

Fig. 3-22: Scene Setting on Function Menu

Once you have the orange highlight on that icon, use the left and right direction buttons or the control dial (or the touch screen) to move through the 9 possible choices.

One good thing about the Scene mode menu system is that each scene setting is labeled or described as you move the selector over it, as shown in Figure 3-23, so you are not left trying to puzzle out what each icon represents. (You can control how detailed these descriptions are with the Hints & Tips item on the Setup menu, as discussed in Chapter 7.)

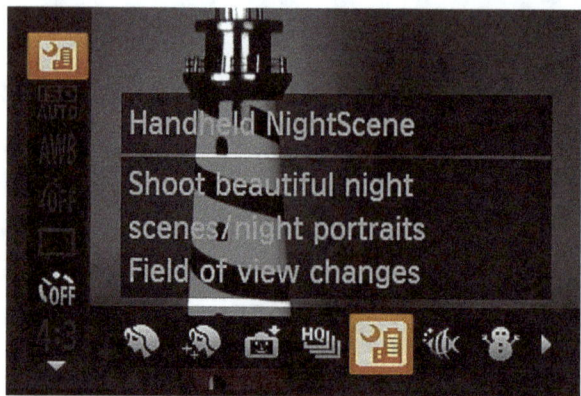

Fig. 3-23: Description Displayed for Scene Setting

As you keep pushing the right button or moving the control dial to move the selector over the other scene types, when you reach the right edge of the screen, the selector wraps around to the first setting on the left and continues going.

That's all there is to do to select a scene type. But you need to know something about each choice to know whether it's one you would want to select. In general, each different scene setting carries with it a variety of values, including things like focus mode, flash status, range of shutter speeds, sensitivity to various colors, and others.

With that introduction, I will describe the various scene settings, moving from left to right through the selections on the Function menu, so you can make an informed choice. I will discuss the main features of each setting, with sample images for some of the settings.

Portrait

The Portrait setting, illustrated by the icon shown in Figure 3-24, is designed to yield rich flesh tones with a softening effect. You should stand fairly close to the subject and set the zoom to some degree of telephoto, so as to blur the background if possible. The flash mode is initially set to Auto, but you can switch the flash off if you want.

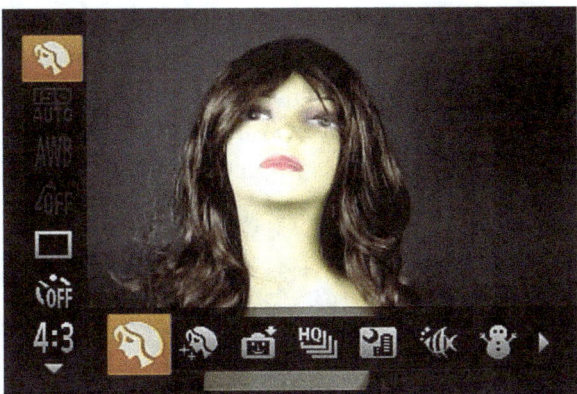

Fig. 3-24: Portrait Setting Icon

The example shown in Figure 3-25 was taken in the early evening under a cloudy sky with no flash.

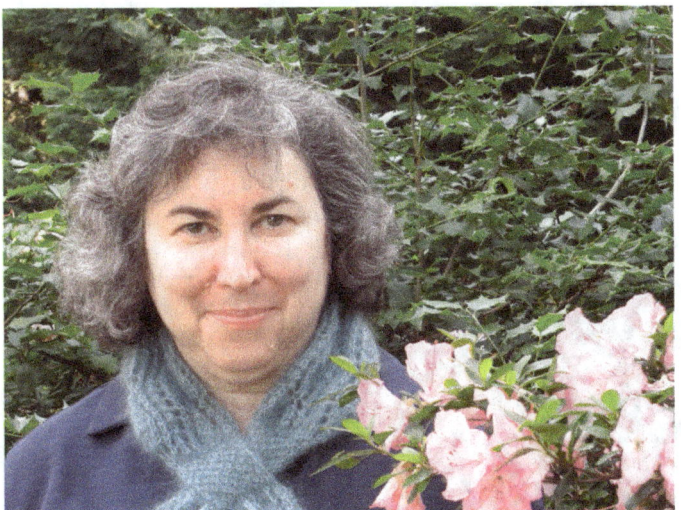

Fig. 3-25: Portrait Example

Smooth Skin

This setting, represented by the icon seen in Figure 3-26, is similar to Portrait, but it provides the added feature of smoothing out areas of skin tones in the image, to reduce wrinkles and other blemishes on faces.

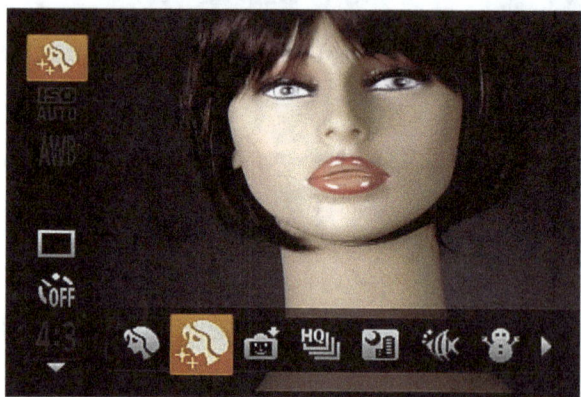

Fig. 3-26: Smooth Skin Setting Icon

This setting is unusual in that it includes controls that let you make adjustments to the processing the camera carries out. To make these adjustments, press the down direction button, marked DISP., and the camera will display two rectangles, the top one for the level of the effect, and the bottom one for the color of the subject's skin, as shown in Figure 3-27.

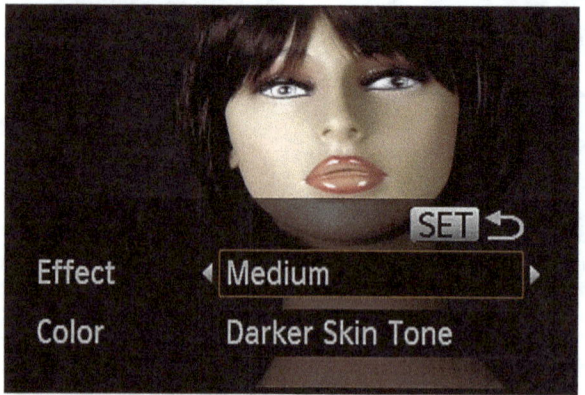

Fig. 3-27: Smooth Skin Setting Adjustment Screen

Using the up and down direction buttons, select the top rectangle; when it is selected, triangles will appear at its ends. Then use the control dial or the left and right buttons to select Low, Medium, or High for the intensity of the smoothing effect. Next, press the down button to highlight the bottom rectangle, and use the dial or the buttons to select Off, Lighter Skin Tone, or Darker Skin Tone. With Off, the effect will be applied to medium-dark areas of the image; with the other settings, the camera will adjust the effect so it is applied to lighter or darker skin tones. Once the settings are made, the camera will show a preview of how the effect will alter the image.

You also can make the settings for this scene type using the touch screen; touch the DISP. icon to start, then touch the triangles to adjust the levels of the settings and press the SET icon on the screen to finish.

Smart Shutter

This setting, whose icon is shown in Figure 3-28, is not designed for a particular type of subject. Instead, it gives you several tools for triggering the camera automatically by smiles, winks, and faces.

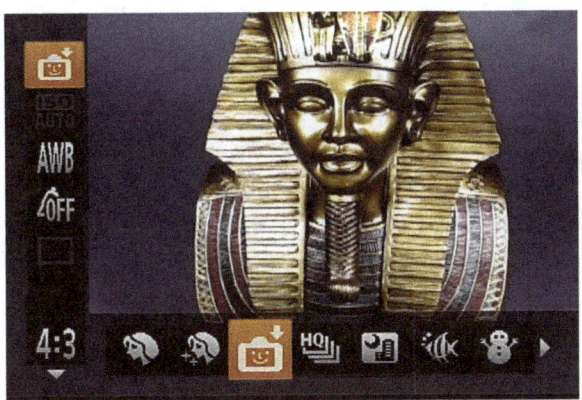

Fig. 3-28:   Smart Shutter Setting Icon

When you select Smart Shutter from the scene icons at the

bottom of the screen, you will see the DISP. label in the lower left corner of the screen. Press the Display button (or touch the DISP. icon on the screen), and you will see a sub-menu with three options: Smile, Wink Self-Timer, and Face Self-Timer, as shown in Figure 3-29.

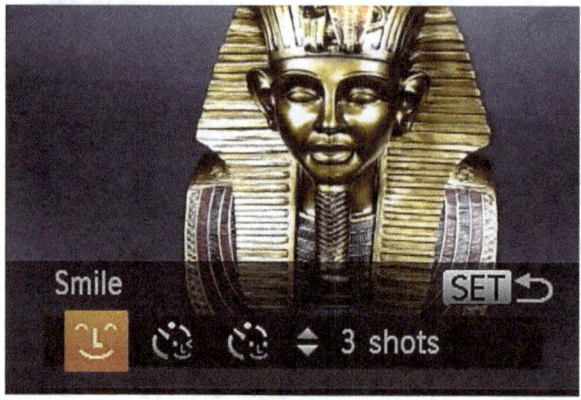

Fig. 3-29: Smart Shutter Settings Screen

These three options work as follows, starting from the left.

With the Smile setting highlighted, press the up and down buttons to change the number of shots the camera will take, from 1 to 10. Once you have set the number of shots, press the Func./Set button again. Now the camera will be in smile-detection mode, waiting until it sees a smile. Once it does, the self-timer lamp on the front of the camera will light up once, and the camera will take the number of shots you set. This function is not perfect, but it works quite well. You may have to tell your subject to open his or her mouth wide and show a lot of teeth to trigger the camera, but this can be a way to make sure the subject smiles. It also can be a good conversation starter.

The next Smart Shutter sub-option is the Wink Self-Timer, which works in similar fashion to the smile detector, except that, for winks, you have to press the shutter button fully. Then the camera will wait until it sees a person wink (closing one or both eyes momentarily); once it does, it will trigger the shutter for the number of shots you have set. The self-timer lamp will blink and the beeper will sound repeatedly while the camera is waiting for the subject to wink. If no wink takes place, the camera will trigger the shutter after 15 seconds anyway.

The third and final sub-option is the Face Self-Timer. This option is similar to the Wink Self-Timer, in that you have to press the shutter button fully down, and the camera will take the picture once it detects a new face. Here again, as with the Wink Self-timer, if the camera doesn't see a new face, it will trigger the shutter after 15 seconds anyway. As with the other options, you can set the camera to take from 1 to 10 shots when triggered.

High-Speed Burst HQ

This mode, whose icon is shown selected in Figure 3-30, is not meant for a particular type of scene, but for a particular type of shooting.

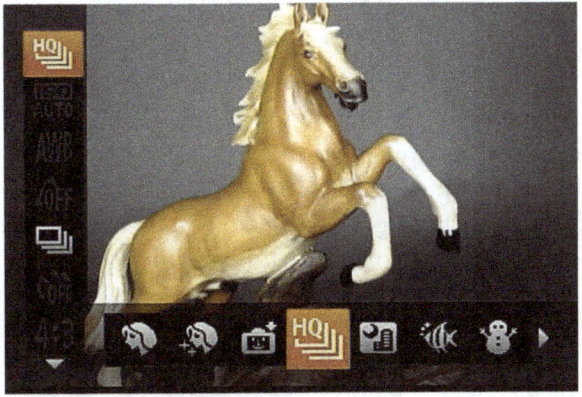

Fig. 3-30: High-Speed Burst HQ Setting

As its name implies, you select this setting when you want to fire off a burst of continuous shots by just holding down the shutter button.

As I'll discuss in Chapter 4, there also are settings on the Function menu for continuous shooting. Here are some pointers on how to choose between this Burst HQ feature and the more standard continuous shooting on the Function menu.

With the Function menu's continuous-shooting options, you can have the camera set to any of several shooting modes for still images: Program, Aperture Priority, Shutter Priority, Manual, Creative Filters, and several of the Scene mode types (Portrait, Underwater, Snow, or Fireworks). If you choose one of the first four (PASM) modes, you have the option of shooting with the Raw format, for maximum quality and flexibility in post-processing your images in software.

In addition, with those standard continuous-shooting options, you can choose continuous shooting with autofocus, in which case the camera will focus for each shot in the series.

Along with those capabilities comes one major trade-off: The maximum speed of the standard continuous-shooting options is 2.1 frames per second, and it drops to a maximum of 0.9 frame per second with continuous autofocus.

With the High-Speed Burst HQ option from the Scene mode menu, you get much faster shooting, at a rate as high as 10 frames per second for a maximum burst of 10 shots. With this option, you get high-quality images of Large size, but you cannot shoot with Raw format and most options on the Function menu are disabled, including i-Contrast, ISO, white balance, My Colors, self-timer, aspect ratio, and ND Filter. You can, however, use the continuous-shooting option on the Function menu to select continuous shooting with autofocus, in which case the camera will adjust its focus for each shot, but at a noticeably slower rate of about 3 or 4 frames per second.

With this setting, I was able to capture the series of rapid-fire shots shown in Figure 3-31 from an "air dog" exhibition, in which the dogs jumped out over a swimming pool in pursuit of a tennis ball or other dog-friendly item.

82

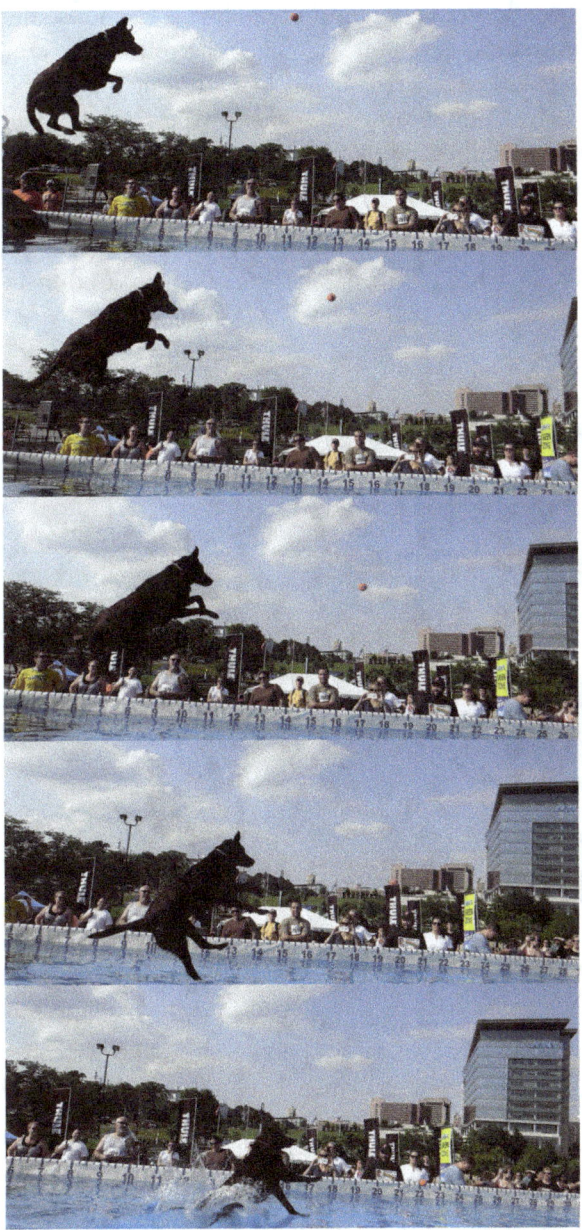

Fig. 3-31: High-Speed Burst HQ Example

To sum up the situation with continuous shooting, choose the High-Speed Burst HQ option if you need maximum speed for a burst of up to 10 shots. If you can live without that speed and can settle for roughly one or two shots per second, you will have more flexibility in making settings with the standard continuous-shooting options that are found on the Function menu.

I will discuss playback options for shots taken in a burst in Chapter 6.

Handheld Night Scene

This mode, whose icon is shown in Figure 3-32, gives you an option for taking pictures in low light without flash or tripod.

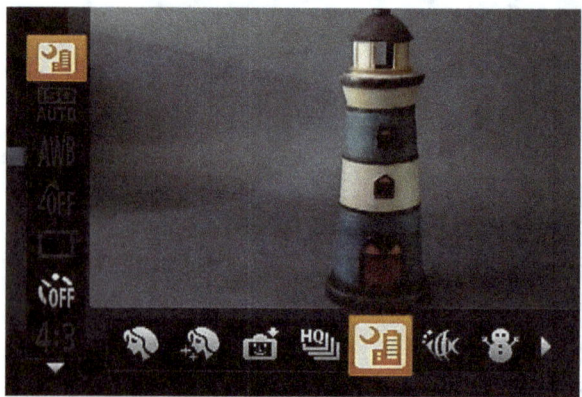

Fig. 3-32: Handheld Night Scene Setting Icon

Ordinarily, the slow shutter speeds that are required to expose the scene properly in those conditions will result in blurring from camera motion, because most people cannot hold a camera steady enough to avoid some movement. With this special mode, the camera boosts the ISO to a high level so it can use a fast shutter speed, and takes four images in rapid succession. The camera then combines these images internally into one composite image in order to counteract the effects of high ISO, which often causes visible "noise" or grain in an image.

84

The resulting image is of Large size, and should be of excellent quality. I took Figure 3-33 using Handheld Night Scene; the camera shot four images at ISO 6400 with a shutter speed of 1/20 second and combined them into the result you see here.

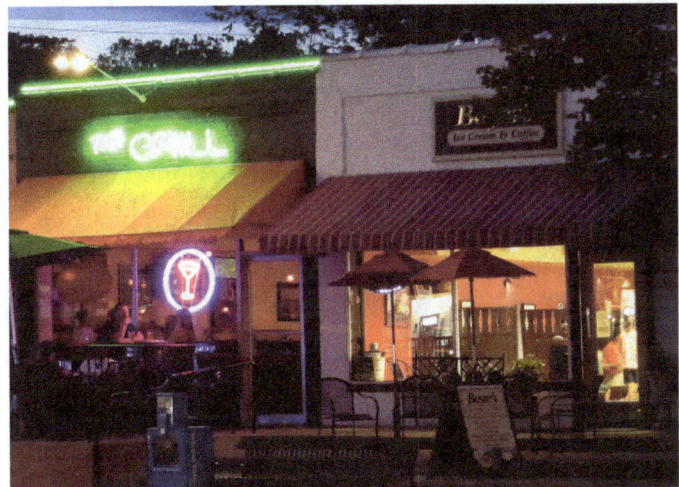

Fig. 3-33: Handheld Night Scene Example

For comparison, I took the image in Figure 3-34, showing the same scene, using AUTO mode. For that image, the camera shot at ISO 1600 for 1/8 second.

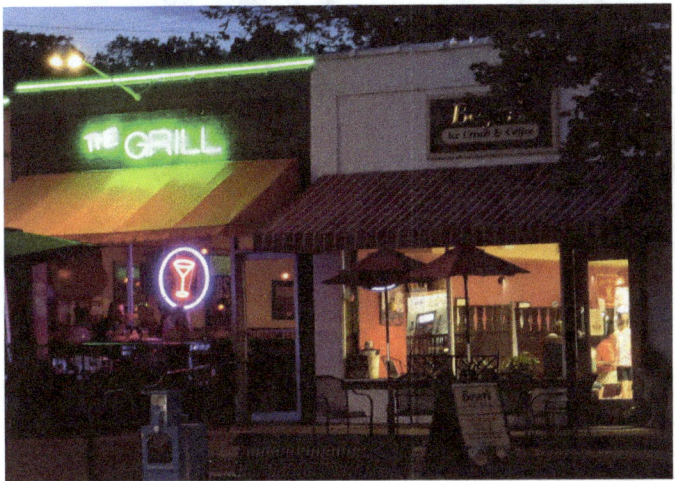

Fig. 3-34: Comparison Shot in AUTO Mode

In this case, the results from the two settings were quite similar. However, the shutter speed of 1/8 second used by the camera in AUTO mode is slow enough that it easily could have resulted in motion blur. If the scene had been any darker, motion blur likely would have resulted.

Handheld Night Scene is a good setting to use if you are caught in a situation in which you cannot use a tripod or flash and the light is very dim. If you can use a tripod, you probably should use AUTO, Program, or one of the more ordinary shooting modes, because Handheld Night Scene will not yield the same quality as a shot at a lower ISO with the camera on a steady support.

Underwater

This scene type, whose icon is shown in Figure 3-35, adjusts the color balance of the shot by emphasizing the reddish part of the spectrum to counteract the blue of the underwater light.

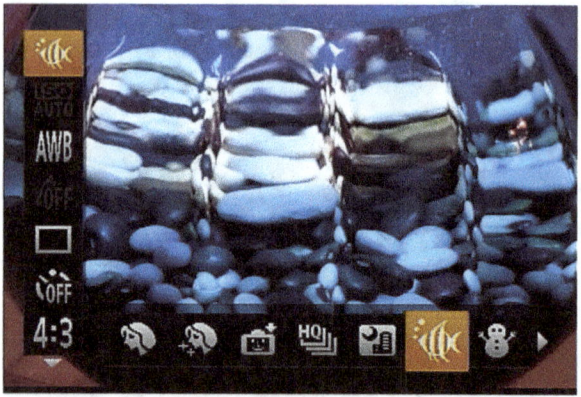

Fig. 3-35: Underwater Setting Icon

The camera also turns on the DR Correction feature, discussed in Chapter 4, set to Auto.

With this setting, the camera also makes available two additional focus modes. To get access to those modes, press the left button, and the enhanced focus menu appears on the screen, as shown in Figure 3-36.

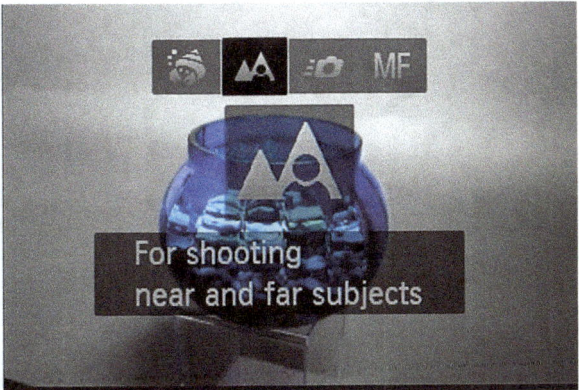

Fig. 3-36: Enhanced Focus Menu with Underwater Setting

You can select one of the icons using the control dial or the left and right direction buttons. The icon at the far left is for underwater macro focusing, when you want to take closeups of things such as shells or sea life. The third icon from the left is for the "quick" focus mode, which is designed for focusing on objects at a distance between 4.9 and 66 feet (1.5 and 20 meters). This range is intended to be used for moving objects or when you may not have much time in which to adjust the focus. With this setting, the camera will still use its autofocus, but having the range narrowed to these values allows it to focus more quickly than normal.

Snow

This scene type, represented by the snowman icon shown in Figure 3-37, uses flash if appropriate and adjusts the colors in an attempt to take photos of people that are not overwhelmed by the brightness of snowy surroundings.

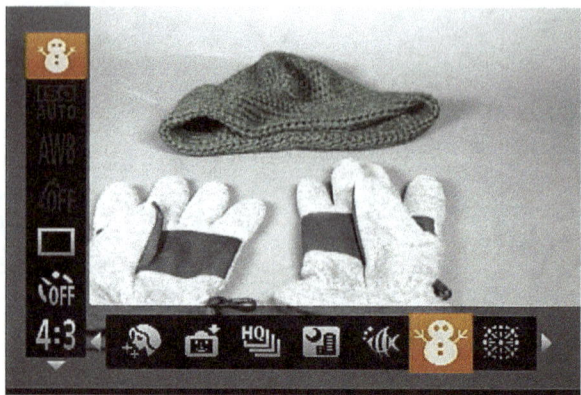

Fig. 3-37: Snow Setting Icon

To illustrate the way in which this option processes your images, I took two shots of the same scene, with and without this setting. Figure 3-38 was taken in AUTO mode with no special settings; Figure 3-39 was taken with the Snow setting. In this case, the differences were not that great.

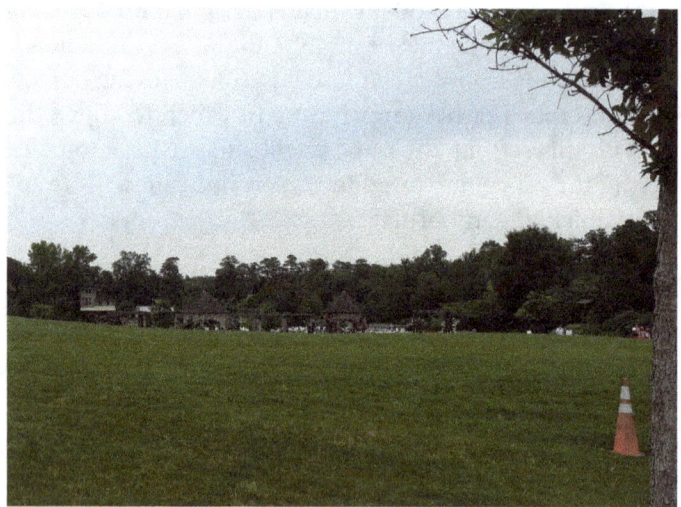

Fig. 3-38: Scene Shot in AUTO Mode

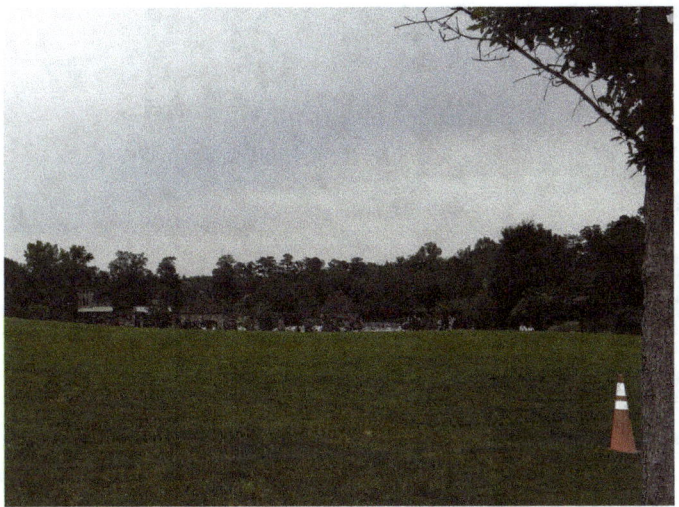

Fig. 3-39: Scene Shot with Snow Setting

Although there appears to be a slight difference in the colors between the two shots, the main difference is that, in the second image, using the Snow setting, the camera used the flash, as can be seen in the lighting of the orange cone at the right of the picture. In any event, this setting is a good one to keep in mind if you need quick shots of the family during a ski trip.

Fireworks

This scene type, whose icon is shown in Figure 3-40, sets the camera to capture vivid images of fireworks bursts. It sets the camera to a 2-second shutter speed and low ISO and intensifies the colors. You should set the camera on a tripod or other sturdy support and turn the image stabilization off in the Shooting menu.

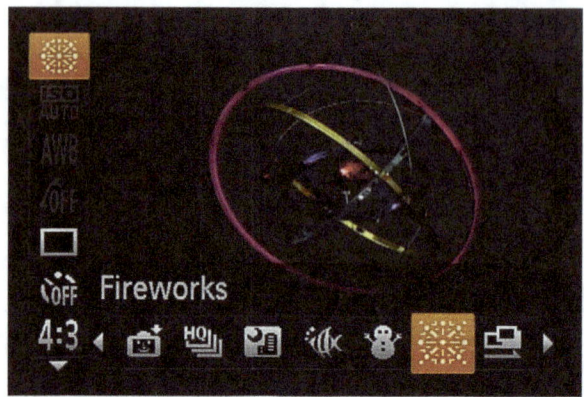

Fig. 3-40: *Fireworks Setting Icon*

Stitch Assist

This setting helps you take a series of images that will be combined later on your computer to form a continuous panorama. There are actually two icons to choose from—panorama from left to right, as shown in Figure 3-41, and panorama from right to left.

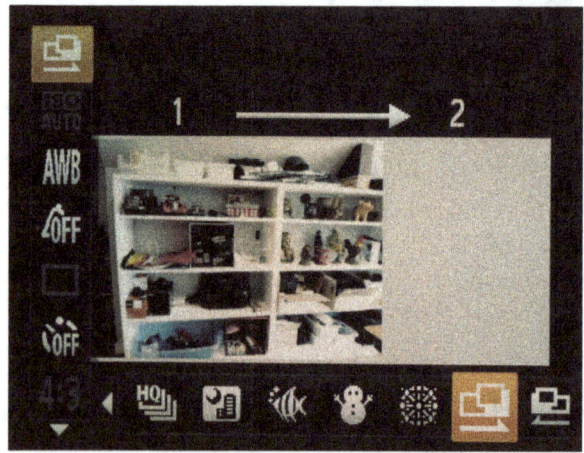

Fig. 3-41: *Stitch Assist Setting L-R on Function Menu*

Choose one of these, and you will see on the screen the live scene, along with a blank gray area. Take the first shot, and the blank area is filled with a portion of the first image, as shown in Figure 3-42.

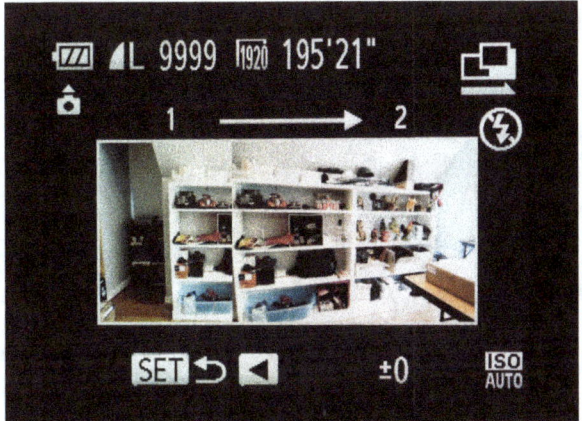

Fig. 3-42: Stitch Assist Screen After First Shot Taken

That partial image will stay on the screen as you move the camera into position for the next image in the panorama. The idea is to take the next image with part of the existing image overlapped, so there will be enough material for the software to use in constructing a seamless panorama later. In other words, make sure that a part of the last image is duplicated by each new image as you take it. You can take a total of up to 26 images in this way.

When you take the series of pictures, you should use a tripod if possible, to keep the images on the same level. Try not to choose a scene with great variations in exposure, because the exposure will be fixed with your first shot. When the images are all taken, use the included PhotoStitch program to weave them together into a panorama. Or, you can use a program such as Photoshop or Photoshop Elements. The image shown in Figure 3-43 was photographed using Stitch Assist, and the parts were merged together in PhotoStitch.

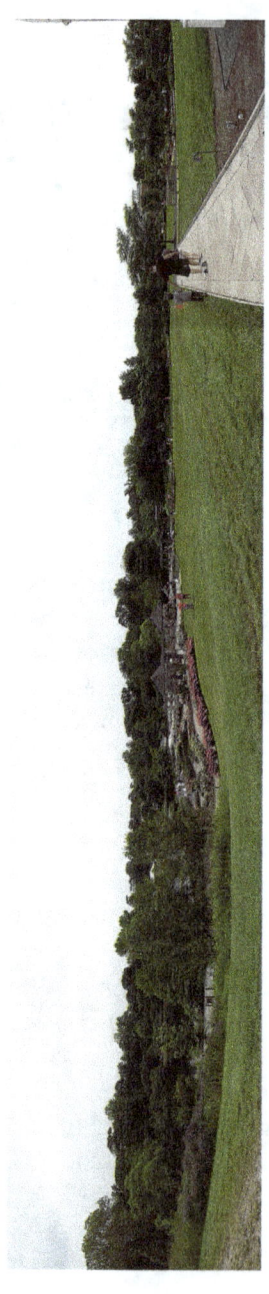

Fig. 3-43: Stitch Assist Panorama Example

Creative Filters Mode

This shooting mode is similar to Scene mode in some ways, because it gives you options for taking pictures with special attributes involving changes in color and other aspects. The essential difference between the modes is a conceptual one—the Scene mode settings involve certain types of subjects in most cases, while the Creative Filters settings provide special effects that you can use for various types of images.

The selection procedure for the Creative Filters settings is the same as for Scene mode.

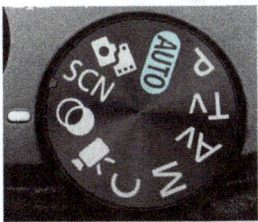

Fig. 3-44: Creative Filters

After turning the mode dial to the Creative Filters icon with two interlocking filters, shown in Figure 3-44, press the Func./ Set button and highlight the top icon on the left of the screen. Then use the Function menu to select from the line of eleven options that are arrayed along the bottom of the display.

Here are notes and examples for each of the eleven settings.

HDR

The first option at the left of the Creative Filters menu is the built-in HDR setting, shown in Figure 3-45, with which the camera automatically takes three shots in rapid succession and then combines them in the camera to produce an enhanced composite image.

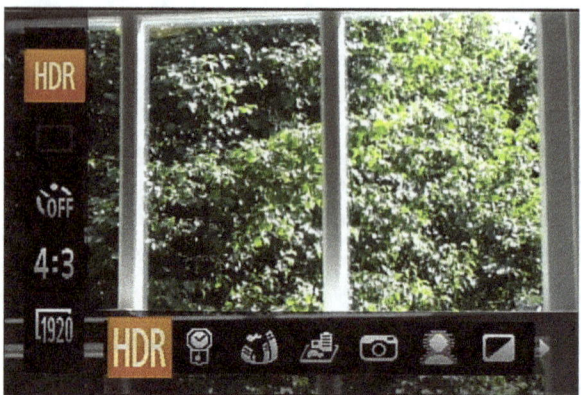

Fig. 3-45: HDR Setting Icon

This is one of the more useful settings on the camera. HDR stands for High Dynamic Range, a photographic technique that involves taking multiple shots at different exposure settings and then combining them, often with software such as Photoshop, so that the best-exposed parts of each shot work together to result in one composite image that exhibits a wide dynamic range—that is, a final image that shows clear details in areas of the scene that were either too bright or too dark in the individual images. The HDR technique is useful for a subject that is partly in bright light, such as sunlight, and partly in deep shadow. The technique also can be used for creative effect to produce a composite image that has a surrealistic quality because of the dramatic effect of lighting that is vibrant and even across a range of unevenly illuminated subjects.

When you select HDR from the menu of Creative Filters settings, the camera forces the flash off and will not let you turn it on. It's also a good idea to go into the IS Mode item on the Shooting menu yourself and set IS Mode to Off—the image stabilization system can interfere with the processing of the three shots. Also, because the camera takes some time to take its three shots and does not align the shots in the camera to eliminate differences among them (as some cameras do), it may not be possible to hold the camera steady long enough for the three shots to be taken without some motion blur. So, you should try to use a tripod or other very steady support while shooting with the HDR setting.

Here is one other point about using the HDR setting that might not be obvious.

With the S110 set for HDR, press the Display button (or touch the DISP. icon on the screen), and the camera puts a short menu on the screen, letting you choose from an abbreviated My Colors selection which, besides Sepia and B/W, includes Super Vivid and Poster Effect as adjustments in addition to the HDR scene type. Super Vivid and Poster Effect are normally considered to be other Creative Filters settings rather than My Colors settings, but in this case you can combine them with the HDR effect. In other words, although you have selected HDR as your Creative Filters setting, you have the ability to se-lect an additional My Colors setting or Creative Filters option to be combined with HDR, in order to create images that not only have enhanced dynamic range, but also have the special look of one of these options. Of course, you can leave this extra My Colors setting at Off and be content with plain HDR. It's worthwhile experimenting with this interesting add-on to the HDR setting; you can achieve some dramatic results by com-bining the heightened impact of an HDR shot with enhanced color effects.

In any event, using HDR alone can be quite sufficient to achieve some useful effects. The series of images shown here illustrates the basic use of this setting and related approaches. I set up a red model truck indoors in front of a window on a sunny day. In Figure 3-46, I took a shot of the truck using Pro-gram mode with no special settings. Clearly, the details on the truck are lost in shadows, and the outdoor part of the scene is washed out in excessive brightness; the dynamic range of the scene was too great for ordinary processing to deal with it.

95

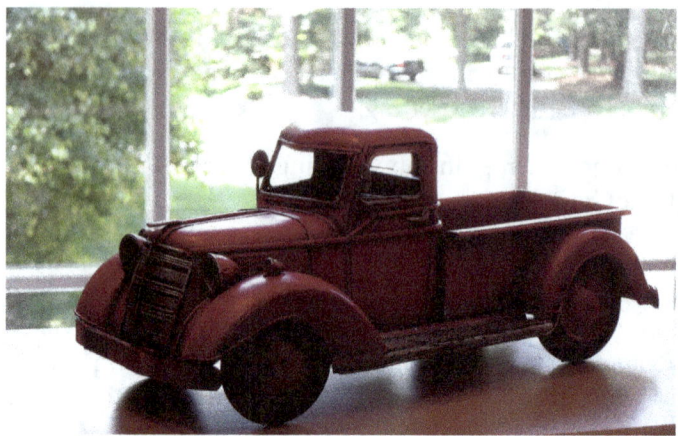

Fig. 3-46: HDR Series - Program Mode

Figure 3-47 shows the same image taken in AUTO mode, to see if the S110 would apply any "intelligent" processing to adjust for the strong contrast between the parts of the scene. In this case, the shot taken in AUTO mode was not any better exposed than the one taken in Program mode.

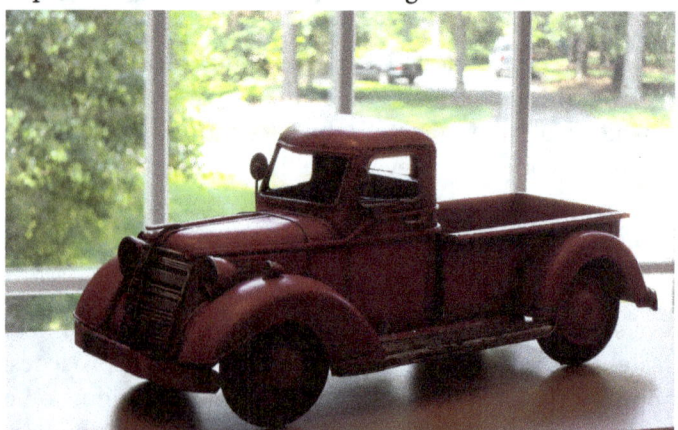

Fig. 3-47: HDR Series - AUTO Mode

Next, Figure 3-48 shows the scene as shot with the HDR setting in Creative Filters mode. This time, the camera clearly compensated for the contrast. The front part of the truck is somewhat brighter than in the first two images, and the outdoor part of the scene is not as badly overexposed as it was in the first two shots.

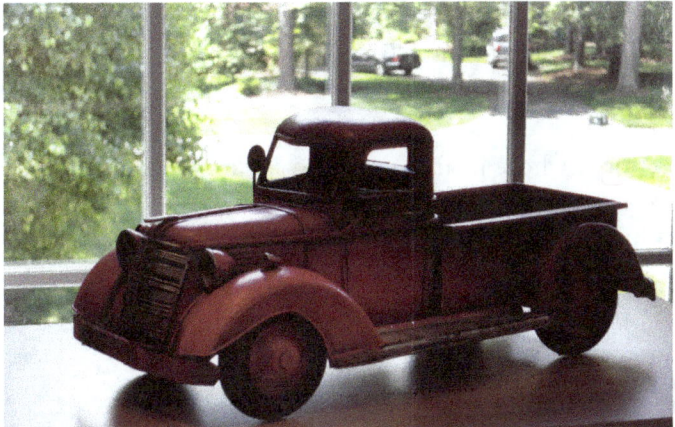

Fig. 3-48: HDR Series - Creative Filters HDR Setting

Finally, I took several shots of the scene using different expo-sures in Manual exposure mode, then combined them in Pho-tomatix Pro, a program designed to create HDR images. After some tweaking, the program produced the final result shown in Figure 3-49, which has brought out the details in the truck and reduced the overexposure of the outdoors area even more.

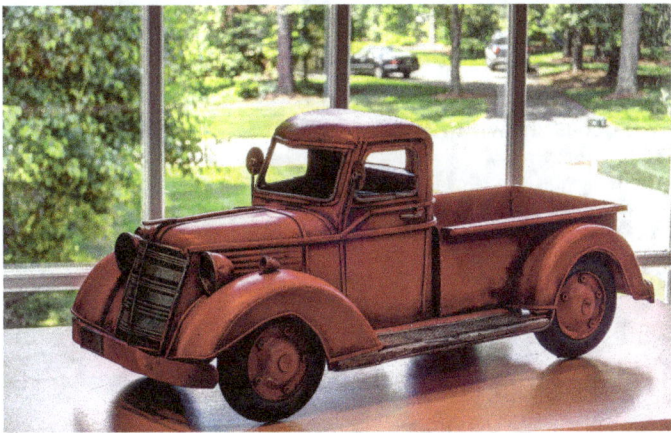

Fig. 3-49: HDR Series - Composite from Photomatix Pro Software

It appears that the HDR setting in Creative Filters mode did a fairly good job in improving the overall exposure of this shot, which was taken in fairly extreme conditions. For daily use, this setting can do an excellent job of dealing with normal situations involving contrasty scenes.

Nostalgic

This option, whose icon is shown in Figure 3-50, is designed to give your images an old-time look by fading the intensity of the colors and "roughening" the image with graininess.

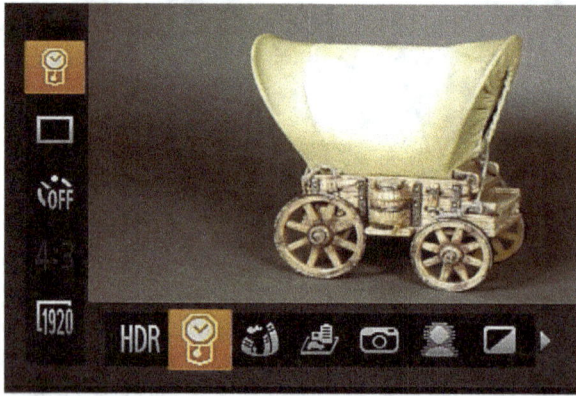

Fig. 3-50: Nostalgic Setting Icon

After you select this option, you will see a scale at the bottom of the screen with white bars that represent how strong the effect will be, as shown in Figure 3-51.

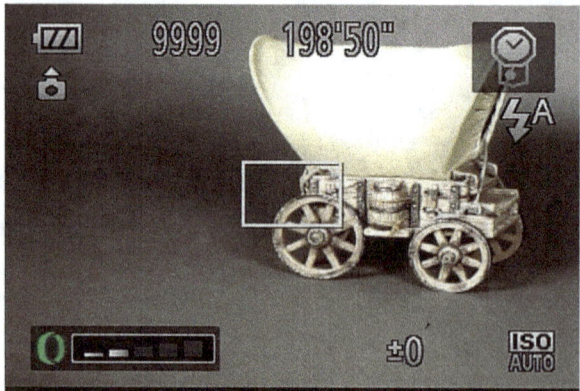

Fig. 3-51: Screen for Adjusting Intensity of Nostalgic Setting

Turn the control ring around the lens to increase or decrease the strength of the nostalgic effect. If you turn the ring to the full extent, the image will be rendered in black and white with a considerable amount of grainy visual noise, or "roughness."

Figure 3-52 was shot with the setting at its mid-level, at which intensity a hint of color remains.

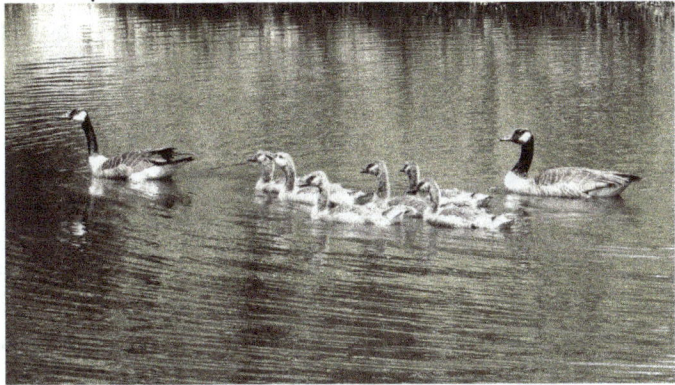

Fig. 3-52: Nostalgic Example

Fish-eye Effect

This effect, whose icon is shown in Figure 3-53, attempts to duplicate the results you can get by using a "fish-eye" lens, an extreme wide-angle lens that makes subjects seem to be stretched as if they were spread around a fish bowl.

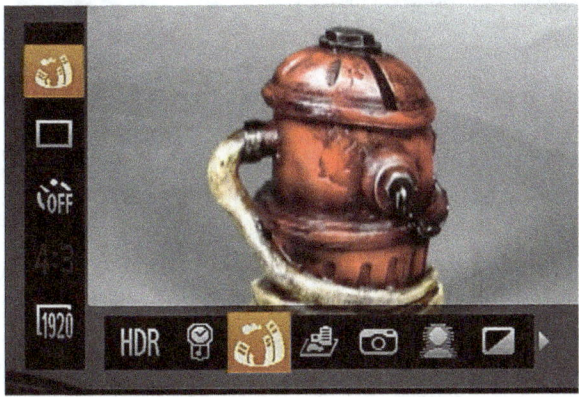

Fig. 3-53: Fish-eye Setting Icon

This is an effect you can achieve through software if you want. For example, in Photoshop you can distort a normal image in this way using the command Filter-Distort-Spherize. It can be fun to experiment with this option in the camera, though. After you first select it, you can use the control ring to select the intensity of the effect. The effect seems to work best with a fairly simple subject that normally would have straight lines, such as a building or bridge. For example, Figure 3-54 is a shot of an old bridge across a river, whose straight lines are strongly distorted by the effect.

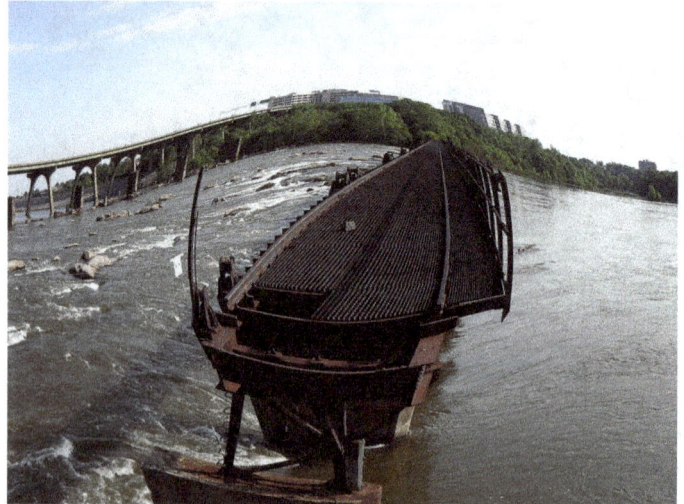

Fig. 3-54: Fish-eye Example

Miniature Effect

This option, whose icon is shown in Figure 3-55, has appeared on a number of cameras in recent years, and appears to be increasingly popular. The Miniature Effect setting lets you select a certain rectangular area in the center of your image to be in sharp focus, and then the rest of the image (top and bottom or two sides) is rendered with a blurred look. The idea is to take a picture of a normal-sized scene and make it have the look of a shot of a tabletop model, or of a scene taken with a large view camera that uses a tilt-shift lens. Pictures of actual models of that sort may have blurred portions because the camera may be close or tilted, meaning the depth of field is very narrow, so only parts of the image can be in sharp focus.

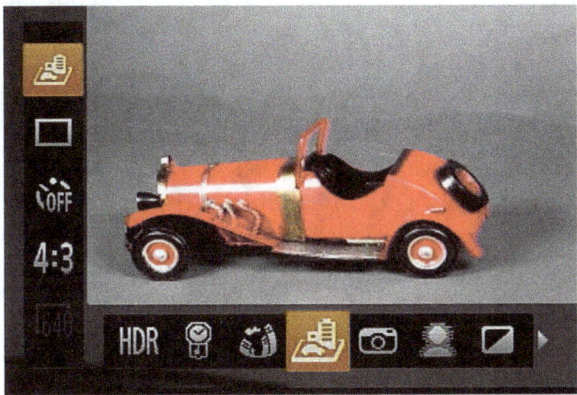

Fig. 3-55: Miniature Effect Icon

After selecting this effect, press the Display button to activate the controls. Use the zoom lever to make the white box on the screen larger or smaller. Everything inside the box will be in sharp focus; areas outside of it will be blurry. Use the direction buttons to move the white box to cover the part of the image that you want to stay in focus. If you turn the camera sideways, the box will turn also. After you're done setting the white box, press DISP. again, and then take the picture.

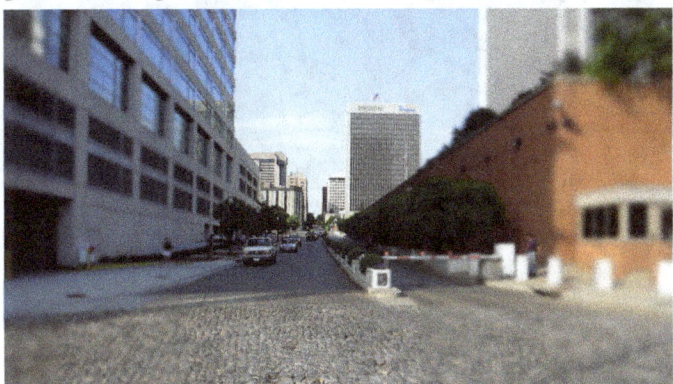

Fig. 3-56: Miniature Effect Example

As you can see in Figure 3-56, this effect can produce an interesting still image. However, probably the more common use of this feature is for making videos that appear to be movies of tabletop models. In that situation, you can set the speed of the movie's playback to be 5, 10, or 20 times faster than normal by turning the control ring to set a speed. The combination of the blurred edges of the scene with the jerky, rapid action of the speeded-up video produces an effect that looks amazingly like a model, rather than real life. Some of the best subjects for videos like this are highway intersections viewed from above, as well as trains, trolleys, and other vehicles that move along straight paths or on tracks, so you can see ahead of time where to set the area of sharp focus. Note that you need to set the camera's aspect ratio to 16:9 if you want a Miniature Effect movie to be recorded in HD.

Toy Camera Effect

This setting, shown in Figure 3-57, darkens the corners of the image and blurs them somewhat to create the vignetting effect that often is seen in images taken with inexpensive cameras with cheap lenses.

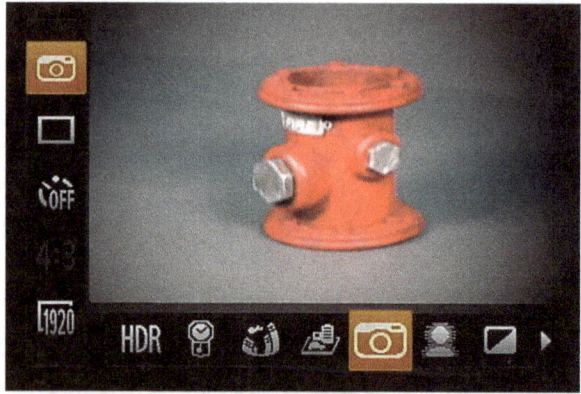

Fig. 3-57: Toy Camera Effect Icon

This effect is probably included with the camera because of the current popularity of cameras such as the Holga and Diana.

Those are "toy cameras" that have somewhat of a cult following among hobbyists who enjoy taking interesting photographs under the constraints imposed by cheaply made equipment. So, in effect, you can convert your sophisticated, high-quality S110 into the equivalent of a low-end snapshooter.

Once you have selected the effect, you can use the control ring to alter the color balance, either to bluish tints (here called "cool" by Canon) or reddish ones ("warm"); or you can leave the setting at its "standard" level. Figure 3-58 was taken with the setting set toward the cooler end of the scale.

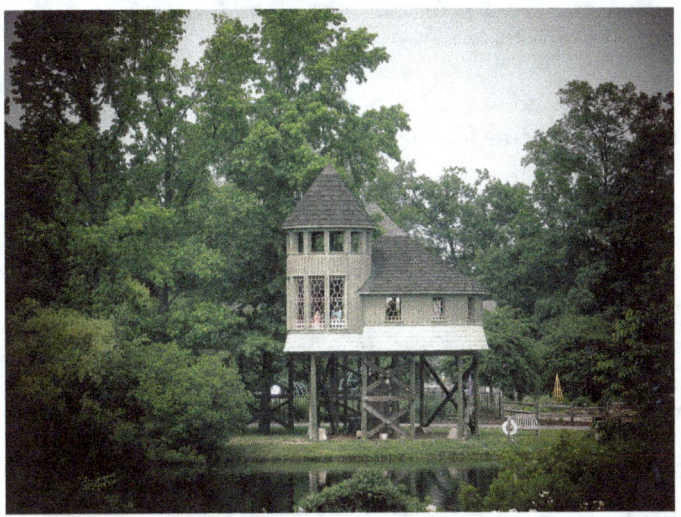

Fig. 3-58: Toy Camera Effect Example

Soft Focus

With this setting, shown in Figure 3-59, the camera defocuses the image to achieve a softer, blurry appearance. As with several other settings, you can use the control ring to adjust the intensity of the effect.

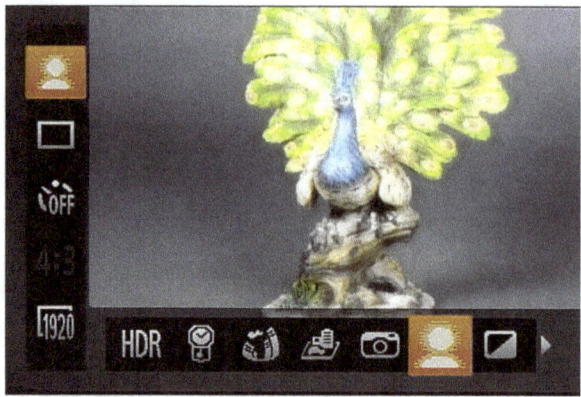

Fig. 3-59: Soft Focus Setting Icon

Figure 3-60 is an illustration of the use of this setting to soften a view of springtime foliage.

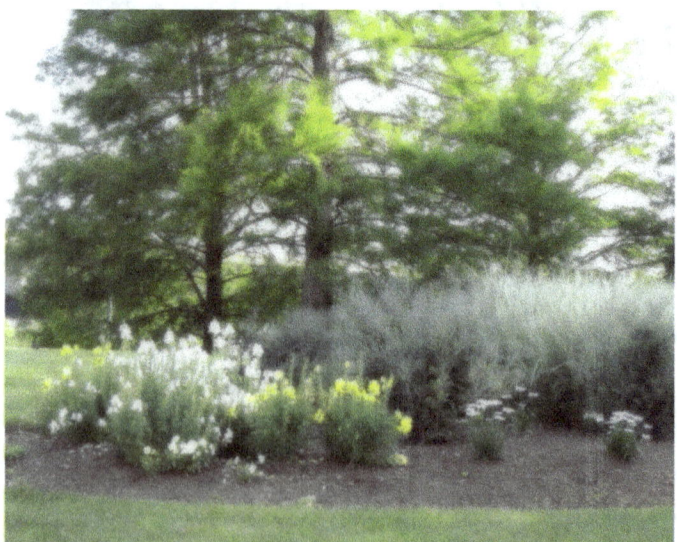

Fig. 3-60: Soft Focus Example

Monochrome

If you are interested in monochrome images, you are in luck with the PowerShot S110, because there are several ways to shoot in black and white. One way is to use the B/W setting of the My Colors option on the Function menu. If you choose that option, you have to shoot in the more advanced (PASM) modes, which gives you access to most other settings in the menu systems. Also, there are several settings in the Creative Filters shooting mode that can produce monochrome, or near-monochrome images, depending on the intensity of their settings: HDR, Nostalgic, and Color Accent, as well as this one, Monochrome, whose icon is shown in Figure 3-61.

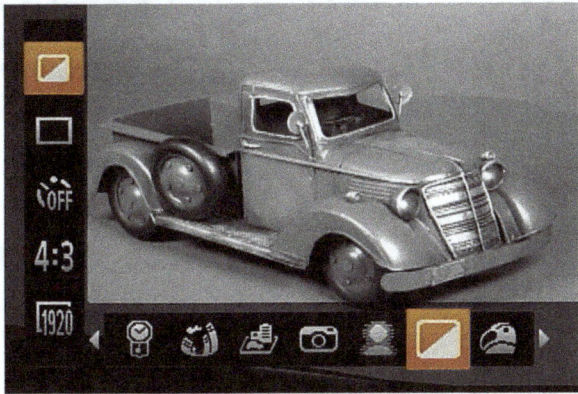

Fig. 3-61: Monochrome Setting Icon

Of course, there are differences among these various settings, involving what modes they can be used in and what effects they include besides monochrome coloring. The Monochrome setting is distinguished from the others because it includes the same "cool" and "warm" control as the Toy Camera Effect setting, discussed above.

In other words, after you select Monochrome from the Creative Filters list, you will see icons in the lower left of the display indicating that you can turn the control ring to select cool or warm to add a bluish or reddish tint to the image, or select standard to leave the image in basic black and white. The example shown in Figure 3-62 was taken with the dial set toward the cool side.

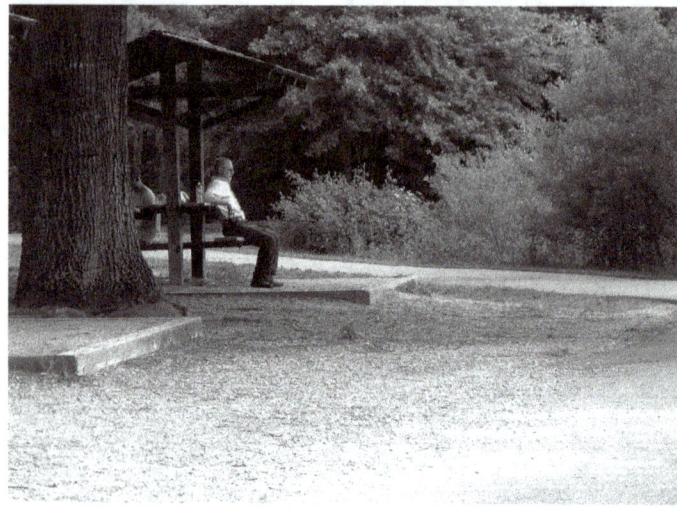

Fig. 3-62: Monochrome Setting Example

Super Vivid

This setting, whose icon is seen in Figure 3-63, intensifies all the colors in your image, giving a dramatic, super-saturated effect.

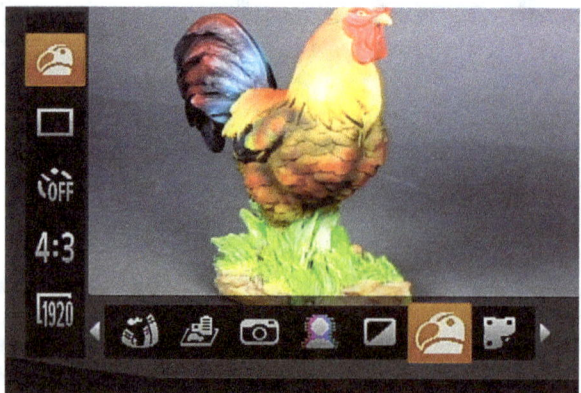

Fig. 3-63: Super Vivid Setting Icon

106

This is the sort of result you could achieve with post-processing software such as Photoshop Elements, but, if you like to experiment with the appearance of your images as they come from the camera, this setting can yield striking results.

Figure 3-64 shows a scene taken using the Super Vivid setting, while Figure 3-65 shows another view of the same scene taken using AUTO mode, to illustrate the difference from using Super Vivid.

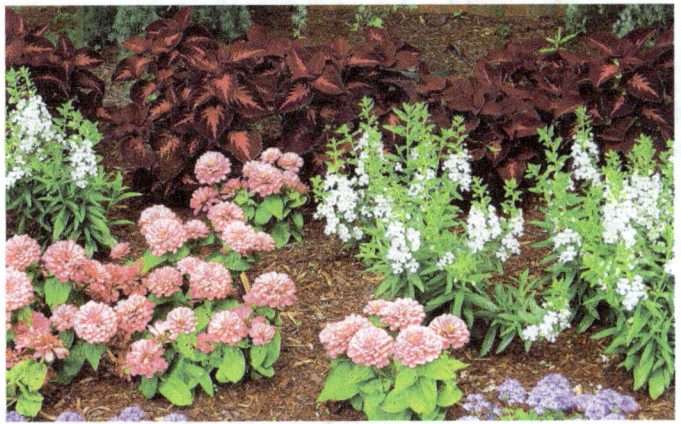

Fig. 3-64: Super Vivid Example

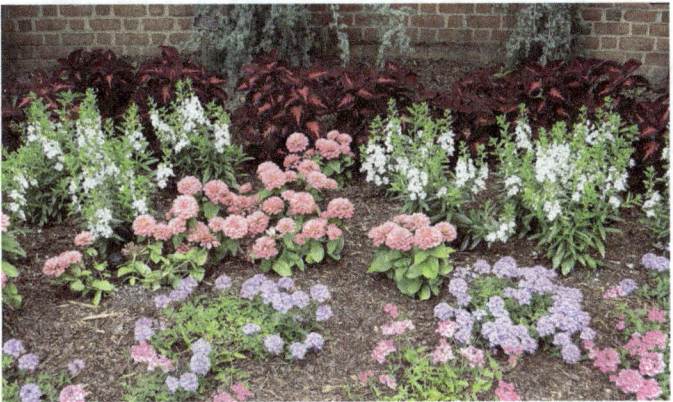

Fig. 3-65: Comparison Shot Taken in AUTO Mode

Poster Effect

This option, whose icon is shown in Figure 3-66, like Super Vivid, alters the appearance of your image in a striking way.

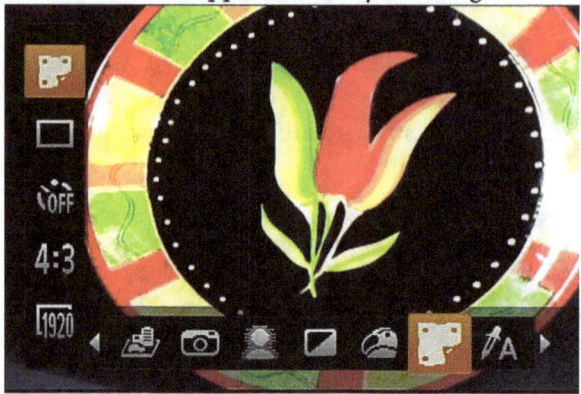

Fig. 3-66: Poster Effect Setting Icon

The "posterized" shot emphasizes the shape and color of your subject and renders it with a stylized look, removing some of the realism and making the scene look more like a painting done with poster colors or pastels. In Figure 3-67 I used this setting to take a picture of a bench in a suburban park. The poster effect seemed to me to create an aura of unreality.

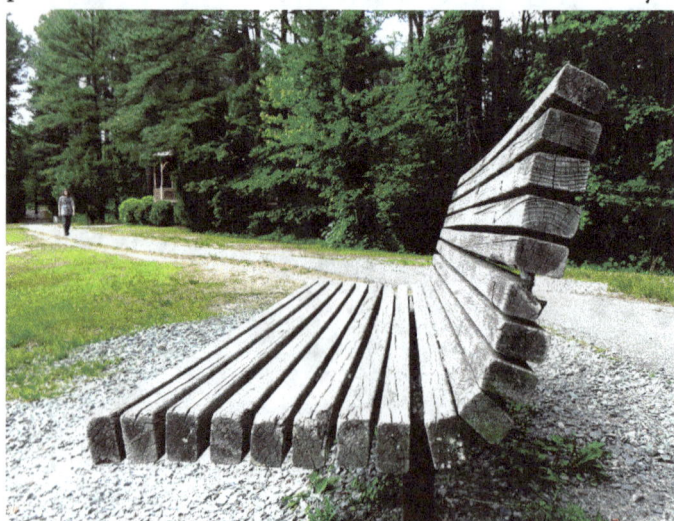

Fig. 3-67: Poster Effect Example

Color Accent

This option also is not meant for a particular type of scene but is more of a procedure. The Color Accent option lets you specify one color or range of colors to be retained; then, when you take the picture, only that color or range of colors keeps its hue, and the rest of the image appears in black and white.

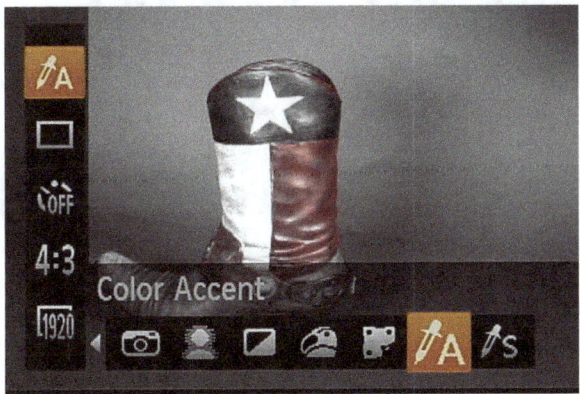

Fig. 3-68: Color Accent Setting Icon

Here is how it works. After highlighting Color Accent from the line of icons at the bottom of the screen, as shown in Figure 3-68, and pressing Func./Set to select it, press the Display button (or touch the on-screen icon) and a small white square appears in the center of the screen, as shown in Figure 3-69.

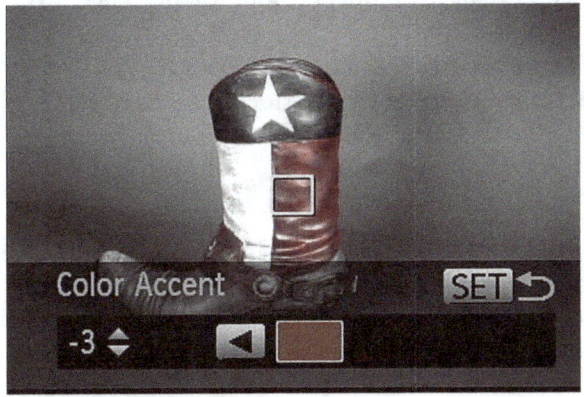

Fig. 3-69: Color Accent Selection Screen

109

Place that square over the color you want to retain, press the left button to lock in your choice, then press Func./Set. For example, for Figure 3-70, I placed the square over one of the red roses in the scene, with the result that only those flowers retained their color in the final image.

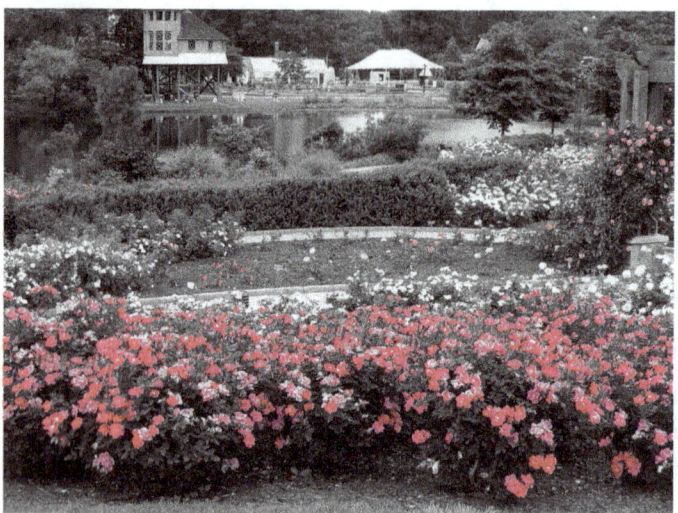

Fig. 3-70: *Color Accent Example*

You can also use the up and down buttons to increase the range of colors that are retained. If you press the up button to increase the number, you increase the range of colors (that is, in this case, more of the reddish colors will be kept); if you press the down button, the number will turn negative, limiting the color to just the particular hue you selected. Then, when you take the picture, every object outside the selected range of colors will be in monochrome.

Color Swap

This procedure, whose icon is shown in Figure 3-71, is like Color Accent except that, instead of keeping one color, it lets you specify one color to change into another.

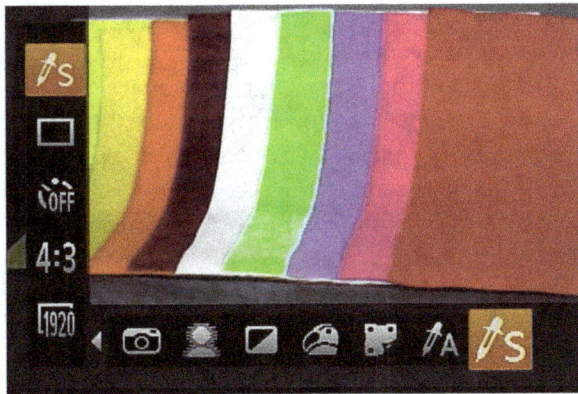

Fig. 3-71: *Color Swap Setting Icon*

In Figure 3-72, I used this feature to change the color of green leaves and grass to light blue, giving the appearance of a coating of frost on the field.

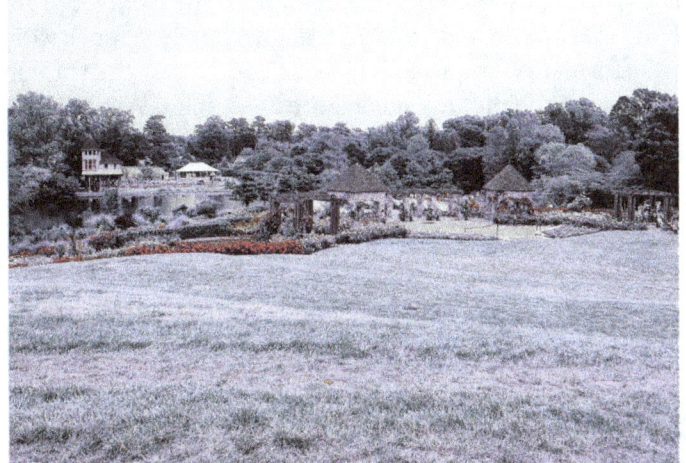

Fig. 3-72: *Color Swap Example*

Here is how to accomplish this exchange. After selecting Color Swap, press the Display button and the screen will show the default settings, with green changed to gray. The screen will be blinking, showing alternately the normal image and the color-swapped image using those settings, if both colors are

111

in the scene. To change the settings, move the small square in the center of the screen over the color to be transformed and press the left direction button. Then place the square over the color the first one is to be changed to, and press the right direction button. Then press Display again to return to the shooting screen, aim at the scene, and take the picture. You may need to experiment a bit to find colors that transform well; I found that some color combinations, such as white and black, don't work very well in some cases.

Note that you don't have to select colors that appear in the scene before you. For example, if you want to see how your red car would look if it were painted yellow, and there's no yellow object near the car, you can go find the perfect shade of yellow anywhere you want—you can travel to the paint store if you want—and set the target color there. Then you can come back to where your car is parked and select its color as the source color. Once the two colors are entered into the camera, press the Func./Set button and you will see how the scene looks with the transformation in place. If it looks good, press the shutter button to take the picture. For Figure 3-72, there was no suitable white object in the outdoor area near the grass, so I used the light blue of my shirt for the target color, to simulate the appearance of frost.

Custom Mode

When you turn the mode dial to the C setting, as shown in Figure 3-73, you take advantage of a very powerful and convenient feature of the PowerShot S110.

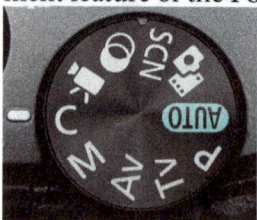

Fig. 3-73: *Custom Mode*

(I call this setting the Custom shooting mode because of the

C on the mode dial, but Canon calls it "Saving Shooting Settings," in case you're looking for the discussion of this mode, which is at page 212 of the Canon user's manual.) You can set up the camera exactly as you want it, with a shooting mode, zoom amount, white balance, ISO, and other settings, and then recall all of those settings instantly just by turning the mode dial to the letter C. The only shooting modes that you can save settings for are Program, Aperture Priority, Shutter Priority, and Manual; you cannot save them for the AUTO, Scene, Creative Filters, Movie, or Movie Digest modes.

Here is how this works. First, take your time and set up the camera with all of the settings you want to be able to recall. For example, suppose you are going to do street photography. You may want to use a fast shutter speed, say 1/250 second, in black and white, at ISO 1600, using continuous shooting with autofocus, using Large and Superfine JPEG images, and shooting in the 4:3 aspect ratio to use all of the available resolution for your shots.

Your first step is to make all of these settings. Set the mode dial to Shutter Priority and use the control ring to set a shutter speed of 1/250 second. Then press the Func./Set button to summon the Function menu, and set ISO to 1600, then go down to white balance and select Daylight, then to My Colors and select the B/W option. Next, move down to the drive mode option and select the icon with the letters AF on a stack of frames. Finally, further down the list of icons, select 4:3 for the aspect ratio, JPEG for format, and Large and Superfine for the image size and quality. You also may want to push the zoom lever all the way to the left, for wide-angle shooting.

Once all of these settings are made, press the Menu button to call up the Shooting menu, and scroll down (or scroll up and wrap around to the bottom) to select the Save Settings item, shown in Figure 3-74, then press OK on the screen shown in Figure 3-75 that asks, Save Current Settings?

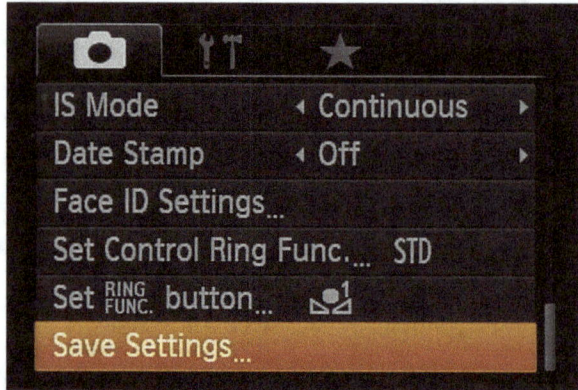

Fig. 3-74: *Save Settings Menu Item*

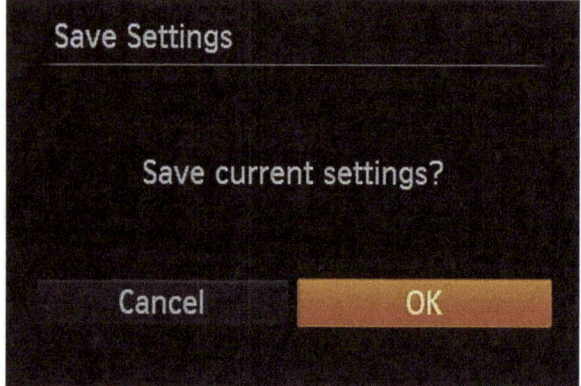

Fig. 3-75: *Save Settings Confirmation Screen*

Now, to check how this worked, try making some very different settings, such as Manual exposure with a shutter speed of
1 second, My Colors set to Vivid, continuous shooting turned
off, the zoom lever moved all the way to the right for telephoto, and image format set to Raw. Then turn the mode dial back
to the C setting, and you will see that all of the custom settings
you made have come back, including the zoom position, shutter speed, and everything else. This is really a wonderful feature, and more powerful than similar features on some other
cameras, which can save menu settings but not settings such
as shutter speed and zoom position. What is also quite amaz-

114

ing is that, if you now switch back to Manual exposure mode, the camera will restore the settings that you had in that mode before you turned to the C mode. (The position of the zoom lens will not revert to where it was, though.)

The single flaw I find with this mode is that there is only one slot for it on the mode dial (some cameras have two or more), and therefore only one group of settings that can be saved at a time. But it's much better than nothing. I suggest you experiment and find one custom settings group that is the most useful to you, and save it to the C mode for instant recall. It also can be useful to jot down some notes on paper with several groups of settings for various situations, so you can quickly program the appropriate group of settings into the camera when you are going to be taking pictures in that type of situation.

Chapter 4: Function menu, Shooting Menu, and My Menu

Much of the power of the PowerShot S110 resides in the many options included in the Function menu and the Shooting menu, which together provide the user with control over the appearance of the images and how they are captured. Depending on your own preferences, you may not have to use these menus too much. You may prefer to use the various Scene mode or Creative Filters mode settings, which choose many of the options for you, or you may prefer, at least on occasion, to use AUTO mode, in which the camera makes its own choices. However, it's nice to know that you do have this degree of control over many functions available if you want it, and it is very useful to understand what types of items you can exercise control over. You also can create a customized menu with a few of your most often-used options, using the feature called My Menu, also discussed in this chapter.

The Function Menu

The first menu system for controlling your settings while shooting images is the Function menu, which is summoned by pressing the Func./Set button, in the center of the control dial, while the camera is in shooting mode. I have already discussed some of the options that are available through this menu, but now it is time to go through each setting in more detail. Note that, as is also true for the Shooting menu, the number of items that are available for selection through the Function menu varies according to the current shooting mode. So, for example, as shown in Figure 4-1, if the camera is set to AUTO mode, only a few options are available (Auto Drive, self-timer, aspect ratio, image size, and movie quality), whereas virtually the whole range of 13 options is available in Program mode.

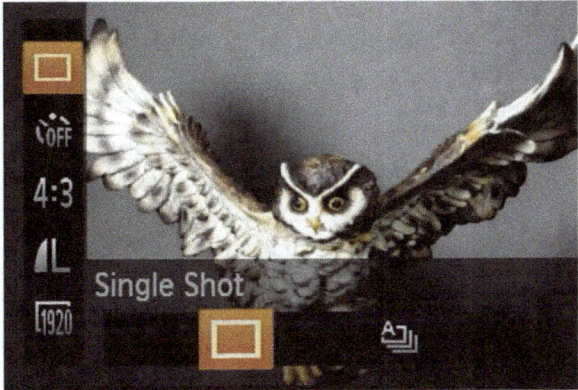

Fig. 4-1: Function Menu in AUTO Mode

(The options are more limited when image quality is set to Raw.) The Scene, Creative Filters, and Movie modes have moderate numbers of menu options available.

In the following discussion, I will describe all of the options that are generally applicable to recording still images. I won't discuss those that are specific to certain settings, such as the scene types, which are selected from the Function menu when the camera is set to Scene mode, or the settings specific to Movie mode, which I will discuss in Chapter 8. In order to follow this discussion and test all of the options, it is helpful to set the shooting mode to Program and the image quality to JPEG, so almost all of the menu options can be selected.

Also, note that the touch screen can be used to make selections from this menu once you have pressed the Func./Set button to call up the menu. I will not mention the touch screen repeatedly in discussing how to make settings; you can always try touching the screen to see if a setting can be made by touch.

With that introduction, following are details about each of the

117

options on the Function menu, starting at the top.

i-Contrast

This is a very useful option that can help you avoid problems with excessive contrast in your images. Such problems arise because digital cameras cannot easily process a very wide range of dark and light areas in the same image—that is, their "dynamic range" is limited. So, if you are taking a picture in an area that is partly lit by bright sunlight and partly in deep shade, the resulting image is likely to have some dark areas in which the details are lost in the shadows, or some areas in which the highlights, or bright areas, are excessively bright, or "blown out," so, again, the details of the image are lost.

One approach to this problem is to use High Dynamic Range, or HDR, techniques, in which multiple photographs of the same scene with different exposures are combined into one composite image that is properly exposed throughout the entire scene. The PowerShot S110 can take HDR shots on its own, or you can take separate exposures and combine them in software on your computer into a composite HDR image. I discussed those approaches in Chapter 3.

The i-Contrast setting gives you another way to deal with the problem of uneven lighting, with special processing in the camera that can boost the details in the dark areas and reduce the overexposure in the bright areas at the same time, resulting in a single image with better exposure than would be possible otherwise. In order to do this, i-Contrast uses two complementary sub-settings, called DR (Dynamic Range) Correction to reduce highlight blowout, and Shadow Correction to pull details out of the shadows.

The i-Contrast setting process is a bit involved; here are the steps. Press the Func./Set button and highlight this option, the top one at the left of the screen, shown in Figure 4-2. (Somewhat oddly, when the Function menu first appears, this item is out of sight, above the ISO item; you have to scroll up to reach i-Contrast.)

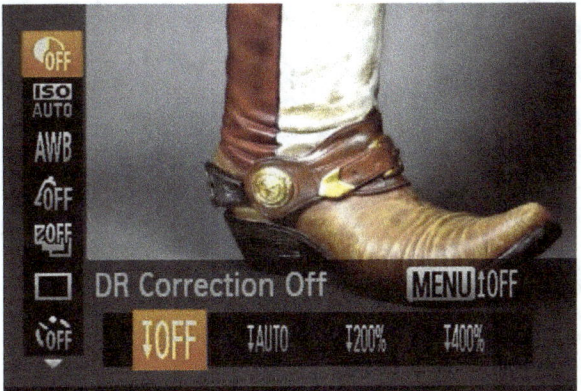

Fig. 4-2: i-Contrast Item on Function Menu

Above the line of icons at the bottom of the screen, when you first highlight the Off icon, you should see the words, "DR Correction Off," as shown in Figure 4-2, meaning you are currently working with the DR Correction sub-setting. (That label may look different and then disappear, depending on the Hints & Tips setting on the Setup menu.)

Scroll through the other settings using the control dial or the direction buttons: Auto, 200%, and 400%. With the Auto setting, the camera will attempt to determine how much processing is needed. The other two settings allow you to choose how much correction is applied.

When you are finished with the DR Correction sub-setting, press the Menu button, and the display switches to let you set the Shadow Correction. For that option, there are only two possible settings: Off and Auto, as shown in Figure 4-3.

119

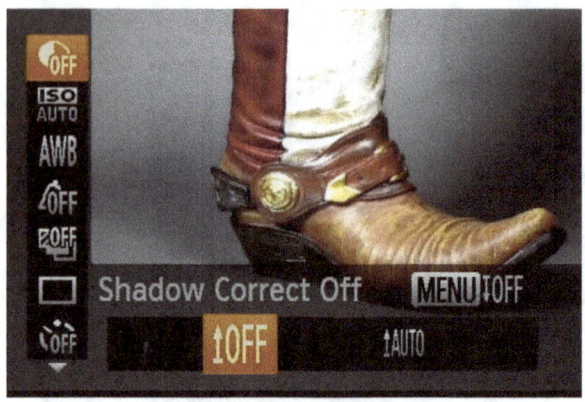

Fig. 4-3: Shadow Correction Option on Function Menu

When you have finished with setting both Dynamic Range and Shadow Correction, press the Func./Set button again to return to the shooting screen. An i-Contrast icon will appear in the lower right of the display, as shown in Figure 4-4, to remind you that you are using this feature.

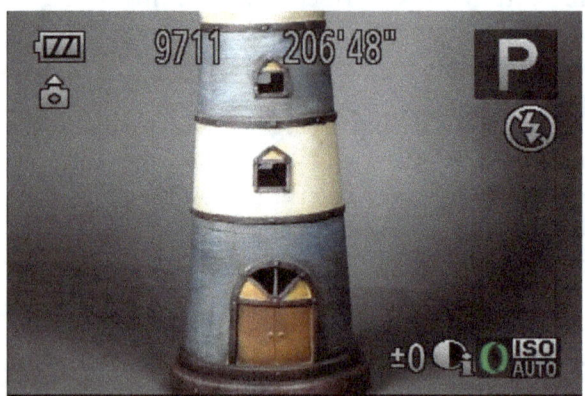

Fig. 4-4: i-Contrast Icon in Lower Right Corner of Screen

To illustrate the effect of the DR setting, I took two photos of cowboy boots in harshly contrasting lighting. In Figure 4-5, DR was turned off; in Figure 4-6, it was set to its maximum value of 400%.

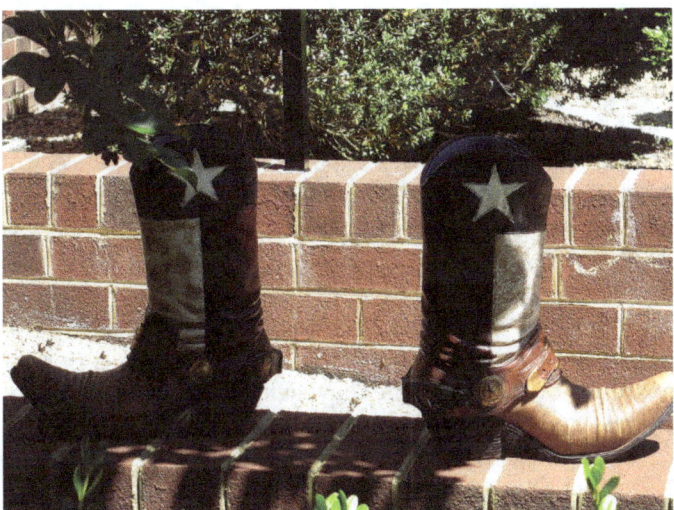

Fig. 4-5: DR Off

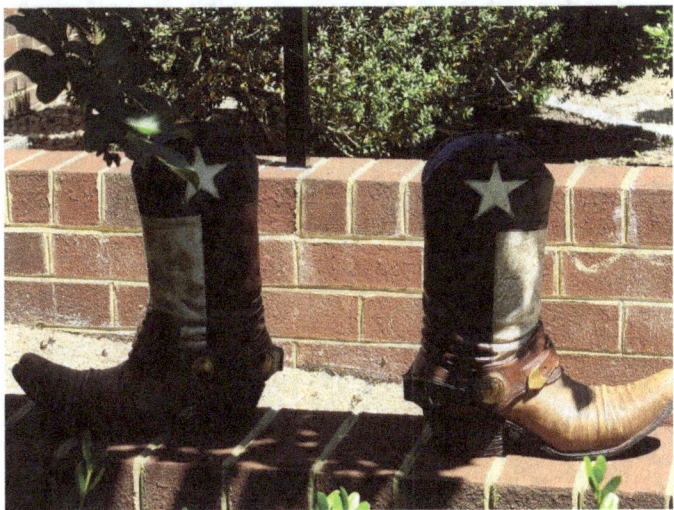

Fig. 4-6: DR 400%

As you can see, the DR setting did not pull details out of the shadows. Instead, it lowered the brightness of the highlights. In these images, this effect appears to be most obvious in the area of light-colored gravel on the ground between the two

121

brick walls. In the image with DR turned off, that area is very bright and washed out; in the image with DR turned on to the maximum, the DR processing reduced the excessive brightness to a more acceptable level. So, if you use this setting, you may be able to increase your exposure somewhat to account for dark areas, relying on the DR setting to keep the highlights from becoming excessively bright. You also can use Shadow Correction if you need to pull details out of the shadows.

Note that i-Contrast cannot be used with Raw images. Also, you can apply a slightly different version of i-Contrast to your images after the fact from the Playback menu, as discussed in Chapter 6.

ISO

These initials represent the International Organization for Standardization, which develops standards for photography and other industries. When I first started in film photography, this standard was called ASA, for American Standards Association. The ISO acronym reflects the more international nature of the modern photographic industry.

The original use of the ISO/ASA standard was to designate the "speed," or light sensitivity, of film. For example, a "slow" film might be rated ISO 64, or even ISO 25, meaning it takes a considerable amount of exposure to light to create a usable image on the film. Slow films yield higher-quality, less-grainy images than faster films. There are "fast" films available, some black-and-white and some color, with ISO ratings of 400 or even higher, that are designed to yield usable images in lower light. Such films can often be used indoors without flash, for example.

With digital technology, the industry has retained the ISO concept, though it applies not to film but to the light sensitivity of the camera's sensor, because there is no film involved in a digital camera. The ISO ratings for digital cameras are supposed to be essentially equivalent to the ISO ratings for films.

So if your camera is set to ISO 80, there will have to be a good deal of light to expose the image properly, but if the camera is set to ISO 1600, a reasonably good (but "noisier" or "fuzzier") image can be made in very low light.

The upshot of all of this is that, generally speaking, you want to shoot your images with the camera set to the lowest ISO possible that will allow the image to be exposed properly. (One exception to this rule is if you want, for creative purposes, the grainy look that comes from shooting at a high ISO value.) For example, if you are shooting indoors in low light, you may need to set the ISO to a high value (say, ISO 800) so you can expose the image with a reasonably fast shutter speed. Otherwise, if the camera uses a slow shutter speed, the resulting image would likely be blurry and possibly unusable.

To summarize: Shoot with low ISO settings (around 100) when possible; shoot with high ISO settings (400 or higher, up to 1600 or even 3200) when necessary to allow a fast shutter speed to stop action and avoid blurriness, or when desired to achieve a creative effect with graininess.

With that background, here is how to set ISO on this camera. As is discussed in detail in Chapter 5, one good feature of the PowerShot S110 is that you can make certain important settings, such as ISO, using the control ring. However, you can also set ISO from the Function menu, and this is not a bad way to make this setting. So, especially if you want to use the control ring for other purposes, it's good to know how to get quick access to the ISO setting with this menu.

Press the Func./Set button and move to the ISO icon, the second one down on the left side of the screen, as shown in Figure 4-7. Then scroll across the menu at the bottom of the screen to select a value ranging from Auto at the left, through 80, 100, 200, and other specific values, to a maximum of 12800 at the right of the scale. There are values between the hundreds, represented by tick marks, such as 160, 250, 320, and 1250.

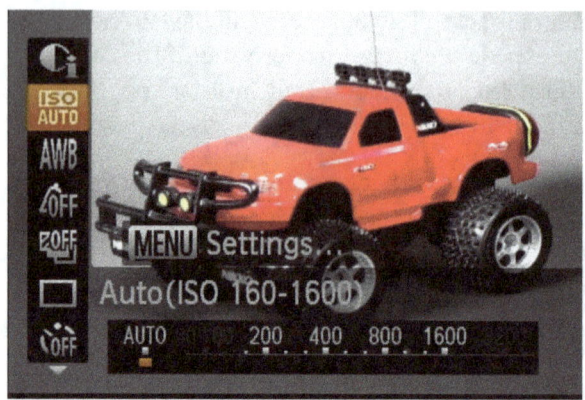

Fig. 4-7: ISO Item Highlighted on Function Menu

If you choose Auto, the camera will select a value from the minimum of 80 to the maximum that you have set with the ISO Auto Settings option. To set the upper level, press the Menu button to display the ISO Auto Settings screen.

On that screen, shown in Figure 4-8, use the right and left direction buttons (or use the touch-screen icons) to set the maximum ISO speed, which can be a value from 400 to 1600.

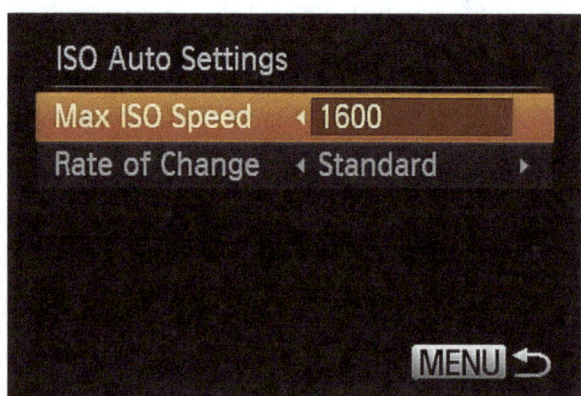

Fig. 4-8: ISO Auto Settings Menu Option

For example, if you set ISO to Auto and set the maximum ISO speed to 1600, the camera will never be able to use an ISO value greater than 1600 when Auto ISO is in effect. If you wanted to use a value higher than that, you would have to set it manually, or use the Handheld Night Scene setting of Scene mode, which uses high ISO values. I discuss the ISO Auto Settings item in more detail later in this chapter, in connection with the Shooting menu, because that menu includes this feature as a separate menu item.

You cannot select Auto ISO in Manual exposure mode; in that shooting mode you have to select a numerical value. In AUTO shooting mode, Movie mode, Creative Filters mode, and Scene mode, Auto ISO is automatically set, and you cannot adjust the ISO setting. Also, when DR Correction is turned on at a level of 200%, ISO can be set only to AUTO or to a level from 160 to 1600. When DR Correction is set to 400%, ISO can be set only to AUTO or to a level from 320 to 1600. Finally, as discussed in Chapter 3, if the shutter speed is set to a time longer than one second, the camera automatically sets the ISO to 80.

White Balance

One issue that arises in all photography is that film, or a digital camera's sensor, reacts differently to colors than the human eye does. When you or I see a scene in daylight or indoors under various types of artificial lighting, we generally do not notice a difference in the hues of the things we see depending on the light source. However, the camera does not inherently have this auto-correcting ability. The camera "sees" colors differently depending on the "color temperature" of the light that illuminates the object or scene in question. The color temperature of light is a numerical value that is expressed in a unit known as kelvins (K). A light source with a lower kelvin rating produces a "warmer" or more reddish light. A light source with a higher kelvin rating produces a "cooler" or more bluish light. For example, candlelight is rated at about 1,800 K; indoor tungsten light (ordinary light bulb) is rated at about 3,000 K; outdoor sunlight and electronic flash are rated at about 5,500 K; and outdoor shade is rated at about 7,000 K.

125

What does this mean in practice? With a film camera, you may need a color filter in front of the lens or light fixture to "correct" for the color temperature of the light source. Any given color film is rated to expose colors correctly at a particular color temperature (or, to put it another way, with a particular light source). So if you are using color film rated for daylight use, you can use it outdoors without a filter. But if you happen to be using that film indoors, you will need a color filter to correct the color temperature; otherwise, the resulting picture will look excessively reddish because of the imbalance between the film and the color temperature of the light source.

With a digital camera, you do not need to worry about filters, because the camera can adjust its electronic circuitry to correct the "white balance," which is the term used in the context of digital photography for balancing color temperature.

The PowerShot S110, like most current digital cameras, has a setting for white balance, which lets the camera set the proper color correction to account for any given light source.

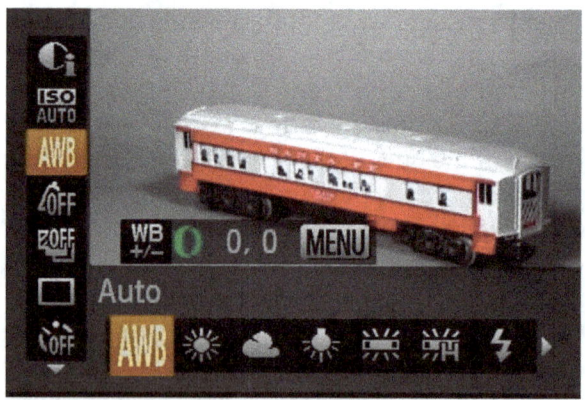

Fig. 4-9: White Balance Option on Function Menu

Here is how to make this setting through the Function menu. Once you have highlighted the white balance setting, which is the third icon down on the left side of the screen, as shown in Figure 4-9, you can scroll across the line of icons at the bot-

126

tom of the screen. These icons correspond to the following choices for the white balance setting, most of them represented by icons: Auto White Balance (AWB); Daylight (sun icon); Cloudy (cloud); Tungsten (round light bulb); Fluorescent (fluorescent bulb); Fluorescent H (same, with letter H); Flash (lightning bolt); Underwater (fish); Custom 1; and Custom 2 (the last two are both represented by a special symbol).

These settings should be self-explanatory, except for Fluorescent H. That setting is for a type of fluorescent bulb that is meant to be closer to the appearance of daylight than normal fluorescents. You may want to experiment, not just with the fluorescent settings, but with all of the presets, to see if the settings listed above produce the results you want. If not, you'll be better off setting the white balance manually.

In my experience, Auto White Balance works quite well when you're shooting outdoors in sunlit or cloudy conditions, and indoors when you're using flash. However, I have occasionally had questionable results with AWB shooting indoors under incandescent lighting. So, when I'm shooting indoors in ordinary room lighting or with photoflood lights, I often use Program or another shooting mode that lets me set the white balance to the proper value; as noted above, with Auto, Creative Filters, and some other modes, the camera is set to Auto White Balance and you have no control over the setting.

If you are faced with an unusual lighting situation, such as mixed lighting or an unknown light source (when you are in a commercial building, for example), or when you want to exercise full control over the white balance setting, you can set a custom white balance by causing the camera to calibrate the setting according to the existing light source or sources.

To set white balance manually, from the white balance menu option on the Function menu, highlight one of the two Custom options, at the far right of the line of icons at the bottom of the screen, as shown in Figure 4-10.

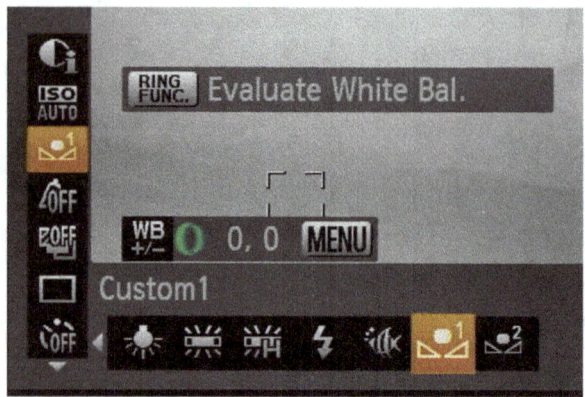

Fig. 4-10: Custom White Balance Icon on Function Menu

Aim the camera at a white (or gray) sheet of paper (or a white or gray wall, or other object) under the light source you will be using, and fill the camera's entire screen (not just the focus frame, if one is visible) with the image of that surface. (You can zoom using the zoom lever if necessary to fill the screen with the chosen surface.) Press the Ring Function button (to the left of the red Movie button) to record and lock in that white balance setting. You will probably see the colors on the screen change, to reflect the use of the new setting. Now, until you change that setting, whenever you select the same Custom white balance icon (number 1 or 2, whichever you used), the camera's white balance will be set for the value you have just selected through this procedure. This system can be very useful if you often use a particular light source, and want to have the camera set to the appropriate white balance for that source.

Figure 4-11 shows all of the various white balance settings, as used for a scene that was lighted with artificial lights balanced for daylight. The Custom setting was based on the gray background that is seen in the images. As you can see, all of the settings produced a reasonably well balanced appearance under this lighting except for Tungsten, which produced an excessively blue tint. However, the best results came from using the Auto White Balance, Daylight, and Custom settings.

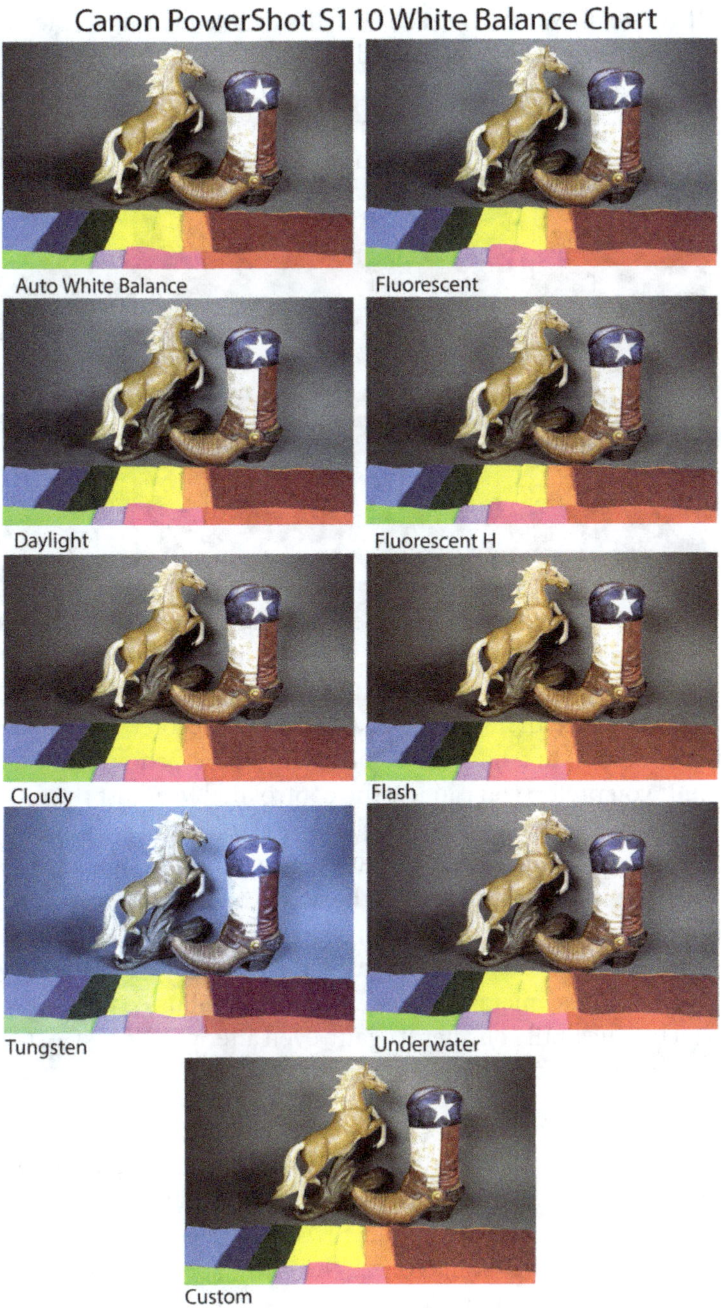

Canon PowerShot S110 White Balance Chart

Auto White Balance

Fluorescent

Daylight

Fluorescent H

Cloudy

Flash

Tungsten

Underwater

Custom

Fig. 4-11: White Balance Chart for Canon PowerShot S110

129

If you really want to tweak the white balance setting to the nth degree, after you have selected your desired white balance setting (whether AWB, a preset, or one of the Custom settings) press the Menu button, and you will be presented with a screen for fine adjustments, as shown in Figure 4-12.

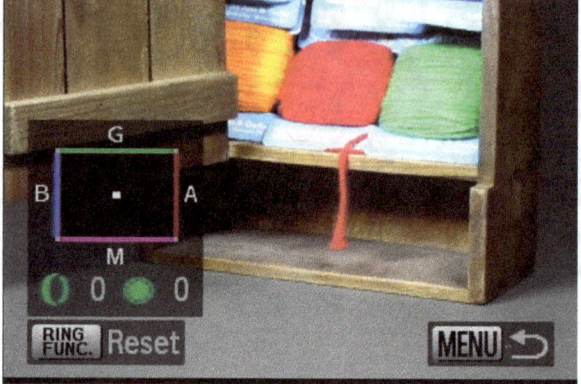

Fig. 4-12: White Balance Adjustment Screen

There are two axes that intersect at a point marked by a white dot. The four sides are labeled G, B, M, and A for Green, Blue, Magenta, and Amber. You can now use all four direction buttons to move the white dot away from the center toward any of the sides, to adjust the color balance exactly how you want it. If you prefer, you can use the control dial to adjust the G-M axis, and the control ring for the B-A axis. (If you only need to adjust the B-A axis, you can use the control ring to make that adjustment without pressing the Menu button; just start turning the control ring while you are still on the main white balance screen.) You also can make adjustments by touching the screen. The camera will remember your adjusted white balance value until you alter it again, even after you have switched to a different white balance preset.

One final note: If you shoot using Raw quality, you can always correct the white balance setting after the fact, in your Raw software. So, if you are using Raw, you really don't have to worry about what setting you are using for white balance. Still, it's a good idea always to check the setting before shooting, to

130

avoid getting caught with incorrect white balance when you are not using the Raw format and to avoid having to adjust the setting with your post-processing software.

My Colors

This next setting on the Function menu offers great options for altering the colors of your JPEG images as you take them. (The My Colors feature does not work and is unavailable for selection when you are shooting Raw or Raw+JPEG images.) Using the fairly wide variety of settings available with this option, you can add or subtract intensity of color or work in subtle changes to the look of your images. Of course, if you plan to edit your images on a computer using software such as Photoshop, you can duplicate these effects readily at that stage. But, if you don't want to spend time processing the images in that way, having the ability to alter the color effects in this quick way can add a good deal to the enjoyment of your photos.

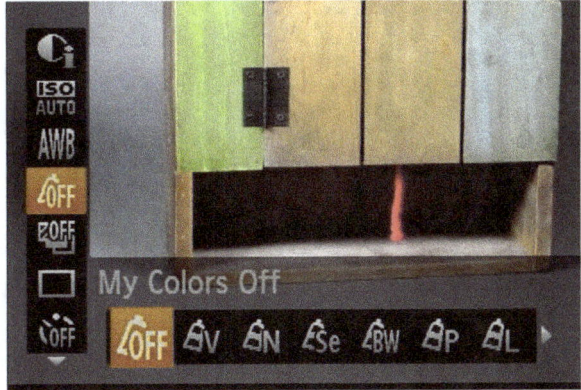

Fig. 4-13: My Colors Icon Highlighted on Function Menu

Using this feature is easy: Just select My Colors, the fourth icon down on the list of icons on the left, as shown in Figure 4-13, then scroll across the icons at the bottom of the screen until you find the one you want to use. To illustrate the different settings, the chart in Figure 4-14 shows the same scene taken with each of the My Colors options. General descriptions of the effects are provided following the chart.

131

My Colors Chart for Canon PowerShot S110

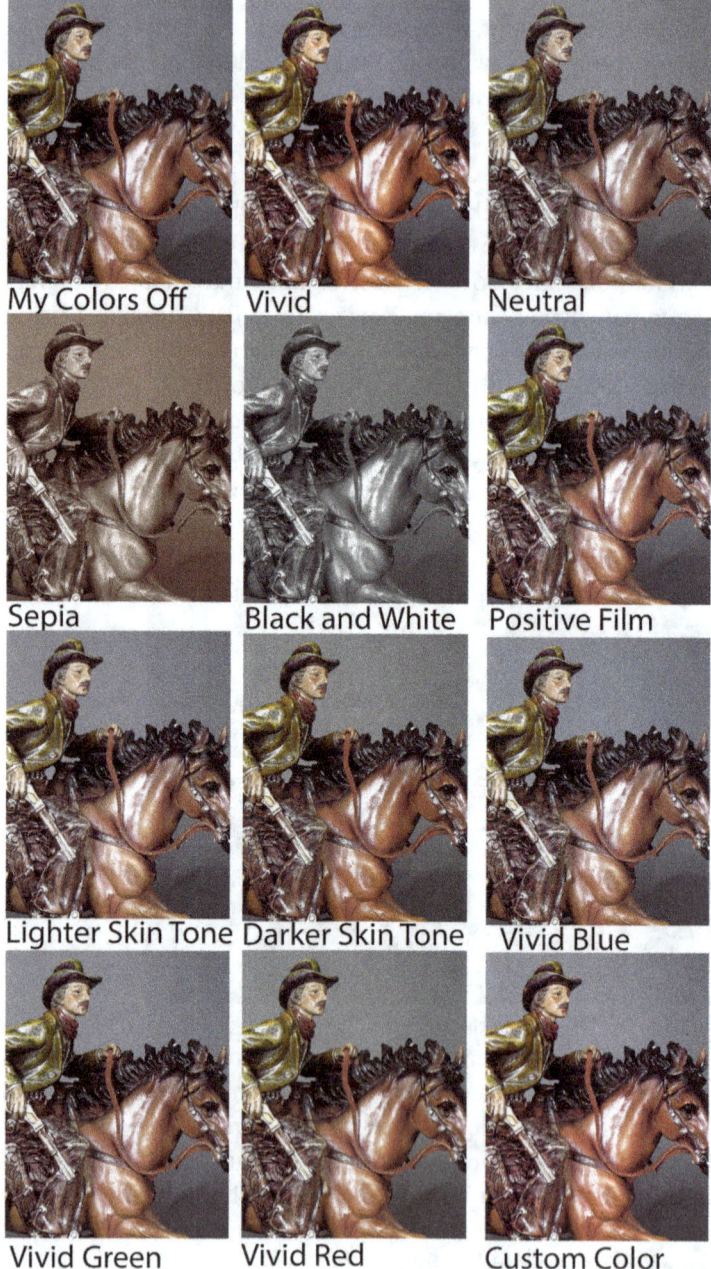

Fig. 4-14: Chart of My Colors Settings for PowerShot S110

My Colors Off

The My Colors Off setting is included on the chart to show the scene with no effects applied, for purposes of comparison with the other options described below.

Vivid

The Vivid setting increases the saturation, or intensity, of all of the colors in the image. As you can see, it calls attention to the scene, though it can easily seem excessive if used in the wrong context. The Vivid setting might work well if you want to emphasize the colors in a birthday party scene or in a bed of colorful flowers.

Neutral

The Neutral setting can be considered the inverse of Vivid. Although it does not drain all color from the scene, it does de-emphasize the colors, ratcheting down the intensity to a more sedate level. You might use this setting to set a mood of calmness or serenity in a scene.

Sepia

When you use the Sepia setting the image is drained of all of its natural colors, and it is rendered monochromatically, but with the added touch of a light brownish tone that is somewhat reminiscent of the appearance of old-fashioned photographs. The Sepia setting can be used to convey a sense of the antique.

B/W

This setting removes all color, converting the scene to black and white. Some photographers use this setting to achieve a realistic look for their street photography. Note that there are several other ways to take monochrome photographs with the PowerShot S110, using the Creative Filters shooting mode. The HDR, Nostalgic, Monochrome, and Color Accent settings all can be used for monochrome shots, depending on their settings. However, the B/W setting for My Colors has the great advantage of being available in the more advanced shooting modes, including Program, Aperture Priority, Shutter Priority, and Manual, so you have access to other settings, such as ISO, white balance, and others. If you want to exercise full creative control over your monochrome photography, there are advantages to using the My Colors B/W option for those shots.

Positive Film

This setting is similar to Vivid, though the intention is to mimic the "natural" colors of slide film.

Lighter Skin Tone

This setting appears to do just what its name implies—it makes flesh-colored tones such as pinks somewhat less intense and more neutral in appearance.

Darker Skin Tone

This setting is similar to the previous one, but the Darker Skin Tone option subtly darkens the tones in the range of pink, red, violet, and the like.

Vivid Blue

This variant of the Vivid setting affects only the blue tones; therefore, as Canon notes in the user's manual, you can use this setting when you want to emphasize the blues of ocean or sky without increasing the saturation of colors such as red and yellow.

Vivid Green

This setting places emphasis on the greens of foliage, including grassy fields, tree-covered mountains, and similar features.

Vivid Red

This last of the Vivid settings can be used to increase the intensity of any reddish subjects, including flowers, decorations, clothing, or sunsets.

Custom Color

This final My Colors setting, whose menu option is shown in Figure 4-15, gives you the opportunity to construct your own version of a My Colors setting by making adjustments to the individual parameters: contrast, sharpness, saturation, red, green, blue, and skin tone.

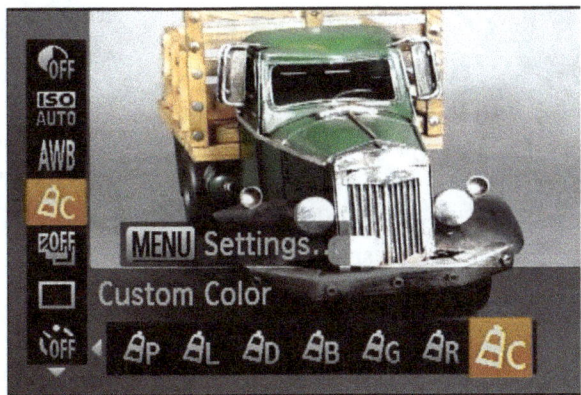

Fig. 4-15: Custom Color Option for My Colors

To set those parameters, once you have chosen the icon for Custom Color, press the Menu button. The camera then presents you with a scale for adjusting contrast, as shown in Figure 4-16.

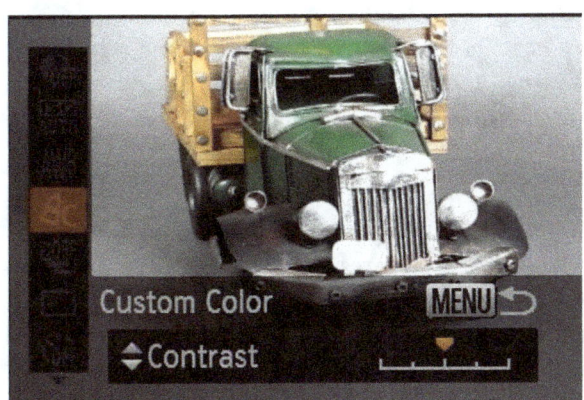

Fig. 4-16: Contrast Adjustment Screen for My Colors

Use the control dial or the left and right direction buttons to increase or decrease the contrast setting by as much as two increments on this scale. Then press the up or down direction button to move to the next parameter. In this way, you can dial in adjustments for contrast, sharpness, saturation (color intensity), red color tone, green color tone, blue color tone, and skin tone. Once you have adjusted all of these settings as you want them, they will stay set that way until you return and change them.

It's important to note that, even though this overall feature of the camera is known as My Colors, you can use this Custom Color setting to adjust contrast and sharpness, two values that are not concerned particularly with colors. So, for example, if you find your images are too sharp or too "soft," you can decrease or increase your sharpness setting in the Custom Color setting of My Colors, and use that setting for your general photography. Of course, you are giving up the ability to shoot your images in Raw format if you take that route, which some photographers would not be willing to do. But it's good to have this setting available as one of the options for tweaking the output of the camera's JPEG processing.

For the example included in the chart in Figure 4-14, I used the Custom Color option with the following settings: contrast, sharpness, saturation, and red were at their maximum settings; green was at its minimum; blue was at one step below the middle setting; and skin tone was at one step above the middle setting.

Bracketing

The next option on the Function menu, Bracketing, is a feature that lets you take three pictures with one press of the shutter button, with three different settings, thereby giving you an added chance of getting a good, usable image. The PowerShot S110 provides two types of bracketing: automatic exposure bracketing, shown as AEB on the Function menu, and focus bracketing, abbreviated as Focus-BKT.

Exposure bracketing

First, I'll talk about exposure bracketing, which is the most commonly used and probably the most useful type of bracketing. If you're shooting with Raw quality, exposure is not that much of an issue, because you can adjust it later with your software, but it's always a good idea to get the exposure as correct as possible when you are shooting. Also, using exposure bracketing is an excellent way to take three pictures that can be combined later in software to produce an HDR (High Dynamic Range) composite, which shows clear details and highlights throughout the image by combining the best-exposed parts of each shot.

To use exposure bracketing, the camera must be set to Program, Aperture Priority, or Shutter Priority mode (not Manual), and the flash cannot be used. Navigate down in the Function menu to the fifth icon, which looks like a stack of images with the word OFF laid on top of it, as shown in Figure 4-17.

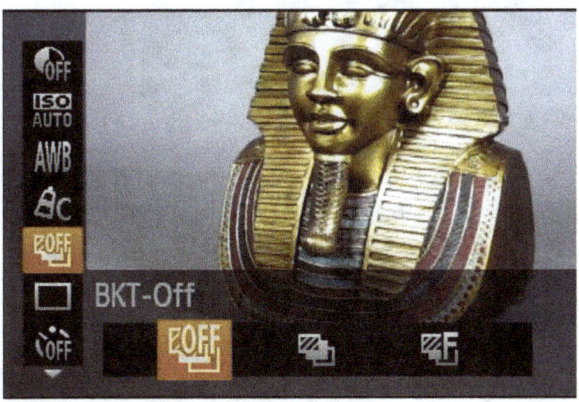

Fig. 4-17: Bracketing Option on Function Menu

Use the control dial or the right direction button, or touch the screen, to move to the icon to the right of that one on the line of icons at the bottom of the screen. That icon shows three image frames, one white, one dark, and one shaded, indicating three levels of exposure.

With that middle icon highlighted, press the Menu button, and the camera will display a scale showing EV (exposure value) numbers from -2 to +2, in increments of 1/3 EV, with three orange dots beneath the scale, as shown in Figure 4-18. Use the control dial or the direction buttons to move those dots so they are separated by the amount of EV difference that you want, up to a maximum difference of 2 EV. Then exit from the Function menu by pressing the Func./Set button. You will see the AEB icon on the shooting screen.

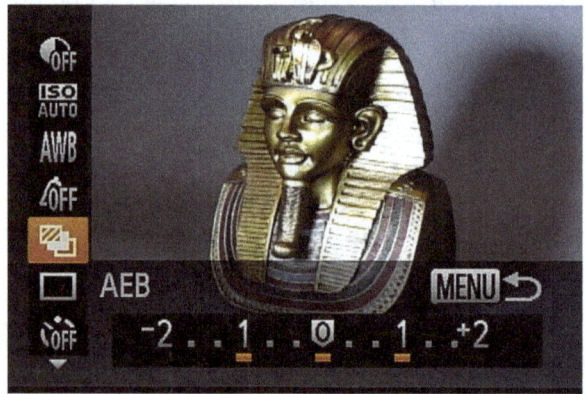

Fig. 4-18: Auto Exposure Bracket Settings Screen

When you are ready, press the shutter button and hold the camera steady (or use a tripod) while it takes the three exposures. The first picture taken is always at the metered level, or 0 change in EV; the second is at the lower EV (darker), and the third is at the higher EV (brighter). If you have added exposure compensation, the bracketed exposures are taken at three levels relative to the adjusted exposure.

Finally, note that there is an alternative way to get access to exposure bracketing: From the shooting screen, press the up direction button to bring up the exposure compensation scale, and you will see the bracketing icon next to the word MENU, as shown in Figure 4-19. If you then press the Menu button, the exposure bracketing screen will appear.

138

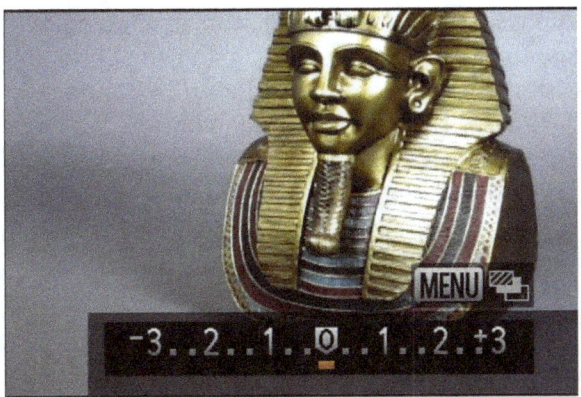

Fig. 4-19: Exposure Compensation Screen with Icon to Call up AEB

Focus bracketing

The other type of bracketing available with the PowerShot S110 is focus bracketing, which lets you take three pictures with different focus settings when you are using manual focus. I don't use this feature often, but it may be useful in tricky focusing situations, such as extreme closeup photography. You also can use it to produce three images that can be merged in software such as Photoshop to produce a composite image with a broad depth of field, using the technique called "focus stacking," which is a focus-oriented version of HDR.

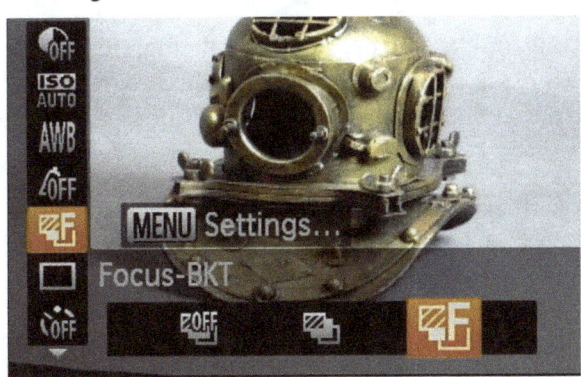

Fig. 4-20: Focus Bracket Option on Function Menu

Focus bracketing works in the same way as auto exposure

139

bracketing. After selecting the bracket icon in the Function menu, navigate to the icon on the far right at the bottom of the screen, with the letter F on the stack of image frames, as shown in Figure 4-20. Then press the Menu button and move the orange dots as needed to set the incremental change in focus among the three shots, as shown in Figure 4-21.

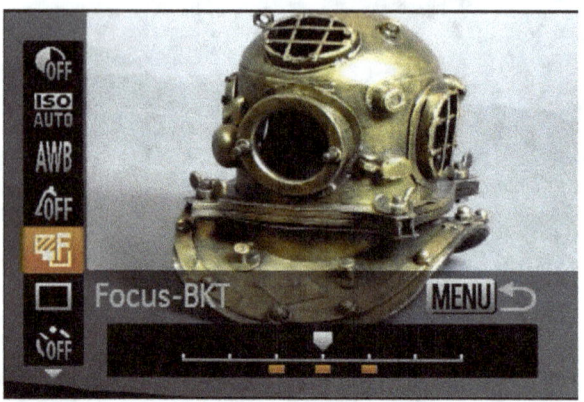

Fig. 4-21: Focus Bracket Settings Screen

When you return to the shooting screen, the camera will take the first shot at the distance you set for manual focus, the second shot with focus set for a farther distance, and the third shot with focus set for a nearer distance.

Focus bracketing, unlike auto exposure bracketing, works with the Manual exposure mode as well as with the Program, Aperture Priority, and Shutter Priority modes. It does not work with flash.

Note that, as with exposure bracketing, there is also a shorter path to the focus bracketing function. After you have used the left direction button to activate manual focus mode, you will see the focus bracketing icon on the screen next to the icon for the Menu button, as shown in Figure 4-22. You can then press the Menu button to be taken directly to the focus bracketing screen.

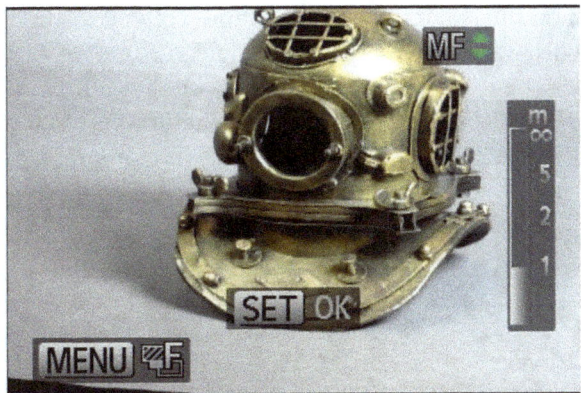

Fig. 4-22: Manual Focus Screen from Which Focus Bracket Can be Set

Continuous Shooting

The next icon down the line on the left side of the Function menu gives you the settings for firing a burst of shots with one press of the shutter button. This feature is known as continuous shooting, and also is sometimes referred to as drive mode, because film cameras need to have a motor drive built in or added on in order to fire a rapid stream of shots.

Start by highlighting the sixth icon down on the left of the Function menu, as shown in Figure 4-23.

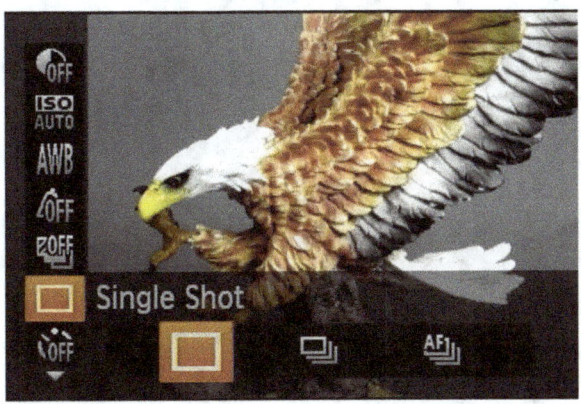

Fig. 4-23: Continuous Shooting Options on Function Menu

141

The first icon on the left at the bottom of the screen is a single white rectangle, which represents the single shot mode, the normal mode when you are taking just one shot at a time. If you navigate over to the middle icon on the bottom of the screen, you will see a stack of white frames, which represents the standard continuous mode, as shown in Figure 4-24.

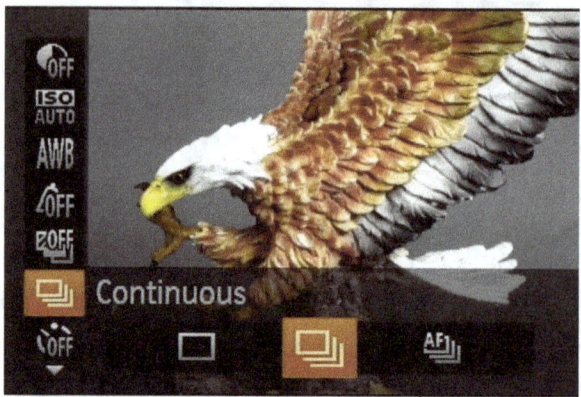

Fig. 4-24: Normal Continuous Shooting Icon Selected

When you select that icon and exit the Function menu, that stack will appear on the screen, indicating that the camera is set for continuous shooting, as shown in Figure 4-25.

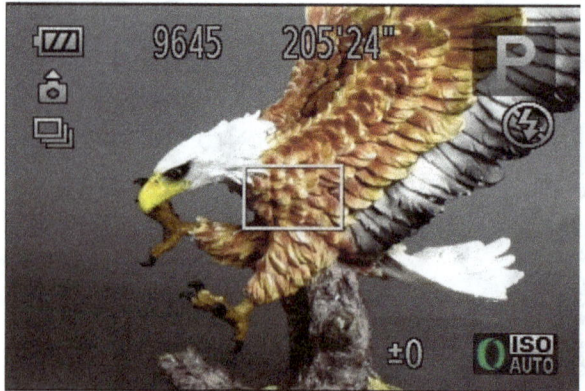

Fig. 4-25: Continuous Shooting Icon in Upper Left Corner of Screen

Now, whenever you hold down the shutter button, the camera will keep taking shot after shot, at a maximum rate of about 2.1 images per second. In this mode, the camera will lock its exposure and focus when you first press the shutter button down halfway, and those settings will not change throughout the continuous shooting. So, if you aim at subjects at different distances from the camera or with varying lighting while shooting, the camera will not adjust its focus or exposure to account for the changing conditions.

This mode is intended to give you the maximum speed for high-quality photographs, but you will get consistently good results only if you are shooting in conditions where changes in lighting and focus will not be an issue. For example, if you are taking photos at a relatively long distance from the subject in daylight, you may not have a problem, because the camera will maintain good focus at that distance and the lighting will not likely change, unless a cloud blocks the sun. On the other hand, if you're indoors at a gathering and want to keep shooting candid photos, the chances are good that some of the images will be poorly focused or poorly lit, or both, because the focus tolerance is more critical at shorter distances, and the lighting may vary considerably in different parts of a room.

The other continuous shooting mode is represented by the icon on the right of the bottom menu.

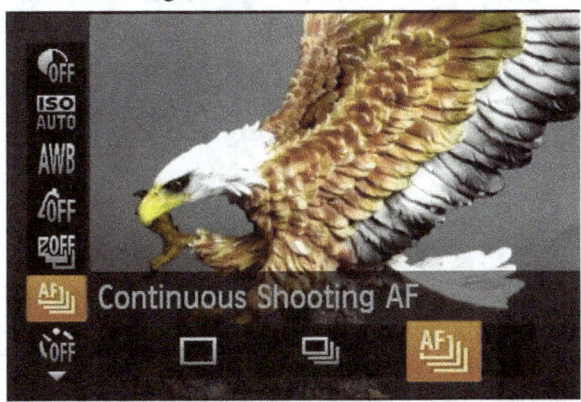

Fig. 4-26: Continuous Shooting AF Icon Selected

That icon is a stack of frames with the letters AF on top, representing autofocus, as seen in Figure 4-26. In this mode, the camera will shoot continuously at a maximum speed of about 0.9 frames per second and will adjust its autofocus for each shot. However, the camera still will not adjust its exposure, which will be locked in when you first press the shutter button down halfway. If the camera is set for manual focus, the Fireworks setting of Scene mode, or autofocus lock (which involves using the manual focus mode), the continuous AF mode is automatically converted to continuous LV shooting mode, in which the camera fires at about 0.9 frames per second, but still locks focus and exposure with the first shot. The LV designation means that the camera displays the live view of the current scene, rather than freezing on the previous shot, as some cameras do when shooting continuously.

Continuous shooting is not fully available in all shooting modes. For example, in AUTO mode, the only continuous-shooting setting available through this menu option is represented by a stack of frames with the letter A, for Automatic. With this setting, called Auto Drive, the camera evaluates the scene and shoots either continuous individual shots or a set of shots that it processes into a single composite shot. In Scene mode, with the High-Speed Burst HQ setting, you can select either normal or AF continuous shooting. You also can use one or both of those settings with the Portrait, Smooth Skin, Underwater, Snow, and Fireworks settings, but not with the Smart Shutter, Handheld Night Scene, or Stitch Assist settings. In Creative Filters mode, you can use either normal or AF continuous shooting with every setting except HDR. You cannot use continuous shooting in Movie or Movie Digest mode.

Note that the maximum shooting speed will slow down in certain conditions, such as when the light is so low as to require a slow shutter speed or when the flash is being used. (The camera will fire continuous shots with flash, though, which is an excellent capability that many other cameras do not have.) The speed also may slow down as the number of shots increases, as the memory buffer fills up and the camera needs to pause to empty it out so more shots can be accepted.

However, in spite of its several limitations, continuous shooting mode can be a very useful tool in some situations, such as when you're shooting scenes with changing action, or people with changing expressions. There's no extra cost involved in taking numerous shots, and you may increase your chances of getting that one priceless image. So you may want to consider using continuous mode on a fairly regular basis, when it might enhance your photographic results.

Finally, remember that there is a way to get considerably faster continuous shooting from the PowerShot S110—by choosing the High-Speed Burst HQ option in Scene mode. In that case, the maximum shooting speed rises dramatically, to 10 frames per second (without autofocus) for a single burst of 10 shots. Of course, as I discussed in Chapter 3, there is a corresponding trade-off with that option, because the images must be JPEG and you cannot use many of the Function menu settings. But, if you need the extra speed, the images are still very usable. So don't overlook this Scene mode option when you need to take a small group of shots at maximum speed.

Self-timer

The next icon down on the line of Function menu options represents the self-timer, as seen in Figure 4-27.

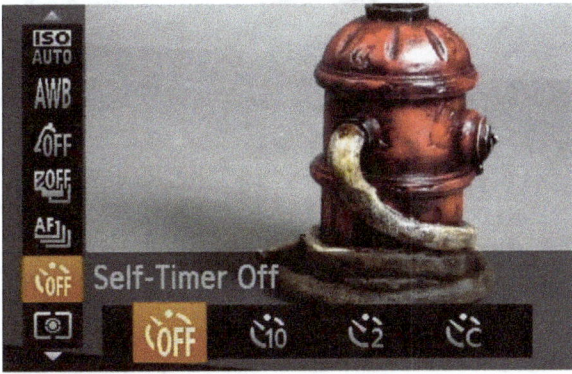

Fig. 4-27: Self-Timer Options Screen on Function Menu

145

The self-timer is useful for occasions when you need to be the photographer and also appear in a group photograph, because you can set the S110 on a tripod, set the timer for 10 seconds or so, and possibly for multiple shots, and then move around to place yourself in the group before the shutter clicks. The self-timer also is helpful in other situations, though, such as whenever you are taking a picture under conditions in which you don't want to cause blur by jiggling the camera as you press the shutter button. For example, when you're taking a macro shot very close to the subject, the focusing can be very critical, and any bump to the camera could throw off the focus. Using the self-timer means the camera has time to settle down after the shutter button is pressed, before the image is actually recorded.

Once you select the self-timer option, you are presented with three choices: ten seconds, two seconds, and C, for custom, as shown in Figure 4-27. If you select ten or two seconds, there are no other settings to make. When you press the shutter button to take a picture, the self-timer will count down for the specified number of seconds and then take the picture. If you highlight the custom setting, you then press the Menu button to get to the screen that lets you select the length of the delay using the control ring, as shown in Figure 4-28.

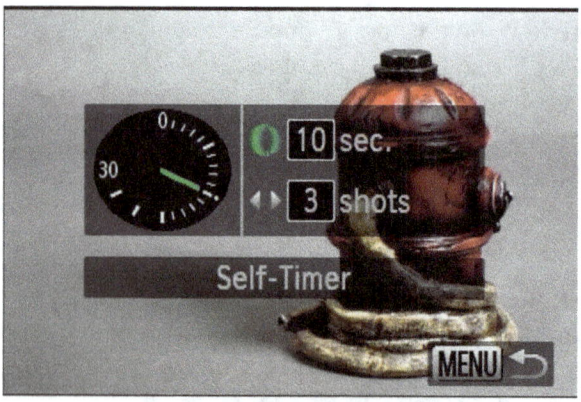

Fig. 4-28: Screen for Setting Self-Timer Shots and Time

The delay can be set anywhere from zero to 30 seconds. You also can set the number of shots that will be taken after the countdown, from one to ten, using the left and right direction buttons.

Also, don't forget that the camera has several other potentially very useful timer functions, completely separate from the self-timer. Those features are included within the Smart Shutter setting of Scene mode, as discussed in Chapter 3: the Smile Self-Timer, the Wink Self-Timer, and the Face Self-Timer.

Metering Method

This option, shown in Figure 4-29, lets you choose among the three patterns of exposure metering offered by the S110: Evaluative, Center Weighted Average, and Spot.

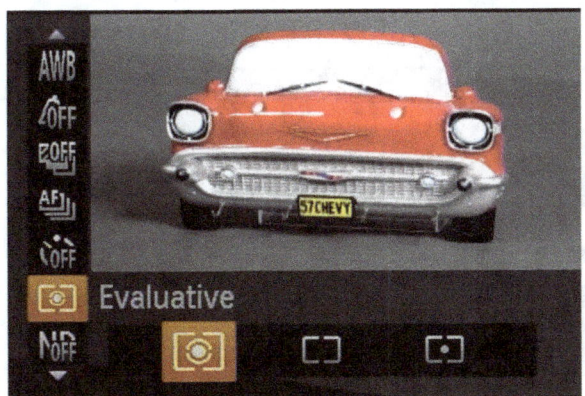

Fig. 4-29: Metering Option on Function Menu

This choice tells the camera's automatic exposure system what part of the scene to consider when setting the exposure. With Evaluative, the camera uses the entire scene that is visible on the LCD, though it uses its built-in programming to evaluate whether the scene is lit from behind ("backlit") or otherwise needs adjustments. With Center Weighted Average, the camera still considers all of the light from the scene, but it gives additional weight to the center portion of the image, on the theory that your main subject is in or near the center. Finally, with Spot, the camera considers only the light that is metered within the spot metering area. In that mode, the camera places a pair of white brackets in the center of the LCD, indicating the metered area. With the Spot setting, you can see the effects of the exposure system clearly by selecting Program exposure mode and aiming those brackets at various points, some bright and some dark, and seeing how sharply the brightness of the scene in the LCD changes. If you try the same experiment in Evaluative mode, you will still see changes, but more subtle and gradual ones.

Note, if you choose Spot metering, the pair of brackets you will see is different from the white frame the camera uses to indicate the 1-point autofocus frame mode. If you make both of these settings at the same time, you will see two white frames in the center of the LCD, as shown in Figure 4-30.

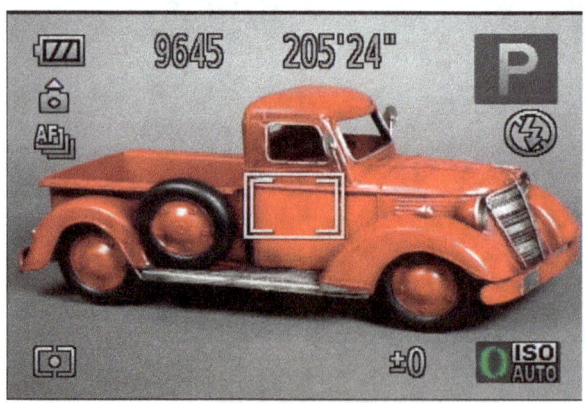

Fig. 4-30: Frames on Screen for Spot Metering and 1-Point AF

So, you may need to be careful to recall which one of these settings is in effect, if only one white frame or pair of brackets is visible in the center of the screen.

If you turn on the AF Point option for the Spot AE Point item on the Shooting menu, you can link the Spot metering brackets to the 1-point autofocus frame. You can then move the Spot

148

metering brackets around the screen as you move the 1-point autofocus frame. That option is discussed later in this chapter.

Note, also, in AUTO mode, Movie mode, Scene mode, and Creative Filters mode, the only metering method available is Evaluative.

ND Filter

This option, shown in Figure 4-31, provides you with a very useful tool for certain types of shots.

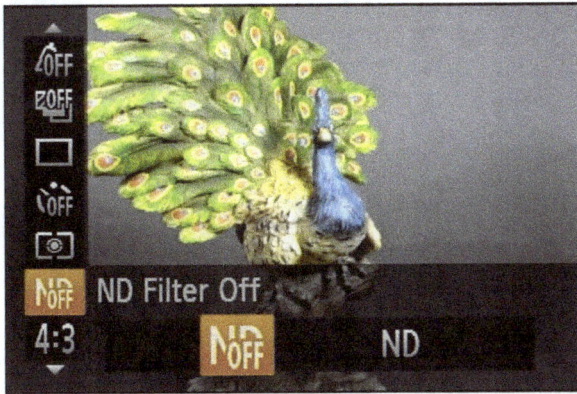

Fig. 4-31: ND Filter Option on Function Menu

When you turn the ND Filter option on, the camera activates an internal neutral density filter, which cuts down the light reaching the sensor just as if you had placed a glass ND filter over the lens. (An ND filter of that type is a gray filter that does not change the color or quality of the image, but just cuts down on light transmission.)

The ND Filter option is of most use when you need to use a slow shutter speed or a wide aperture, but the lighting conditions are so bright that you cannot do so without overexposing the image. For example, you may want to take a picture of a waterfall using a shutter speed of ½ second so the water will appear as a continuous, smooth flow, rather than as a rough, choppy stream with droplets flying around. If the light is too intense, you may not be able to take a properly exposed shot at that slow shutter speed, even at the lowest available ISO setting and the narrowest aperture. If you activate the ND Filter option, the camera reduces the light by three full f-stops, which means the light is cut down to one-eighth the normal amount. (Each stop cuts the light in half, and cutting it in half three times equates to cutting it to one-eighth.) So, for example, if you were shooting at f/5.6 and 1/15 second, once the ND Filter is turned on, you will be able to shoot at about ½ second, producing the effect you are looking for.

In the images shown here, I was trying to use a slow shutter speed to smooth out the water in a fountain. For Figure 4-32, the S110 was set to f/8.0, the smallest possible aperture, at a shutter speed of 1/6 second. ISO was set to 80, the lowest setting available.

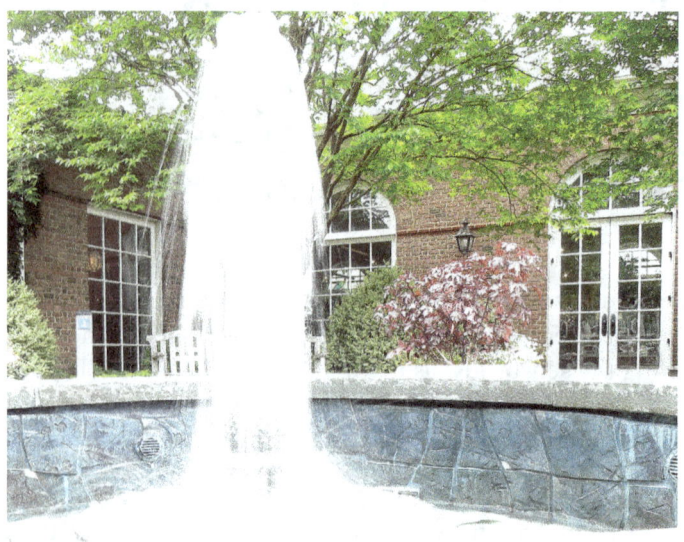

Fig. 4-32: Image Taken with ND Filter Off

As you can see, the image was noticeably overexposed, and I had no further options for decreasing the exposure, because I needed to use a slow shutter speed. So I turned the ND Filter option on, and the resulting exposure was fine for the image in Figure 4-33.

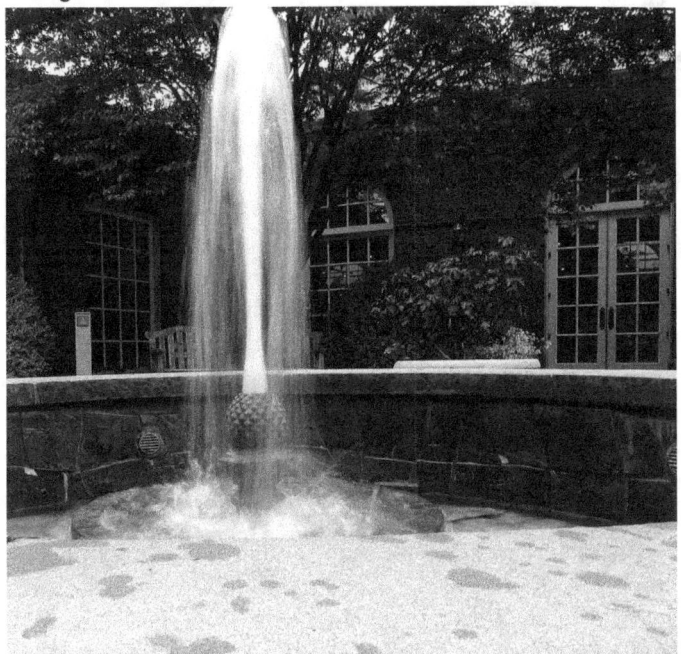

Fig. 4-33: Image Taken with ND Filter On

With the ND Filter turned on, I was able to shoot the photo at f/7.1 at 1/8 second without overexposing the image.

Aspect Ratio

This setting controls the proportions of the images you record with the camera. The choices are 16:9, 3:2, 4:3, 1:1, and 4:5, as shown in Figure 4-34. These numbers represent the ratio of the units of width to the units of height. So, for example, with the first setting, the image is 16 units wide for every 9 units of height. The aspect ratio that covers the entire LCD is 4:3; with any other aspect ratio, some of the pixels are cropped out.

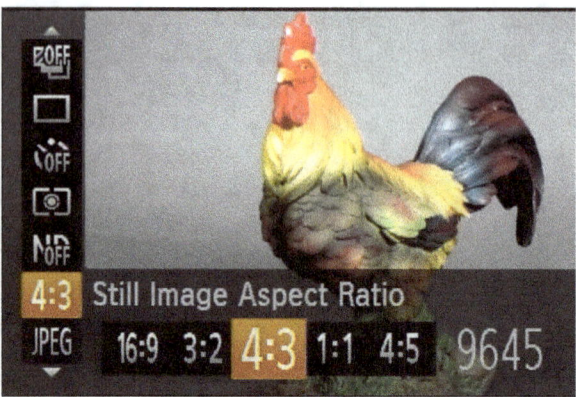

Fig. 4-34: Aspect Ratio Option on Function Menu

So, if it matters to you to record every possible pixel, you might want to use the 4:3 setting. That is the setting that is used for all Raw images; you can't set any other aspect ratio when shooting Raw. You should also note that, if you shoot in Raw or in the 4:3 aspect ratio, you can always alter the aspect ratio of the image later in editing software such as Photoshop, by cropping away parts of the image. However, if you want to have your images in a certain shape, will be shooting in JPEG, and don't plan to do post-processing in software, these aspect ratio settings may be just what you want. The PowerShot S110 is notable for providing more options in this area than many other cameras do, so let's go through the list of possibilities. After each of the aspect ratios discussed below, I am including an image I took of a mural using that setting, to illustrate what parts of a scene are included with each of the different settings. Because the camera was firmly attached to a tripod in the same location for each shot, you can see clearly what parts of the image are included or cut off for each of the various aspect ratio settings.

The 16:9 setting, illustrated by Figure 4-35, is the first choice on the left when you select the Aspect Ratio icon on the Function menu. That ratio is normally considered to be the "widescreen" mode, like that found on many modern HD television sets. You might use that setting when you plan to show your images on an HDTV set. This setting includes all pixels at the left and right, but excludes some from the top and bottom of the image.

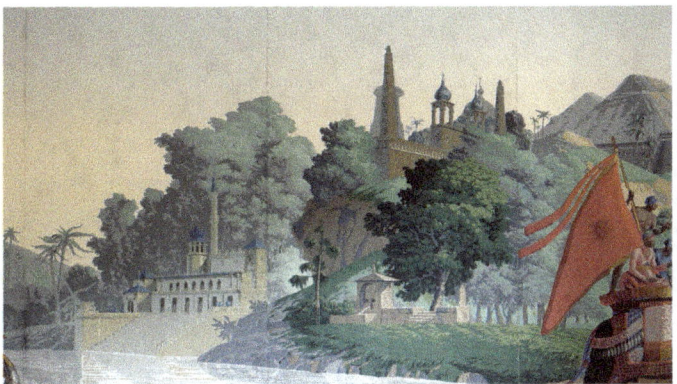

Fig. 4-35: Aspect Ratio 16:9

The 3:2 setting, shown in Figure 4-36, is the same ratio used by traditional 35mm film, and can be used without cropping to make prints in the common U.S. size of 6 inches by 4 inches (15 cm by 10 cm). This setting also includes all pixels at the left and right, but omits some at the top and bottom.

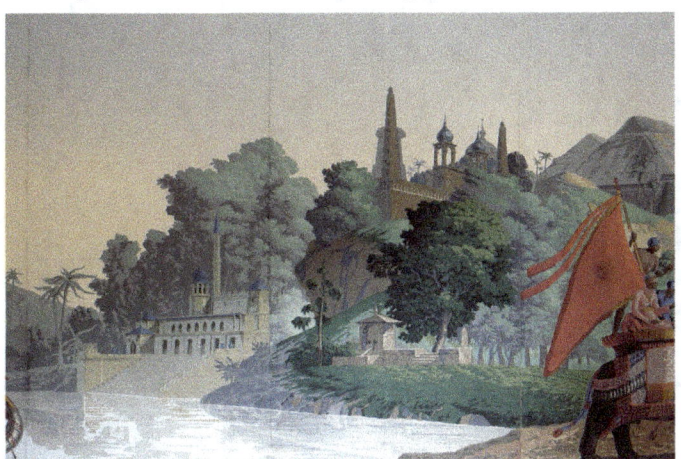

Fig. 4-36: Aspect Ratio 3:2

The 4:3 setting, used for Figure 4-37, is in the shape of the S110's LCD, so, if you want to use the full expanse of the LCD, this may be your preferred aspect ratio. This setting includes all pixels without cutting off any parts of the scene.

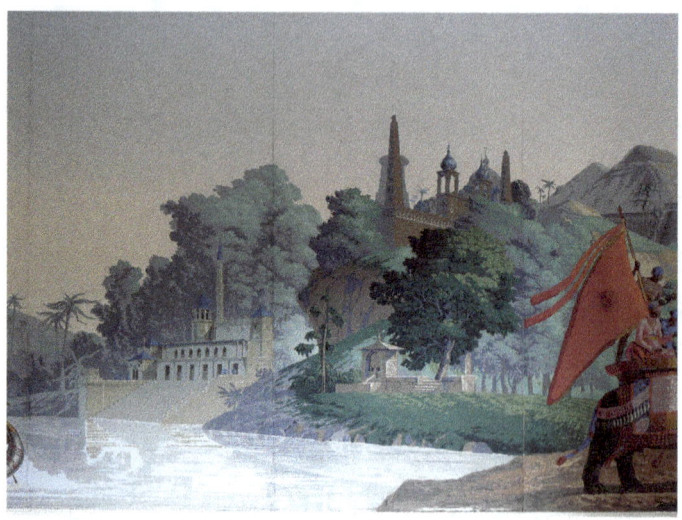

Fig. 4-37: Aspect Ratio 4:3

The 1:1 aspect ratio is illustrated in Figure 4-38.

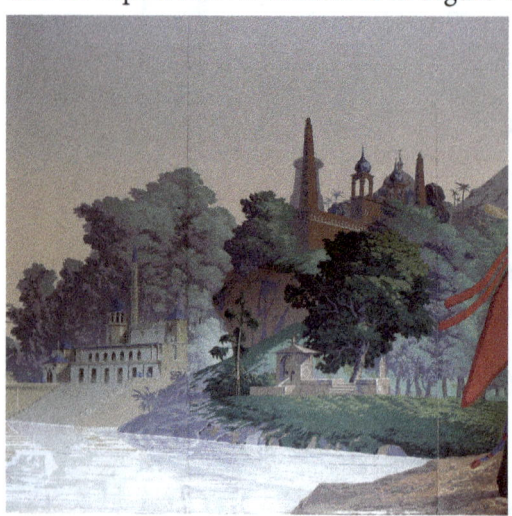

Fig. 4-38: Aspect Ratio 1:1

This setting represents a square shape, which some photographers prefer because of its symmetry and because the neutrality of the shape leaves open many possibilities for using the images. With the 1:1 setting, all pixels from the top and bottom of the image are included, but some of the scene is cut off at the left and right sides of the image.

Finally, the 4:5 aspect ratio, shown in Figure 4-39, the only setting available that is taller than it is wide, may be well-suited for portraits and other scenes with a narrow or tall subject. Of course, you can achieve a similar effect by holding the camera with its left or right side up and shooting with the long side of the frame held vertical. In that case, though, you would have to rotate the images to view them comfortably. This setting includes all pixels from the top and bottom, but, like the previous setting, cuts off areas on the left and right.

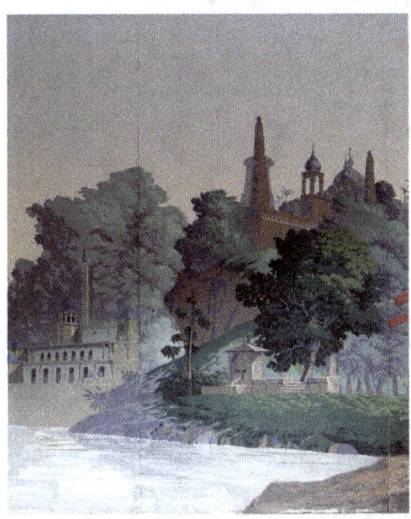

Fig. 4-39: Aspect Ratio 4:5

The Aspect Ratio setting is available in all shooting modes for still images except a few of the Scene and Creative Filters types, including Smooth Skin, High-Speed Burst HQ, Hand-held Night Scene, Stitch Assist, Nostalgic, Fish-eye, Toy Cam-

155

era, and Soft Focus. With the Miniature Effect setting, only the 16:9 and 4:3 settings are available for Aspect Ratio. For movies, the aspect ratio is determined by the setting for the movie format, which is either widescreen (16:9) or VGA (4:3).

Image Type

This setting, just below Aspect Ratio on the Function menu, is one of the most important ones you can make. The choices are JPEG, Raw, and Raw+JPEG, as shown in Figure 4-40.

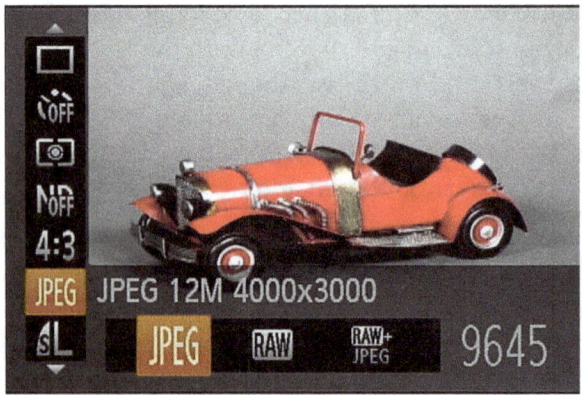

Fig. 4-40: *Image Type Option on Function Menu*

Before I discuss this option, though, I need to mention two other settings that are closely related to this one.

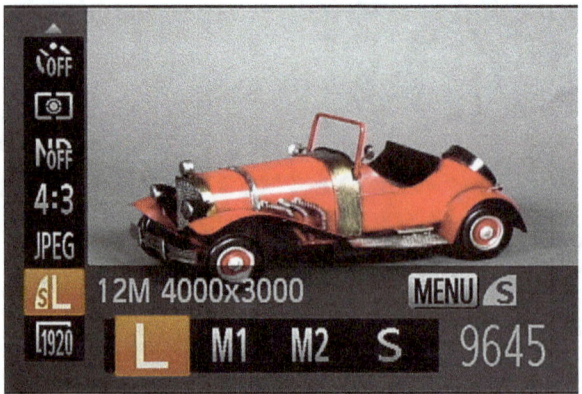

Fig. 4-41: *Image Size Option on Function Menu*

The next icon down on the left side of the Function menu, which is the next-to-last icon at the bottom of the menu, is a capital letter L, M (with a number 1 or 2), or S, preceded by a rounded-triangle shape, either with or without the letter S inside it, as shown in Figure 4-41. That icon, in its two parts, represents image size (Large, Medium, or Small), and quality (plain shape for Fine and shape with S for Superfine). All of these settings go hand-in-hand to determine several attributes of your images.

Here are some guidelines about these settings and what they mean. First, you need to choose between Raw and JPEG images. Raw files are larger than other files, so they take up more space on your memory card, and, later, on your computer, than JPEG files. But Raw files offer some great advantages over JPEG files. When you shoot in the Raw format, the camera records as much information as it can about the scene before it, and preserves that information in the file that it saves to the memory card. Then, when you open the Raw file later on your computer, you will have the ability to extract that information in various ways. What this means, for example, is that you can actually change the exposure or white balance of the image when you edit it on the computer, just as if you had changed your settings while shooting. In effect, the Raw format gives you what almost amounts to a chance to travel back in time to improve the settings that you didn't get quite right when you pressed the shutter button.

Raw is not a cure-all; you can't fix bad focusing or really excessive under- or overexposure. But you can improve exposure-related issues such as brightness and white balance very nicely with your Raw-processing software. (You can use the Digital Photo Professional software that comes with the PowerShot S110, or any of several other software packages, such as Adobe Photoshop, Photoshop Elements, Lightroom, or Apple Aperture.) Using Raw may have some disadvantages as well, depending on your needs. As noted above, the files take up a lot of storage space on your memory card or computer; some

157

Raw images I recently took with the camera were between 16 and 18 megabytes (MB) in size, while Large JPEG images I took at the same time ranged in size from about 4 MB to 7 MB each. Also, Raw files have to be processed on a computer; you can't take a Raw file and immediately send it as an image by e-mail or print it on photo paper; you first have to use Raw-processing software to convert it to .jpg, .tif, .psd, or some other standard file format for printing and manipulating digital photographs. If you are pressed for time, you may not want to take that extra step. Finally, as noted earlier in this book, some features of the PowerShot S110 are not available when you are using the Raw format, including the AUTO, Creative Filters, or Scene shooting modes, or the digital zoom, i-Contrast, My Colors, or aspect ratio settings.

If you're undecided as to whether to use Raw or JPEG, you have the option of selecting Raw+JPEG, the third option on the right in the line of icons on the Function menu. With that setting, the camera records both a Raw and a JPEG image when you press the shutter button. The advantage with that system is that you have a Raw image with the highest quality and with the ability to do extensive post-processing manipulation of some settings, and you also have a JPEG image that you can use more quickly for viewing, e-mailing, printing, and the like. The disadvantage is that this setting consumes your storage space more quickly than saving your images in just the Raw or JPEG format.

If you decide not to use Raw, the other option for image type is JPEG files, which are compressed; that is, some information is digitally "squeezed" out of them in a way that reduces their size so they don't take up too much storage space on a memory card or computer hard drive, but that does not remove crucial information. JPEG images can be of excellent quality, although they do not carry with them the possibility for after-the-fact corrections of exposure problems, at least not nearly to the extent that Raw files do. (An experienced user of Photoshop or similar software can still do wonders in improving the appearance of a JPEG image, just not to the same degree as with a Raw file.) If you do decide to use JPEG files, you still have a few more choices to make about the size and quality of your images, as discussed next.

Image Size and Compression Amount

This option on the Function menu lets you choose the size and compression level of your JPEG images, when you have chosen either JPEG alone or Raw+JPEG for your image type on the previous item. If you have decided to use Raw images only, there are no other choices to make. Raw files come in one size and one quality only. So, if you selected Raw on the previous Function menu item, you will see that the next menu item below that one becomes darkened and unavailable, as shown in Figure 4-42.

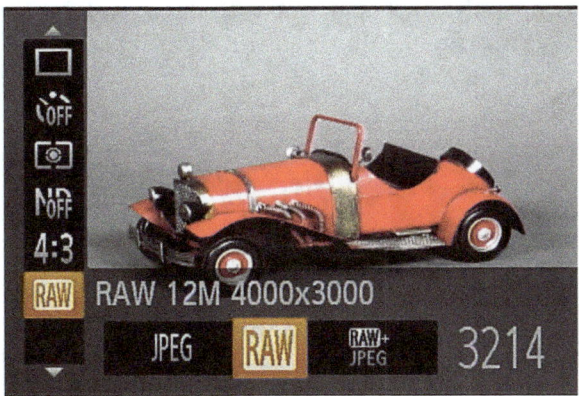

Fig. 4-42: Image Size Blacked Out When Raw Selected

If you decide to use JPEG images (either alone or with the Raw+JPEG setting) and are concerned more with quality than with storage space, I recommend that you choose the largest size and quality for those images. You will gain the ability to store more files if you choose the smaller sizes and the lower quality for your JPEG files, but, unless you are absolutely certain that you won't want to crop the images to emphasize just a small part of them, or to make large prints from them, you

159

might as well use the best-quality settings you can. If you record a picture in a small, low-quality file, you can never recover the quality you would have realized from using the higher-quality settings, but you can always produce lower-resolution copies of high-quality images if you need smaller file sizes for sending by e-mail or storing on a computer disk.

You set the size and quality of JPEG files using the next-to-bottom option on the left side of the Function menu. When you first highlight that icon, you will likely see the menu on the bottom of the screen listing the file sizes from left to right: L, M1, M2, and S, for Large, Medium 1, Medium 2, and Small, as shown in Figure 4-41. Once you have scrolled through those settings and made your selection, press the Menu button, and the camera will replace the menu of image sizes with a choice of two levels of quality, represented by the rounded-triangle (or quarter-circle) shapes, one with the letter S inside it, representing Superfine quality, and the other representing Fine quality, as shown in Figure 4-43.

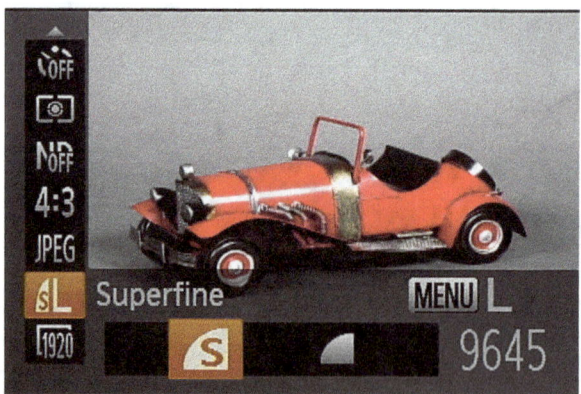

Fig. 4-43:   Fine and Superfine Options

With Superfine quality, the compression of the JPEG file is kept to a minimum; with Fine quality, the file is compressed further, resulting in a loss of additional information from the file and a corresponding reduction in the quality of the image.

To get an idea of the relative sizes of the files that result from these settings, look at the chart at page 334 of the Canon Camera User Guide. The chart shows that, using an 8 GB memory card, you can store 1379 Large images, 2431 Medium 1 images, 7442 Medium 2 images, or 27,291 Small images, all at Superfine quality. So, clearly you are not likely to run out of space on your memory card very quickly, even if you are shooting JPEG images at the largest size and highest quality. (If you shoot with the Raw format, you can store 446 images on the card.)

In short, your best bet in terms of preserving the quality of your images and your options for post-processing and fixing exposure mistakes later is to choose Raw files. However, if you would prefer to let the camera do more of the work and process the files in the camera using features such as i-Contrast, digital zoom, My Colors, the Scene and Creative Filters shooting modes, and others, which are not available with Raw files, then choose JPEG. If you do choose JPEG, I strongly recommend that you choose the Large size and Superfine quality, unless you have an urgent need to conserve storage space on your memory card or on your computer.

Movie Resolution

The final option on the Function menu lets you choose the resolution of your movie clips. This option is available on the regular Function menu along with other options for still shooting because, with the PowerShot S110, you can record a movie while the camera is set to any of the still shooting modes. You just press the red Movie button, and a movie will start recording. Therefore, the camera always needs to have a movie format selected for use when you press that button.

I will discuss the video shooting options in detail in Chapter 8. For now, all you need to know is that the highest numbers produce the highest-quality video. If you want full HD video, select 1920, the option on the left of this menu item, as shown in Figure 4-44.

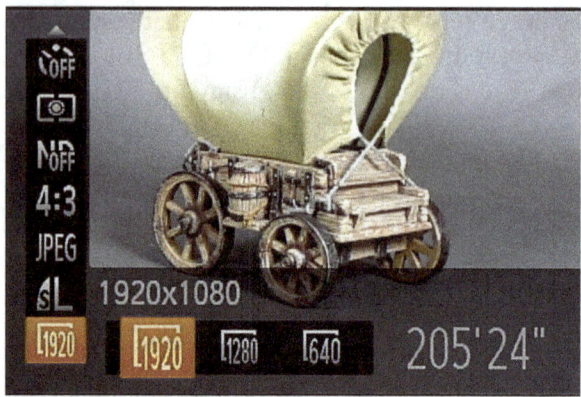

Fig. 4-44: 1920 Option Selected for Movie Format

The Shooting Menu

The next menu system to discuss is the Shooting menu, which gives you access to several options that are important but not likely to be used as frequently as the items on the Function menu.

The Shooting menu is easy to use once you have played with it a bit. As I mentioned earlier, the menu options can change depending on the setting of the shooting mode dial on top of the camera. For example, if you're using AUTO mode, the Shooting menu options are very limited, because that mode is for a user who wants the camera to make almost all of the decisions without input. For the following discussion, I'm assuming you have the camera set to Program mode (mode dial turned to the P setting), because with that setting you have access to most of the power of the Shooting menu. (Though some menu options will be unavailable in certain situations.)

Turn the mode dial on top of the camera to P for Program mode, then enter the menu system by pressing the Menu button—the one at the lower right of the camera's back.

In the menu system, when the camera is in shooting mode, besides the Shooting menu, there is the Setup menu, marked at the top by the wrench and mallet icon, as seen in Figure 4-45.

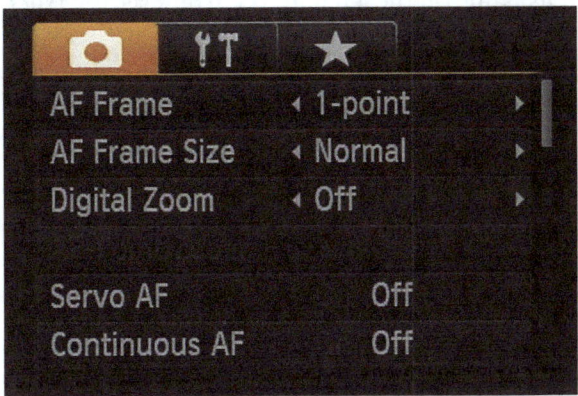

Fig. 4-45: Shooting Menu Tab Selected

The third menu option, marked by a star, is called My Menu; it is a collection of menu items that you can customize as you wish. When the camera is in playback mode (reached by pressing the Playback button) the three choices are the Playback, Print, and Setup menus. For now, I will discuss only the Shooting menu, marked by the camera icon.

On the Shooting menu, whose first screen of options ready for selection is shown in Figure 4-46, you'll see a fairly long list of options.

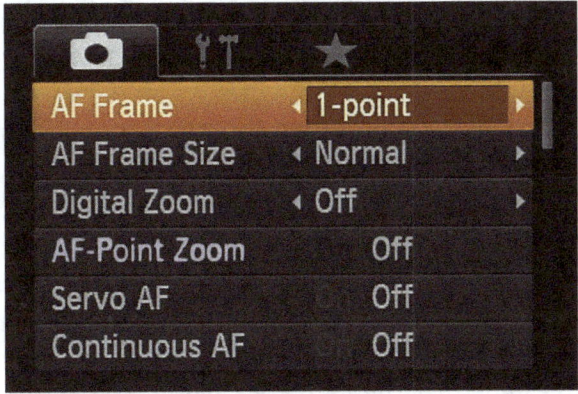

Fig. 4-46: First Screen of Items on Shooting Menu

163

In most cases, each option (such as AF Frame Size) occupies one line, with its name on the left and its current setting (such as Normal or Small) on the right. In other cases (such as Flash Settings), the option is followed by three dots, meaning you have to press the Func./Set button or the right direction button to see more options on another screen.

You have to scroll through several screens to see all of the Shooting menu's options. If you find it tedious to scroll with the up and down cursor buttons, you can turn the control dial on the back of the camera, which may help you get through the menus faster. Also, depending on the menu option, you may be able to reach it more quickly by reversing direction with the cursor buttons, and wrapping around to reach the option you want. In other words, if you're on the top line of the menu, you can scroll up to reach the bottom option. Or, if the highlight is already near the bottom option, you can scroll down to get to the options at the top of the menu.

Here's one more tip for navigating the menus: If you have scrolled down into a menu screen, away from the tabs at the top, and you want to switch to a different menu (such as from the Shooting menu to the Setup menu), you don't have to scroll all the way to the top of the menu screen and then move over to the next menu tab with a direction button; instead, you can just push the zoom lever briefly to the right or left, and you will scroll immediately over to the next menu tab.

Finally, you can take advantage of the S110's very convenient touch-screen capability for navigating the menu system. You can touch a tab at the top of a menu screen to move from one menu system to another, and you can touch an item on any line of the menu to select it and to change its setting. You also can scroll a menu screen up and down by dragging a finger over it.

Some of the menu's lines may have a dimmed, "grayed-out" appearance, meaning they cannot be selected under the present settings. For example, if you have set the AF Frame menu option to Face AiAF, you cannot change the AF Frame Size option, which is automatically set to Normal, so the AF Frame Size line on the Shooting menu is grayed out, as shown in Figure 4-47.

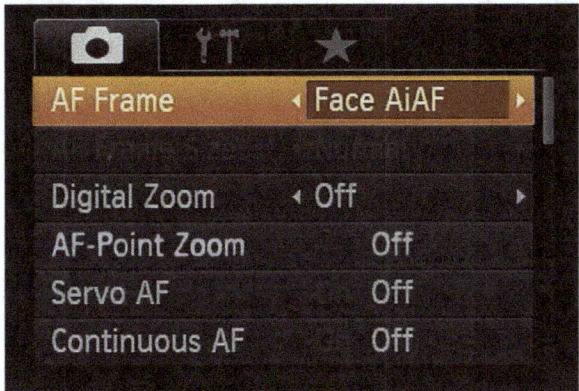

Fig. 4-47:   Frame Size Grayed Out when Face AiAF Selected

Also, if you have set the shooting mode to AUTO, some options do not even appear on the Shooting menu—they just disappear (such as AF Frame Size and Servo AF, among others), as seen in Figure 4-48.

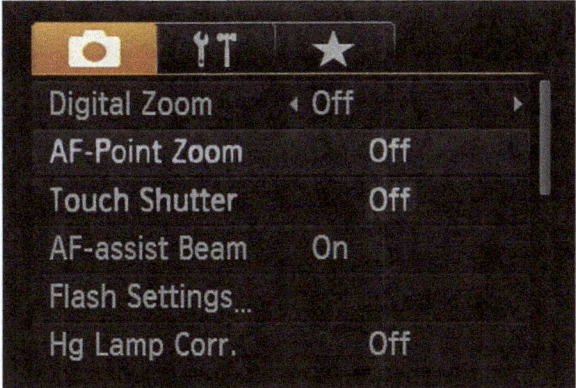

Fig. 4-48:   First Screen of Shooting Menu in AUTO Mode

If you want to follow along with the discussion of the options on the Shooting menu, leave the shooting mode set to Program and the image type set to JPEG in the Function menu. With these settings, you can get access to just about every option on the Shooting menu. (Some options are available only in Movie mode, discussed in Chapter 8, and some are available only in other modes; I'll mention those as I come to them.) I'll start at the top and discuss each option on the way down the list.

AF Frame

This first item on the Shooting menu gives you several options for controlling how the autofocus frame is set up when the camera is in autofocus mode. Once this menu option is highlighted, press the left and right direction buttons or use the touch screen to select from the two options, as follows:

Face AiAF

With Face AiAF, the camera looks for human faces. If it detects what it believes are faces, it puts a white frame on what appears to be the main subject, and up to two gray frames on other faces, as shown in Figure 4-49.

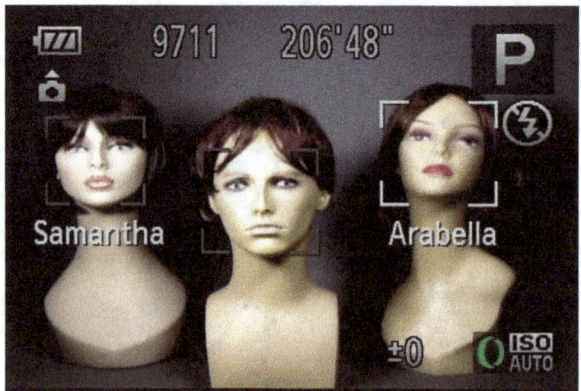

Fig. 4-49: *Face Detection in Operation with Multiple Faces*

When you press the shutter button halfway, the camera will

166

focus on the main faces and set the exposure and white balance. The LCD will display up to nine green frames to show the faces it has chosen to focus on. This is a good option to choose when you're at a picnic or other group function and you need to take a quick snapshot with as many faces in focus as possible. In other situations, you may want to take more time and select the focus point and other options yourself.

Tracking Subjects or Faces

When the Face AiAF option is activated, you can set the camera to maintain its focus on a particular subject, including a person's face. To do this, aim the camera at the scene, and touch the screen where the chosen subject or face appears. The camera will then display a focus frame with double brackets at its corners, as shown in Figure 4-50.

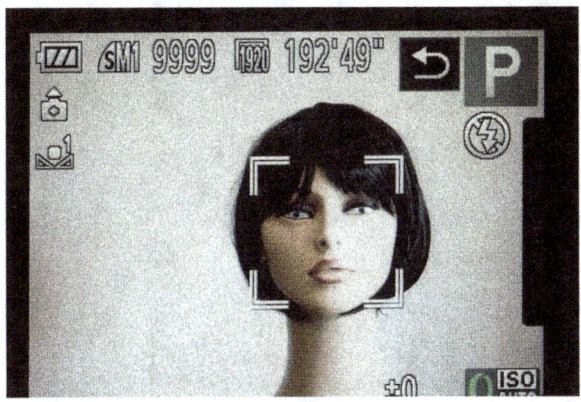

Fig. 4-50: Double Focus Bracket for Face Tracking

That frame will move around the screen as the subject (or the camera) moves, to keep the subject within the focus frame. When you are ready to take the picture, press the shutter button to take it. If you want to cancel the tracking before taking a picture, touch the curved arrow in the upper right corner of the screen.

Note: This tracking function will not work if you turned on the Touch Shutter option using the Shooting menu, which is dis-

167

cussed later in this chapter. If that option is turned on, touching the screen in shooting mode and then removing your finger will take a picture. So, you must have that option turned off if you want to use focus tracking.

You also can use the Face AiAF option in conjunction with the Face Select function, with which the camera focuses on a specific person's face. To do this, you have to assign the AF Frame Adjustment option to the Ring Function button, as discussed later in this chapter. Then, aim the camera at the person's face; the camera should place a single focus frame around the face. Next, press the Ring Function button, and the focus frame will change to a double frame, as shown in Figure 4-51, and the camera will track that face even as the person (or the camera) moves around.

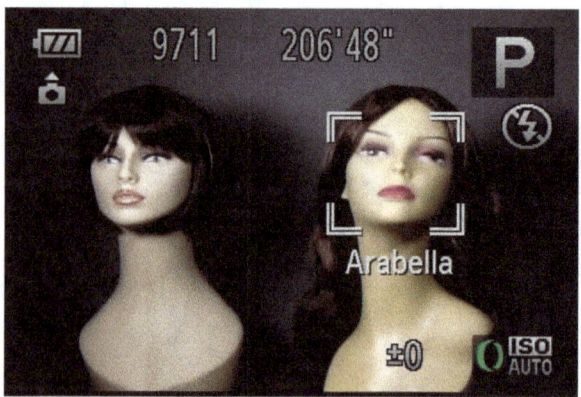

Fig. 4-51: Face Select Function in Use

To switch the focus to a different person's face, you can press the Ring Function button again. Once all faces have been selected in turn, pressing the Ring Function button again will cancel the Face Select function.

1-point

With this option, the camera places an autofocus frame in the center of the screen, as shown in Figure 4-52. You can then place this frame over the area of the scene that you want to be in sharpest focus.

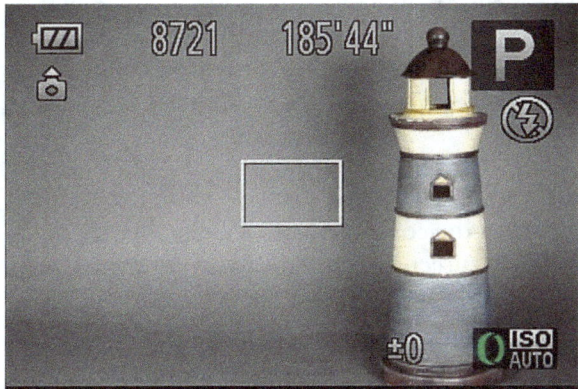

Fig. 4-52:   1-Point AF Frame in Center of Screen

The advantage of this setting is that you can move the focus frame around the screen. To do this, touch the focus frame with your finger; the frame will then turn orange and the message Change size/Move frame will appear briefly on the screen.

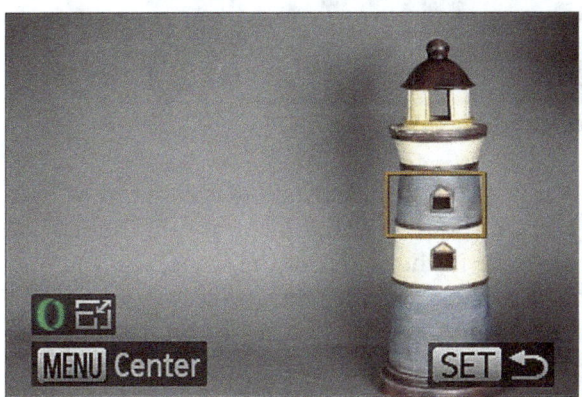

Fig. 4-53:   1-Point AF Frame Moved Over Subject

You can then move the frame to any location on the screen, as shown in Figure 4-53, by dragging it with your finger, by turning the control dial or by pressing any of the four direction buttons. When you have the frame located where you want it,

169

press the Func./Set button, or touch the SET icon in the lower right corner of the screen, to fix the frame in place. It will then turn white again. If you want to return the frame quickly to the center of the screen, press the Menu button or touch the Menu icon while the frame is orange, and it will jump back to the center.

In addition, as also noted on the display, while the frame is orange, you can turn the control ring to change the size of the frame if you need to direct the camera's focus on a small area. The small frame is shown in Figure 4-54.

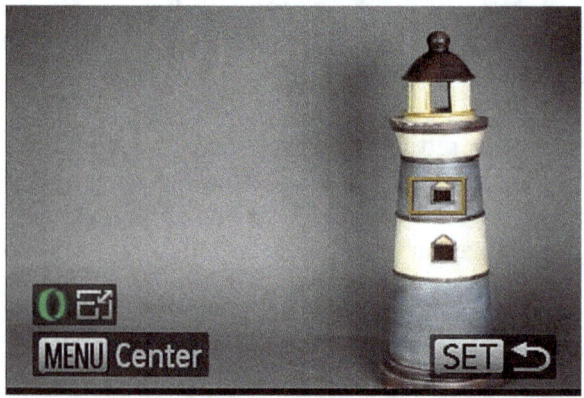

Fig. 4-54:   1-Point AF Frame at Small Size

There is another way you can change your focus point, without moving the 1-point frame. If the point you want to focus on doesn't happen to be in the center of the scene, you can lock focus on it by pressing the shutter button halfway while aiming at it, and then move the camera back to compose the shot as you want; the focus will be locked on the target you chose.

AF Frame Size

This second option on the Shooting menu is one you may not need very often, because its function can be handled by the control ring. This option is related to the autofocus frame type, which is set using the AF Frame option, discussed above. As

I noted earlier, if you set the autofocus frame type to 1-point, you can change the size of the frame by turning the control ring after the frame is activated through the touch screen. However, if you want to set the size of the autofocus frame through this menu option, you can do that as well. For example, if you know you will want to use the smaller frame size, you can make that setting through this menu item, and then you will not have to bother changing the frame's size using the control ring. You can, however, still change the size back to normal using the control ring when the frame is activated. Of course, this setting will take effect only when the AF Frame option is set to 1-point, as noted above.

The autofocus frame cannot be made smaller when the camera is set to use digital zoom, digital tele-converter, or manual focus.

Digital Zoom

This feature lets you zoom in on a scene electronically, beyond the reach of the camera's optical zoom capability. Because it is an electronic zoom and not an optical one, it does not really increase the information received by the camera; instead, it just magnifies the pixels so they appear larger, which can result in a blocky, pixellated look. That's not to say that digital zoom is completely useless. It can help you compose a scene the way you want to, or to measure the exposure on a small part of the scene before you zoom back out to take the picture without the digital zoom effect, for example. But don't be misled by the notion that this feature lets you zoom in to a super magnification with no drop-off in quality of the image.

To use digital zoom for still images, first of all, you have to have the camera set to use JPEG files through the Function menu. You can't use digital zoom with the Raw (or Raw+JPEG) setting, and digital zoom also is unavailable in Creative Filters mode and with all of the Scene types except for Smart Shutter, Portrait, Underwater, Snow, and Fireworks. The digital tele-converter settings, discussed below, are not available in any

171

shooting modes except P, Av, Tv, and M.

When you select Digital Zoom from the menu, you will have several options to choose from: Off, Standard, 1.5x and 2.0x. The Standard setting is for digital zoom; the other two settings are for a different function called digital tele-converter, discussed below.

When you turn on digital zoom using the Standard setting, you will notice that you can zoom the lens, using the zoom lever, to a greater focal length than before. In fact, when you use the zoom lever with that setting turned on, the focal length of the lens is changed from its normal range of 24mm to 120mm. Instead, the range becomes four times the normal range, or 24mm to 480mm, yielding a maximum zoom factor of 20 times the wide-angle 24mm focal length.

When you use digital zoom, you will see some changes in the zoom scale that appears at the top of the display screen. As shown in Figure 4-55, when the Digital Zoom menu option is turned off, the zoom scale is one continuous white rectangle, indicating that the entire zoom range consists of optical zoom.

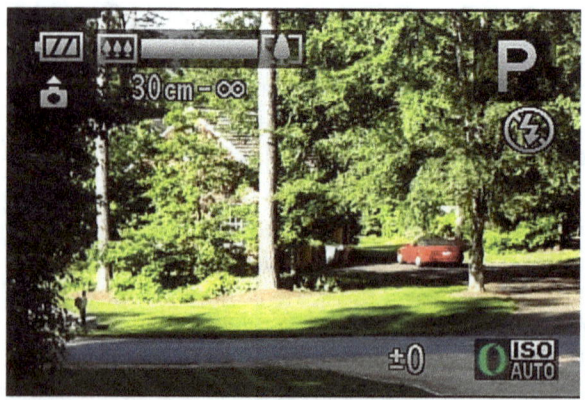

Fig. 4-55: Zoom Scale with Digital Zoom Turned Off

When the Digital Zoom option is turned on, as shown in Figure 4-56, the zoom scale is divided into two parts, with a vertical white line between them.

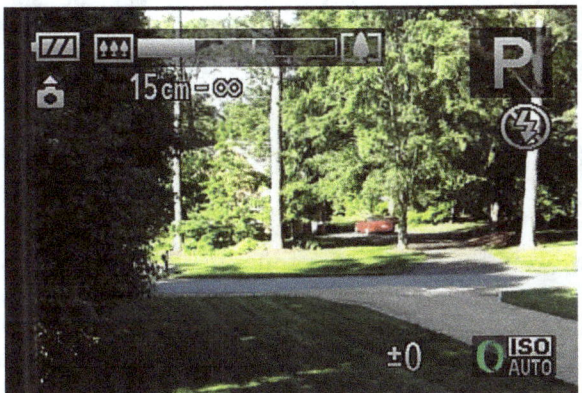

Fig. 4-56:   Zoom Scale with Digital Zoom Turned On

As long as you keep the zoom bar to the left of the line, the bar will be white, indicating that only optical zoom is in use.

However, if you keep pressing the zoom lever to move the zoom bar past the small vertical line, the zoom scale will turn yellow and then blue as it progresses to higher levels of magnification, as shown in Figure 4-57.

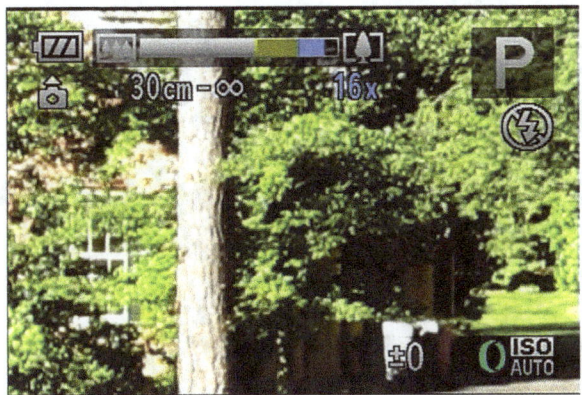

Fig. 4-57:   Zoom Scale with Yellow and Blue Parts when Digital Zoom On

173

The yellow area means that the image should not be very much degraded by the use of extra pixels. Canon attempts to achieve this result by using its technology to enhance the size of the image without the excessive enlargement that results in pixellation. When the zoom bar turns blue, that indicates that the image will be degraded because of the camera's electronic enlargement of the area of pixels that make up the image.

The point that divides the yellow area from the blue area changes as the resolution of the image changes. When the image size is set to Large through the Function menu, the zoom bar turns yellow in the area from 5 times to 10 times magnification, and turns blue in the area above 10 times magnification. However, when the image size is set to a smaller level, the camera is using fewer of the available pixels on the image sensor to produce the image, so it can use the excess pixels to create the zoom effect without as much deterioration of the image.

So, when the image size is set to the M1 level, the zoom bar stays yellow in the range from 5 times to 13 times zoom; only above 13 times does it turn blue, indicating greater deterioration. When the image size is set to M2 or S, the zoom bar stays yellow for all zoom levels above 5 times; it never turns blue, as illustrated in Figure 4-58.

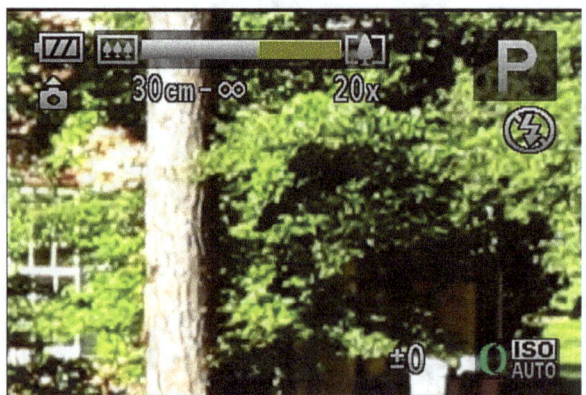

Fig. 4-58: Zoom Scale with Yellow but no Blue

The two numerical settings under the Digital Zoom menu option (1.5x and 2.0x) activate a function that Canon calls "digital tele-converter," which is supposed to provide better quality than digital zoom, with less likelihood of image deterioration. What the digital tele-converter option does is increase the magnification of the normal lens throughout its range, instead of just providing greater magnification at the upper end of the range, as digital zoom does. Therefore, with the digital tele-converter, you can actually use the lens at its shortest optical focal length of 24mm, which allows you to achieve a blurred background and to use faster shutter speeds than otherwise, because the aperture can be wider open.

This can be confusing, so I'll use an example. Suppose you set the lens to its widest-angle focal length of 24mm. At that focal length, you can set the aperture to its widest value of f/2.0 and use relatively fast shutter speeds, because a lot of light is coming in through the wide aperture of the lens. Now suppose you move the optical zoom to a range of 50mm. At that range, the aperture will close down to about f/4.0, because you cannot have a wide-open aperture with the lens zoomed in optically. However, if, instead of using the optical zoom, you turn on the digital zoom feature to its 2.0x tele-converter setting, the normal optical focal length (unzoomed) of 24mm is converted to 48mm. So, without using the optical zoom at all, you have achieved the equivalent of a zoom to about 50mm. Because you have not used the optical zoom, you can still set the aperture to its widest setting of f/2.0, and use faster shutter speeds.

When you use the digital tele-converter settings, the zoom scale remains white throughout its entire range, indicating that there is no deterioration of the image due to enlarging of pixels.

I prefer to avoid using digital zoom and digital tele-converter and just rely on the optical zoom, although there are some situations in which it's good to have these options available. For example, as noted above, using the digital tele-converter function in some cases can allow the camera to use a faster shutter speed than otherwise, because you can use the 24mm focal length setting, but still magnify the image to the equivalent of 48mm. In this way, the camera can use its widest aperture, letting in enough light to allow the wider shutter speed. Also, composing with a digitally zoomed image may allow you to meter the exposure of your subject properly; you can then zoom back out to take the picture without the quality loss that results from using digital zoom.

AF-Point Zoom

When you turn this option on, the camera enlarges the area that it uses to focus on the scene. So, for example, if you are using Face AiAF for your AF Frame setting, the camera enlarges the face it is focusing on.

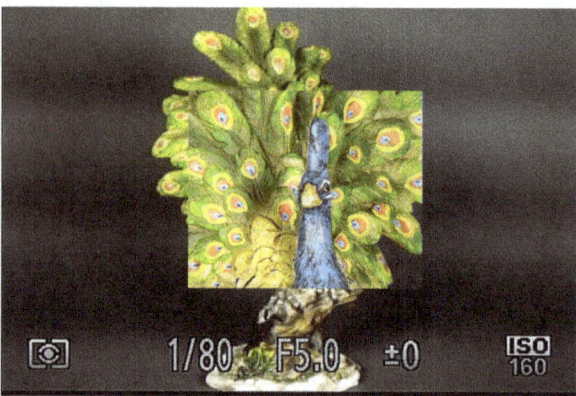

Fig. 4-59: AF-Point Zoom Feature in Use

(It won't enlarge the area if it doesn't detect a face.) If you are using 1-point for the AF Frame setting, the camera enlarges the center of the frame, as shown in Figure 4-59. The enlarged view does not appear until you press the shutter button down halfway to cause the camera to focus.

The focus area will not be enlarged if you are using the digital tele-converter function or if the camera is connected to a

176

TV set. It also will not be enlarged if the Digital Zoom menu option is set to Standard and the lens has been zoomed into the range where the zoom scale turns yellow or blue; it will be enlarged if that option is turned on, as long as the lens has not been zoomed into the yellow or blue range.

I find AF-Point Zoom to be helpful, because it lets me see the area being focused on quite clearly, though some people may find it distracting to have the image distorted by the enlargement of a square area in the middle of the scene.

Servo AF

With the Servo AF option turned on, when you press the shutter button down halfway to evaluate focus, the camera places a blue focus frame on the screen and continues to adjust focus as long as you keep the shutter button down halfway, as shown in Figure 4-60.

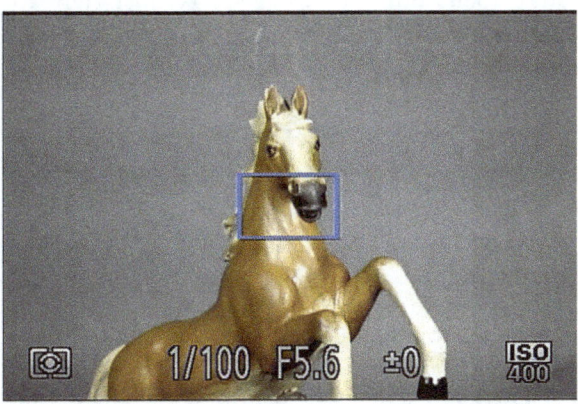

Fig. 4-60: Blue Frame for Servo AF

If you use this feature when AF Frame is set to 1-point, the blue frame will stay in one place, and focus will be adjusted for any object that remains within that frame.

If you use this feature when AF Frame is set to Face AiAF, then, if the camera detects a face, it will turn the focus frame blue when you press the shutter button down halfway, as shown in

177

Figure 4-61, and it will keep adjusting focus on the face, even if the person moves, while the button is held halfway down.

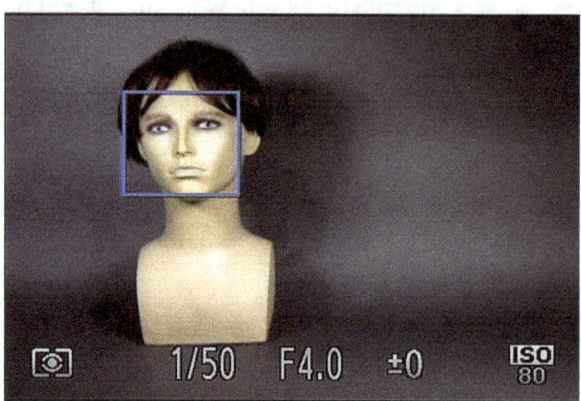

Fig. 4-61: *Blue Frame Moved with Servo AF and Face AiAF in Use*

So, if you are trying to photograph a child, say, and you want to keep adjusting focus until the image looks just right for your scrapbook before pressing the shutter all the way down, you can press the shutter halfway and keep the camera trained on her until the perfect moment arrives. Note, though, that if the camera does not detect a face, the blue frame will stay in the center of the screen and the frame will not move as the subject moves. Therefore, you cannot use the Servo AF setting to track an object such as a bicycle or car; the frame will move only when the camera has detected a face.

The key point to note for this feature is that it lets the camera continue to adjust focus after the shutter button is pressed halfway down. Normally, when this feature is not turned on, when you press the button halfway down, the camera locks in the focus at that point and will not adjust it further. It's important to distinguish the Servo AF function from the continuous focus adjustment that takes place before the shutter is pressed halfway down. That sort of continuous adjustment takes place when you use the Touch AF function, discussed earlier in this chapter, and when you turn on the Continuous AF feature, discussed immediately below.

Of course, the Servo AF option uses up the battery rapidly, because the autofocus mechanism keeps working constantly, so you may not want to use it too much unless you have an extra battery at the ready.

Continuous AF

The Continuous AF menu option is similar to Servo AF in that it causes the camera to focus continuously, but the difference is that, with this option, the camera focuses continuously before you press the shutter button halfway down to evaluate focus. Then, when you press the button halfway down, the camera locks in its focus. With this option, you may be able to get a bit of a head start on the focusing operation by having the camera constantly refocusing as you move it around, or as your subject moves. In that way, when you finally decide to press the shutter button down halfway to lock in the focus, the camera should already have the focus nearly adjusted for the subject, so the final adjustment can be quick and accurate. Of course, this option, like Servo AF, uses up battery power quickly, so I recommend you use it only if you find it important to save some time on the final focus adjustment when it comes time to press the shutter button to take the picture.

Note that you can, if you want, turn on both Servo AF and Continuous AF, in which case the camera will focus continuously before you press the shutter button down halfway, and then will continue to adjust the focus while the button is held down halfway; it will lock in the focus only when you actually take the picture. If your subject is quite mobile and you are afraid it will move out of focus before you can press the shutter button down fully, you might try using both options together, but, for me, the drain on the battery ordinarily would not be worth the slight gain in accuracy that you might obtain.

One other point to keep in mind is that, if you activate the Touch AF feature, discussed earlier in this chapter, the camera focuses continuously on the subject that you have selected, even if the Continuous AF menu option is turned off. The

Continuous AF option comes into play for other situations, such as when you are not yet sure where you will be focusing the camera, and you want to make sure the lens keeps focusing on whatever subjects come into view.

Touch Shutter

The Touch Shutter menu option is used to turn on the camera's ability to take a picture when you touch the screen with your finger. I will discuss this feature in Chapter 5, in connection with the discussion of the various touch-screen features of the PowerShot S110.

AF-Assist Beam

This menu option lets you turn on or off the reddish light beam that emanates from the AF Assist/Self-timer lamp on the front of the camera.

This beam comes on when the camera is trying to focus in a dark area; the light helps the autofocus mechanism find the patterns and shapes it needs to evaluate in order to achieve proper focus. You should usually leave this setting turned on, but you may want to turn it off when you're taking pictures in a place where the beam could be distracting or annoying to others, or where it might alert the subjects of your candid photography. I like to disable it when doing street photography, for example, because it is not of much use outdoors and can call attention to the camera. Note that, even if you turn off the lamp with this menu option, the lamp still will light up when you use the self-timer; you cannot disable the lamp from illuminating for that function. The lamp also fires when the Red-Eye Lamp menu option, found under the Flash Settings menu item, is turned on.

MF-Point Zoom

This option is similar to AF-Point Zoom, discussed above. When you turn this feature on through the menu, the camera places an enlarged square in the center of the screen when you are focusing manually, so you can judge the sharpness of the focus more readily. This capability is actually probably more useful with manual focus than with autofocus, because it's up to you to make sure the focus is accurate. But, you may prefer not to be distracted by this distortion of the normal image. One way to deal with the situation is just to zoom in on the scene yourself while focusing, and then zoom back out again after the focusing is done.

Safety MF

When Safety MF is turned on, the camera will "fine-tune" the focus using its autofocus mechanism when you press the shutter button to evaluate the exposure, after you have made the focus as sharp as possible using manual focus. If you turn Safety MF off, then the camera will not assist you with auto-focusing in this situation. Whether you use this option or not depends on your particular situation. For example, you may want to start the focusing process manually in order to make sure the camera is focusing on the proper part of your subject, but then still have the camera make the final adjustment to get the focus sharp. In that case, leave Safety MF turned on. On the other hand, you may want to get the manual focusing done all on your own, without the possibility that the camera will make it worse by adjusting the focus in a way that is not helpful when you press the shutter button halfway to evaluate exposure. So, evaluate any particular photographic task to see whether this function might be helpful.

Flash Settings

This menu item is followed by three dots, meaning you have to press the Func./Set button or the right direction button to get access to the next screen, where the specific settings are located. As an alternative, you can get access to that screen directly from shooting mode, by pressing the Flash (right) button, and then immediately pressing the Menu button.

Some or all of the following six settings may be available on the Flash Settings screen, depending on the shooting mode.

Flash Mode

This option can be a bit tricky to understand, because the camera has quite a few different flash settings, several of which could be considered "modes," such as Forced Off, Forced On, Auto Flash, etc. But the Flash Mode setting on the Shooting menu is none of those. This option is only available on the menu screen in two shooting modes—Shutter Priority and Aperture Priority. In all other modes it is automatically set to one or the other of the two available settings, and this menu item does not even appear on the screen. In Auto mode, Program mode, and most of the Scene mode and Creative Filters mode settings, Flash Mode is preset to Auto. In Manual exposure mode, only, Flash Mode is preset to Manual. In Shutter Priority and Aperture Priority shooting modes, you have the choice of setting Flash Mode to Auto or Manual.

When Flash Mode is set to Auto, that means that the camera automatically calculates how much flash power to use to expose the image properly. When Flash Mode is set to Manual, the camera does not make that calculation. Rather, it is up to you to set the power of the flash's output using the next item down on the Flash Settings menu, whose name and function change depending on how Flash Mode is set.

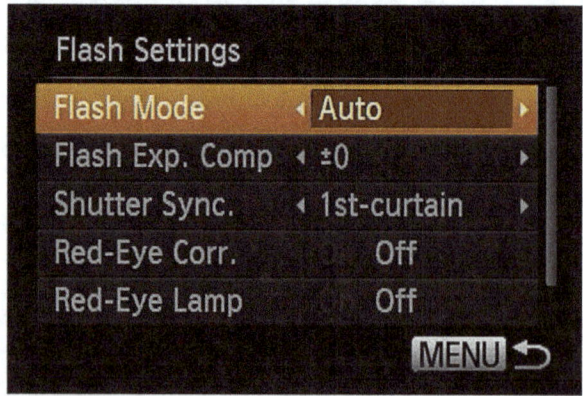

Fig. 4-62: Flash Mode Set to Auto

182

If Flash Mode is set to Auto, meaning the flash output is automatically controlled by the camera's exposure system, the next item down on the menu is called Flash Exposure Compensation, as shown in Figure 4-62. That option works in similar fashion to standard exposure compensation without flash. That is, you can dial in an amount of flash exposure compensation up to 2 EV units, in increments of 1/3 EV. When you do that, you are telling the camera, in effect, "Okay, you go ahead and calculate the correct exposure with the flash, but then add in (say) 1 1/3 EV extra, to make the picture brighter."

On the other hand, if Flash Mode is set to Manual, then the flash output is not automatically controlled, and the next item down on the menu changes to Flash Output, as shown in Figure 4-63.

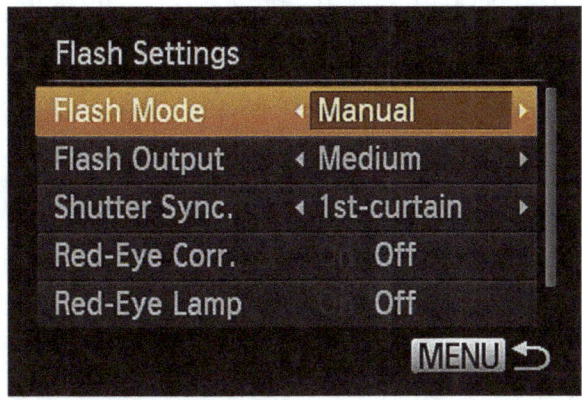

Fig. 4-63: Flash Mode Set to Manual

This option has three settings: Minimum, Medium, and Maximum. As you can see from the names, it is up to you to make an absolute setting of flash power, as opposed to the relative setting that you make using the Flash Exposure Compensation setting. In this case, you are saying to the camera, "Okay, I will tell you how much flash to fire—go ahead and use (say) your Medium setting—that seems about right to me."

There is one extra benefit to having the Manual setting for

183

Flash Mode. When Flash Mode is set to Auto, the camera fires a pre-flash before it fires the actual flash that is used for the exposure. The camera needs to fire this pre-flash so its automatic exposure system can measure the light from the flash and set the camera's aperture and shutter speed to account for the light from the flash. However, when Flash Mode is set to Manual, the camera fires only the actual flash for the exposure; it does not need to fire a pre-flash.

The benefit to having a flash that can fire without a pre-flash is that you can use the S110's flash to trigger an optical "slave" flash unit. That sort of unit can be a self-contained flash with a built-in optical trigger, or it can be an add-on optical trigger to which an external flash unit is attached. When the Power-Shot S110's flash fires, the light from its flash activates the slave and triggers the other flash unit. If a pre-flash were fired, the pre-flash would trigger the slave too soon, before the actual exposure is taken with the S110. I will discuss this setup in Appendix A.

Flash Exposure Compensation and Flash Output

These two menu options are discussed above, in connection with the discussion of the Flash Mode setting.

Shutter Sync.

This menu option is available only in the Program, Aperture Priority, Shutter Priority, and Manual exposure modes, as well as in the Movie Digest mode. This setting is one you may not often need, unless you encounter the particular situation it is designed for. Shutter Sync. has two settings—1st-curtain and 2nd-curtain. The normal setting is 1st-curtain, which causes the flash to fire early in the process when the shutter opens to expose the image. If you set it to 2nd-curtain, the flash fires later, just before the shutter closes.

The reason for having the 2nd-curtain sync setting available is that it can help you avoid having a strange-looking result in some photographic situations. This issue arises when you are taking a relatively long exposure, such as one-half second, of a subject with taillights, such as a car or motorcycle at night, that is moving across your field of view. With 1st-curtain sync, the flash will fire early in the process, freezing the vehicle in a clear image. However, as the shutter remains open while the vehicle keeps going, the camera will capture the moving tail-lights in a stream that appears to be extending in front of the vehicle. If, instead, you use 2nd-curtain sync, the initial part of the exposure will capture the lights in a trail that appears behind the vehicle, while the vehicle itself is not frozen by the flash until later in the exposure. Therefore, with 2nd-curtain sync in this particular situation, the final image is likely to look more natural than with 1st-curtain sync.

In the images shown here, I used a model truck with a red taillight to demonstrate this effect. In Figure 4-64, I used the 1st-curtain setting (flash set to Forced On) for an exposure of 1/4 second in Shutter Priority mode. As you can see, the flash fired early in the exposure, catching the truck early in its mo-tion, and the taillight then continued moving in the direction of the truck, tracing a bright trail in front of the vehicle.

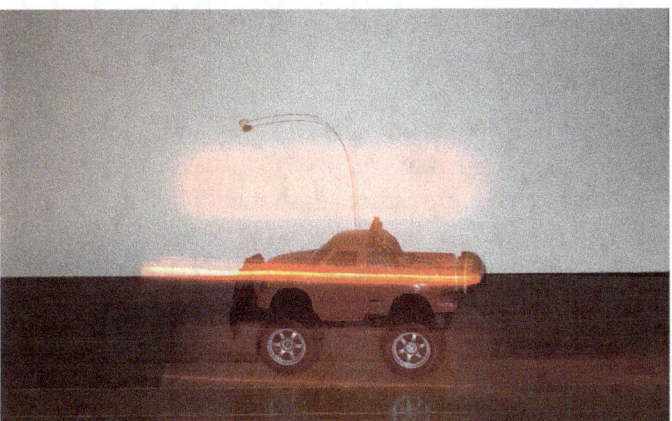

Fig. 4-64: Image Taken with First-Curtain Setting

In Figure 4-65, with 2nd-curtain sync, the flash fired later, so the camera captured the trail from the taillight first, and then the flash fired, capturing the truck in front of the trail of light.

185

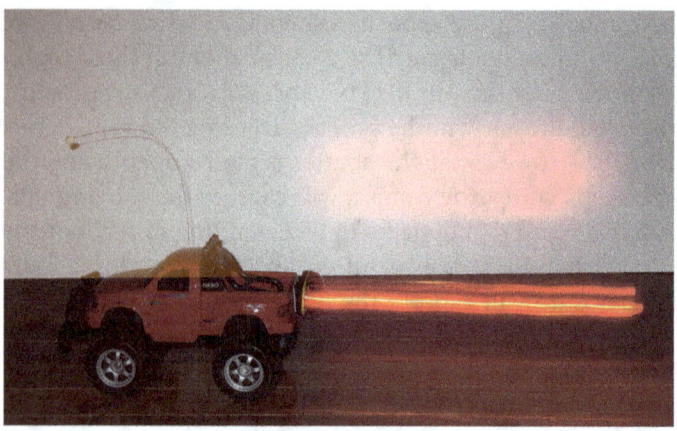

Fig. 4-65: Image Taken with Second-Curtain Setting

To sum up the situation with the 1st-curtain and 2nd-curtain Shutter Sync. settings, a good general rule is to always use the 1st-curtain setting unless you are sure you have a real need for the 2nd-curtain setting. Using the 2nd-curtain setting makes it harder to compose and set up the shot, because you have to anticipate where the main subject will be when the flash finally fires late in the exposure process.

Red-Eye Correction

This option is one of the two measures the PowerShot S110 offers against the problem of "red-eye"—the red cast to human eyes that results from on-camera flash that lights up the blood vessels on the retina. The name of this option is "Red-Eye Correction," which implies that the red-eye effect occurs, but then is "corrected" digitally. That is, the camera applies digital processing to remove the red tint after the eyes are reddened by the penetrating flash. As the Canon user's manual points out, there is some chance that this option will "correct" not only red-eye problems, but also other red patches in your shot, such as reddish makeup on a person's face. I rarely use this option, but it could be useful if you want to take some shots with flash at a party and don't want to bother with correcting any red-eye effects after the fact. Note that the Playback menu provides another option for red-eye correction, which can be applied to images that were previously captured. That option is discussed in Chapter 6.

Red-Eye Lamp

This next Flash Settings menu option is the camera's second approach to solving the red-eye problem. When you have this option turned on in the menu, before taking a flash picture the camera fires the reddish lamp near the lens that also serves as the AF-Assist lamp. The idea is that the burst from this bright light will cause the subject's pupils to constrict enough to keep the light of the flash from penetrating to the retinas, thereby reducing or eliminating the red-eye effect. You can have both this option and the previous one turned on if you want to use all available options to combat the red-eye problem.

Safety FE

This final option on the Flash Settings sub-menu is, as its name implies, a safety precaution that you can turn either on or off. If you turn it on using this menu option, then, when the flash fires, the camera is supposed to gauge the exposure and adjust the shutter speed or aperture to avoid an overexposed shot with washed-out highlights. Although I have rarely noticed the camera change its settings because of this feature, I recommend you leave the feature turned on in case you encounter a shot in which there is a risk of blown highlights without this safety measure.

Hg Lamp Correction

This Shooting menu option is unusual because it appears on the menu screen only when the camera is set to AUTO mode; if you have the camera in Program or any other mode, this item will not appear at all, because it is intended for use only in that one mode.

This setting is meant to be used when you are shooting at night

187

under mercury lamps, such as might be found outdoors in a park, to correct for a green tint that may be caused by such lamps. I have not found any situations in which this setting made a difference in the appearance of my images, but, if you encounter lighting that seems to cast a green tint, you might want to try turning on this option.

ISO Auto Settings

This selection does not appear on the Shooting menu unless the Auto ISO setting is available on the Function menu. So, unless the camera is set to Program, Aperture Priority, Shutter Priority, or Movie Digest mode, you won't find this entry on the menu. When you do see it, it has three dots after it, meaning there are other options that can be set on the next screen after pressing Func./Set—Max ISO Speed and Rate of Change.

I mentioned these two settings earlier in this chapter, in connection with the ISO setting on the Function menu.

The first of these options, Max ISO Speed, shown in Figure 4-66, lets you set the maximum ISO level that will be set when the camera is set to Auto ISO.

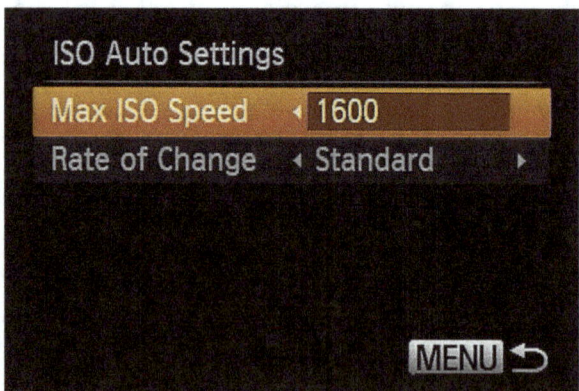

Fig. 4-66: Max ISO Speed and Rate of Change Menu Options

You can set this maximum level to ISO 400, 500, 640, 800, 1000, 1250, or 1600. You might want to set it to one of the

188

lower levels if you need to avoid the sort of visual "noise" that tends to show up in images taken at higher ISO settings.

The other option available through this menu choice, Rate of Change, is a fairly important option, though its function is not obvious from its name or from the discussion in the Canon Camera User Guide. First, note that this option is available only when the camera is set to Program, Aperture Priority, or Movie Digest mode. In Shutter Priority mode, the ISO Settings menu selection is available, but Rate of Change is not. What the Rate of Change feature does is let you specify a preference for higher or lower ISO settings, resulting in faster or slower shutter speeds. If you set this option to Slow, the camera will prefer low ISOs, likely resulting in slow shutter speeds, depending on the available light. Conversely, with the Fast setting, you are likely to see higher ISO settings, allowing the use of faster shutter speeds. Standard leaves the ISO settings in the moderate range. This option is useful, for example, if you don't mind some added noise, and want to be sure the camera sets a high ISO so you can use a fast shutter speed to avoid motion blur. So, if you are photographing action at a sports event, you might want to set this option to Fast; if you are taking pictures of scenery, you probably can leave it set to Slow.

High ISO NR

This next option on the Shooting menu gives you a way to control how much noise reduction the camera applies to its images when you are shooting with higher ISO values. As the ISO level is set higher, there is increased likelihood that visual noise will be introduced into your images. Normally, the camera processes images with digital noise reduction techniques, which reduce the noise in higher-ISO shots but also can reduce the details in the images. This menu option lets you decide whether to value the noise reduction above the details. Personally, I like to leave this setting at Low, because I usually do not mind a certain amount of noise when shooting at high ISOs; the grainy look can be appealing. But there undoubtedly will be times when you prefer to reduce the noise level as much as possible by setting this option to High.

This setting will be grayed-out and unavailable for selection if you are shooting with Raw or Raw+JPEG images, because, with the Raw format, the camera does not process the images with noise reduction; you can use your Raw processing software to reduce the noise in the images as you see fit.

Spot AE Point

This option has a very specific purpose and can be used only when certain other conditions exist. Specifically, you must have the metering method set to Spot on the Function menu, and you must have AF Frame set to 1-point on the Shooting menu. If both of those conditions are in effect, then you can use the Spot AE Point option to link the metering frame with the autofocus frame. If you do that, then, whenever you move the 1-point AF frame around the screen using the touch-screen procedure described earlier in this chapter, the Spot metering frame will move with it, as shown in Figure 4-67.

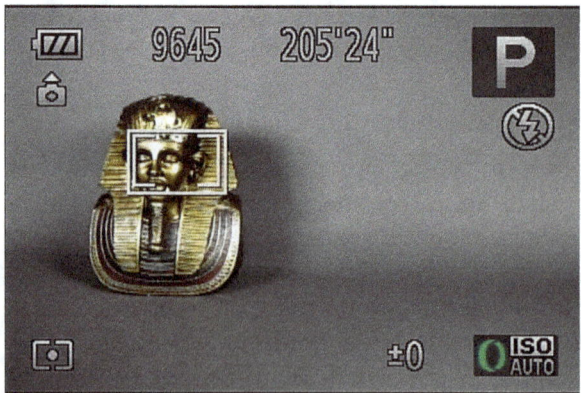

Fig. 4-67: *Spot Metering and 1-Point Focus Frames Linked*

Therefore, you will have the ability to set the camera's exposure and focus together on a small area that is not in the center of the display.

To accomplish this linking of the two frames, set the Spot AE Point option to AF Point. If, instead, you set it to Center, then the Spot metering point will remain in the center of the display, even if you move the AF frame, as shown in Figure 4-68.

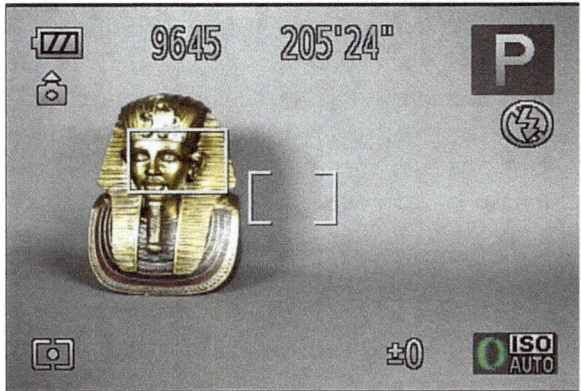

Fig. 4-68:   Spot Metering and 1-Point Focus Frames Not Linked

Safety Shift

This menu option, like the previous one, does not appear on the menu screen at all unless the context permits its use. Therefore, you will only see it on the menu when the camera is set to Aperture Priority or Shutter Priority mode. In those modes, if you turn Safety Shift on, the camera will override your setting of aperture or shutter speed if necessary for a proper exposure.

For example, suppose you have the camera in Shutter Priority mode with ISO set to 80 and the shutter speed set to 1/250 second in a relatively dimly-lit room. With Safety Shift turned off, the shutter speed setting will stay as it was set, and the aperture number (2.0 if the lens is zoomed out to wide-angle) will turn orange, indicating underexposure. But, if you have Safety Shift turned on in the same situation, the shutter speed will shift to something like 1/4 second, despite your having set it to 1/250 second, so the image can be exposed properly.

Whether to use this setting or not depends on your intentions

191

in a given situation. If you are experimenting with a particular shutter speed or aperture and want to use it whether or not the image will be well exposed, then leave Safety Shift turned off. If you would rather let the camera take over to save the image, turn this option on. My own preference is to control the camera's settings myself, so I leave Safety Shift turned off and change the settings when conditions call for changes, but this safety feature can be helpful if you prefer that the camera use its technology to help rescue shots from underexposure or overexposure. Note that this menu option does not have any effect when the flash is fired, although the menu option still can be turned on in that situation.

Wind Filter

This option appears on the regular Shooting menu, but it applies only to recording videos; it is discussed in Chapter 8 in connection with video options.

Review

This setting controls whether, and for how long, a newly captured image stays on the LCD screen when you take a picture. The possible settings are Off, Quick, any value from 2 through 10 seconds, and Hold. If you set this option to Quick, then the image you have just taken will stay on the display only as long as it takes for the camera to process it and become ready to shoot another image. If you select Hold, the image stays on the screen until you press the shutter button halfway down to return the camera to shooting mode. In Hold mode, the image will stay on the screen, but you can't move back or forward to other images. You can, however, change the display of information for that image using the Display button, and you can erase that image by pressing the Trash button (Ring Function button). Remember that you can always exit immediately from the Review display by pressing the shutter button down halfway.

Review Info

This next setting determines what information is displayed along with images when they are displayed on the screen immediately after shooting. The choices are Off, Detailed, and Focus Check. With Off, only the image itself is displayed. With Detailed, the screen shows a lot of information, including shooting settings and a histogram that provides a graphic representation of the dark and light areas in the image. The Focus Check setting displays a special screen that shows the image in two windows. The larger window shows the overall scene, and the camera places rectangular frames in this window—a white frame where the focus was set, a gray frame on any face that was detected, and an orange frame that acts as an inset to show what area is enlarged in the other large window on the LCD.

If you move the zoom lever to the right, the other window will become active, showing the area within the orange inset frame at large size. You can scroll around within that window to check the focus in that area, while also moving the area around so you can eventually check the entire image through the window. When you are done checking the focus, press the Menu button to return to the original Focus Check display. Then press the shutter button to return to shooting mode.

The Review Info menu option controls only which screen is displayed immediately after you take a picture. You can always call up the other displays of the image by pressing the Display button.

Blink Detection

This option can be set to either On or Off. When it is turned on, the camera will alert you by displaying an icon of a blinky-faced person if it detects that your subject's picture was taken with his or her eyes closed, as shown in Figure 4-69. This feature can serve as a useful check to see if you need to re-take a shot, because it can be difficult to tell if someone's eyes are closed while you are concentrating on taking the picture, or on examining the small LCD screen after it has been taken.

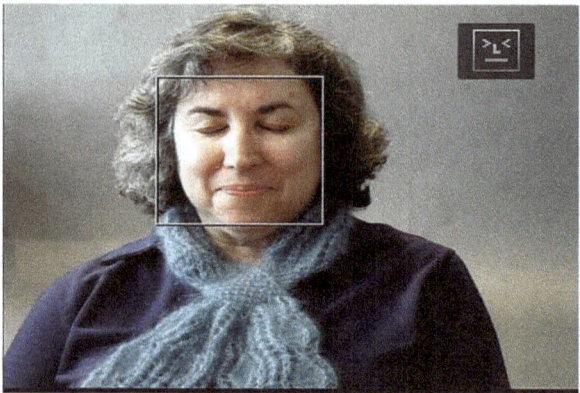

Fig. 4-69: Blink Detection Screen

Custom Display

This menu option controls the information displayed on the LCD screen in shooting mode. Move to the option's main screen, shown in Figure 4-70, by pressing the right direction button or the Func./Set button, or by touching the option's line on the menu screen.

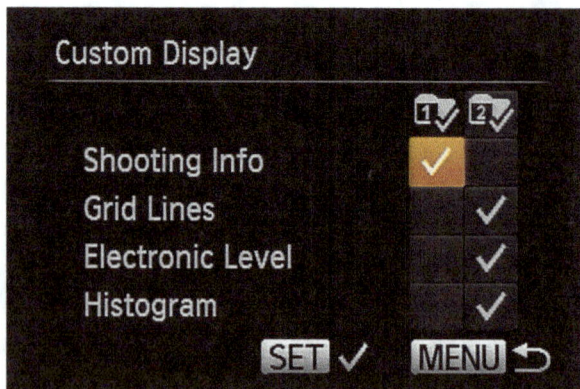

Fig. 4-70: Custom Display Menu Option - Settings Screen

Then, using the control dial or the direction buttons, navigate between the two columns with the numbers 1 and 2 at their

194

tops, and press the Func./Set button to add or remove a check mark for any one of the three items listed— Shooting Info, Grid Lines, Electronic Level, or Histogram. You also can touch the screen to mark or unmark items.

Items with check marks will display on that screen, and items with no check marks will not display. For example, with the setup shown in Figure 4-70, only the shooting information will show on the first screen, as seen in Figure 4-71.

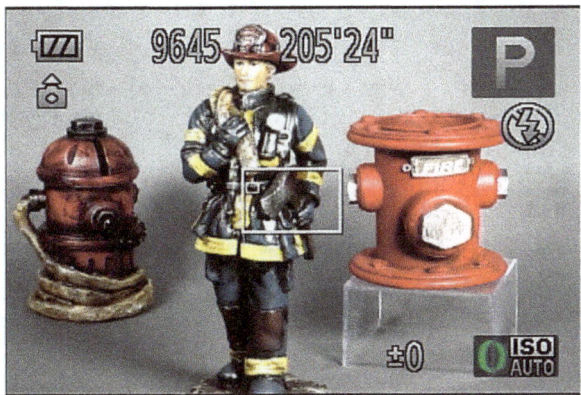

Fig. 4-71: Screen with Shooting Info Only

The second screen will display the grid lines, level, and histogram, as seen in Figure 4-72.

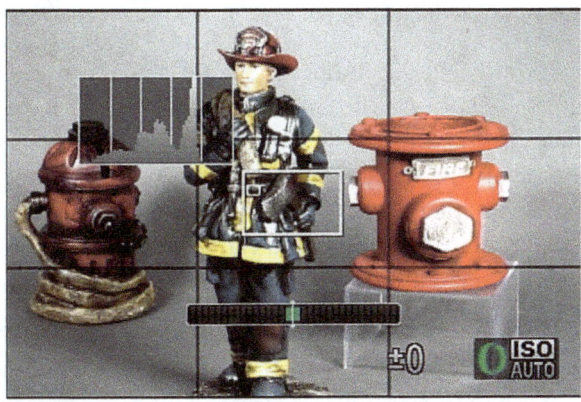

Fig. 4-72: Screen with Grid, Histogram, and Electronic Level Only

195

As you can see from Figure 4-71, the shooting information that displays, if selected, includes shooting mode, image size and quality, number of images remaining, minutes of video that can be recorded, video format selected, flash status, battery status, exposure compensation value, ISO setting, and a few other items, some of which appear only when certain settings are in place, such as the self-timer, i-Contrast, a white balance setting other than Auto White Balance, or a My Colors setting other than Off.

If you turn on the Grid Lines option, the camera displays the lines shown in Figure 4-72. They can be very helpful with orienting straight lines in your image, such as the horizon or the edge of a building or other structure. In addition, you may want to use the intersections of the lines to assist in aligning important subjects at points one-third of the way from the edges of the image in order to place them where they may have the most visual impact, in accordance with the Rule of Thirds.

The histogram, also shown in Figure 4-72, is a graphic display of how the dark and light tones in your image are distributed. A graph with most of the peaks toward the left indicates that there is an abundance of dark areas; a graph with many peaks at the right means there may be too many highlights, with the possibility of overexposure. I will discuss the histogram more fully in Chapter 6, in connection with the histogram that displays for images in playback mode.

Finally, the electronic level, seen near the bottom center of the screen in Figure 4-72, is useful when it is important to have the camera level. As you tilt the camera to the right or left, the white marker on the level moves to the opposite side of the scale. When the camera is level, the marker remains in the center of the scale and turns green. You can calibrate the level, if necessary, using the Setup menu, as discussed in Chapter 7.

Once you have finished setting up these items as you want them, return to the shooting screen by pressing the shutter button halfway. You can then alternate between the two displays by pressing the Display button.

IS Mode

With this option, you can set up the camera's image stabilization system as you want it. The three available options are Off, Continuous, and Shoot Only. You probably should turn IS off when the camera is on a tripod, because the IS system can actually generate image blur in that situation. Continuous is a good setting for everyday shooting, because the system will help reduce the risk of blur from camera motion for all of your shots, and you can gauge the effects of stabilization as you compose the image on the LCD. Shoot Only can be used to save power, because the camera will not stabilize the image while you are viewing a scene; the stabilization system will start to work only at the moment you actually press the shutter button to record the image. The Shoot Only setting also can be useful because it can force you to be more aware of the camera's movement, causing you to hold it as steady as possible.

When the camera is set to AUTO mode, it displays icons indicating the status of the IS system. For example, Figure 4-73 shows the hand icon in the upper right corner of the screen that indicates that stabilization is in effect and the camera is not panning.

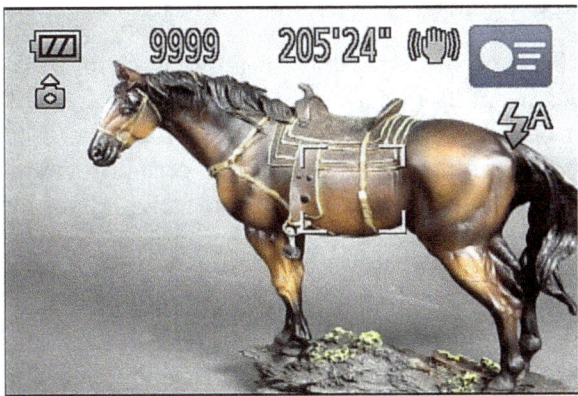

Fig. 4-73: Hand Icon in Upper Right Corner in AUTO Mode

197

See page 103 of the Canon user's guide for a key to these icons. One notable feature in AUTO mode is that, if the camera detects that it is on a stable support, it will turn off the IS system automatically and display an icon that shows a small tripod, as shown in Figure 4-74.

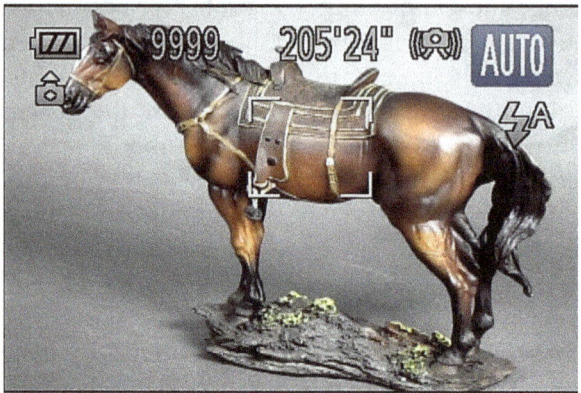

Fig. 4-74: Tripod Icon in Upper Right Corner in AUTO Mode

In all other shooting modes, you have to turn the IS system off yourself when the camera is on a tripod.

Date Stamp

This setting can be used to embed the current date, or the date and time, in the lower right corner of your images.

This embedding is permanent, which means that the information will appear as part of your image that cannot be deleted, other than through cropping or other editing procedures. You should not use this function unless you are certain that you want the date and time recorded on your images, perhaps for images that are part of a scientific research project. You can always add the date and time in other ways after the fact in editing software if you want to, because the camera always records the date and time internally with each image (if the date and time have been set accurately), so think twice before using this function. When you are shooting with this option activated, the word "DATE" appears in the lower right corner of the screen as you compose your shot. Figure 4-75 was taken with this option turned on, with both date and time embedded.

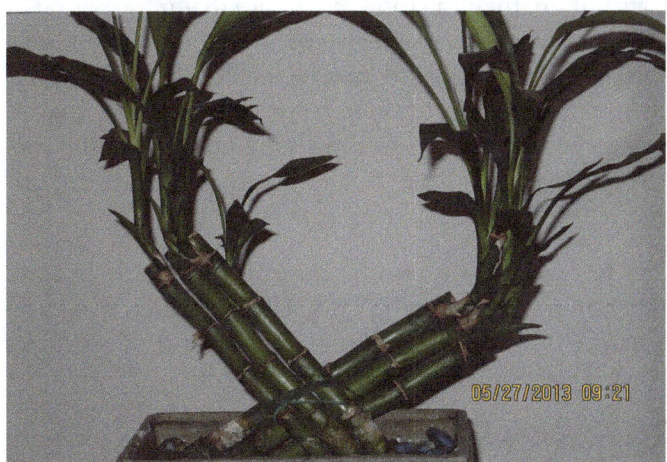

Fig. 4-75: Image with Date Stamp Option in Use

Face ID Settings

This option is followed by three dots, meaning more settings are on the next screen, reached by pressing the right button or the Func./Set button, or by touching the screen. On the next screen, seen in Figure 4-76, there are four options: Face ID, Add to Registry, Check/Edit Info, and Erase Info.

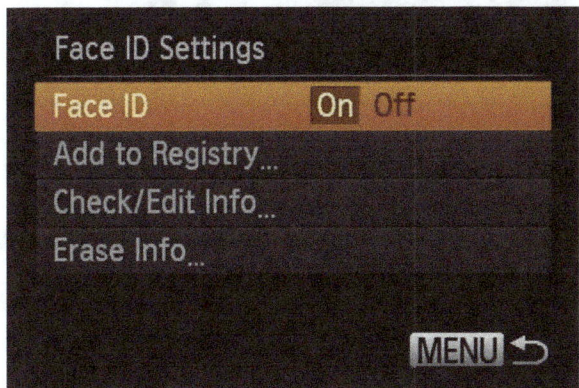

Fig. 4-76: Face ID Settings Menu Option

199

The first option, Face ID, lets you turn the Face ID function on or off. If you turn it off, then the camera does not use any information you have entered using the Add to Registry option. If you turn it on, then the camera will use that information to identify faces that you have registered in the camera and will adjust its focus and exposure for a recognized face. It also will display the names of up to three registered people in images, and will record the information with the images. In addition, you can use this function to search through your recorded images to find pictures of a particular person.

In order to register a face in the camera, you use the Add to Registry option. First, you have to set the Face ID option to On. Then, select the Add to Registry option and Select Add a New Face on the next screen, shown in Figure 4-77.

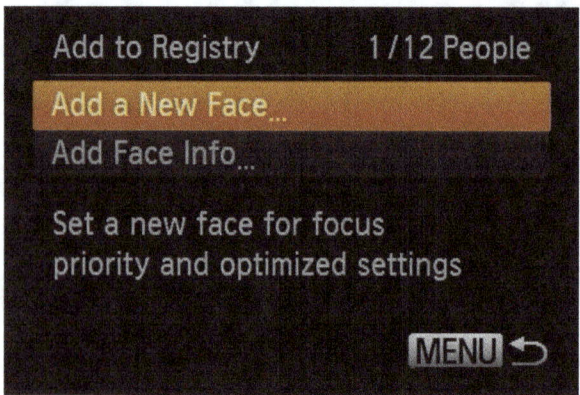

Fig. 4-77: Add a New Face Menu Option

The camera will then display the screen shown in Figure 4-78, with a square in the middle and a message prompting you to place the frame over the face you want to register. You can zoom the image in or out as needed to fill the frame with the face. When the face is well centered, press the shutter button to capture the face; the camera then displays a screen asking if you want to register the face. If the image looks okay, select OK and press the Func./Set button.

200

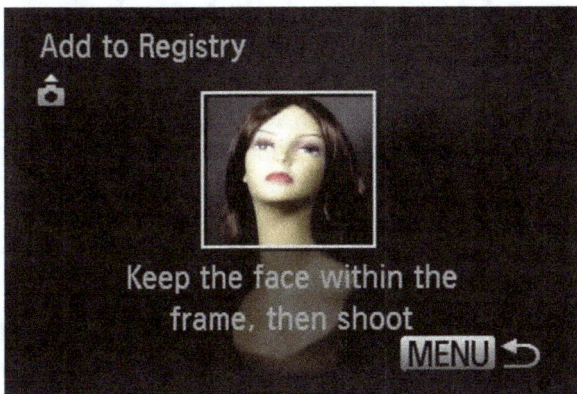

Fig. 4-78:   Screen for Capturing Image of New Face

On the next screen, shown in Figure 4-79, you can enter a name for the person whose face you just registered.

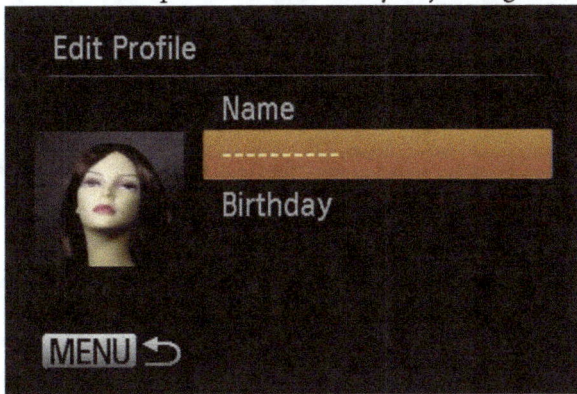

Fig. 4-79:   Option to Enter Name for New Face

When you press Func./Set, you will see a screen with a set of letters for data entry. You can enter up to 10 characters for the name, so you may want to include only the first name. The easiest way to enter the name is to use the touch screen and just touch the letters, space bar (if needed) and shift key (upward arrow at lower left) with your fingers. If you prefer, though, you can enter the characters by scrolling through them using the direction buttons or the control dial and entering them by pressing the Func./Set button.

201

When you have entered the name, press the Menu button (or touch its icon) to go back to the previous screen; now you can enter the person's birthday if you wish; if you select that option, the camera displays a screen where you can use the direction buttons or control dial to enter the birth date. Then navigate back to the main profile screen and select Save. The camera will display a message saying the person has been registered. Next, it will ask if you want to register additional face information by taking photos of the person's face from other angles, with or without a smile, and under indoor lighting versus outdoor lighting. If you do this, the added data should improve the camera's ability to recognize the person in various situations. If you proceed, you will have the opportunity to shoot up to four additional photos using the same procedure as before, keeping the face within a square on the screen.

When you are taking photographs and the camera recognizes a face that has been registered (and the Face ID Settings menu option is turned on), the camera will display a screen like that in Figure 4-80, showing the name of the person.

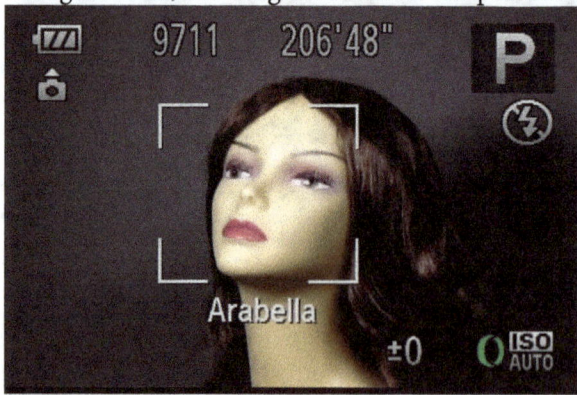

Fig. 4-80: Face Recognition in Operation

After you take a picture of a registered person, the camera will display the name and birth date, if any, on the screen with basic image information.

Finally, you can use the Check/Edit Info and Erase Info options if you need to change or delete the data that was entered for a particular person.

I do not use the Face ID feature myself, but it could be useful if you want to keep track of your children's school activities with a good photographic record, for example.

Set Control Ring Function

This menu option gives you a way to change the behavior of the control ring, which is the large, ridged ring around the lens, right next to the camera's body. This ring can have several very useful functions; I will explain these options in detail in Chapter 5, where I discuss the camera's physical controls. For now, you should just be aware that this menu option gives you a way to change the function, or set of functions, performed by this extremely convenient control.

Set Ring Function Button

This is a very useful feature that you will probably want to take advantage of. The Ring Function button is the button marked RING FUNC., just to the left of the red Movie button on the back of the camera. In shooting mode, this button will take on any one of the 19 functions that are available through this menu option, as shown in Figure 4-81.

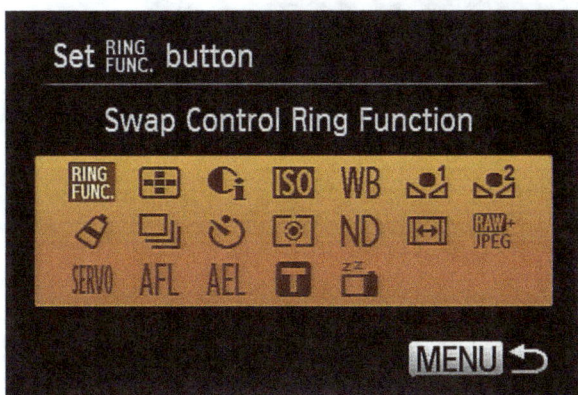

Fig. 4-81: Ring Function Button Options Screen

I suggest you try setting it to various choices and see which ones are the most useful to you. Also, you may find that setting the button to one particular function is especially useful for a certain type of shooting session. To set the button's function, select this menu option, then use the direction buttons, the control dial, or the touch screen to navigate to the option you want to set, and press the Func./Set button to assign it.

In certain cases, such as when you have the image type set to Raw, you will notice that some of the settings on the screen have a diagonal negative sign through them, indicating that they are not available with the current settings. For example, Figure 4-82 shows the screen of options when the Raw setting is in effect; the icons for i-Contrast, My Colors, and digital tele-converter have the negative sign through them.

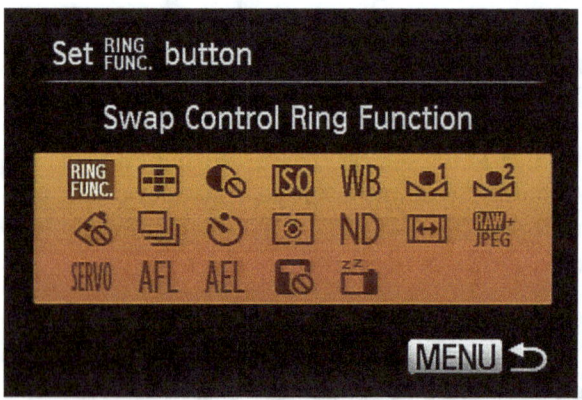

Fig. 4-82: Ring Function Button Options When Raw is Selected

Here are the details about each of the possible settings, starting at the upper left of the chart on the menu screen and proceeding left to right along each of the three rows:

Ring Function

By default, naturally enough, the Ring Function button is programmed to let you change the function of the control ring. So, if you select the first option on the menu screen, RING FUNC., that is what this button will do. When you press it, it will bring up a screen with a line of icons for the various sets of functions the control ring can take on, including STD and eight others. I will discuss all of those options in Chapter 5, in connection with the discussion of the control ring.

AF Frame Adjustment (Face Select)

This function is available only if you assign it to the Ring Function button. Once you have assigned it to this button, make sure the camera is set to use Face AiAF focusing through the shooting menu. Then aim the camera in shooting mode at one or more people and press the Ring Function button. The message Face Select On will appear and the camera will find a face and place a tracking frame over it, as shown in Figure 4-83.

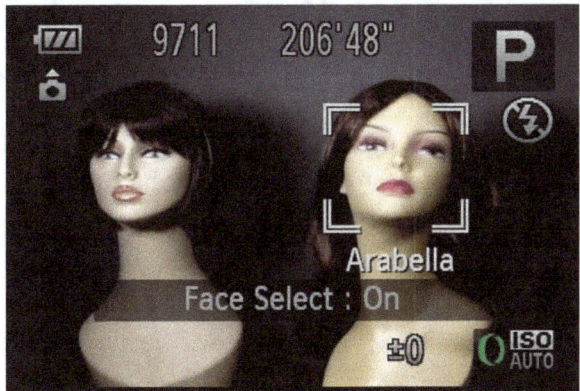

Fig. 4-83: Face Select Function in Operation

If that is the face you want to track, leave the frame on that face and let the camera track it until you're ready to take the picture. If you want to track a different face instead, press the Ring Function button, and the camera will search for another face to place into a tracking frame. If there are no other faces available, pressing the button will turn Face Select off.

To summarize the use of this feature, it can be helpful if you are taking shots of a group of people and you want to make sure the camera keeps its focus on one particular person; with this function, you can aim at your desired subject, press the

205

Ring Function button, and keep focus locked on that person, even as he or she moves around in a group of people. If you are taking photos of an individual with no other people around, you can just use the normal Face AiAF setting on the Shooting menu.

i-Contrast

If you set the Ring Function button to the i-Contrast option, you can summon that setting directly by pressing the button, rather than having to use the Function menu to get to the options for this feature. I discussed the use of i-Contrast earlier in this chapter, in connection with the Function menu.

ISO Speed

If you assign this setting to the Ring Function button, pressing it will call up the ISO settings screen. You can then set ISO to any value from Auto to 12800. To set ISO quickly to the Auto ISO setting, just press the Ring Function button again. To get to the ISO Auto Settings screen, press the Menu button.

Using this button for ISO can be a very handy thing, especially if you have decided not to use the Control Ring to control the ISO setting. Many cameras have a dedicated ISO button, and with this setting, your S110 can have one, too.

White Balance

With this option assigned to the Ring Function button, pressing the button calls up the white balance setting screen. Because the white balance setting is an important one, this is a useful way to assign your Ring Function button. I discussed the details of setting white balance earlier in this chapter, in connection with the discussion of the Function menu.

Custom White Balance 1 and 2

These two possible assignments for the Ring Function button each let you assign one specific white balance setting to the button—Custom White Balance, either slot 1 or slot 2. In my opinion, these assignments for the button are more useful than the previous one, which just takes you to the general white balance setting screen. With either of these settings, one press of the Ring Function button cuts through the need to navigate through the white balance settings to get to the Custom 1 or Custom 2 setting.

When you press the Ring Function button with either the Custom White Balance 1 or the Custom White Balance 2 setting assigned to it, while filling the entire screen with a white or neutral object that is lit by the same light as your scene, you are immediately causing the camera to evaluate the white balance of the lighting for that scene. Once you press the Ring Function button, you will hear a beep and the icon for the selected Custom White Balance slot (1 or 2) will appear on the screen. At this point, the camera will have evaluated the current lighting and set the white balance to an appropriate value, while storing that setting for future reference.

If you will be shooting in a situation in which the white balance is uncertain and you may need to evaluate a custom white balance more than once or twice, assigning that function to this button can be a real convenience. You need to remember, though, that the camera will not give you any prompting messages or other indications of what is taking place; once you press the Ring Function button, the custom white balance is immediately evaluated and stored in either slot 1 or slot 2.

My Colors

Assigning the Ring Function button to My Colors lets you call up the My Colors settings immediately, rather than having to use the Function menu. I discussed the My Colors option earlier in this chapter.

Drive Mode

This option gives you the ability to call up single shot mode, continuous shooting, or continuous shooting with autofocus as your drive mode, without having to use the Function menu.

Self-timer

If you assign the Ring Function button to the self-timer, one press of the button brings the menu of timer selections right up on the screen, which is a real time-saver as opposed to using the Function menu and scrolling down to the self-timer option.

Light Metering

If you assign the Ring Function button to Light Metering, you can quickly get to the screen with three choices for your metering mode: Evaluative, Center Weighted Average, and Spot.

ND Filter

This option causes the Ring Function button to bring up the ND Filter screen, letting you quickly turn the ND Filter on or off. This is one of the more useful and powerful of the possible assignments for the Ring Function button, because you may at times have a need to activate the ND Filter quickly when the lighting is too bright to accomplish what you are trying to do, whether it be smoothing out a waterfall by using a slow shutter speed or blurring a background by using a wide aperture.

Aspect Ratio

This function could be a very useful one to assign to the Ring Function button if you are likely to change the aspect ratio of your shooting fairly often. As I discussed earlier in this chapter, the PowerShot S110 can shoot still images in any one of five aspect ratios: 16:9, 3:2, 4:3, 1:1, and 4:5. There are some situations in which you are likely to need a particular aspect ratio. For example, you may want to use the 16:9 setting for a broad riverfront vista, or the 4:5 setting for a portrait. So, it could be helpful to be able to select a particular aspect ratio by pressing the Ring Function button and moving to that setting without delay.

Raw or JPEG

This option is another possible assignment for the Ring Function button that is very useful. In this case, one press of the button takes you directly to the selection screen where you can choose JPEG, Raw, or Raw+JPEG for your image format. In my case, I prefer to shoot in Raw whenever possible, but if I want to use certain features, such as i-Contrast or My Colors, that are not available with Raw images, it's good to be able to switch quickly into JPEG, so I can use those features.

Servo AF

This option can be of considerable use as a quick-access setting. You might want to switch quickly into Servo AF for your focusing mode when you encounter a subject that is likely to keep moving as you track it. When the Ring Function button is assigned to this item, one press of the button turns Servo AF on, and another press turns it off.

AF Lock

This setting is meant for a situation when the Autofocus Lock function is not available through the normal controls, so you would need to assign it to the Ring Function button. Normally, to lock autofocus you press the shutter button halfway to focus, then press the MF button (left direction button) to enter manual focus mode, locking the focus at the distance the autofocus mechanism measured. However, when you are using the Stitch Assist category of the Scene mode, manual focus is not available. Therefore, for that one situation, Canon has made it possible for you to assign the AF Lock option to the Ring Function button. If you're using Stitch Assist and want to lock focus, first assign AFL to the Ring Function button. Then, when you press that button, the camera will adjust the focus and lock it in; you don't have to half-press the shutter button to focus. Personally, I have a hard time imagining a time when I would need to do that, because a panorama is likely to be at a long distance from the lens in any event, and focus locking would not likely be necessary. But there may be some occasion when this function would be useful.

Of course, if you assign the AF Lock setting to the Ring Func-

209

tion button, you can use it at any time, not just with Stitch Assist. So, if for some reason you prefer to lock focus by using this button rather than by pressing the shutter button down halfway, you will have that option.

AEL

With this setting, Auto Exposure Lock, you can lock the exposure as you aim the camera at one object, and then move the camera to a new position with the exposure locked at the initial reading. Ordinarily, to do this you need to press the shutter button down halfway and then press the up direction button to lock the exposure setting. If you assign the AEL function to the Ring Function button, you can lock your exposure with one press of that single button, thereby saving a step. This might be useful if you encounter repeated situations in which you need to set your exposure by aiming away from your final subject, and then returning to your subject to take the picture with the locked exposure.

Note that, when using this setting for the Ring Function button, the exposure lock is cleared when you press the shutter button to take a picture, just as with the normal AEL function. You also can cancel the AEL by pressing the up direction button, just as with the normal AEL procedure. When you assign AEL to the Ring Function button, the button activates FE (flash exposure) Lock if you press the button while the flash is turned on. FE Lock is discussed in Chapter 9 along with other flash-related topics.

Digital Tele-converter

With this option, one press of the Ring Function button sets the camera to the 1.5x setting of the digital tele-converter, and a second press sets it to the 2.0x setting. A third press turns it off. If you have occasion to use the digital tele-converter, it is considerably more convenient to activate it with the Ring Function button than by going in to the Shooting menu and navigating to its location on the list of options. One problem, however, is that the digital tele-converter feature is not avail-

210

able unless the file type is set to JPEG, and the shooting mode is set to Program, Aperture Priority, Shutter Priority, or Manual exposure, as discussed earlier. So, if this function is assigned to the Ring Function button, you may press the button and find that nothing happens. But, if you have kept track of your other settings and know that digital tele-converter is available with the current settings, assigning it to the Ring Function button can be very convenient.

Display Off

This final option for setting the Ring Function button provides a quick and easy method to turn off the camera's display screen. This can be a very convenient way to darken the screen to avoid distracting others, or to conserve power if your battery is running down. To restore the screen, you can press the Ring Function button or any button other than the power button, or you can just rotate the camera vertically or horizontally, which also will wake up the display.

Save Settings

I discussed this final Shooting menu option in Chapter 3, in connection with the discussion of the Custom shooting mode (the C position on the mode dial). As a reminder, this menu option is what you use when you want to register, or save, a group of shooting settings to the camera's memory, so they can be recalled instantly by rotating the mode dial to that position. The settings that can be saved are the shooting mode (Program, Aperture Priority, Shutter Priority, or Manual); the various shooting settings made through the Function menu or the Shooting menu, including ISO, white balance, AF Frame, i-Contrast, and others; the position of the zoom lens; the manual focus setting; and the My Menu settings (custom menu setup, discussed later in this chapter).

Here is an example to illustrate the kinds of settings that you might want to save in this way. Let's say you are working on a project to take photographs of some pieces of pottery in a friend's studio. Because of the lighting conditions and arrangement in the studio, you found the best settings to use are Shutter Priority at 1/30th second, with +1.0 EV of exposure compensation added, with the ISO set to 200. Let's say you are using the self-timer, because you have the camera on a tripod and want to minimize camera shake that comes from pressing the shutter button as the picture is taken. (With the self-timer, there is a 2-second delay before the shutter is tripped, so you will not be touching the camera at that point.) Also, say you're shooting JPEG images of Large size, with a 1:1 aspect ratio, and the lens is zoomed in to the 50mm point. Finally, you have the camera set to manual focus, at a distance of 10 centimeters (4 inches).

Then, because it would be a nuisance to duplicate all of those settings individually, you had the foresight to use the Save Settings option on the Shooting menu to save the above settings to the C slot on the mode dial. Later on, you have the opportunity to go outside and photograph a colorful horse and carriage. For those images, you switch to Program mode, using Raw images with a 16:9 aspect ratio, autofocus, and no self-timer. When you return to the pottery studio, all you have to do is turn the mode dial to the C setting, and voilà! All of your settings are restored exactly as you need them. As I said earlier, this is a very powerful feature of the S110—more powerful than similar features on some other cameras in this class—so you should take advantage of it if you have a group of settings that you may need to recall from time to time.

My Menu

There is one other menu to be discussed now; the others—the Playback, Print, Setup, and Movie menus—will be discussed in Chapters 6, 7, and 8. Right now it's time to talk about My Menu, a special system for setting up your own menu with up to five of your own favorite settings, for quick access.

The My Menu system occupies its own place on the menu screen, and is available only when the camera is in shooting mode. My Menu is designated by a five-pointed star at the top of the menu tab on the right of the screen. When the camera is first set up, if you select this menu tab you will find only one entry, called My Menu Settings, as seen in Figure 4-84.

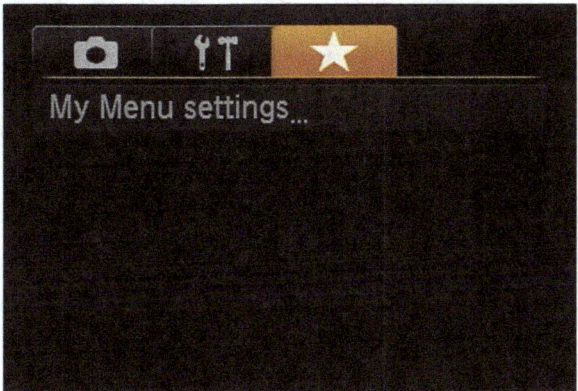

Fig. 4-84: My Menu Screen with No Entries Added

If you select that menu item by pressing the Func./Set button, you will be taken to a sub-menu with two active lines: Select Items and Set Default View, shown in Figure 4-85.

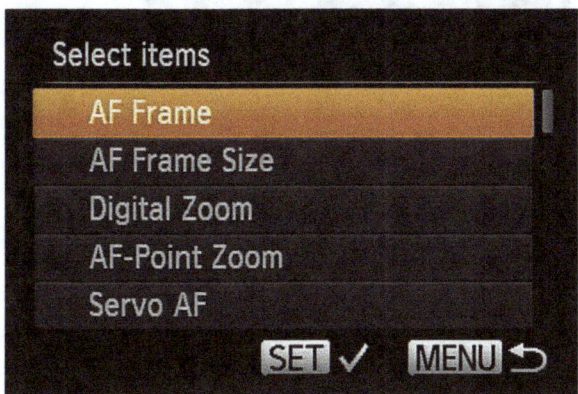

Fig. 4-85: First Screen of Selections for My Menu

To get started, highlight Select Items and press Func./Set or the right button, or just touch the Select Items option on the screen. The camera will then display a sub-menu with 26 items, from which you can choose any five (or fewer) to include on your list of "favorites" for the My Menu screen. The items on this list are AF Frame, AF Frame Size, Digital Zoom, AF-Point Zoom, Servo AF, Continuous AF, AF-assist Beam, MF-Point Zoom, Safety MF, Flash Settings, ISO Auto Settings, High ISO NR, Hg Lamp Correction, Spot AE Point, Safety Shift, Wind Filter, Review, Review Info, Blink Detection, Custom Display, IS Mode, Date Stamp, Face ID Settings, Set Control Ring Function, Set Ring Function button, and Save Settings. The first screen of options is shown in Figure 4-86.

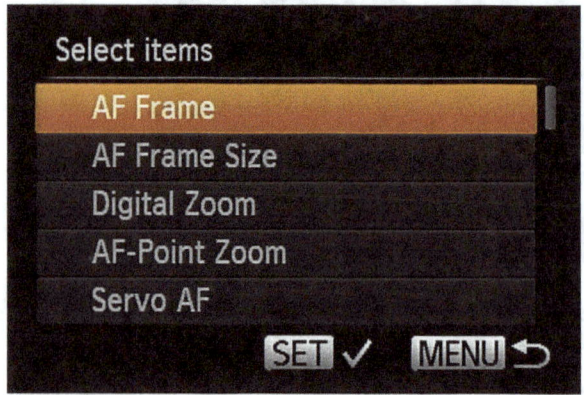

Fig. 4-86: First Screen of Selections for My Menu

Just scroll through this list using the direction buttons or the control dial and press Func./Set when any item you want to select is highlighted. Or, scroll using the touch screen and press the name of the item you want to select. A check mark will appear to the left of the item, as shown in Figure 4-87.

One slightly odd feature of this setting screen is that some of the items on the list may be grayed out, making them appear unavailable, but you can still select them for your My Menu collection. The camera shows them as grayed out to remind you that these items are not currently available because of the current settings of the camera. In fact, if you select an item that is grayed out, when you later go to the My Menu screen that item will not appear on the list at all, if it is not available for selection at the time you go to the My Menu list.

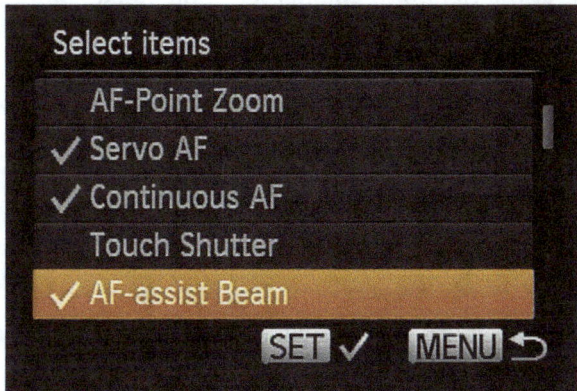

Fig. 4-87: *My Menu Items Selected for Menu*

Once you have selected up to five items for the My Menu Screen, you can get quick access to them at any time (if they are available under current conditions) by pressing the Menu button and navigating to the My Menu tab at the right of the menu tabs, as shown in Figure 4-88.

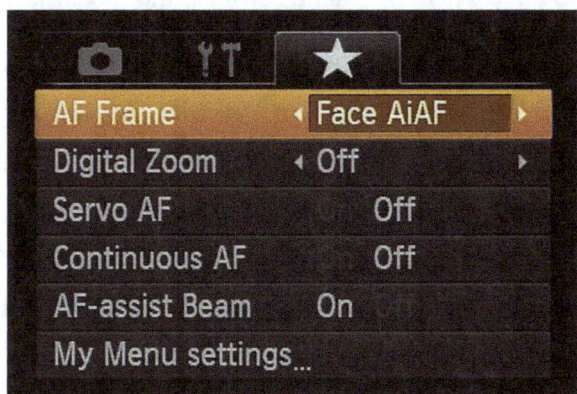

Fig. 4-88: *My Menu with Several Items Added*

You can also sort the My Menu list in order to get your most-used items nearer the top of the list; just select the Sort option from the My Menu screen, then highlight any item on your list and press Func./Set. You will see a pair of up and down triangles appear at the right of the item's selection bar, as shown in Figure 4-89, indicating that you can now use the up and down direction buttons to move that item to a different position on the menu.

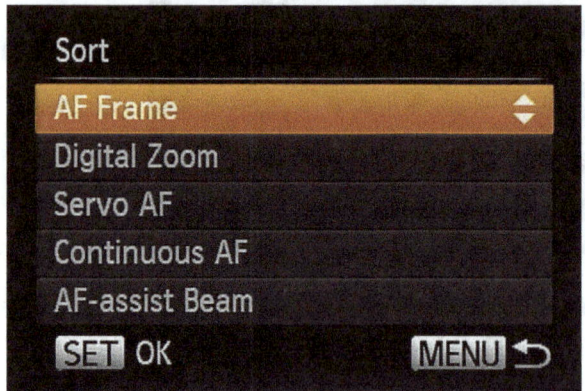

Fig. 4-89: *Sort Option for My Menu*

If you want to have the options on your My Menu list as readily available as possible, select My Menu Settings, and then select Set Default View, the last option on that settings screen. Use the direction buttons to set this option to Yes; from then on, when you press the Menu button while in Recording mode, you will go immediately to the My Menu screen.

Finally, don't forget that you can use the Custom shooting mode to store a particular set of My Menu settings. So, if it's important to you to have a group of up to five menu settings within quick reach on this menu, but you sometimes use other settings for My Menu, you can quickly restore your favorite group of My Menu settings by saving it to the Custom mode, and you can then recall it just by turning the shooting mode dial to the C position.

Chapter 5: Other Controls

The PowerShot S110, like other very compact cameras, does not have a great number of physical controls. It relies to a large extent on its system of menus to give you the ability to change settings. But the S110 is at the upper end of the scale of high-quality compact cameras, and one aspect of its quality is that it has more actual controls than many cameras of this size. Advanced photographers generally prefer to be able to make settings with a knob or a dial whenever possible, for speed of access. In this chapter, I'll discuss each of these controls and how they can be used to best advantage, starting with the controls on top of the camera, as seen in Figure 5-1.

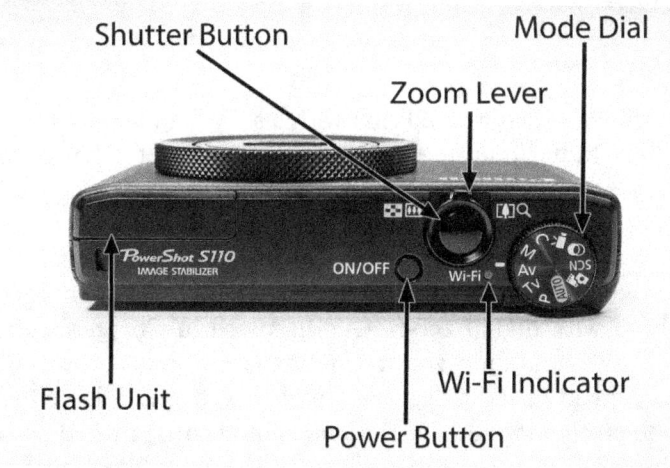

Fig. 5-1: Controls on Top of Camera

Mode Dial

The mode dial, located at the right side of the camera's top, has a single function—to switch the camera from one shooting mode to another. The shooting modes were discussed in Chapter 3. If you need to take a quick still picture, just turn this dial to the AUTO position and fire away with the shutter button. If you want to take a quick video sequence, turn the dial to AUTO or P, and then press the red Movie button.

Shutter Release Button

The shutter release button is the single most important control on the camera. When you press it halfway down, the camera evaluates exposure and focus (unless you're using manual exposure or manual focus). Once you are satisfied with the settings, you press the button all the way down to take the picture. When the camera is set for continuous shooting, you hold this button down while the camera fires repeatedly. You also can press this button halfway to exit from playback mode, to get the camera set to take its next picture. Also, you can press this button to stop recording a movie, though this button cannot start a recording.

Zoom Lever

The zoom lever is a small ring with a short handle, surrounding the shutter button. Its primary function is to change the focal length of the lens to values between the wide-angle setting of 24mm and the telephoto setting of 120mm. If you have the camera set for digital zoom or digital tele-converter, the lever will take the zoom to higher levels, up to a maximum of 480mm with digital zoom. (As discussed in Chapter 4, that impressive-sounding zoom amount is illusory, because the image quality will be degraded by the electronic enlargement of the pixels.) If you have the step zoom feature turned on by assigning it to the control ring with the Ring Function button, you can zoom to a specific focal length with each click of the control ring: One click to the left zooms to 28mm, the next click to 35mm, then 50mm, 85mm, 100mm, and finally 120mm, the limit of the optical zoom. Even if you are using the step zoom feature, though, you can still zoom to other intermediate settings using the zoom lever. You also can use the zoom lever to reach higher focal lengths using the digital zoom or digital tele-converter options.

In playback mode, moving the zoom lever to the left produces index screens with increasing numbers of images, and moving the lever to the right enlarges your current image. These operations are discussed in Chapter 6. The zoom lever also is used to make adjustments to the settings in the Miniature Effect category of the Creative Filters shooting mode. Finally, the zoom lever can be used to switch quickly between the tabs at the heads of the camera's menu screens.

Power Button

This button in the middle of the camera's top is used to turn the camera on and off. If you press and hold the Func./Set button while turning the camera on, the camera's built-in digital clock of rotating cubes will display, as shown in Figure 5-2.

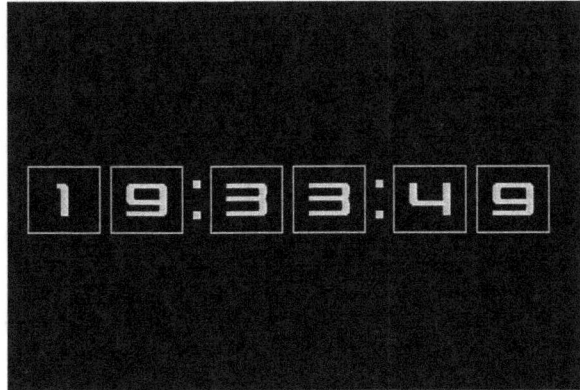

Fig. 5-2: Digital Clock Display

Press the Func./Set button again to cancel that display and proceed to shooting mode. Note that, once the lens is retracted

219

in playback mode, you can also turn the power off by pressing the Playback button. If you turn on the power while pressing the Display button, the camera's sounds will be muted.

Next, I will discuss the few items on the front of the camera, as shown in Figure 5-3.

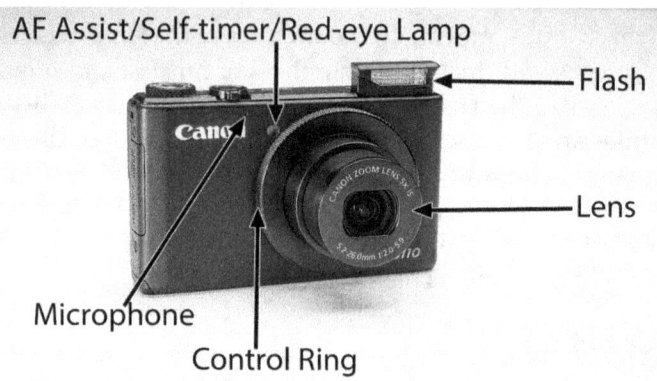

Fig. 5-3: *Items on Front of Camera*

AF Assist/Self-timer Lamp

The small lamp on the front of the camera next to the control ring has numerous functions. Its reddish light blinks to signal the operation of the self-timer, smile detection, the Wink Self-Timer, and the Face Self-Timer. It also turns on in dark environments to assist with autofocusing, and it serves as the red-eye reduction lamp by lighting up to constrict your subject's pupils, thereby cutting down on the risk of red reflections of the flash burst from his or her retinas. You can control the use of the lamp for autofocusing and red-eye reduction through the Shooting menu. To turn it off for autofocusing, use the AF-Assist Beam option on that menu. You can use the Red-Eye Lamp option on that menu to prevent the lamp from illuminating before a flash shot.

220

Control Ring

The control ring is the very useful ridged dial that surrounds the lens. As I noted earlier, it is a sign of a more advanced camera to have physical controls that let you make adjustments without navigating through menus. This particular control is of great use, first, because it is large and easy to find and turn by feel, and, second, because you have the option of assigning various functions to it, so it can suit your particular needs as a photographer.

The control ring is closely related to the Ring Function button, which I will discuss next, along with the other controls on the back of the camera, shown in Figure 5-4. First, I will discuss how you can use the Ring Function button to set the function of the control ring.

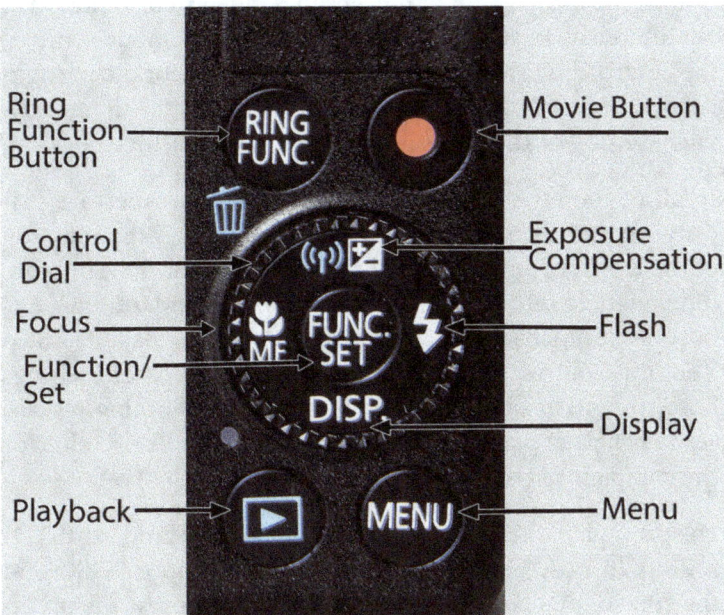

Fig. 5-4: Controls on Back of Camera

Ring Function Button

The Ring Function button, sitting to the left of the red Movie button, has several purposes, depending on how you have it set using the Set Ring Func. Button item on the Shooting menu, as discussed in Chapter 4. If you have that menu option set to its first choice, which is called Swap Control Ring Function, then pressing this button lets you select the function or functions assigned to the control ring.

The functions available for the control ring vary according to the shooting mode that is set on the mode dial. In addition, when you change the setting for the control ring, the setting for the control dial, on the back of the camera, will change as well in some cases.

In the Auto, Movie, and Scene modes, the control ring is permanently set to control the step zoom function, which lets you change the focal length of the lens in defined steps rather than continuously. In several of the Creative Filters mode settings, the control ring is used to change the intensity of the particular effect, such as the fading of the image's colors with the Nostalgic setting or the intensity of the Fish-eye setting.

In all of the other shooting modes (Program, Aperture Priority, Shutter Priority, and Manual), you can set the function of the control ring using the Ring Function button. There are nine possible settings for the control ring: Standard, ISO, Exposure Compensation, Manual Focus, White Balance, Step Zoom, i-Contrast, Aspect Ratio, and Custom. These settings have somewhat different effects in different shooting modes; see the chart at page 207 of the Canon Camera User Guide for the complete list of those effects.

For example, with the control ring set to its Standard (STD) setting, in Program mode, the control ring controls ISO and the control dial controls nothing (unless you press the up direction button to activate exposure compensation). In Aperture Priority mode, the control ring controls the aperture and the control dial still controls nothing (unless exposure compensation is activated). In Shutter Priority mode, the control ring controls the shutter speed and the control dial controls nothing (again, unless you activate exposure compensation). In Manual exposure mode, the control ring controls aperture and the control dial controls shutter speed.

If you change the control ring's setting to ISO, then, in the PASM modes, the control ring controls ISO. The control dial controls aperture or shutter speed in all modes except Program, in which it does not control anything. (In Manual exposure mode, you need to press the up direction button to toggle the function of the control dial between setting aperture and setting shutter speed.)

If you set the control ring's function to its last possible value, C, for Custom, and then press the Ring Function button, you are presented with the screen shown in Figure 5-5, where you can choose which of the 7 available functions is assigned to the control ring for each of the four PASM shooting modes.

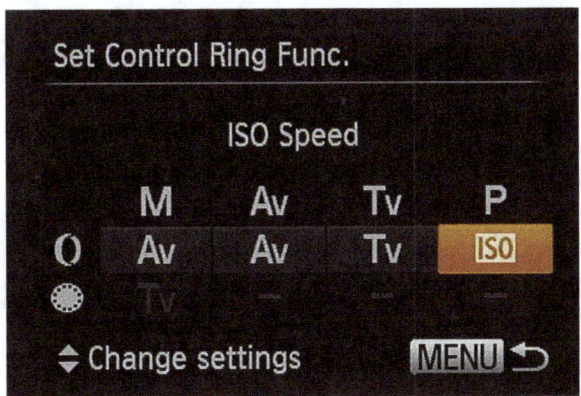

Fig. 5-5: Custom Setting Screen for Control Ring Function

For example, you could set up the C value so that, when you select C from the Ring Function button's menu, the control ring controls manual focus in Manual mode, ISO in Aperture Priority mode, white balance in Shutter Priority mode, and

223

step zoom in Program mode.

The control ring also has some subsidiary functions that are not set using the Ring Function button. For example, when you are fine-tuning white balance using the four color axes, you can begin adjusting the colors along the blue and red axis by turning the control ring, without first pressing the Menu button to get access to the adjustment screen.

The control ring and its accompanying Ring Function button give you many options for effectively setting up your own set of physical controls. In my case, I am very pleased to be able to adjust aperture with the control ring and shutter speed with the control dial when using Manual exposure mode, so I tend to leave the ring set at its Standard setting, but I'm also glad to have available the option of assigning different functions to the ring in other situations.

If, using the Shooting menu, you have assigned the Ring Function button to one of its 18 other possible duties, pressing the button lets you quickly call up that one function. I discussed all of the possible assignments for the button in Chapter 4; they include items such as ISO, Face Select, i-Contrast, white balance, aspect ratio, and ND Filter.

The Ring Function button's third identity is as the Trash button, as indicated by the small trash can icon located below and to the left of the button. In playback mode, or in shooting mode when you are displaying a single image using the Review function, pressing this button produces a message asking if you want to erase that picture; you can then select Cancel or Erase using the direction buttons, the control dial, or the touch screen, and confirm the operation with the Func./Set button.

Finally, the Ring Function button has a special duty in connection with the setting of a custom white balance. When you have selected that option, you press this button to cause the camera to evaluate and store the new white balance setting.

Playback Button

This button, marked with a small blue triangle, is used to put the camera into playback mode, which allows you to view your images on the LCD and lets you get access to the Playback menu. The button also can be used in slightly different ways, depending on the context. For one thing, you can use this button instead of the power button to turn the camera on, placing it immediately into playback mode with the lens retracted. Whenever the lens is retracted, either because you turned on the camera with the Playback button or because the camera entered playback mode and the lens has therefore retracted automatically, pressing the Playback button will turn the camera off. If the lens is not retracted, pressing the Playback button will put the camera into playback mode, and pressing it again will put it back into shooting mode. When the camera is in playback mode, you can always press the shutter button down halfway to change into shooting mode.

Menu Button

The Menu button, at the lower right of the camera's back, is straightforward in its basic function. Press it to enter the menu system, and press it once more to exit back to whatever mode the camera was in previously (shooting mode or playback mode). The button also cancels out of sub-menus, taking you back to the main menu screen for items that have sub-options, such as Sound Options on the Setup menu. There are some other variations as well. For example, if you want to get quick access to the Flash Settings sub-menu, press the Flash button (right direction button) and then quickly press the Menu button; this action takes you directly to the sub-menu for setting items such as Flash Mode, Shutter Sync., etc.

The Menu button is also used to switch to other settings from some menu screens. For example, when you are setting white balance on the Function menu, pressing the Menu button gives you access to the screen for fine-tuning the white balance setting along two axes for color adjustments. When

225

you are setting the image size through the Function menu to Large, Medium, or Small, you can press the Menu button to get access to the setting for image quality as Superfine or Fine. The button also is used to switch views when using the Focus Check display in playback mode. And, after you press the left direction button to invoke manual focus mode, pressing the Menu button will switch the camera to focus bracketing. In addition, after pressing the up direction button to call up the exposure compensation scale, pressing the Menu button will select exposure bracketing. This button also is used to return the 1-point autofocus frame to its center position after you have moved the frame to a different position on the screen.

In playback mode, when an image has been enlarged using the zoom lever, you can press the Menu button to return the image immediately to its normal size.

Movie Button

The red button at the upper right of the control area on the camera's back has just one function—to start and stop the recording of movie sequences. You do not have to switch the camera into the Movie shooting mode; just press this red button at any time to start a video recording, and press it again to stop the recording. You can also use the shutter release button to stop a recording, but not to start one. There are differences in how the camera operates for recording videos in different shooting modes, though. I will discuss movie-making in detail in Chapter 8.

Control Dial and Its Buttons

The main controls on the back of the camera are within the perimeter of the control dial, the ridged wheel with several icons in its interior. In the center of the wheel is the Func./Set button, a much-used control. At the four points of the wheel (up, down, left, and right), the edges of the wheel function as buttons. That is, if you press down on the wheel's rim at any of those four points, you are, in effect, pressing a button. These buttons all have at least two functions—as direction controls along with one or more other specific assignments. When they act as direction controls, the buttons are used to navigate through menu options and other choices for controlling the camera's settings. The other functions of the buttons are indicated by one or more icons at each button's position on the control dial. I will discuss all of these various controls in turn.

Control Dial

This wheel is one of the most versatile controls on the S110. In many cases, when you are able to choose a menu item or a setting, you can do so by turning this dial. In some cases, you have the choice of using this dial or pressing the direction buttons. One helpful feature of the S110 is that it places a green icon on the screen representing the control dial when there is a value that can be adjusted at that point by the dial. For example, in Figure 5-6, the icon, which looks like a green disk with holes around its perimeter, is positioned next to the value for exposure compensation in Movie mode. This indicates that you can turn the dial to adjust exposure compensation.

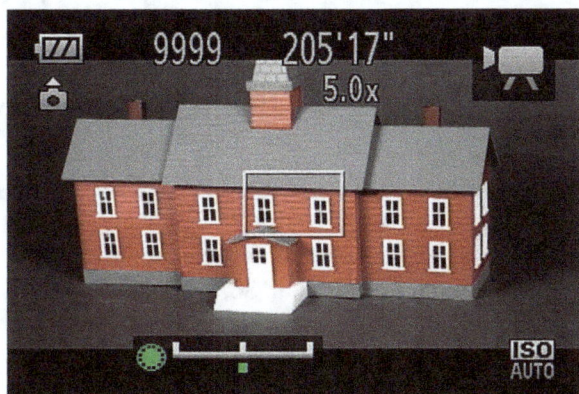

Fig. 5-6: Control Dial Icon in Movie Mode

Figure 5-7 shows the camera's display screen in Manual exposure mode, in which the icon for the control dial is next to the shutter speed value, indicating that you can adjust the shutter speed by turning the control dial.

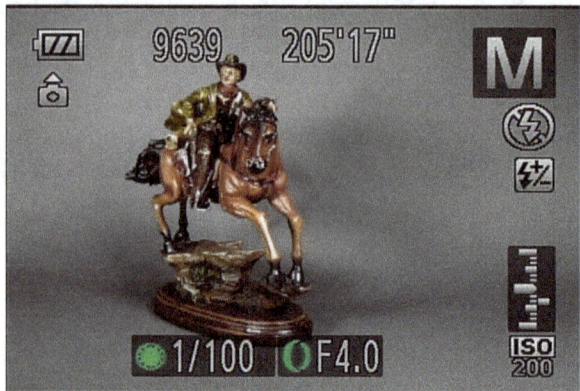

Fig. 5-7: Control Dial Icon in Manual Exposure Mode

The control dial also has many other functions. When you are viewing a menu screen, you can navigate up and down through the list of options by turning the dial. When you are adjusting items using the Function menu, you can navigate across the menu at the bottom of the screen with the dial. When you are using manual focus, the control dial can be used to adjust the focus. In Movie mode, when you have locked exposure using the up direction button, you can then use the control dial to adjust exposure compensation on a scale, as discussed in Chapter 8.

Also, as noted earlier in the discussion of the control ring, when you use the Ring Function button to change the functions of the control ring, in some cases you automatically change the functions of the control dial. So, for example, if you want to use the control dial to adjust aperture instead of shutter speed in Manual exposure mode, use the Ring Function button to change the function of the control ring to Exposure Compensation, which causes the control ring to be used to adjust shutter speed and the control dial to be used to adjust aperture.

In playback mode, the control dial is used to navigate from

one image to the next on the LCD. If you turn the dial rapidly, the images scroll by in a format called Scroll Display, discussed in Chapter 6. (That option can be disabled through the menu system, as discussed in that chapter.) The dial is also used to jump ahead to specified groups of images, and to select images when using functions such as protecting, erasing, and marking images as favorites, all of which are discussed in Chapter 6.

Func./Set Button

This button in the center of the control dial serves many purposes. On menu screens that have additional options, such as the Flash Settings screen, this button takes you to the next screen. It also acts as a selection button when you choose certain options. For example, after you press the left direction (MF) button and then navigate to your desired focus option, you can press the Func./Set button to confirm your selection.

The Func./Set button is also used to get access to the Function menu. Press this button once, and that menu appears along the left and bottom edges of the screen. Then, after you navigate to the setting you want, you can select it or confirm it by pressing this button to use its Set operation.

This versatile control also can produce one screen on its own—the clock display, which shows the time through rotating cubes with digits for the hours, minutes, and seconds, as shown in Figure 5-2. You can summon this display by pressing and holding the Func./Set button. Press the button again briefly to cancel the clock display. When the camera is powered off, you can bring up the clock display by holding down the Func./Set button while pressing the power button to turn the camera on. If you rotate the camera to a vertical position while the clock is displayed, the year, month, and day are added to the information displayed.

In playback mode, you can press this button to start playback of a movie or to "open up" a series of continuous shots so they can be viewed individually. You also can pause and resume a

229

slideshow, among other functions.

Direction Buttons

Each of the four edges on the control dial—up, down, left, and right—is also a "button" that you can press to get access to a setting or operation. This is not immediately obvious, and sometimes it can be tricky to press in exactly the right spot, but these four direction buttons are very important to your control of the camera. You use them to navigate through menus and through screens for settings, whether moving left and right or up and down.

You also use them in playback mode to move through your images and, when you have enlarged an image using the zoom lever, to scroll around within the magnified image.

In addition to these navigational duties, the direction buttons are used for several miscellaneous functions in connection with various settings. For example, when you are using the Creative Filters mode's Color Swap function, you use the left and right direction buttons to select the source and target colors for the swap. With the Color Accent operation, only the left direction button is needed, to select the single color to be retained in the image while the rest of it is converted to black and white. Also, in order to lock exposure, you press the up direction button, after pressing the shutter button halfway to evaluate the exposure.

Finally, each of the direction buttons has its own separate identity, as indicated by the one or two icons that appear on or near each of the buttons, as discussed below.

Up Button: Exposure Comp./Wi-Fi Settings/Histogram

When not acting as the up direction button, this control has several duties. In shooting mode, it serves as the exposure compensation button. As I discussed in Chapter 2, you press this button to bring up an EV scale on the screen, as shown in Figure 5-8, and then use the control dial to adjust the value.

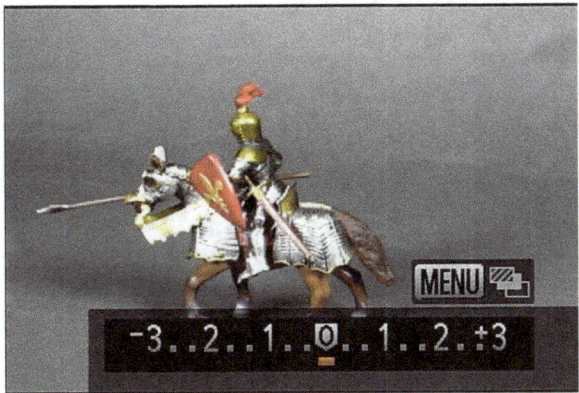

Fig. 5-8: Exposure Compensation Scale

Or, depending on the settings for the control ring, you can bypass this button and just use the control ring to adjust exposure compensation.

Also, in shooting mode, you can use this button to lock the exposure setting that the camera has made, which is sometimes known as the AEL (auto exposure lock) function. You might want to do this to make sure your exposure will be calibrated for a particular object that is part of a larger scene, such as a painting on a wall. You could move close to the painting and lock the exposure while aiming the camera only at it, then move back to take the overall picture of the wall with that locked exposure, ensuring that the painting will be properly exposed. To do this, while aiming just at the painting, press the shutter button down halfway until the aperture and shutter speed appear on the screen. Then, while still holding the shutter button in that position, press the up direction button. You will hear a beep, and an asterisk (*) will appear on the screen, as shown in Figure 5-9, indicating that exposure lock is in effect. Now you can move back (or anywhere else) and take your photograph using the exposure setting that you locked in.

231

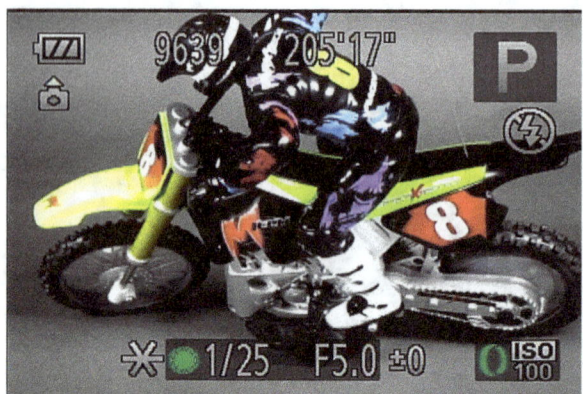

Fig. 5-9: AEL Icon on Screen

And, there is one more feature you can use when the exposure is locked, called Program Shift, but only if the camera is set to Program mode. Once you have the exposure locked, you can turn the control dial on the back of the camera, and a pair of matched dials will appear, as seen in Figure 5-10, showing apertures on top and shutter speeds on the bottom. As you turn the control dial, you will see the two dials move at the same time, and the green line they pass through will show matched pairs of values that are equivalent to the values that were originally locked in.

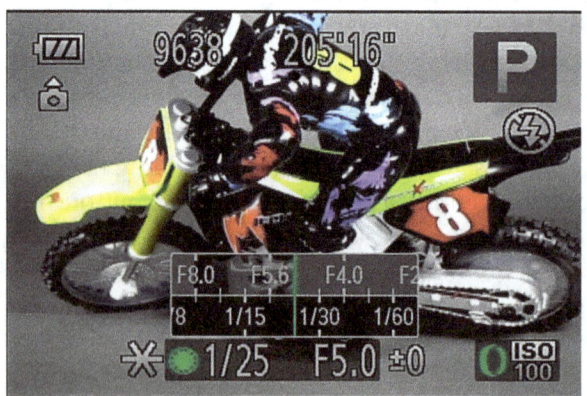

Fig. 5-10: Program Shift Dials on Screen

In other words, the camera lets you "shift" the original expo-sure to any of the matched pairs that appear as you turn the control dial while AEL is in effect. For example, if the original exposure was f/2.0 at 1/30 second, you will see equivalent pairs of f/2.2 at 1/25, f/2.5 at 1/20, and f/2.8 at 1/15, among others.

Why would you want to do this? You might want a slightly faster shutter speed to stop action better, or a wider aperture to blur the background more, or you might have some other creative reason. Of course, if you really are interested in set-ting a particular shutter speed or aperture, you probably are better off using Aperture Priority mode or Shutter Priority mode. However, having the Program Shift capability available is a good thing for a situation in which you're taking pictures quickly using Program mode, and you want a fast way to tweak the settings somewhat.

In playback mode, pressing the up button gives you access to the Wireless LAN screen. (This does not work if you are view-ing the detailed information screen; in that case, pushing this button brings up the RGB histogram, as discussed below.) As I'll discuss in Chapter 9, the Wireless LAN screen is where you set up the camera's wireless connection to another Canon camera, a smartphone, a computer, a printer, or an internet portal through the S110's built-in Wi-Fi capability.

The up button has other specialized functions in playback mode. First, when you are viewing images with the detailed in-formation display, which shows a standard histogram, pressing the up button produces an additional RGB histogram, which breaks down the brightness values for each of the primary colors—red, green, and blue. This color histogram appears on the right side of the screen in place of the detailed shooting information, as shown in Figure 5-11. If you press the button again, the camera displays the GPS information screen, but only if the image being displayed contains that information, as discussed in Chapter 9. Press the same button again to switch back to the information display.

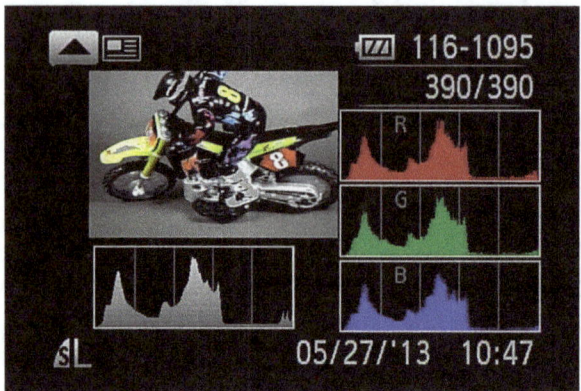

Fig. 5-11: RGB Histogram

When you are viewing a group of images taken in High-Speed Burst HQ mode with the Group Images option turned on in the Playback menu, you cannot move out of a group of images until you press the up button to exit from the group.

Right Button: Flash Settings

When the camera is in shooting mode, pressing the right button brings up a small menu showing the options for setting the behavior of the flash unit, as shown in Figure 5-12.

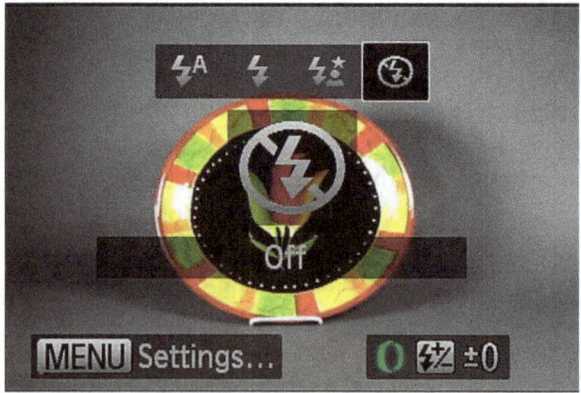

Fig. 5-12: Flash Mode Menu

Depending on the shooting mode, these options may include

Auto Flash, Forced On, Slow Synchro, and Forced Off, or just two or three of those. If you would prefer to go straight to the full menu screen for Flash Settings, you can press this button and then quickly, within about a second, press the Menu button to call up the Flash Settings screen from the Shooting menu.

One important point to note about the Flash button is that you have to use this button and its menu to bring the flash unit up into firing position, and to send it back down into the camera. With some cameras, there is a physical button to pop up the flash, and the flash unit can just be pushed back into place inside the camera. That is not the case with the Power-Shot S110—you have to use the settings on the little menu that comes up when you press this button. Don't try to force the flash unit back down into the camera by pushing on it.

Down Button: Display

The down direction button, marked DISP., is used to switch among the various displays of information on the camera's LCD screen, in both shooting and playback modes. As I discussed in Chapter 4, you can change the contents of the shooting mode screens to some extent using the Custom Display setting on the Shooting menu.

You can also use the Display button to adjust the brightness of the LCD, as an alternative to using the LCD Brightness setting on the Setup menu. In either shooting or playback mode, just press and hold the Display button for more than one second and the screen will increase to its maximum brightness. Press and hold it again to restore it to the prior brightness setting. To conserve battery power, you might want to set the display to a dim level through the Setup menu and then use this shortcut to restore the screen's brightness only when you need it.

And, if you hold down the Display button while turning the camera on, you can disable the camera's normal operational sounds, so you can keep the camera quiet from the outset.

Left Button: Focus Options

This final button is labeled with the MF icon for manual focus and an image of a flower, representing macro (closeup) focusing mode. When you press this button in shooting mode, the three icons for focusing modes appear near the top center of the screen, as shown in Figure 5-13.

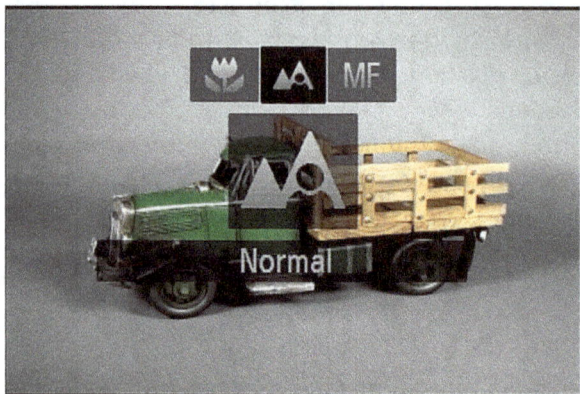

Fig. 5-13: Focus Mode Menu

You can navigate among them using the control dial, the direction buttons, or the touch screen, and either confirm your choice with the Func./Set button or just do nothing, and let the camera use the icon that you highlighted. The three choices are, from left to right, macro autofocus, normal autofocus, and manual focus.

Indicator

It isn't really a "control," but the little light above and to the left of the Playback button, which Canon calls the "Indicator," is worth discussing because its information can be important to understand.

The light can glow steadily or blink, in either green or orange. If it blinks green, that means that image data is being sent to or from a memory card or being transmitted by an Eye-Fi card. A steady green glow means either that the camera is ready to take pictures (that is, focus has been achieved) or that the display has been turned off, and the light is there to let you know that the camera is still powered on.

If the light blinks orange, that is a warning that camera shake could be a problem under the current conditions. That is, the camera has set a slow shutter speed, presumably because of dim lighting, and you should use a tripod or find some other firm support to avoid blurring of your images from a shaky camera. The blinking orange light does not mean that camera shake is actually taking place, only that it's a risk. A steady orange light means that the camera is ready to take pictures when the flash is being used; that is, the flash has recycled and is ready to fire, and focus has been achieved.

Touch Screen

The last "control" to discuss in this chapter is the camera's touch screen, which provides you with a very convenient alternative to using the S110's buttons and dials in many situations. There is no special setting you have to make in order to enable the touch-screen operations of the camera, other than the touch shutter, discussed below. To control the camera's menu options, you can just touch the screen as an alternative to using the buttons and dials.

For example, suppose you want to turn on flash exposure compensation to a level of +1 2/3 EV. First, with the camera turned on in shooting mode, select Program mode and press the Menu button to bring up the shooting menu. Then, touch the menu screen with your finger and drag lightly until the Flash Settings... item appears in the middle of the screen as shown in Figure 5-14. Next, press your finger or thumb lightly down on the Flash Settings... menu item, until the next screen appears, shown in Figure 5-15. On that screen, use your finger to touch lightly at the left or right side of the rectangle that contains a number from 0 to plus or minus 2. You don't have to touch exactly on the triangle at either side, just near it. The number will increase as you touch on the right side, and de-

237

crease as you touch on the left side. When the value you want to set appears, touch the Menu icon at the bottom right of the screen and the main menu screen will appear. Now, you need to press the Menu button or press the shutter button down halfway to exit back to the shooting menu.

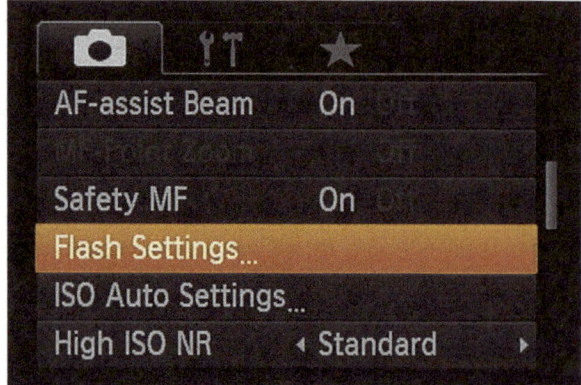

Fig. 5-14: Flash Settings Menu Item

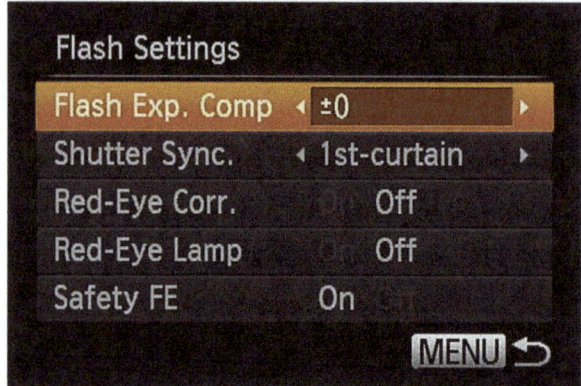

Fig. 5-15: Flash Exposure Compensation Menu Item

You can control any other menu option in the same way. For those options that do not have a second screen with settings, such as Digital Zoom, you can just touch the item's line on the menu screen and then touch the value frame to change the setting.

There also are several other items that can be controlled by

238

the touch screen. As I discussed in Chapter 4, you can control the focus frame by touch. When the AF Frame menu option is set to Face AiAF, you can activate focus tracking by touching the focus frame. When that option is set to 1-point, touching the frame turns it orange and activates it so you can move it around the screen. When you press the up, right, or left direction button to bring up the menu for exposure compensation, flash, or focus, you can then touch the icon for the option you want to select. For example, for flash, you can touch the lightning bolt icon for the Forced On mode. To make the menu disappear immediately, touch the chosen icon again. If you don't do that, the menu will disappear within a few seconds anyway, and the setting will stay in place. For exposure compensation, you can touch a value on the scale to set that amount of exposure compensation.

When you call up the Function menu using the Func./Set button, you can use a finger to scroll through the menu on the left of the screen and touch the option you want to set, and you can then touch an icon on the menu at the bottom of the screen to make the actual setting.

In playback mode, you can scroll through your images by dragging a finger across the screen, and you can enlarge an image using the "pinch and zoom" technique that is familiar from other devices, such as the iPhone and iPad. To do this, you place two fingers on the screen close together, and then drag them apart on the screen, enlarging the view. You can reverse the enlarging by starting with two fingers wide apart and pinching them together. Once the image has returned to its normal size, if you continue pinching in this way, the camera will display its series of index screens. All of these functions can be accomplished using the zoom lever, as discussed in Chapter 6, but it is very convenient to use the touch screen for these purposes.

You also can play a movie using the touch screen. When a movie is displayed, you will see a large "Play" button in the center of the screen, as shown in Figure 5-16.

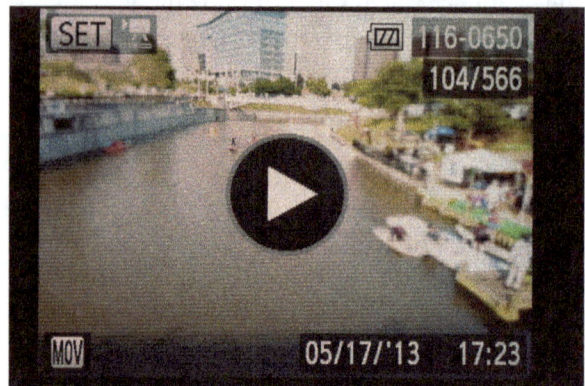

Fig. 5-16: Movie Ready to Play

To play the movie, just touch that icon. You can then pause the movie by touching the screen, and you can move through it quickly using the orange slider that appears when it is paused, as shown in Figure 5-17.

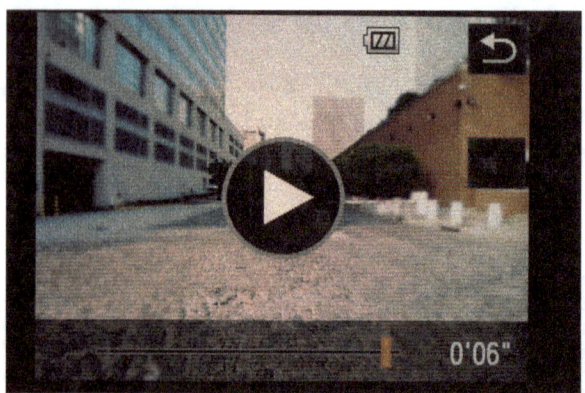

Fig. 5-17: Movie Paused with Orange Slider on Screen

You can control the volume by touching the speaker icon at the right side of the screen, and then touching the up or down arrows on the volume scale that appears. You also can change the volume quickly by just dragging a finger up the screen to

240

raise the level, and down the screen to lower it.

If you want to change the sensitivity of the touch screen so that a firmer or lighter touch is required to activate an item, you can use the Touch Response item on the Setup menu, discussed in Chapter 7.

Touch Shutter

In addition to the numerous settings that you can always control with the touch screen, you also have the option to trigger the shutter by touching the screen. In order to use this capability, you first have to turn it on through the Shooting menu. Using the direction buttons, the control dial, or the touch screen, scroll to the Touch Shutter option, shown in Figure 5-18, and choose On, then press the Menu button or press the shutter button down halfway to return to the shooting screen.

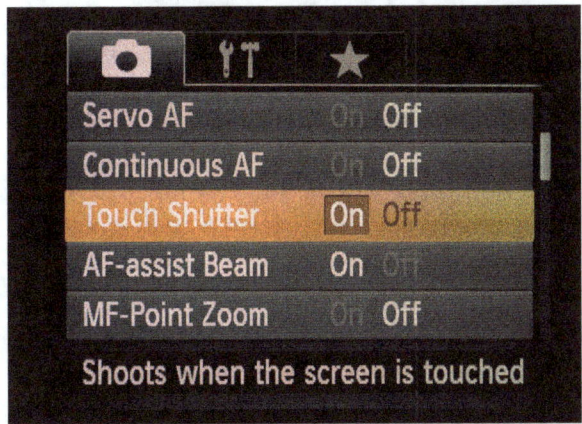

Fig. 5-18: Touch Shutter Menu Option

At that point, the Touch Shutter icon will appear in the upper left corner of the screen, as shown in Figure 5-19.

Now, when you are ready to take a picture, place your finger on the screen where the subject is located. Hold your finger in place until the camera confirms focus with a beep, then release your finger, and the camera will trip the shutter, taking the picture. After the image has been captured, the camera will

241

display the return-arrow icon in the upper right corner. You can touch that arrow to return to the shooting screen, or you can wait for the camera to return to that screen by itself, which it will do within a few seconds if the Review option on the Shooting menu is set for a specific number of seconds.

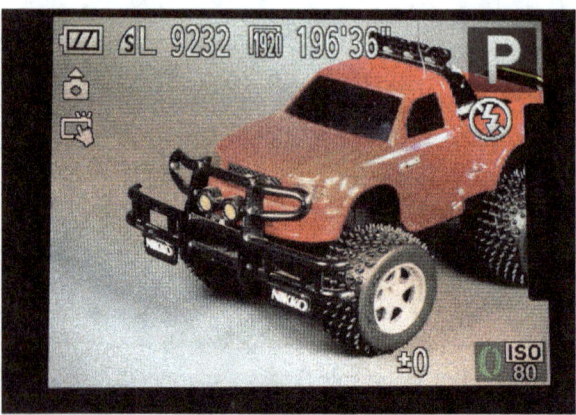

Fig. 5-19: Touch Shutter Icon in Upper Left Corner of Screen

If you have Face AiAF and Servo AF both turned on in the Shooting menu, the camera will use focus tracking and track the subject, even it moves out from under your finger, until you remove your finger from the screen; at that point, the camera will trip the shutter. If you have 1-point autofocus and Servo AF turned on, then the focus frame will not move, but the camera will keep adjusting focus on whatever subject is within the blue frame until you remove your finger from the screen, tripping the shutter.

If you have continuous shooting turned on through the Function menu, Touch Shutter will work, but only one image will be taken when you remove your finger from the screen. If you have the self-timer turned on, the specified period of delay will start when you remove your finger from the screen.

I find the Touch Shutter option to be a very interesting one, with pluses and minuses. On the plus side, it is convenient to be able to direct the camera's focus to a particular point on the screen and take the picture in one continuous movement. On the minus side, it can be awkward to hold the camera steady while touching the screen with a finger, and you cannot see the screen clearly with a finger on top of it, so you may not capture the scene exactly as you were planning to. My own preference is to use the shutter button to capture images in most situations. However, when the camera is firmly fixed on a tripod, it can be convenient to direct the focus to a particular subject and then continue on to take the picture using the touch-screen system.

Chapter 6: Playback and Printing

Whan I return from a session of shooting images, I usually insert the memory card into a card reader and import the images into a new folder on my computer that is named for the location and date of the session. Then I edit the images as needed with software and post them on the web, print them out, e-mail them, or do whatever else the occasion calls for. I generally don't spend too much time viewing images or videos in the camera. But it's still useful to know how the various in-camera playback functions work. Depending on your needs, there may be plenty of times when you take a picture and then need to examine it closely in the camera. Also, the camera can serve as a viewing device like an iPod or other gadget that is designed, at least in part, for storing and viewing photos. So it's worth taking a good look at the various playback functions of the PowerShot S110. I'll also discuss options for printing images.

Normal Playback

I'll begin with a brief summary of basic playback techniques. First, you should be aware of your setting for the Review function, found on the Shooting menu. This option determines whether, and for how long, the image stays on the screen for review when you take a new picture. If your major concern with viewing images in the camera is to check them right after they are taken, this setting is all you need to be concerned with. As discussed in Chapter 4, you can leave Review turned off, set it to any time from 2 to 10 seconds, or set it to hold the image on the screen until you press the shutter button halfway down to return the camera to shooting mode. You also can choose the Quick setting, which leaves the new image on the screen only until the camera is ready to shoot another image.

If you want to control how your images are viewed later on, you need to work with the settings that are available in playback mode. For ordinary review of your images, the process is very simple. Just press the Playback button, marked by a blue triangle, to the left of the Menu button on the back of the camera. Once you press that button, the camera is in playback mode, and you will see the most recent image saved to the memory card that is in the camera. (If you change the setting of the Resume option on the Playback menu, the camera will show the last image you viewed rather than the last one that was shot.)

To move back through older images, press the left direction button or turn the control dial (the dial on the back of the camera). (You can also move through images using the control ring, but that process works differently; I'll discuss it later in this chapter, in connection with the discussion of "jumping" through images.)

To move back to the more recent images, use the right direction button or turn the control dial to the right. You can hold down either the right or left direction button to move through your images more rapidly.

You also can use the touch screen, which is easy to work with. Once the camera is in playback mode, just touch the screen with your fingers and drag to the right or left to view newer or older images.

Index View and Enlarging Images

In normal playback mode, you can press the zoom lever on top of the camera to view an index screen of your images or to enlarge a single image. When you are viewing an individual image, press the zoom lever once to the left, and you will see a screen showing four images, one of which is outlined by an orange frame, as shown in Figure 6-1. You can then press the Func./Set button to bring up the outlined image as the single image on the screen, or you can move through your images with the four-image index screen by pressing the left and right direction buttons, by turning the control dial (on the back of the camera), or by dragging your fingers over the screen.

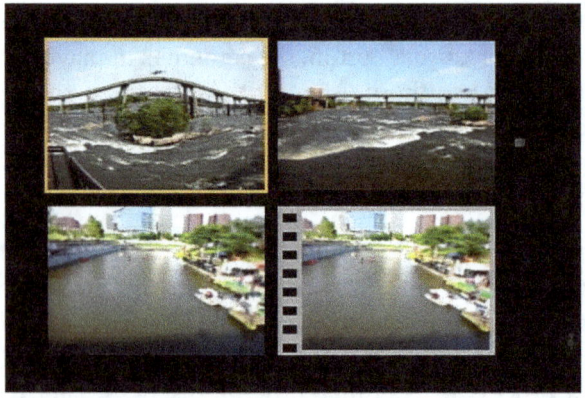

Fig. 6-1:   Index View with 4 Images

If you press the zoom lever to the left once more, the camera will display an index screen of 9 images; another press brings 36 images; and a last press brings a 100-image index screen (assuming in each case that you have that many images; if not, there will be blank spaces on the screen). You can maneuver through any of these screens to select a single image for viewing. If you want to reduce the number of images per screen, just press the zoom lever to the right repeatedly to reverse the progression of index screens.

You also can produce the index screens using the touch screen. To do that, place two fingers on the screen separated by a couple of inches or a few centimeters, and then drag them together, using the "pinching" motion that is familiar to users of iPhones, iPads, and similar devices. You can reverse the order

246

of screens back to a single image by starting with your fingers together on the screen and dragging them apart in an expanding motion.

Once you are again viewing a single image, another press of the zoom lever to the right enlarges that image. Then, as in Figure 6-2, you will see a display in the lower right corner of the image showing an inset white block that represents the portion of the image that is now filling the screen in enlarged view. You also can produce this enlarged view of an image by dragging your fingers apart on the touch screen.

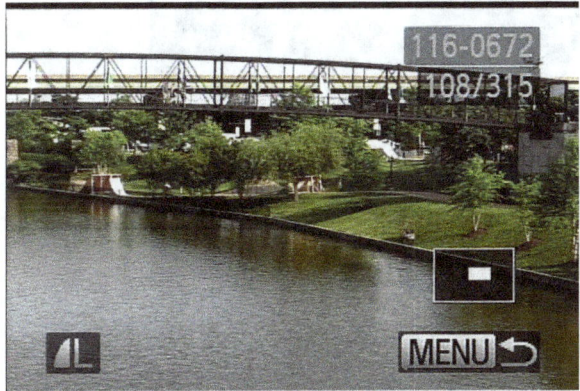

Fig. 6-2: Enlarged View in Playback Mode

If you press the zoom lever to the right repeatedly or continue to drag your fingers apart, the image will be enlarged up to a maximum of about 10 times normal size. While it is magnified, you can scroll in it with the direction buttons or the control dial, or by dragging the screen around with your finger; you will see the white block move around within the white rectangle that represents the whole image. To reduce the image size again, just press the zoom lever to the left as many times as necessary or press the Menu button (or touch the Menu icon on the screen) to revert immediately to normal size. To move to other images while the display is magnified, turn the control dial.

Scroll Display

If you use the control dial to move through your images, you will notice that, if you turn the dial rapidly, the display changes, so that the images become smaller and begin to flow in a fluid stream, similar to what happens on an iPod when viewing the images of album covers. You also can start this stream of images moving by dragging quickly with your fingers in one direction on the touch screen.

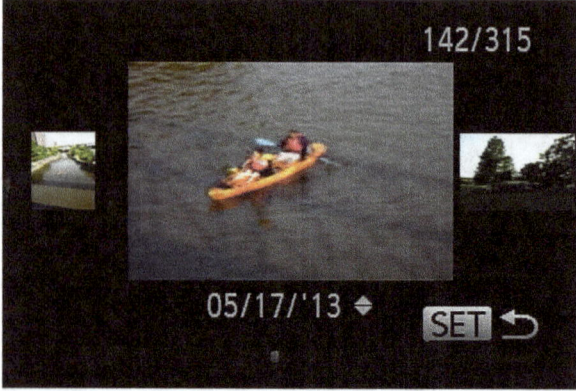

Fig. 6-3: Scroll Display Option in Use

This feature is what Canon calls Scroll Display. It lets you move very quickly through your images, and, as shown in Figure 6-3, it places the date on the screen along with a pair of up and down triangles, indicating that you can press the up or down direction button to move to another date and scroll through images from that date. You also can scroll up or down with a finger on the touch screen to move to images from another date. If you press the Func./Set button or touch your finger to the largest image on the screen while in the Scroll Display mode, the camera returns to the normal single-image display mode. You can disable the Scroll Display feature by turning it off in the Playback menu.

Playing Movies

It is easy to recognize a movie on the playback screen of the S110, because it has a large "Play" icon superimposed in the middle of the screen, as shown in Figure 6-4.

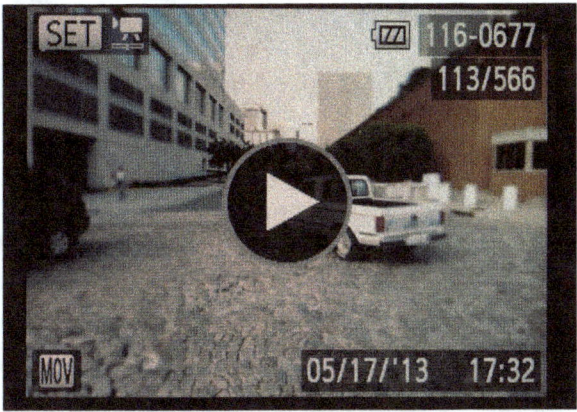

Fig. 6-4: Movie Ready to Play

To play a movie when it is displayed like this, you have two options: either press the Func./Set button, or touch the Play icon with a finger. If you press the Func./Set button, the camera will display the screen shown in Figure 6-5, with a line of control icons at the bottom of the screen.

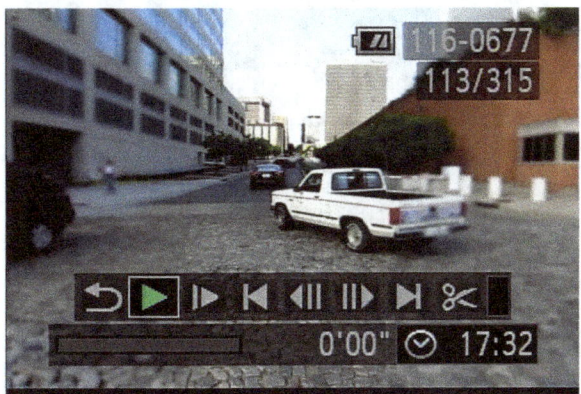

Fig. 6-5: Movie Playback Controls on Screen

249

From left to right, these icons represent Exit, Play, Slow Motion, Skip Backward, Previous Frame, Next Frame, Skip Forward, and Edit. Navigate through the line of icons using the left and right direction buttons or the control dial, and press the Func./Set button when the control you want to use is highlighted. The stack of orange bars at the far right indicates the volume control; you can change the volume by pressing the up and down direction buttons while the icons are on the screen.

If, instead of using the Func./Set button to start the playback process, you touch the large Play icon on the screen with your finger, the movie will immediately start playing. While the movie is playing, you can adjust the volume by swiping a finger up the screen to raise the volume or down the screen to lower it. You can pause the movie by touching the screen; at that point you will see the screen shown in Figure 6-6.

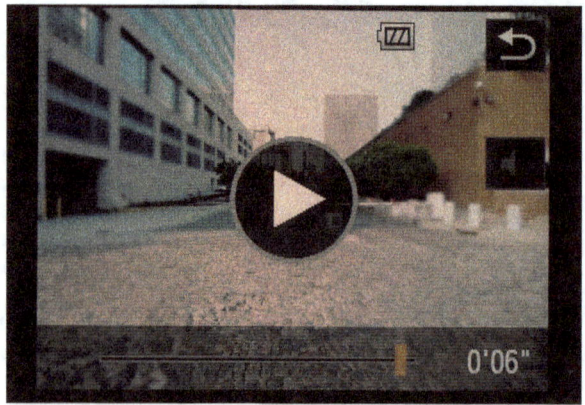

Fig. 6-6: Movie Paused with Orange Slider on Screen

You can touch the curved arrow in the upper right corner of the screen to exit back to the main playback screen, or you can press the Play icon again to resume playback. You also can use a finger to slide the orange bar at the bottom of the screen to the left or right, which will scroll through the video at any speed you choose. You can touch the speaker icon at the right side of the screen, and then use your finger to move the orange volume bars up or down.

Different Playback Screens

When you are viewing a still image in single-image display mode, pressing the Display button repeatedly cycles through the four different screens that are available: just the full image with no added information, as seen in Figure 6-7; the full image with basic information, including date and time it was taken, image number, and image size and quality, as shown in Figure 6-8; a reduced-size image with detailed recording information, including aperture, shutter speed, ISO, recording mode, white balance, and other data, plus a histogram, as shown in Figure 6-9; and the Focus Check screen, which lets you examine the image closely to check for sharp focus, as shown later in this chapter in Figure 6-14.

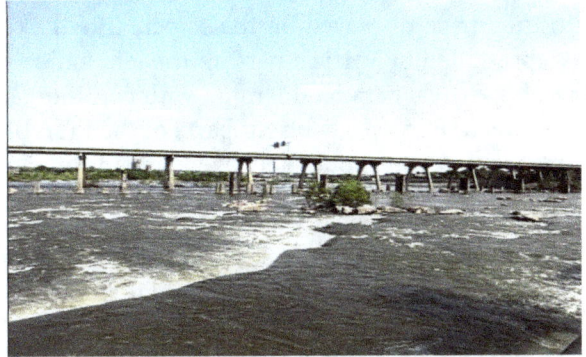

Fig. 6-7: Playback Screen with No Information

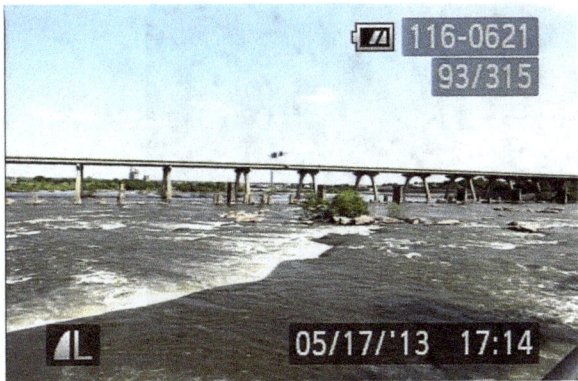

Fig. 6-8: Playback Screen with Basic Information

251

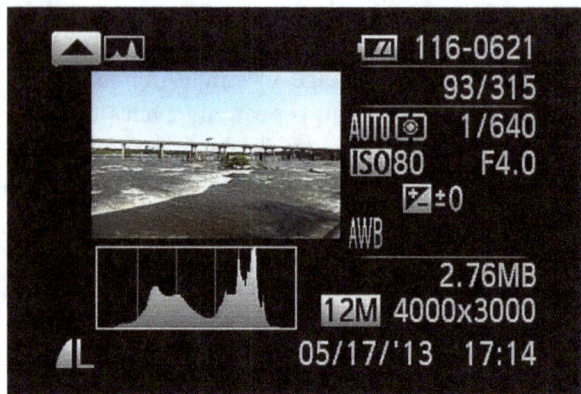

Fig. 6-9: Playback Screen with Detailed Information

A histogram is a graph showing the distribution of dark and bright areas in the image displayed on the screen. The darkest blacks are represented by vertical bars on the left, and the brightest whites by vertical bars on the right, with continuous gradations in between. Excessively bright parts of the thumbnail image blink to warn you about likely overexposure.

If you have a histogram in which the brightness values are clearly bunched toward the left of the scale, that means there is an excessive amount of black and dark areas (high points on the left side of the histogram), and very few bright and white areas (no high points on the right). Figure 6-10 illustrates this degree of underexposure.

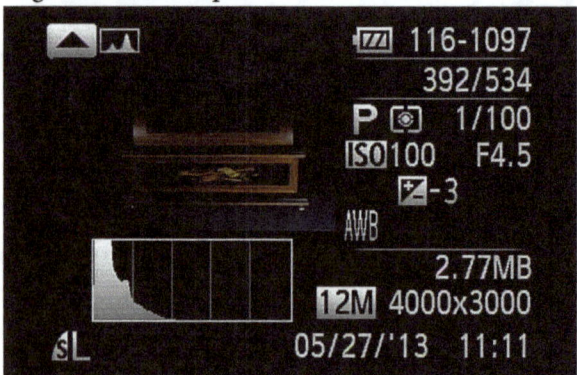

Fig. 6-10: Histogram for Underexposed Image

A histogram with high points bunched on the right side of the screen means the image is too bright, as seen in Figure 6-11.

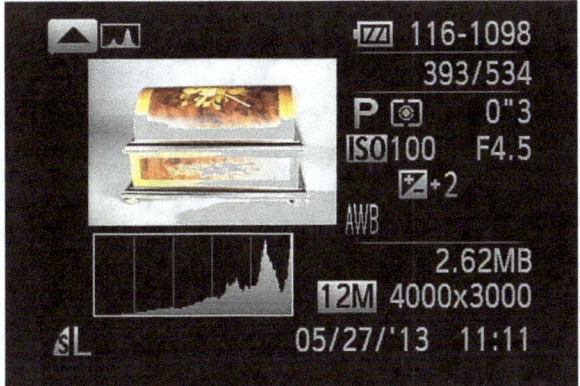

Fig. 6-11: Histogram for Overexposed Image

A histogram for an image with normal exposure has its high points arranged evenly in the middle of the chart. That pattern, as illustrated in Figure 6-12, indicates a good balance of whites, blacks, and medium tones.

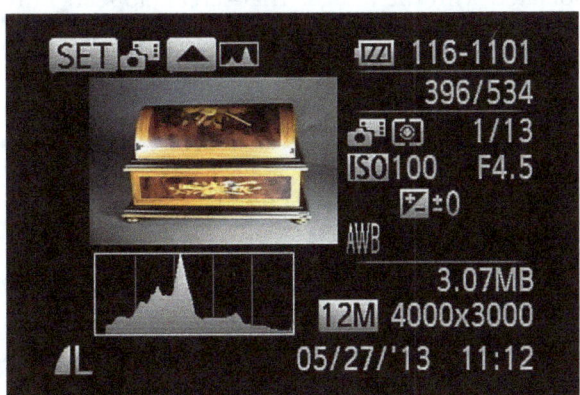

Fig. 6-12: Histogram for Normally Exposed Image

The RGB histogram, shown in Figure 6-13, appears when the up direction button or icon is pressed while the detailed-information screen is displayed. This version of the histogram in-

253

cludes the standard information for blacks and whites as well as similar information for the three basic colors, red, green, and blue.

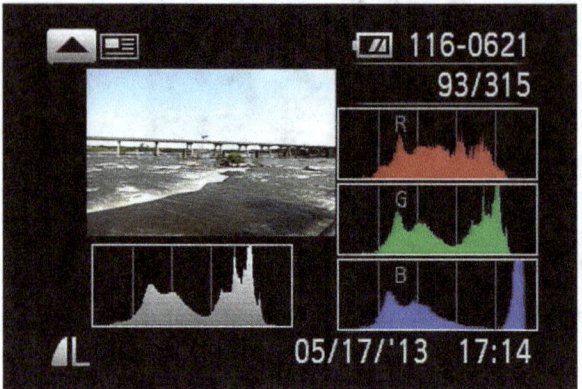

Fig. 6-13: RGB Histogram

If you press the up direction button or icon once more with the RGB histogram displayed, you will see the GPS information screen, which provides information about the location and time associated with the image. That screen appears only for images that have had GPS information added to them through a wireless connection to a GPS-enabled smartphone.

The histogram is an approximation, and should not be relied on too heavily. It may be useful to give you some feedback as to how evenly exposed your image is likely to be. Also, there may be instances in which it is appropriate to have a histogram skewed to the left or right, for intentionally "low-key" (dark) or "high-key" (brightly lit) scenes.

The Focus Check screen, as seen in Figure 6-14, is a special display that gives you an opportunity to examine an image very closely for sharp focus. The screen has two windows. The large one at the upper left shows the whole image, and the camera places two or more rectangular frames in this window—a white frame where focus was set, a gray frame on any face that was detected, and an orange frame that outlines the area that is shown enlarged in the other window on the lower right of the LCD.

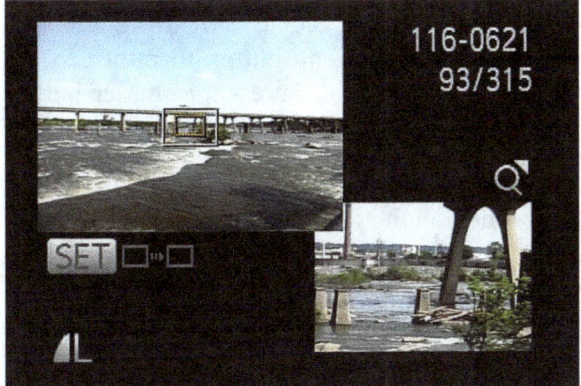

Fig. 6-14: Focus Check Screen

If you move the zoom lever to the right, the right window becomes active and larger, as shown in Figure 6-15, displaying the area contained within the orange inset frame in the other window.

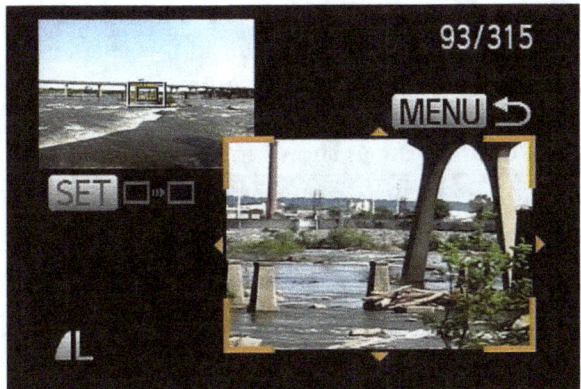

Fig. 6-15: Focus Check Screen with Right Window Enlarged

You can now use the direction buttons to scroll around within the right-side window to check the focus in that area, while moving the inset area around so you can eventually check

255

the entire image through this window. If you want to check the focus within a different inset rectangle, (if there are any) press the Func./Set button to change to another rectangle, and proceed in the same way to check focus. When you are done checking the focus, press the Menu button to return to the original Focus Check display. Then press the shutter button halfway to return to shooting mode.

You also can move between the two rectangles in the Focus Check display by touching the screen within the rectangle you want to make active; you can touch the Menu icon to switch screens, also. You can touch the SET icon to switch focus rectangles, if the image contains more than one of those rectangles.

For movies, the camera displays 3 screens: the plain image, the image with shooting information, and the detailed image with histogram. There is no Focus Check screen for movies.

Jumping

The PowerShot S110 provides a system for using the control ring to "jump" through your images by 10 or 100 images, by date the image was shot, or by finding images marked as Favorites (if there are any), as described later in this chapter. In single-image playback mode, turn the control ring and the camera will display an orange icon of a curved arrow along with a down and/or up arrow, as shown in Figure 6-16.

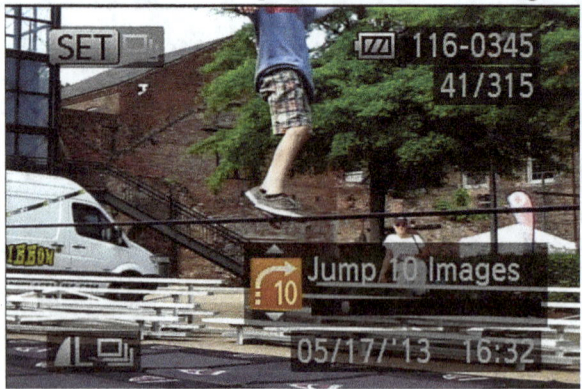

Fig. 6-16: Option to Jump 10 Images

This icon indicates the current jump option and shows that you can select a different jump option with the down direction button, and, sometimes, also with the up button. For example, in this case, the icon shows that turning the control ring will jump ahead 10 images (if that many exist), and that you can press the up or down button to select one of the other three jump options.

In this mode, if you select jumping by shot date and you keep turning the control ring, you will move to different dates. You can then move through the images on a given date using the control dial or the left and right direction buttons. The images will not be filtered, so you will eventually move to images on other dates; you have just "jumped" to the selected date as a starting point, rather than limiting the images displayed to only those from that date.

If you use the control ring to select jumping by Favorites or by 10 or 100 images, you then need to keep turning the control ring to move through your images by the selected number of images, or to move through the Favorites. In this case, if you use the control dial or the direction buttons, you will move through your images one at a time, rather than jumping. If no images are marked as Favorites, then that option will not appear on the screen when you turn the control ring.

You also can use the touch screen to jump to other images. To do this, swipe two fingers together across the screen to the left or right; the jump icon will appear, just as if you had turned the control ring.

The Playback Menu

The other options that are available for controlling playback on the PowerShot S110 appear as items on the Playback menu. You get access to this menu by pressing the Menu button when the camera is in playback mode. You enter playback mode by pressing the Playback button when the camera is turned on in shooting mode. Or, if the camera is turned off, you can turn it on in playback mode by just pressing the Playback button instead of the power button. The Playback menu is represented by the triangle icon at the top left of the menu screen, as shown in Figure 6-17.

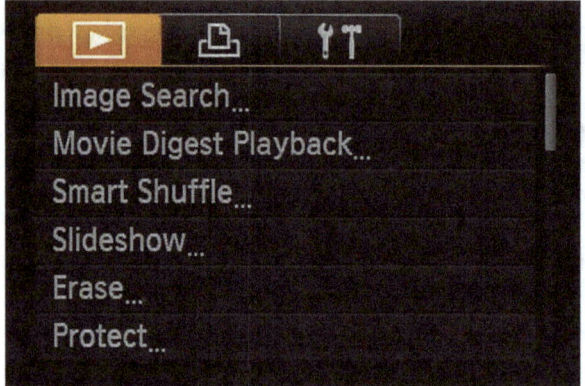

Fig. 6-17: Playback Menu Tab Highlighted

Here is information about the items on the Playback menu, the first screen of which is shown in Figure 6-18 with the top option highlighted.

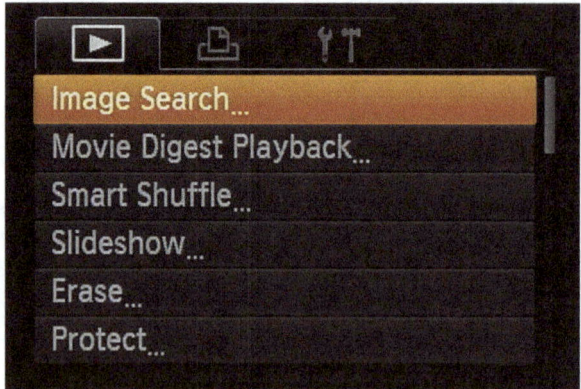

Fig. 6-18: First Screen of Options on Playback Menu

Image Search

This first option on the Playback menu gives you a way to filter your images so you can view them according to criteria that you specify. If you have a lot of images saved on your memory card and would like to view them according to their dates, image categories, or some other criteria, this menu option is the way to do so. Here is how this works.

Highlight the Image Search option on the Playback menu, press the Func./Set button or the right direction button or touch the menu item with your finger, and, on the next screen that appears, you will see a line of icons along the left side of the screen, as shown in Figure 6-19.

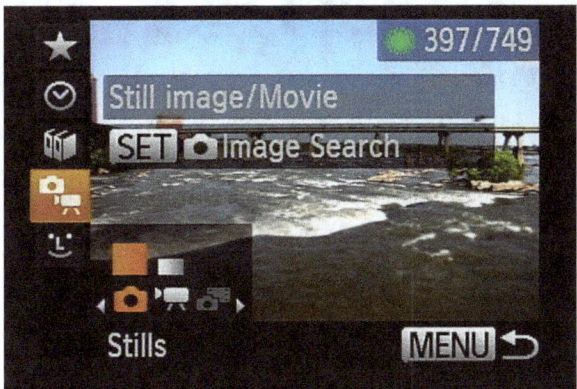

Fig. 6-19: Image Search Screen with Icons at Left

Those icons represent filters, or selection criteria, for choosing images to view. From the top, the icons represent Favorites, Shot Date, My Category, Still Image/Movie, and Name. You scroll through this list using the up and down direction buttons and highlight the filtering choice you want. You also can use the touch screen to select your chosen filtering criterion.

If you choose Favorites, and some images have been marked as Favorites, just press the right direction button or turn the control dial to start viewing the images that are a match for this selection. That is, if you press the right direction button or turn the control dial, the camera will display the first image that is marked as a Favorite, as shown in Figure 6-20.

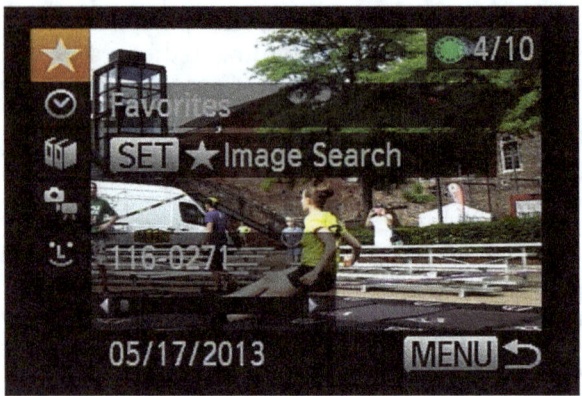

Fig. 6-20: Images Selected by Favorites

A number such as 4/10, shown here, will display in the upper right corner, indicating that that image is the fourth of ten Favorite images. (Of course, if you haven't marked any images as Favorites, no images will be displayed.) You can then keep moving through all of the images marked as Favorites.

If you highlight Shot Date, the second icon down on the list at the left of the screen, you will see a display of columns at the lower left of the screen, as shown in Figure 6-21. The columns will vary in height from zero, shown as a dash, to taller bars, indicating the relative numbers of pictures for each date. Press the left or right direction button to start the process of filtering by date. As you press the left and right direction buttons, a different column is highlighted in orange, and the date for that group of images appears below the line of columns. When you have highlighted the column for the date you want, press the Func./Set button to choose that date.

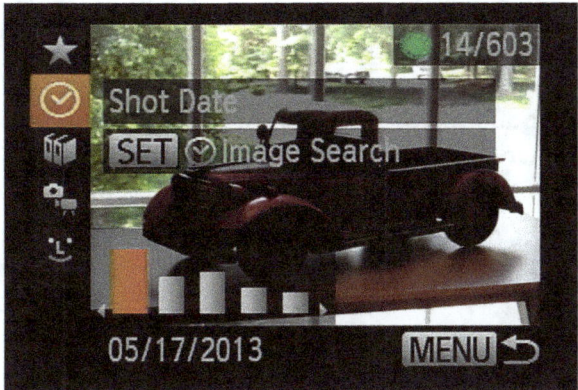

Fig. 6-21: *Images Selected by Shot Date*

The camera places a yellow frame around each image from that date, as shown in Figure 6-22, which shows image 18 of 603 from the selected date.

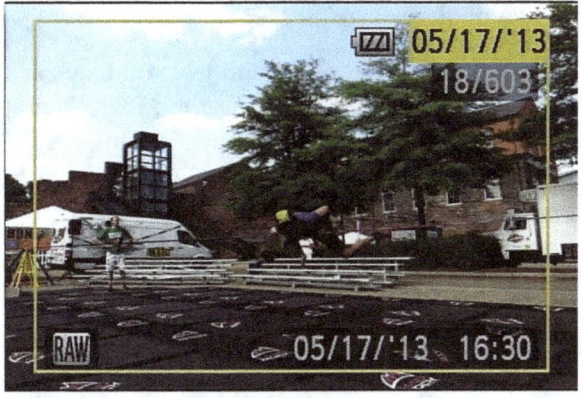

Fig. 6-22: *Selected Image in Yellow Frame*

You can then turn the control dial, press the direction buttons, or drag a finger on the screen to move through all images from that date. As a shortcut to this process, you can just start turning the control dial once the date you want is displayed on the screen. In that case, the camera does not display the yellow frame.

261

If you select the icon for My Category, Still Image/Movie, or Name, the process is the same as for Shot Date. You can use the direction buttons to select a filter (a category of images for My Category; or Still Image, Movie, or Movie Digest for Still/ Movie; or registered names of recognized faces), then press Func./Set to choose that filter and view the images with yellow frames around them, or just turn the control dial to view images matching the filter of the current image. (I will discuss the various categories and how they work later in this chapter.)

Once you have finished viewing your images using the filtered playback procedure, press the Menu button to end the process. Press the Func./Set button to select Cancel Image Search on the Playback menu and return to normal playback. (If you just used the control dial to view your images, and did not bring up the yellow frame around your images, then just press the Menu button twice to return to normal playback.)

Movie Digest Playback

This second option on the Playback menu lets you play back any "movie digest" that you created using the Movie Digest shooting mode. As I will discuss in Chapter 8, this special mode causes the camera to record a video clip of about 2 to 4 seconds along with every shot you take in that mode. The camera then assembles all of those brief clips from any given day into a single movie that gives you a video record of all of your events for the day. This mode gives you an easy way to recall a day of sightseeing in an unfamiliar city, for example.

When you want to view the movie digest for a particular day, select this option from the Playback menu, and then use the control dial or the up and down direction buttons to select a date from the list that appears, as shown in Figure 6-23. (If there is only one date, no list appears.) Once you have selected the date, press the Func./Set button and the movie will play. At that point, you can control its playing using the same controls as for any other movie. For example, you can pause it and bring up the playback controls by pressing the Func./Set button, or you can use the touch-screen controls.

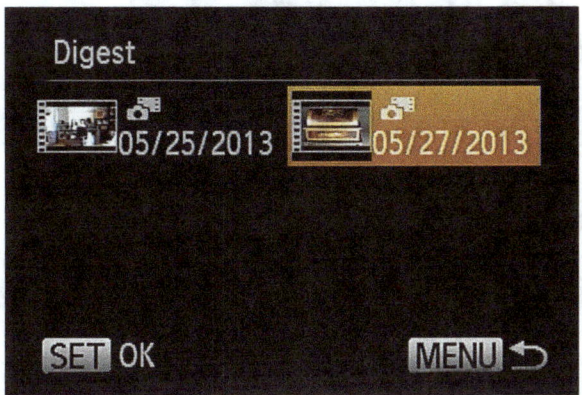

Fig. 6-23: Movie Digest Playback Screen

Another way to select movie digests for playback is to use the Image Search menu item discussed above, and select the Still Image/Movie option, which lets you select stills, movies, or Movie Digest videos.

Smart Shuffle

This next menu option is really a novelty in my opinion, probably best suited for entertaining your family and friends when you're viewing the images from your camera on a large-screen TV. When you select the Smart Shuffle option from the menu, the camera displays five still images selected at random, as shown in Figure 6-24. One of the images is in the center of the screen at a large size, and the other four are shown as small thumbnails at the four sides of the large one. You can then press any of the direction buttons to select which one of the small images to display in large size, and keep repeating the process as long as you want to. You also can touch one of the small images with your finger to select it. You can touch the center image to display it full-screen; touch it again to return to the shuffle display. When you're done, press the Func./Set button or the Menu button to return to single-image view.

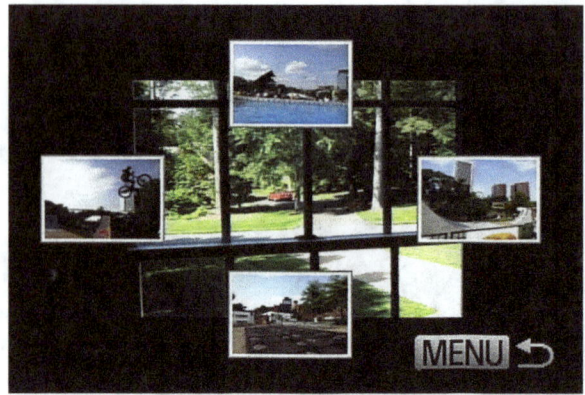

Fig. 6-24: Smart Shuffle Feature in Use

Slideshow

This feature lets you play your images in sequence, at an interval you specify and with transitions that you can choose. When you select the Slideshow menu item, the next screen, shown in Figure 6-25, has three options that you can set: Repeat, Play Time, and Effect.

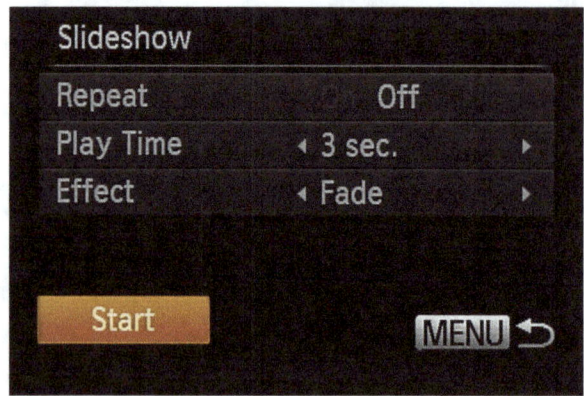

Fig. 6-25: Slideshow Settings Screen

Repeat can be set either on or off. If it is turned on, the show will keep repeating; otherwise, it will play only once. The camera will not power off automatically in this mode, so be sure to stop the show when you are done with it. Play Time, which controls how long each image stays on the screen, can be set to any interval from 3 to 10 seconds; 15 seconds; or 30 seconds. The Effect setting lets you choose what transition, if any, marks the change from one image to the next. If you turn effects off, then each image just "cuts" to the next. The other possibilities are Fade, Bubble, Cross, Letterbox, Scroll, and Slide. (If you choose Bubble, which "floats" the images across the screen in circle shapes, you cannot set the playing time.)

Once the options are set, navigate to the Start box at the bottom of the screen using the control dial or the direction buttons, and then press the Func./Set button to start the show, or just press the on-screen Start icon to start the show. You can pause and restart the show with the Func./Set button, and move forward or back through the images with the left and right direction buttons. Hold those buttons down to fast-forward or fast-reverse through the images. You stop the show by pressing the Menu button or by touching the screen with your finger.

Here's an important note for setting up slideshows: There is no setting in the Slideshow menu option for selecting what images to include in the show. If you want to show only certain images, you have to select them first using the Image Search menu option. Once you have the Image Search selection in effect, you can go to the Slideshow menu and set up your show; only the images in the Image Search set will be displayed in the slideshow. So, for example, you can set up a show with only images marked as Favorites, or only those from a certain date or category. You can set up three user-defined categories, as discussed later in this chapter, and you could use one of those categories to select the images for your slideshow if you wanted to do so. (Or, you could set up all three categories for images to be seen in three different slideshows.) When the slideshow has ended, cancel the Image Search selection using the Playback menu.

Erase

The Erase command is useful when you want to delete multiple images from your memory card in one operation. (If you just want to delete a few images, it's easier to display each image on the screen, then press the Trash button and confirm the deletion.) When you select the Erase command, the menu offers you the choices of Select, Select Range, and Select All Images, as shown in Figure 6-26.

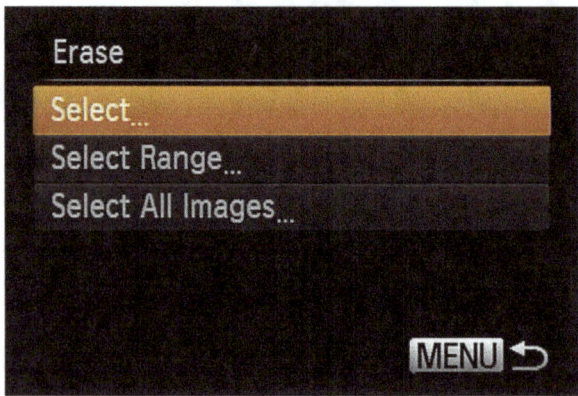

Fig. 6-26: Erase Menu Option

If you choose Select, the camera displays an image with three items in its upper left corner: a trash can icon, a black box for a check mark, and a box containing a number.

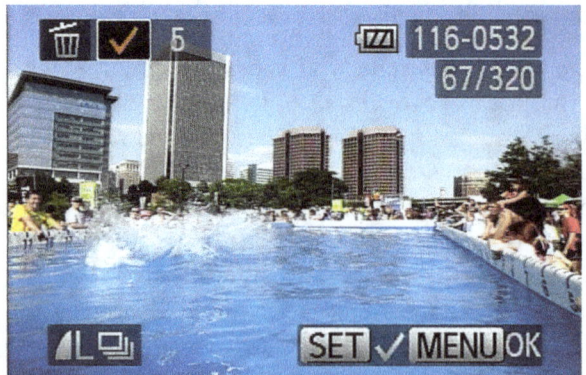

Fig. 6-27: Erase Selection Screen with Check Box

266

If you want that image to be erased, press the Func./Set button or touch the black box with your finger. An orange check mark will appear in the black box, and the number 1 will appear in the box on the right, indicating that there is now 1 image to be erased. You can then scroll through your remaining images using the normal methods (buttons, control dial, or touch screen), marking those that you want to be erased, as shown in Figure 6-27. If you change your mind about any images, you can press the Func./Set button again to remove the check mark. When you are finished marking images, press the Menu button (or touch its icon), and the camera will take you to a screen asking you to confirm the operation. On that screen, you can highlight OK to proceed or Stop to abort the operation, and press Func./Set to confirm.

If you choose Select Range, the camera displays a screen with blocks for two small images and a white dash in between the blocks, as shown in Figure 6-28.

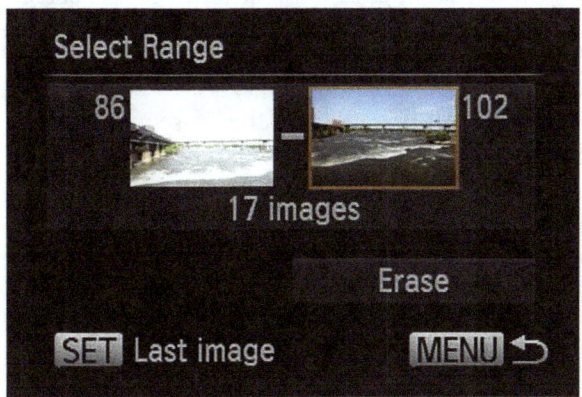

Fig. 6-28: Select Range Option Screen

You need to select a range of images to be erased, based on their image numbers. The first block will be filled with an image. Press the Func./Set button while that first block is highlighted, and then scroll through your images until you find the first image in the range to be erased. The words "First image" will appear in the upper left of the screen as you scroll. When

267

you find the first image to be erased, press the Func./Set button or the SET icon while the image is displayed. The camera will then take you back to the selection screen with two blocks, with that image now filled in as the first image in the range to be erased. Next you need to use the right direction button to move to the second block (or touch the second block with your finger), and press Func./Set to activate the selection process for the last image in the range to be erased. Then scroll through your images until you find that image. Note that the last image has to have a higher image number than the first one, or you will get an error message. Of course, it's also important to note that this process will delete all images in the selected range, including the first one, the last one, and all of those in between. So, be certain that all of those images are ones you want to erase.

Once you have pressed Func./Set to select the last image to be erased, the camera will fill the second block with that image. At that point, you can highlight the Erase block on the screen and press Func./Set to confirm, or you can press the Menu button to cancel and return to the menu screen.

Finally, you can select All Images from the Erase menu. If you make this choice, on the next screen you will see a message asking you to confirm the operation, and letting you cancel if you have changed your mind, as shown in Figure 6-29.

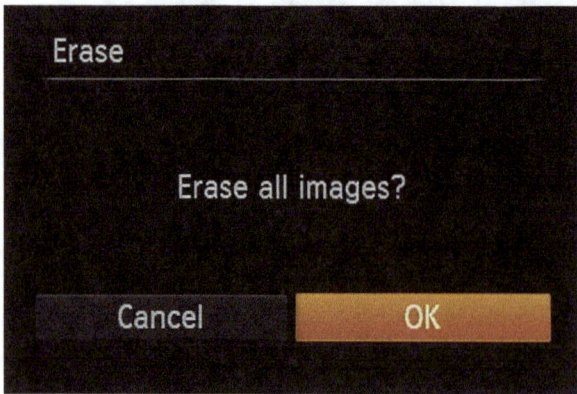

Fig. 6-29: Erase All Images Confirmation Screen

268

If you highlight and confirm with the OK selection, all images on the card will be erased except any that have been protected using the Protect function, discussed below.

Protect

With the Protect feature, you can "lock" selected images so they cannot be erased with the normal erase functions, including using the Trash button and using the Erase option on the Playback menu, discussed above. However, if you format the memory card using the Format command, all data will be erased, including Protected images.

To protect images using this menu option, the procedure is the same as for erasing images, discussed above. You have the same three options of selecting images individually, selecting a range, or selecting all images, before confirming the protect operation.

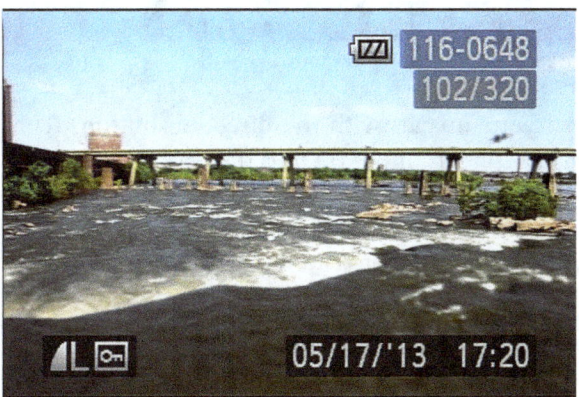

Fig. 6-30: Key Icon in Lower Left Corner of Protected Image

Any image that is protected will have a key icon in the lower left corner, as shown in Figure 6-30, which will be visible when the image is viewed with the detailed information screen or the basic information screen; the icon will not appear in the image-only view or in the focus-check view.

Rotate

With the Rotate option, you can rotate any image in 90-degree increments and save that new orientation with the image. Once you have selected Rotate from the Playback menu, you will see a screen showing an image with the word "Rotate" in the upper left corner, as shown in Figure 6-31.

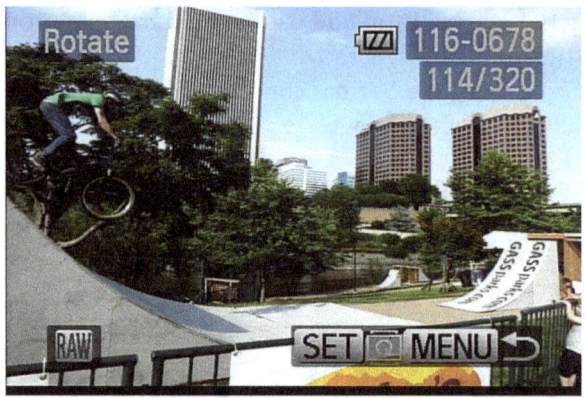

Fig. 6-31: Rotate Option in Use

Scroll through your images with the direction buttons, control dial, or touch screen until you find the first one you want to rotate. When that image is displayed, press the Func./Set button or press the SET icon on the screen with your finger. The image will rotate 90 degrees clockwise each time you press that button. When the image is in the position you want it to remain in, you can keep scrolling to find others to rotate. When you have finished, press the Menu button to return to the menu screen. Any image you rotated will remain in its new orientation unless you use the Rotate command again to change the orientation. This option will not function if you have turned off the Auto Rotate option on the Playback menu, discussed later in this chapter.

Favorites

The Favorites menu item lets you mark any or all of your images, up to a maximum of 500, as Favorites.

Once they are marked, you can use the Image Search menu option or jump option to find them or to view them in a slideshow. This menu option does not provide procedures for selecting a range of images or selecting all images; you have to scroll through your images individually and mark those that you want to classify as Favorites by pressing the Func./Set button (or touching the SET icon) for each chosen image.

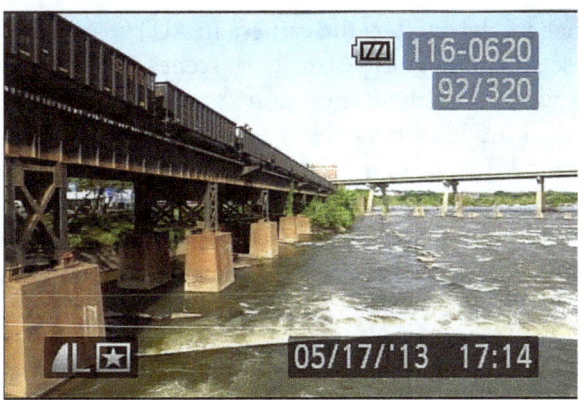

Fig. 6-32: Star in Lower Left Corner of Image Marked as Favorite

Once it is marked as a Favorite, an image will have a star displayed in the lower left corner, as seen in Figure 6-32.

My Category

The My Category menu option is a powerful way to tag any or all of your images with one or more categories. Once the images are categorized in this way, you can view the images from any category using the Image Search option, discussed earlier. You can also view that grouping of images in a slideshow after using the Image Search feature.

There are a few points you need to know about categories in

general before I discuss the procedure for assigning images to categories. First, the camera automatically places some images into categories that are set up without your input. Those categories are the following.

People

All images that include faces detected by the camera and that were shot with the Portrait or Smooth Skin setting, or for which the camera detected a face using its face detection feature. The icon for this category is a pair of faces.

Scenery

All images that are detected by the camera in AUTO shooting mode as sunsets, dark landscapes, or dark scenes with people in them (see page 245 of the Canon user's manual), as well as images shot with the Handheld Night Scene setting. The icon for this category is a scene of mountains with clouds above.

Events

All images shot with the Underwater, Snow, or Fireworks setting. The icon for this category is a tennis racket with a ball.

The other categories, which are left for you to assign to images if you choose to, are called Category 1, Category 2, Category 3, and To Do. The icon for each of the three numbered categories looks like a three-leaf clover with a number 1, 2, or 3 inside it. The icon for the To Do category looks like a list of items with check marks on it.

You can remove any image from a category even if the camera assigned it to that category, and you can assign any image to any category, including those that are automatically assigned.

Here is how to use this feature. When you select My Category from the Playback menu, the camera shows you a screen with two options: Select and Select Range. These options work in the same way as the similar options for Erase and Protect, discussed above.

If you choose the Select option, the camera proceeds to display an image, with the words My Category at the upper left and the icons for the various categories displayed on the left of the image, as seen in Figure 6-33.

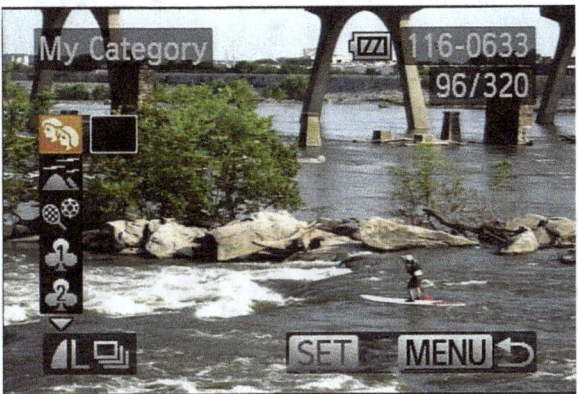

Fig. 6-33: My Category Selection Screen

There is a triangle at the bottom of the list of icons, indicating that you will have to press the down direction button to scroll through the complete list of icons. If the camera has automatically assigned the image to any category, you will see a check mark beside the icon for that category. You can now scroll down through the list of icons and clear any check mark from an icon, or add a check mark for an icon, using the Func./Set button. When you are done with that image, you can continue scrolling through your other images with the direction buttons or the control dial and assigning or un-assigning categories for each image. When you are done, press the Menu button to return to the menu screen. As with other menu options, you can use the camera's touch-screen features to make selections and to scroll through the images.

Once images are assigned to categories, you can take advantage of those assignments whenever you need to deal with a particular group of images. For example, if you have just finished taking pictures of a valuable collection of antiques and you want to protect those images from accidental erasure, you can use the My Category menu option to assign each of those images to a category, such as Category 1. (You could use any category for this purpose, even one such as Scenery or Events, but it might make more sense in this case to use a generic one like Category 1.) Then, use the Image Search menu option and search for all images in Category 1. Next, while the search is in effect (with the yellow frame surrounding each image), select Protect from the Playback menu, and, from the sub-options, choose the option for Select All Images in Search, as shown in Figure 6-34.

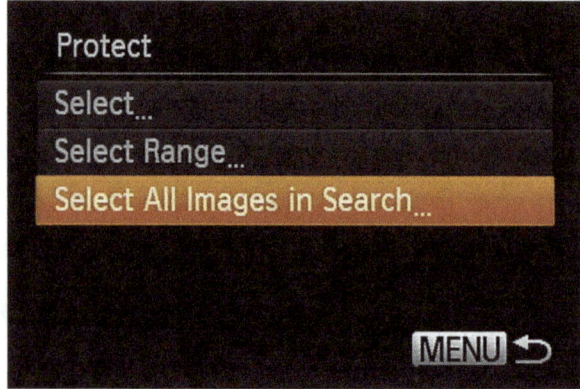

Fig. 6-34:   Select All Images in Search Menu Option

When you have finished, all of your photos of the antique collection will have the key icon, indicating their protected status.

Part of the power of the My Category feature is that you can assign images to multiple categories. Therefore, you can establish various sets of images that overlap each other. For example, if you want to set up one slideshow for your relatives with all of your photos from a vacation trip, and another show for co-workers that includes only some of the more scenic photos from that trip, you can assign all of the trip photos to, say, Category 1, and then assign just the more scenic trip photos to Category 2. Some images will be assigned to both categories, but you can select one category or the other for a given slideshow, and only the images from that category will be shown.

Photobook Setup

This feature is intended to let you create a Photobook, which is a group of images that can be imported into Canon's software and used by a service that prints photo books with high-quality images. As with the Erase and Protect options discussed above, you can use various selection methods to choose the images to place into the Photobook: You can browse through all images and mark them with the Func./Set button; you can select all images on the memory card; or you can first use the Image Search feature and then use the option to Select All Images in Search, as was shown above in Figure 6-34.

Once you have set up the Photobook with your chosen images, you can use Canon's ImageBrowser EX software to upload those images to your computer from the memory card, or directly from the camera using the USB cable. When you do this, the software will display a message like that shown in Figure 6-35, asking if you want to have those images imported into a Photobook folder.

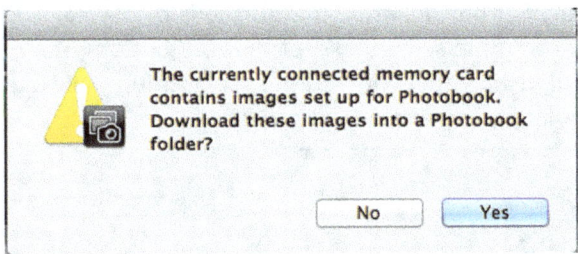

Fig. 6-35: Computer Message for Photobook Option

If you click on the Yes button, the software will do this. Then, if you want to have those images printed by a commercial printing company in a book format, or if you just want to print this group of images yourself, they will be organized together in a folder one level under your main location for images named Photobook, and in a sub-folder named according to the date the Photobook was created. For example, I created a Photo-

275

book made up of several images that had faces detected. After I imported those images into ImageBrowser EX, the software created a folder named Photobook_2013_05_13, inside a folder named Photobook, which was placed in the Pictures folder on my computer. Now, if I wanted to print those images as a group or to send them to a printer as the images for a commercially printed photo book, I could easily find them.

To summarize, this feature provides a good way to keep a selected group of images together so they can easily be found and printed from your computer or printed in a photo book by a commercial company.

i-Contrast

This menu option lets you apply post-processing to your images in the camera, to correct situations in which an image is too dark or lacking in contrast. To use this process, select i-Contrast from the Playback menu. At this point, the camera will display the term "i-Contrast" in the upper left corner of the screen. Scroll through your images until you find one that seems as if it would benefit from this sort of processing, and press the Func./Set button while that image is displayed. You will then see the same screen, except that the bottom line of the screen will display the word Auto, Low, Medium, or High at the bottom left, as shown in Figure 6-36.

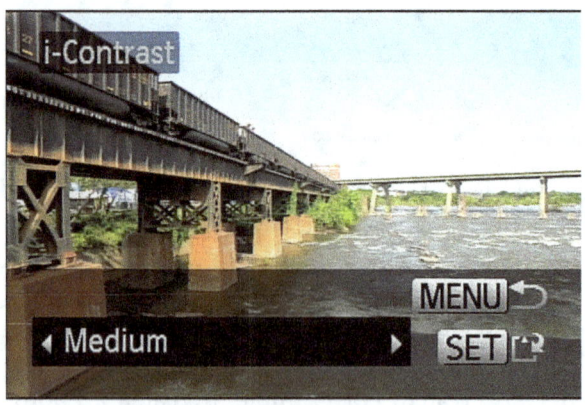

Fig. 6-36: i-Contrast Setting Screen

You can then use the control dial or the left and right direction buttons, or touch the arrows on the touch screen, to select one of those settings.

When your desired setting is highlighted, press the Func./Set button to confirm and apply the process. The camera will then prompt you to save the new image by highlighting and selecting OK, or to cancel. If you select OK, the camera will process the adjustments to the dark areas and contrast and save the image with a new file name, so the original image is not overwritten or deleted. When you are done applying i-Contrast processing to your images, press the Menu button and the camera will ask if you want to have the new image displayed. If you say yes, the camera will display the adjusted version of the last image that you applied changes to. You can then scroll back to any earlier images you corrected with this feature.

Note that you can use a similar feature when recording photos, as discussed in Chapter 4. However, although that feature is also called i-Contrast by Canon, it has two sub-components, DR Correction and Shadow Correct, whereas the playback mode version of i-Contrast only deals with dark areas. Also, of course, you can apply post-processing of this sort using software such as Photoshop and Photoshop Elements. Note also that you cannot use this feature to adjust Raw format photos.

Red-Eye Correction

This option, like i-Contrast, lets you apply editing in the camera to fix a specific type of problem—in this case, the redness in human eyes that comes from the flash reflecting off people's retinas. There are no sub-options to be selected. Just highlight and select this menu item, and the camera displays the first image, as shown in the top frame of Figure 6-37. You can then scroll through your images until you find the first one you want to apply correction to. When that image is displayed, press the Func./Set button, and the camera will attempt to apply correction. If it does not find what it considers to be correctable red-eye areas, it will show an error message, saying the image

277

cannot be modified. The camera will display a similar error message for any Raw image, because this sort of correction cannot be applied to Raw files. If the camera does find and correct red-eye, it will then place a frame around the corrected area, and ask if you want to save a new file or overwrite the existing one, as shown in the middle frame of Figure 6-37.

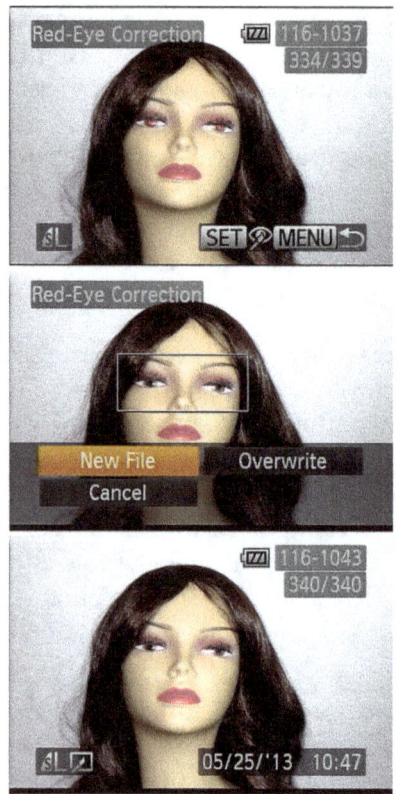

Fig. 6-37: Red-eye Correction Option in Use

I don't recommend ever overwriting your original file, because it cannot later be restored. I don't often use this feature, because such corrections can be easily accomplished in post-processing software, including the software that comes with the PowerShot S110. However, if you do not have access to a computer and need to touch up some photos for a quick showing, this feature works well and can be quite useful.

As was discussed in Chapter 4, a similarly named option is available from the Flash Settings screen of the Shooting menu, for applying correction as you are taking your pictures.

Cropping

The Cropping option allows you to perform a certain amount of trimming of your images in the camera. Here is the procedure. Select Cropping from the Playback menu, and the camera displays the first available image, with the word Cropping at the upper left. Scroll through your images using the control dial, the direction buttons, or the touch screen until you find an image you want to crop. Press the Func./Set button (or touch its icon on the screen), and the camera puts two yellow frames on the screen, as shown in Figure 6-38.

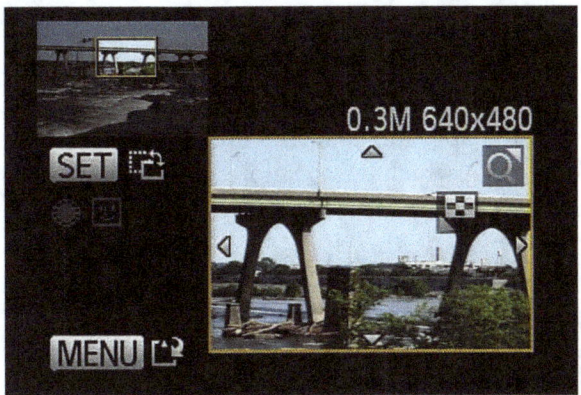

Fig. 6-38: Cropping Menu Option in Use

The frame on the upper left shows the area of the original image that will remain after cropping. You can change the size of that frame using the zoom lever on top of the camera, and you can move the frame around within the original image with the four direction buttons. You also can move it by touching it with a finger on the screen. You can change the frame to a vertical orientation by pressing the Func./Set button. The larger

279

yellow frame on the right contains the enlarged view of the image as it will look after the cropping. When you are satisfied with how the cropping frame is arranged, press the Menu button (or touch its icon) to carry out the operation. The camera will then prompt you to save the new image or cancel. If you confirm the crop, the camera will save the new image. You can then move on to crop other images if you want to. When you are done, press the Menu button. The camera will then ask if you want to display the last new image that was cropped.

This option will not work on Raw images or those already at the smallest sizes. The new images that result from cropping will have lost resolution, because the cropping process reduces the number of pixels in an image. The Cropping function can provide a rough-and-ready sort of editing if nothing else is available, if you need to crop an image for e-mailing or sending directly to a printer.

Resize

This feature lets you save a copy of an image in a smaller size. It does not alter the appearance of the image; it just saves it with a smaller file size, which may be more convenient to send as an attachment to an e-mail message or to store on a cellular phone, for example. To do this, select the Resize option from the Playback menu, then scroll to find the image to resize.

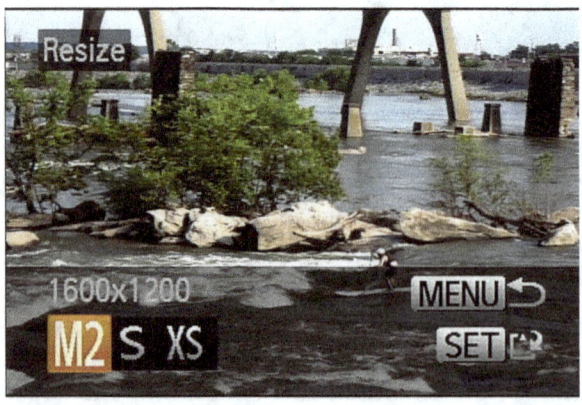

Fig. 6-39: Resize Options Screen

When that image is displayed, press Func./Set, and, depending on the size of the original image, the camera gives you up to 3 options at the lower left of the screen: M2, S, and XS, as shown in Figure 6-39. Select the new size you want with the direction buttons, control dial, or touch screen, and then press Func./Set to confirm. As with other features discussed above, you can then move on to other images, or press Menu to end the Resize operations. At that point the camera will ask you if you want to display the last new image that was saved.

This option does not work with Raw files or with files that have already been saved to the XS size using this operation.

My Colors

In Chapter 4, I discussed the use of the My Colors option on the Function menu, which lets you apply a broad range of color effects to your images as you record them. The My Colors option on the Playback menu lets you apply those same effects to your images after the fact, in the camera, rather than applying them as the images are recorded. To use this function, select it from the Playback menu, then scroll to an image you want to apply one of the My Colors effects to. When your chosen image is displayed, press the Func./Set button or touch its icon on the screen, and the camera will display a line of the My Colors icons along the bottom of the screen, as shown in Figure 6-40.

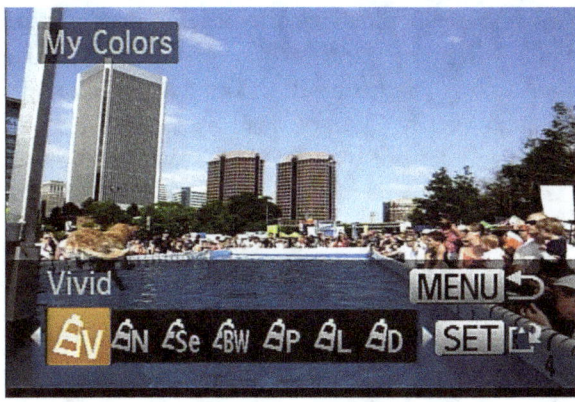

Fig. 6-40: My Colors Icons at Bottom of Screen

281

Scroll through those icons for the various color settings using the control dial or the left and right direction buttons. As you move from one icon to another, the displayed image will change to reflect the use of the setting represented by that icon. When you have highlighted the icon you wish to select, press Func./Set again to apply it, or you can just touch the icon on the screen to select it. The camera will ask you if you want to save the new image with that color setting; select OK to proceed or Cancel to abort. You can then move through other images to carry out the same process. Press Menu when you are finished with all images, and the camera will ask if you wish to display the last changed image.

I ordinarily don't do this sort of post-processing function in the camera, because I can use Photoshop or other software for that function. However, I do like the My Colors process for some purposes. If you are taking photographs in a particular situation and you have the time to experiment a bit, you can take one image without any My Colors settings, then display it on the screen and call up the My Colors feature in Playback mode. At that point, as discussed above, you can scroll through the various My Colors settings, and instantly see how the image would be altered with each of those settings. Then you can go back and take some new pictures using the My Colors settings that you tested in Playback mode.

Also, using this feature in playback mode lets you combine My Colors effects with other settings that do not let you use My Colors when taking pictures. For example, with Creative Filters settings such as Toy Camera, Fish-eye, Color Accent, and Poster Effect, you cannot use My Colors when shooting. However, once an image is recorded, you can enter playback mode and try out My Colors settings in combination with the Creative Filters effects. For example, Figure 6-41 shows an example for which a shot taken with the Fish-eye setting was combined with the Black and White setting of the My Colors item on the Playback menu.

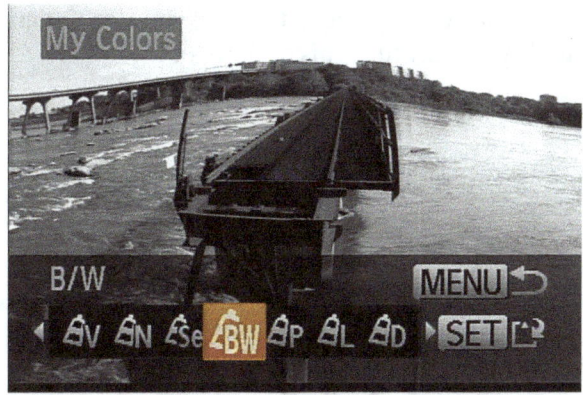

Fig. 6-41: My Colors BW Setting Applied to Fish-eye Image

As you might expect, the My Colors feature works only with JPEG images, not Raw files.

Face ID Info

This menu option gives you a way to edit and control the display of information concerning detected faces. When you select this option and navigate to the next screen, the camera presents you with two options: to turn the name display on or off, and to edit the name information, as shown in Figure 6-42.

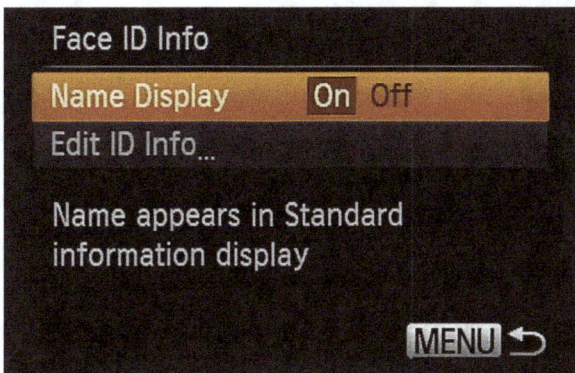

Fig. 6-42: Face ID Info Options Screen

If you leave the name display turned on, the names of faces that you registered with the camera will display in any images

283

in which the camera detected those faces. If you don't want those names to display, just turn this option off.

The second menu option provides a way to erase or overwrite the names that are associated with detected faces. After you select this option, you need to scroll to an image that has a name displayed for a recognized face.

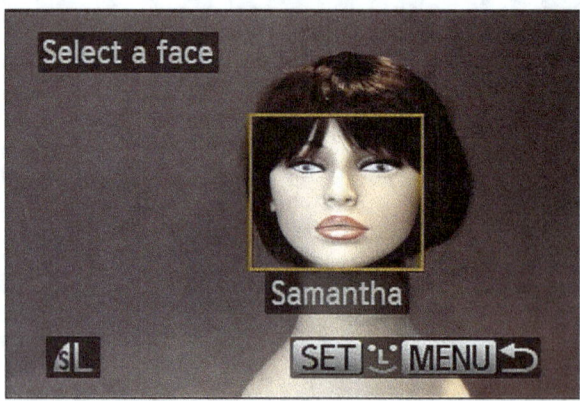

Fig. 6-43: Selected Face in Orange Frame

As seen in Figure 6-43, the camera then places an orange frame around a detected face. You can use the left and right buttons or the control dial to move the frame to a different face if necessary.

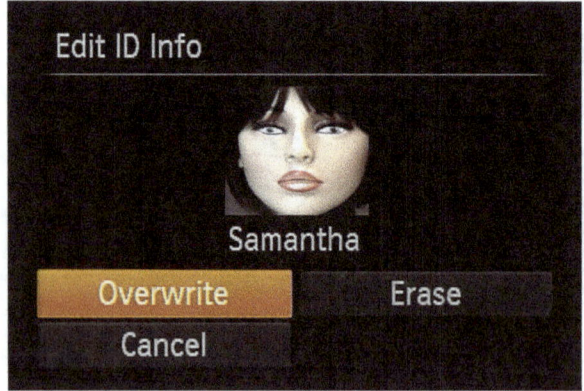

Fig. 6-44: Edit ID Info Confirmation Screen

Then press Func./Set, and the camera displays the screen shown in Figure 6-44, giving the options to overwrite or erase the name, or to cancel the operation. If you choose Erase, the name is deleted. If you choose Overwrite, the camera will display a screen showing the available names to use to overwrite the name. Select the one you want, and carry out the operation with the Func./Set button or icon.

Scroll Display

I have mentioned this feature a couple of times previously. When you scroll through your images using the control dial, if you start scrolling rapidly, the images will shrink and start to flow in a stream, as shown in Figure 6-45.

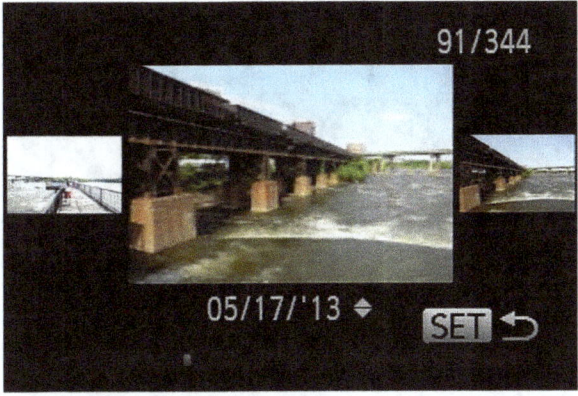

Fig. 6-45: Scroll Display Feature in Use

The camera will show the date of the images below the central image; you can switch to images from a different date by pressing the up or down direction button. You also can activate this effect by scrolling rapidly with a finger on the touch screen.

If you find this effect distracting, you can disable it with this menu option. Just set this option to Off, and no matter how fast you turn the control dial or scroll on the touch screen, the images will stay at their full size and scroll in the normal fashion.

285

Group Images

This option can be turned either on or off. If it is on, then any images you took using the High-Speed Burst HQ setting from Scene mode will be displayed in group format. That is, only one image from the group will appear in playback mode. It will be labeled with the word SET and an icon showing multiple files, as shown in Figure 6-46.

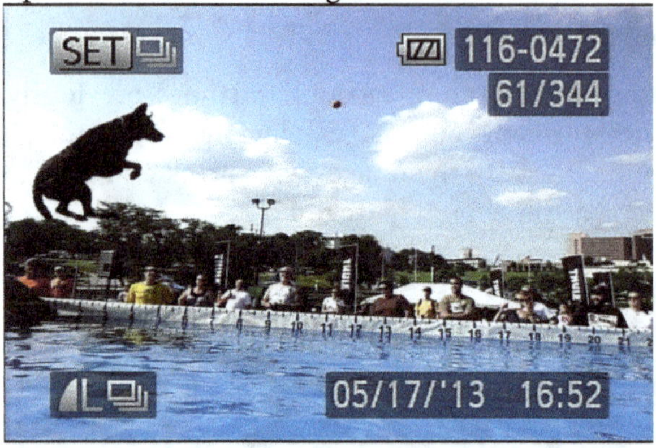

Fig. 6-46: Group of Continuous Shots Ready to Play

To view the other images in the group, you have to press the Func./Set button and then scroll through the individual images. To exit from the group so you can view images outside of the group, you have to press the up direction button.

If, on the other hand, you set the Group Images item on the Playback menu to Off, then each image in the group shows up as an individual image, just like any other.

Which setting to use here is a matter of personal preference. I prefer to leave it turned off, because this particular burst mode is limited to ten shots and I don't use it that much, so it's not a burden to view the individual shots. If you take many high-speed bursts, then you might want to turn this option on so you can scroll through just one image from each group. Also, when you use some features, such as the My Colors processing on the Playback menu, you have to have this option turned off so you can apply the processing to an individual image.

Auto Rotate

This menu item controls whether images shot with the camera held vertically appear in that orientation when you play them back on the camera's horizontal screen. By default, this option is turned on, meaning the images taken vertically are automatically rotated so that the vertical shot appears right side up on the horizontal display, as shown in Figure 6-47.

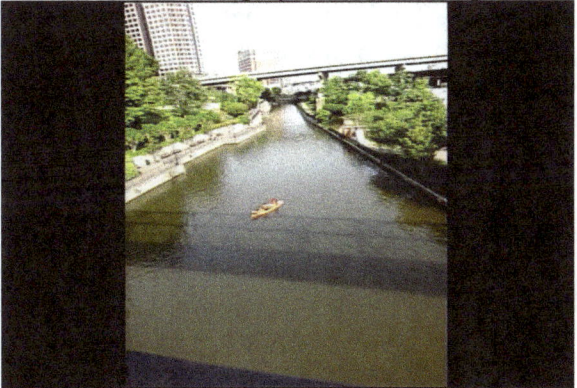

Fig. 6-47: Vertical Image on Horizontal Screen

If you turn this option off, then the images will appear sideways on the screen, as shown in Figure 6-48.

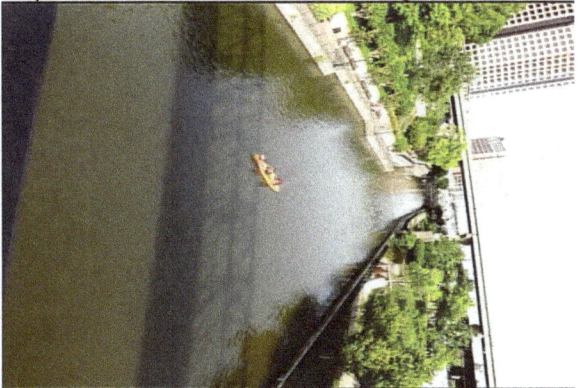

Fig. 6-48: Vertical Image Displayed at Full Size

Also, if this option is turned off, you cannot rotate images using the Rotate command, discussed earlier in this chapter.

Resume

This option has two possible settings: Last Seen and Last Shot. If you set it to Last seen, then, whenever you enter Playback mode, the camera will display the last image that you viewed on the screen. If you choose Last shot, then the camera will initially display the last image that was recorded with the camera. I generally like to set this item to Last Shot, so I can review my most recent images. But there may be times when you are spending a lot of time reviewing your images in the camera and you want to keep going back to the images you were reviewing most recently.

Transition

This menu option lets you choose the transition that is used between images when they are displayed on the LCD screen in single-image playback mode. The choices are Off, which means they will just "cut" from one to the next; Fade; Scroll; and Slide. Note that this transition setting is different from the setting for slideshows, which is set independently through the Slideshow option discussed above.

Set Touch Actions

This menu option gives you the opportunity to assign specific actions to each of four gestures you can make on the touch screen of the S110. When you select this menu option and move to the next screen, you will see the display shown in Figure 6-49, which shows the four gestures at the left. Each one is represented by an icon with a line representing a right-angle movement; each line has an arrow indicating the direction in which it is made. For example, the first gesture at the top of the list is made by moving your finger from the bottom of the screen upward, and then to the left.

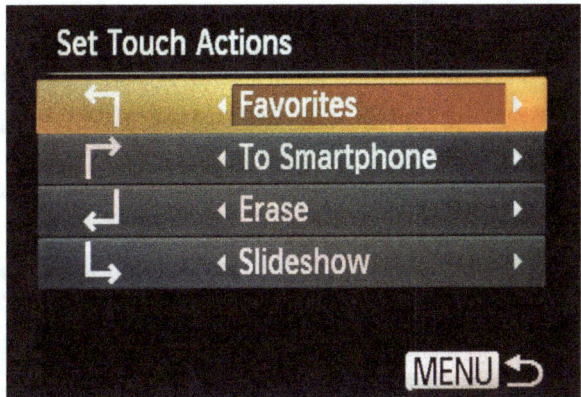

Fig. 6-49: Set Touch Actions Menu Option

The right side of the screen has a box for selecting which action is assigned to each of these four gestures. By default, the camera assigns the four gestures to the following actions, in order from top to bottom on the menu screen: Favorites; To Smartphone; Erase; and Slideshow. So, for example, if you drag your finger up and to the left over an image in playback mode, it will be marked as a Favorite; if you drag up and to the right, it will be sent to your phone using the wireless connection functions, discussed in Chapter 9; if you drag down and to the left, the image will be erased (with a chance to cancel first); and if you draft down and to the right, the camera will start a slideshow. I have found that this feature works best if you drag at a fairly moderate rate in the middle of the screen; when you do that, the camera will prompt you at the left and right with messages showing what will happen if you drag in either direction; then you can complete the motion in your chosen direction.

Each of the four gestures can be assigned to any one of 15 possible actions. You can assign the same action to more than one gesture, if you want. For my purposes, the most useful actions are Favorites, Erase, Protect, and Slideshow, but you may prefer to try several of the others to see if they are useful to you.

Printing Images

There is a lot of variation among photographers with respect to how often they print their photographs on a printer. Some people are content to view their images on the camera's screen; many save them to a computer and share them on sites such as Flickr, Pinterest, and Facebook; others send them to friends by e-mail.

If you want to produce copies of digital photographs on paper, there are various ways to do so. You can import the images into a program such as Adobe Photoshop or Photoshop Elements, or use the ImageBrowser EX software supplied by Canon with the S110, or any of many other programs that are available for photo editing. Once you have edited the images to your satisfaction, you can print the finished products from that software.

However, in some cases you may not want to spend the time to edit the pictures in software before printing them. You may have access to a printer that will connect directly to the camera, and you may prefer to print out copies on photo paper without going through the time-consuming process of transferring the images to a computer first. Or, you may want to try a service that will take your memory card and produce high-quality prints directly from that card. The following discussion covers the high points of these procedures.

Printing Directly from the Camera

The PowerShot S110 uses the PictBridge printing protocol, which lets it communicate directly with a wide variety of printers. The basic procedure is quite simple: Just plug the USB cable that came with the camera into the AV/USB port inside the door on the right side of the camera. (This is the upper of the two ports in that location.) Then plug the other end of the cable into the USB port of a PictBridge-compatible printer. (This USB port is different from the one for the cable that connects the printer to a computer: This one is rectangular; the

290

port for the cable to the computer has more of a square shape.) The printer does not have to be made by Canon; I plugged the S110 directly into my HP Photosmart C6180 printer, and the two devices communicated with no problems.

Once the connection is made, press the Playback button on the camera to display images, and use the various techniques discussed earlier in this chapter to display the image you would like to print. The camera will display a special screen that appears only when it's connected to a PictBridge printer, as shown in Figure 6-50, giving you various options for selecting landscape or portrait orientation, paper size, number of copies, and other options.

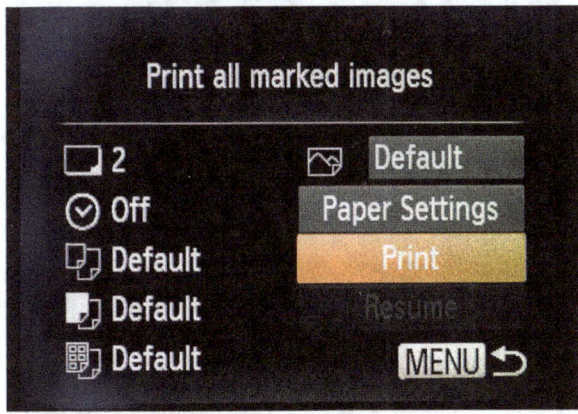

Fig. 6-50: Screen When Camera Connected to Printer

For complete details about these settings, see Canon's Personal Printing Guide, which is available for download at http://support-th.canon-asia.com/contents/TH/EN/0300304403.html.

Once you have all the settings as you want them, press the Func./Set button on the camera to print out the photograph. If you want to select multiple images before sending them to the printer, use the DPOF (Digital Print Order Format) function, which is built into the camera. That system lets you mark images on your memory card to be added to a print list, which can then be sent to your own printer. Or, you can take the memory card to a print shop to print out the selected images.

The Print Menu

To mark images for the DPOF list, while the camera is in Playback mode press the Menu button and highlight the tab for the Print menu, headed by a printer icon, as shown in Figure 6-51.

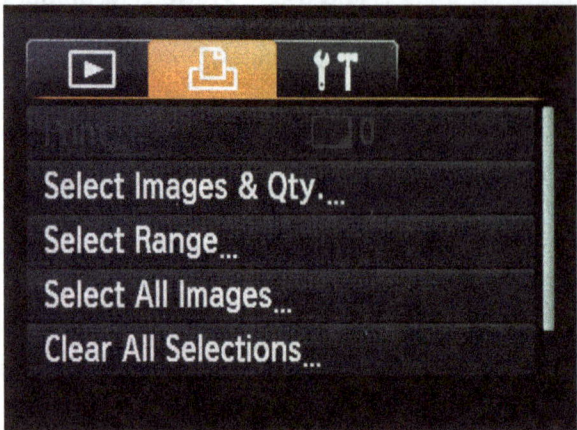

Fig. 6-51: Print Menu

Start the DPOF process of specifying images to be printed from this menu, using the Select Images & Quantity item near the top of the menu screen. The camera will present you with a selection screen similar to that used for the Erase, Protect, and Favorites procedures. Scroll through your images and mark those that you want to print, along with the number of copies of each image to print. You can then use the Print Settings item on this menu to set options for printing, including Standard or Index (that is, whether to print whole-page images or indexed thumbnails), whether to print the date, and others.

Once you have added all of the chosen images to the print list and set the options as you want them, you can either connect the camera to a PictBridge-compatible printer and print them out by selecting Print from the Print menu, or take the memory card to a photo store or printer who can handle this process, and have the photos printed there.

Chapter 7: Setup Menu

I n previous chapters I discussed the Function, Shooting, My Menu, Playback, and Print menu systems. The next system to discuss is the Setup menu. (I'll discuss menu options for Movie mode in Chapter 8.)

The Setup menu gives you various choices for housekeeping matters like screen brightness and operational sounds. As a reminder, you enter the menu system by pressing the Menu button. The available menus change depending on whether the camera is set to shooting mode or playback mode. However, no matter what other options are available, you can always enter into the Setup menu. After pressing the Menu button, use the direction buttons, the zoom lever, or the touch screen to select the wrench and mallet icon, as shown in Figure 7-1.

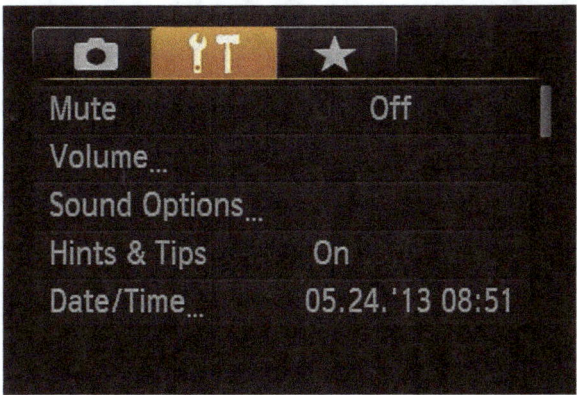

Fig. 7-1: Wrench and Mallet Icon for Setup Menu Highlighted

Once that icon is highlighted, use the control dial, the up and down direction buttons, or the touch screen to navigate through the various options on the menu.

Mute

This first option on the menu, highlighted on the first screen of the Setup menu in Figure 7-2, is a quick way to silence the beeps and chirps that sound off when the camera performs actions such as turning on, achieving focus and exposure, having a control button pressed, or having the shutter pressed to take a picture.

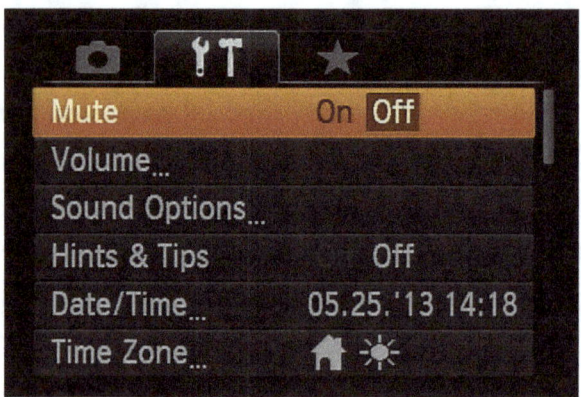

Fig. 7-2: First Screen of Options on Setup Menu

When you turn the Mute option on, the camera becomes very silent; there is a faint click when the shutter is pressed to take a picture. There still will be some mechanical sounds, like a soft whirring when the flash pops up or down, or a slight clicking when the flash is fired, but no sounds of any magnitude. The Mute feature is useful when you want to take pictures without attracting attention, such as for candid photography or photography in a museum or other quiet area.

What if you suddenly find yourself in a place where you need to be quiet but haven't yet activated the Mute option? You can keep the camera completely silent in that situation by holding down the Display button while turning the camera's power on. (If the camera was already on, you can turn it off first; it does not make any electronic sounds when turning off.)

Volume

This option is grayed out when Mute is turned on. If Mute is not on, then you can use the Volume menu item to adjust the loudness of camera sounds on a scale of 1 to 5, with 1 being quiet and 5 being loud. The four categories that can be adjusted are Start-up Volume, Operation Volume (beeps that accompany presses of controls), Self-timer Volume, and Shutter Volume.

Sound Options

With this item, you can choose the electronic sounds that the camera uses in the four categories discussed above under Volume. You can choose from three different clicks, beeps, and chirps for each option; as you move the highlight from one numbered option to another, you will hear a sample of the chosen sound, so you can customize the audio experience in using the camera.

Hints & Tips

This option can be turned either on or off. When it is turned on, the camera uses one line at the bottom of each menu screen for a brief statement about the function of the menu item that is currently highlighted by the selection bar. For example, as shown in Figure 7-3, when the orange bar rests on the Sound Options menu line, the Hints & Tips area at the bottom of the screen says "Sets various camera sounds." For some menu items it takes two lines to fit all of the words in the tip; in those cases, the camera displays one line at a time and scrolls from one to the next. For all items, the hint disappears after displaying for about 10 or 15 seconds. If you want to see the hint again, you have to move the highlight bar off the item and then back on again.

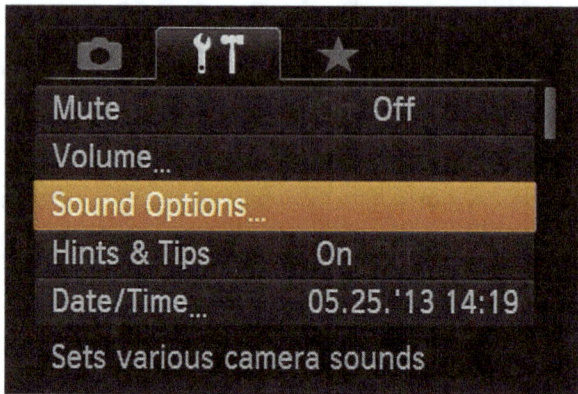

Fig. 7-3: Hints & Tips Information Displayed at Bottom of Screen

Note that in some cases, when you turn Hints & Tips off, the camera displays more information in some ways than when it is turned on. For example, when the camera is set to Scene mode, as you use the Function menu to scroll through the various scene types, if Hints & Tips is turned on, then the camera displays a short description of the setting above its icon, as seen in Figure 7-4 for the Portrait setting.

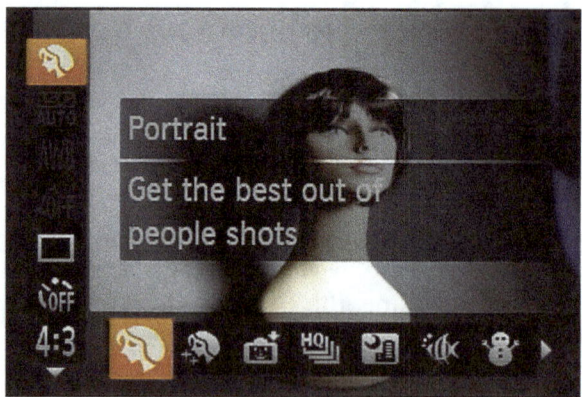

Fig. 7-4: Portrait Setting with Hints & Tips Turned On

This description, including the Portrait label, disappears after a few seconds, and no information about the setting remains on the screen. However, if Hints & Tips is turned off, there is less information displayed—just the Portrait label—but that label remains on the screen, just above the Portrait icon, indefinitely, as shown in Figure 7-5.

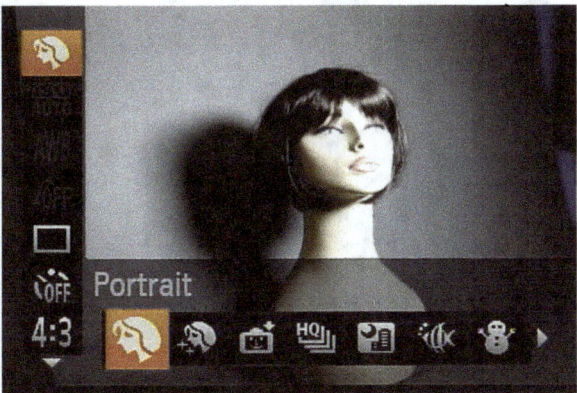

Fig. 7-5: Portrait Setting with Hints & Tips Turned Off

So, if you would like to keep the labels above the Scene mode settings, turn Hints & Tips off. You will get less information, but the information you get will not disappear. This same situation holds true for the other options on the Function menu.

Date/Time

This menu item is where you set the current date and time, which will be recorded with your images in data that can be read by your Canon ImageBrowser EX software and by many other programs, such as Adobe Photoshop and Photoshop Elements. (The date and time will not appear on the images unless you take further steps to make that happen, either by using the Date Stamp function from the Shooting menu or by selecting the option to include them when printing from the camera.) To set the date and time from this menu item, as seen in Figure 7-6, adjust each highlighted value by using the control dial, the up and down direction buttons, or the touch screen, then move to the next item using the right direction button or the touch screen. The last item on the right is the setting for Daylight Savings Time. If you set that block to On, the time will move one hour later.

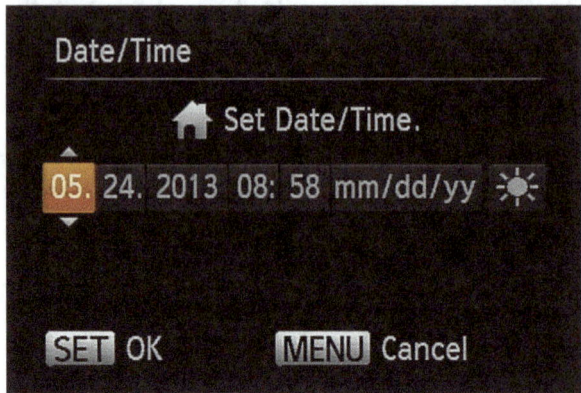

Fig. 7-6: Date/Time Settings Screen

When you have adjusted all items to the correct values, press the Func./Set button or the SET icon on the touch screen to save them.

Time Zone

This menu option lets you set two time zones, labeled Home and World, so you can switch back and forth between them if you travel and thereby keep your camera's date and time settings accurate for local conditions. To use this feature, select the Time Zone option on the Setup menu and then select Home on the next screen by pressing Func./Set.

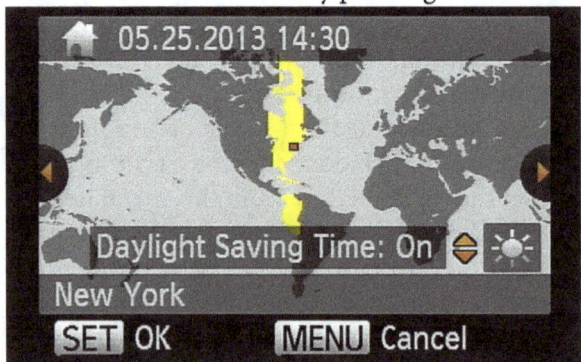

Fig. 7-7: Time Zone World Map

298

On the next screen, shown in Figure 7-7, use the left and right direction buttons or the control dial to move the yellow highlight through the world map until your home time zone is highlighted and its name appears in the lower left of the screen. Then press Func./Set to accept that setting, and repeat this operation for the World time zone. Once those two time zones are set and the date and time are set accurately for the local time zone, whenever you travel you can just use the Time Zone screen to select either Home or World, depending on your present location. Any photographs you take using those settings will include accurate date and time information in the image files.

LCD Brightness

This menu item, shown in Figure 7-8, lets you adjust the brightness of the LCD screen.

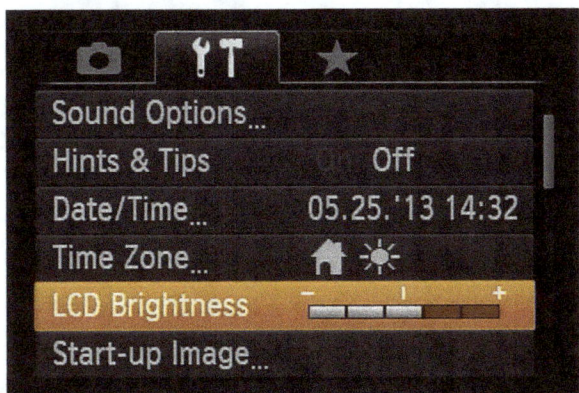

Fig. 7-8: LCD Brightness Menu Option

To adjust the setting, press the right or left direction button or the Func./Set button, or touch this menu item, to activate the brightness scale, then turn the control dial, use those two direction buttons, or touch either side of the scale to raise or lower the brightness. You can set the brightness at any level from 1 (dimmest) to 5 (brightest). The standard setting is 3. If you can manage with the dimmer settings, you can save some battery power by turning down the brightness. You may need to use the brightest setting when you are shooting outdoors in sunlight.

If you need to increase the brightness of the screen temporarily without having to use the menu, you can press and hold the Display button for more than one second; that will boost the screen to its brightest level (if it wasn't already set there). You can reverse this operation by pressing and holding the Display button one more time. The increased brightness setting will last only until the camera is powered off.

Start-up Image

When the camera comes from the factory, the image it shows as it turns on is a blue and black globe with an HS System icon in its center, to promote Canon's high-sensitivity digital sensor system. This menu option gives you a way to change the start-up image to either of the two standard ones provided by Canon, to one of your own images, or to no image at all. To use one of the Canon images, select the number 1 or 2 from the menu screen.

To use one of your own images, the image must be on the memory card that is in the camera. Select the Start-up Image option from the Setup menu while the camera is in Playback mode.

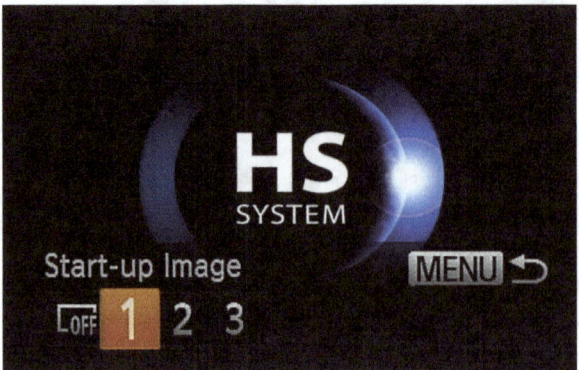

Fig. 7-9: Start-up Image Menu Option

On the Start-up Image menu screen, shown in Figure 7-9, select image number 3, press the Func./Set button, and then navigate through the images on your memory card; the words "Start-up Image" will appear at the upper left of the screen during this process. When you find the image you want, press the Func./Set button (or touch the SET icon on the screen) to select it. That image will then appear every time you start up the camera, unless you change it again using the same process.

Format

The Format command is one of the more important menu options. Choose this process only when you want or need to completely wipe all of the data from a memory storage card. When you select the Format option, the camera will ask you to confirm that you want to format the memory card, as shown in Figure 7-10.

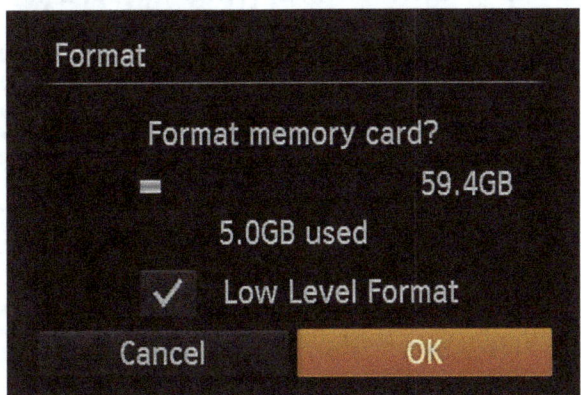

Fig. 7-10: Format Confirmation Screen

If you reply by selecting OK, the camera will proceed to carry out the formatting operation, and the result will be a card that is empty of images and is properly formatted to store new images from the camera. With this procedure, the camera will erase all images, including those that have been protected from accidental erasure with the Protect function on the Playback menu. It's a good idea to save your good images and videos to your computer or other storage device and then re-format your memory card from time to time, to make sure it is properly set up to start recording new images and videos. You should certainly format any new memory card before using it in the camera, and some photographers format their card after transferring the images from it to a computer.

You also can select the option for Low Level Format, which takes longer but may speed up the performance of the memory card and correct any problems that may have arisen with the card's performance.

File Numbering

This option controls how the camera assigns numbers to your images and videos. There are two choices: Continuous and Auto Reset. If you choose Continuous, then the camera continues numbering where it left off, even if you put a new memory card in the camera. For example, if you have shot 112 images on your first memory card, the last image likely will be numbered 100-0112, for the folder number (100, the first folder number available), and the image number. If you then switch to a brand new memory card with no images on it, the first image on that card will be numbered 100-0113, because the numbering scheme continues in the same sequence. If you choose Auto Reset instead, the first image on the new card will be numbered 100-0001, because the camera resets the numbering back to the first number. Each folder can hold up to 2,000 images, and the camera can number the images up to 9,999. It's important to note that the Auto Reset function may not work properly if the new card you use already contains images and is not newly formatted before being placed in the camera. With Auto Reset, the image numbers will also reset when the camera creates a new folder, as discussed below.

Create Folder

With this option, you choose how often the camera creates new folders—daily or monthly. Which one works best for you may depend on how often you shoot, and how many images you shoot at a time. If you shoot large numbers of images at a time, you may want to choose the Daily option, so you will have a separately numbered folder for each shooting date. If you take photos only occasionally, the monthly choice may make more sense. Of course, if you are in the habit of saving your new images to your computer and organizing them using software such as Canon's ImageBrowser EX or Adobe Photoshop Lightroom, you don't need to worry too much about how the image folders are numbered on the camera.

Lens Retract

This menu option gives you control over the behavior of the lens-retraction mechanism. With the normal setting, when you switch the camera from shooting mode to playback mode, the lens will retract after about one minute, on the theory that you aren't using the lens for shooting, and it might as well be pulled back inside the camera's housing for protection if you don't need it at the moment. If you want, you can change this setting to 0 seconds, so the lens retracts immediately when you change into playback mode. However, if you have adjusted the lens through focusing or zooming to a certain point and want to preserve that value, you might want to leave this option set to delay for one minute, so you don't immediately lose your lens setting.

Power Saving

With the settings available through this menu item, you can control whether the camera will stay powered up or will turn itself off if you don't touch the controls for a period of time, and you can specify how long the camera will sit idle before the display blanks out to save power. These functions are controlled by two sub-options of the Power Saving item on the

303

Setup menu, as shown in Figure 7-11: Auto Power Down and Display Off, which work independently of each other. They work somewhat differently in shooting mode and playback mode.

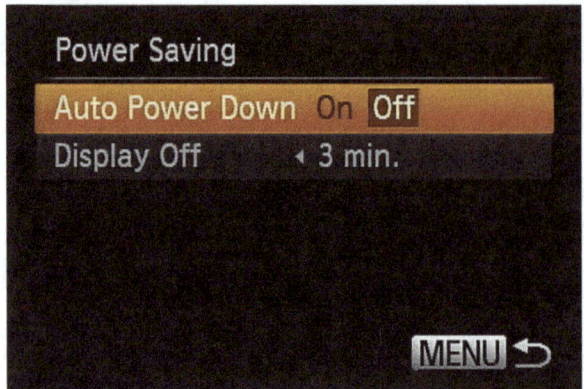

Fig. 7-11: Power Saving Options Screen

When the camera is in shooting mode, if you leave Auto Power Down turned on, the camera will turn itself completely off after about 3 minutes of inactivity, regardless of the setting for the Display Off option. You have no control over the 3-minute time; this option can be set only on or off. You can set the Display Off option to 10 seconds, 20 seconds, 30 seconds, or 1, 2, or 3 minutes. You cannot turn this option off.

If the display goes blank, you can restore it by pressing the shutter button halfway. However, once the camera turns off, you have to turn it back on to keep working; you can't revive it just by pressing the shutter button or some other control.

When the camera is in playback mode, the Display Off option has no effect. However, the camera will turn itself off after about 5 minutes of inactivity, if the Auto Power Down option is turned on in the menu. If that option is turned off, the camera will stay powered on as long as the battery holds its charge, just as it will in shooting mode. If you're using an AC adapter, the camera will stay powered on indefinitely if that option is turned off. However, even with an AC adapter plugged in, the Auto Power Down option will shut down the camera after the prescribed time if that option is turned on.

It may be convenient at times to turn the Auto Power Down option off, but you then run the risk of running the battery all the way down if you forget to turn the power off. So, it may be a good idea to leave Auto Power Down turned on, and to just remember to press a control button every couple of minutes if you want the camera to stay powered up for the time being.

Units

This option gives you the choice of meters and centimeters or feet and inches for the units of distance used by the camera for focusing and for the elevation of a smartphone that is connected to the camera wirelessly to provide GPS data. Just select the units of measurement you are most comfortable with.

Electronic Level

As was discussed in Chapter 4, one of the options that can be turned on using the Custom Display menu option is the electronic level. Once it is turned on through that menu item, the level will appear on the shooting screen with the more detailed screens, when you press the Display button to summon it. A screen with the level in use is shown in Figure 7-12.

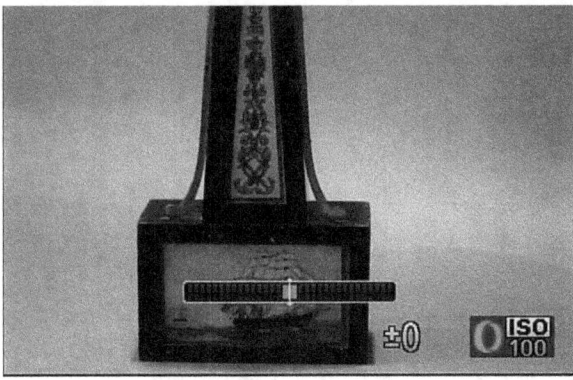

Fig. 7-12: Electronic Level in Use

This option on the Setup menu lets you calibrate the electronic level in case it no longer seems to be finding a true level reading. To use this option, make sure the camera is placed on a steady, level surface, then navigate to the second screen and choose the Calibrate option, as shown in Figure 7-13.

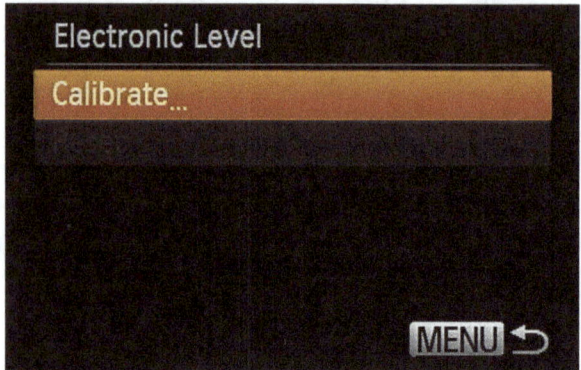

Fig. 7-13: Electronic Level Calibration Screen

Once you have calibrated the level, the Reset option will become available for selection; you can use that option to restore the level to its factory setting in case the calibration does not appear to have been successful.

Video System

This item gives you the option of selecting the appropriate system for the television to which you are connecting the camera by means of the audio-visual cable. There are only two options available: NTSC and PAL. NTSC is the system used in the United States, Canada, most of South America, South Korea, Japan, Taiwan, and some other countries; PAL is used in Europe and most other areas. A third standard, SECAM, used in some countries, is not available on the PowerShot S110.

CTRL via HDMI

This setting is of use only when you have connected the camera to an HD (high-definition) TV set and you want to control the camera with the TV's remote control, which is possible in some situations. If you want to do that, set this option to Enable and follow the instructions for the TV and its remote control. See the list of items that can be controlled at page 283 of the Canon Camera User Guide.

Touch Response

This menu option lets you adjust the sensitivity of the S110's touch screen. If you change the setting to High instead of the default setting of Standard, the camera will respond to a lighter touch. I have found the Standard setting to work very well for me. When I tried High, I felt the camera was responding too readily to a very light touch, which seemed to increase the risk of triggering an unintended action, but you may find the High setting to work well for you.

Wireless LAN Settings

This menu option helps you control the S110's ability to connect to other devices over a wireless (Wi-Fi) local area network, or LAN. The camera has a considerable set of features for connecting wirelessly to other devices for the transfer of images. I will provide some information about using those features in Chapter 9. This option on the Setup menu does not control most of the wireless functions of the camera; it only concerns a few technical matters.

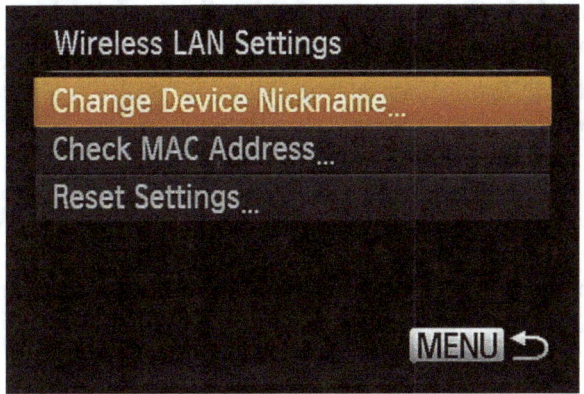

Fig. 7-14: Wireless LAN Settings Screen

307

As seen in Figure 7-14, the main screen of this menu option has three choices. The first selection, Change Device Nickname, is used if you want to change the nickname that you assigned to the camera while setting up the wireless LAN capabilities. This nickname is a short name using letters and numbers to identify the camera when it is connecting to other devices.

The second option, Check MAC address, is for use in case you are having difficulty connecting the camera wirelessly through a Wi-Fi access point (router). In some cases, it can be useful to get access to the router's settings through a computer, to make sure that the router is set up to accept a connection from a particular MAC address. (Some wireless access points are configured to accept connections only from certain MAC addresses.) If you are having difficulty with the connection between the camera and the computer through a wireless network, you may want to use this option to check the camera's MAC address in order to diagnose the problem.

The third and final menu option, Reset Settings, is to be used when you want to wipe out all wireless LAN settings you have made and return those settings to the default state. You might want to do this if you sell the camera, for example.

Copyright Info

This menu option gives you a way to record copyright information along with all images taken with the camera. Using these options, shown in Figure 7-15, you can enter your name under Enter Author's Name, and you can enter further details under Enter Copyright Details. For example, I entered my name, and, as further details, "Copyright 2013. All rights reserved." You can use the first option, Display Copyright Info, to check the information you have entered. Once you have entered the information through this menu option, any images you take will include the information in their metadata.

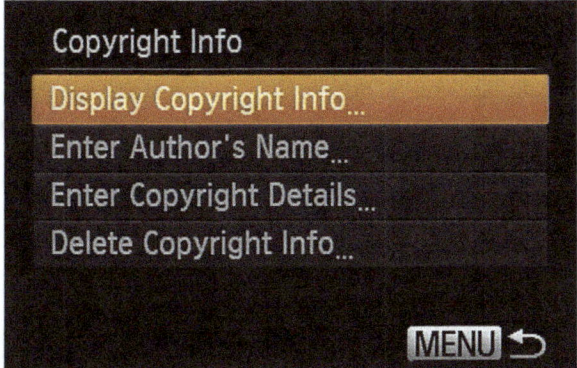

Fig. 7-15: Copyright Info Menu Option

For example, when I used Adobe Bridge software to view some pictures I took with the copyright menu option in use, my name showed up on the Author line in the Metadata area, and the other information showed up on the Copyright line. The information also showed up in the Shooting Info area when I viewed the images with Canon's ImageBrowser EX software.

The final menu option lets you delete copyright information.

Certification Logo Display

This menu option displays the logos for certain certification requirements met by the camera, as shown in Figure 7-16. It is included for legal or contractual reasons and has no application for your photography.

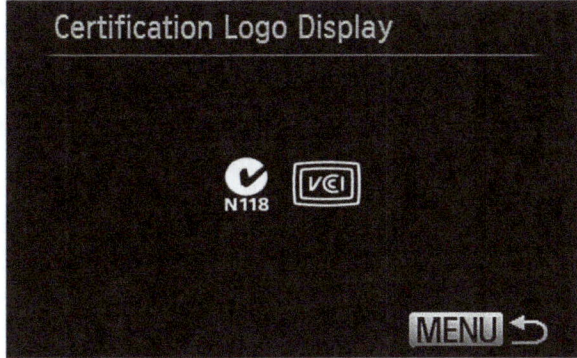

Fig. 7-16: Certification Logo Display Menu Option

Eye-Fi Settings

This menu option, shown in Figure 7-17, does not appear at all unless you have an Eye-Fi card installed in the PowerShot S110. As I discussed in Chapter 1, an Eye-Fi card is a special type of SD memory card with a built-in transmitter that can transfer images from the card directly to your computer over a wireless (Wi-Fi) network. Ordinarily, you should not need to change these settings on the menu.

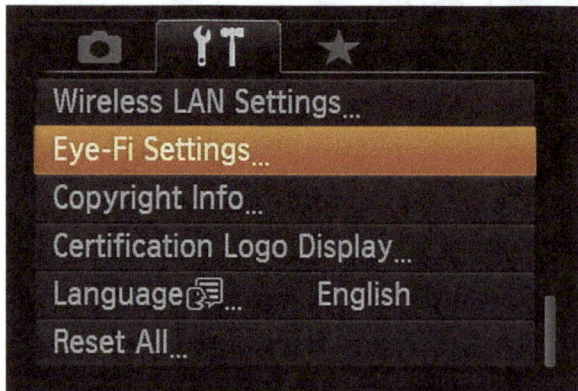

Fig. 7-17: Eye-Fi Settings Menu Option

The first sub-option for this item is Eye-Fi Transmission Enable/Disable, shown in Figure 7-18.

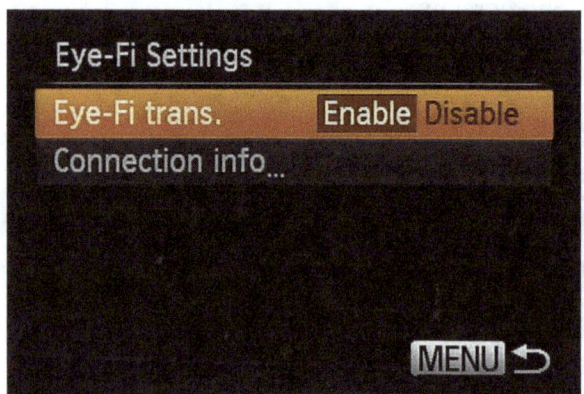

Fig. 7-18: Eye-Fi Transmission Enable Menu Option

You can save some battery power if you have an Eye-Fi card installed in the camera but don't currently need to transmit images to a computer. According to Canon's user's manual, using this option to disable the card is not sufficient to comply with warnings against using transmission devices, such as on airplanes in flight or in hospitals; you may have to remove the card from the camera in those situations.

The second menu sub-option, Connection Info, reports details about the Eye-Fi card's current connection to a wireless network, if any. For example, this menu item may report the name of your network and a message such as "Transferring" or "Connected," as shown in Figure 7-19.

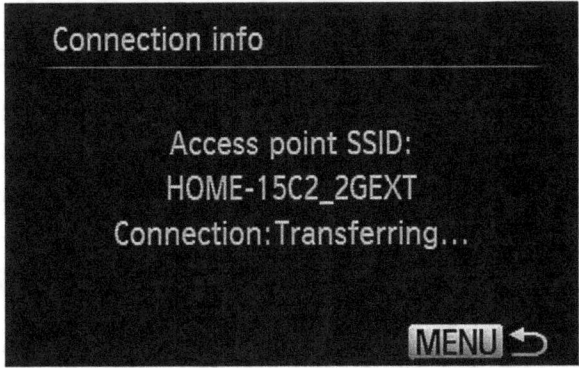

Fig. 7-19: Display When Eye-Fi Card is Transferring Images

This information may help you diagnose a problem with the functioning of your Eye-Fi card.

Language

This option gives you the choice of the language that is used for the display of commands and information on the camera's LCD screen. Once you have selected this menu item, scroll through the numerous language choices, shown in Figure 7-20, using the control dial or the direction buttons, or just touch your choice on the screen, and press the Func./Set button when your chosen language is highlighted.

311

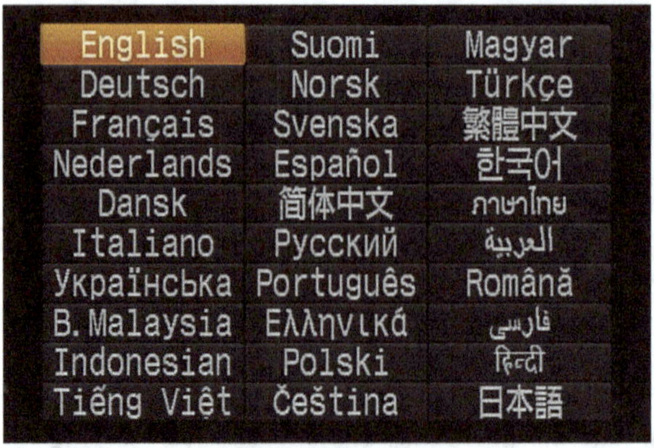

Fig. 7-20: *Language Selection Screen*

If you prefer a quicker route to the Language option, you can press the Playback button to enter playback mode, then press the Menu button while holding down the Func./Set button, to take you directly to the Language screen.

Reset All

Choose this menu option when you want to reset all of the camera's settings back to their original (default) values. This action can be useful if you have been playing around with different settings and you find that something is not working as expected. The Reset All command will give you a fresh start with known values for all of the major settings on the menus and for shooting. There are a few settings that will not be reset, including items such as date and time, time zone, language, video system, and the scene type chosen in Scene mode. The complete list is at Page 276 of the Canon Camera User Guide.

Chapter 8: Motion Pictures

Nowadays it seems that it's a necessity for any advanced compact digital or DSLR camera to include movie-making capabilities. Most recently, it's become standard practice for camera manufacturers to incorporate high-definition (HD) video recording into their premium cameras, and the PowerShot S110 is one example of that trend. The S110's video abilities provide you with a substantial tool for capturing motion clips in high definition, along with a few refinements. I will go through the various options for movie-making in this chapter. Before I discuss the specific settings you can make for your movies, I'll begin with a brief overview of the process.

Movie-making Overview

In one sense, the fundamentals of making videos with the S110 can be reduced to four words: "Push the red button." Having a dedicated motion picture recording button makes things very easy for the user of this camera, because anytime you see a reason to take some video footage, you can just press that easily accessible button while aiming at your subject, and you will get results that are very likely to be quite usable. You do not need to worry about making any particular settings, particularly if you have set the camera to AUTO mode. When you're done recording, press the red button again. You also can press the shutter release button to stop recording, though you cannot start recording with that button; if you press that button when a movie is not being recorded, even when the camera is set to Movie mode, the camera will take a still photo.

If you're mainly a still photographer and not that interested in movie-making, you don't need to read any further. Be aware that the red button exists, and if an interesting event starts to unfold in your vicinity, you can press that button and record the action for posterity.

But for those S110 users who would like to delve further into their camera's motion picture capabilities, there is considerably more information to discuss.

Before I get into details about how to record videos, I should note that the PowerShot S110 has built-in limitations that prevent it from recording any sequence longer than just under 30 minutes for HD footage, or about one hour for standard-quality footage. You can, of course, record multiple sequences adding up to any length, depending on the amount of storage space available on your memory cards. If you plan to record a significant amount of HD video, you should get one of the highest-capacity and fastest memory cards you can find. For example, a 16 GB card can hold about one hour of Full HD video, about 85 minutes of standard-quality HD video, or about 3 hours of the lower-quality 640 (VGA) video. If you want to fit both still images and HD video sequences on a card, you might be better off with a 32 GB card, or even with an SDXC card having a capacity of up to 256 GB. You should try to get a card rated in Class 6 or higher, so it will have the necessary speed for recording HD video.

Recording in Non-Movie Shooting Modes

One aspect of motion picture recording with the S110 that is somewhat confusing is what to do about choosing a shooting mode. For still photography with this camera, when you choose a shooting mode with the mode dial on top of the camera, that is the mode that you will shoot your pictures in. That is not quite how it works with movie recording. In the motion picture arena, where you set the mode dial has some effect on your shooting, but not as direct an effect as for still photos.

Here is the situation. If you look at the mode dial on top of the camera, you will see the various shooting modes for still photography: AUTO, Program, Shutter Priority, Aperture Priority, Manual, Custom, Scene, and Creative Filters. There is also one entry on the dial for Movie mode, represented by the movie camera icon, and another one for the Movie Digest mode. However, because of the red Movie button, you do not have to set the mode dial to Movie mode to record a movie (though you certainly can, as I'll discuss shortly). In fact, you can have the mode dial set to any of its settings and still record a movie. But, the results may not be what you might expect based on the name of the shooting mode.

For example, if the mode dial is set to M for Manual exposure mode, if you press the red button you will not be shooting a movie in Manual exposure mode. In fact, you'll be shooting a movie with the camera adjusting the exposure automatically by setting the aperture and shutter speed. This is the same result you'll get with any of the four PASM shooting modes on the mode dial (Program, Aperture Priority, Shutter Priority, and Manual).

Here is where the situation gets slightly complicated. As I just noted, when you set the mode dial to some of the major still-shooting modes, such as Aperture Priority, Shutter Priority or Manual, the camera does not follow that mode's behavior for setting exposure when you press the red movie button. But the camera does use some (not all) of the other settings that have been made in that shooting mode. For example, if you have the mode dial set to A for Aperture Priority, when you press the red button to make a movie, the camera does not let you set the aperture; instead, it chooses both aperture and shutter speed. However, the camera does use some of the settings that were chosen through the Function and Shooting menus while the camera was in Aperture Priority mode, such as white

315

balance, My Colors, and ND Filter. You can even use the self-timer. However, all of these settings have to be made before you press the red Movie button to start recording the movie, and once the recording is underway you cannot change those settings unless you end the recording.

What about recording movies using the more automatic still-shooting options, such as AUTO mode, the Scene mode types, and the Creative Filters mode settings? Here, again, you can press the red Movie button and record your video in any of those modes. However, in some cases, the special aspect of the mode will not have any effect. For example, you can turn the mode dial to the Creative Filters setting (two interlocking circles) and then use the Function menu to select the Fish-eye effect, which makes the scene look distorted as if seen through a fishbowl. If you then press the red button, a video will be recorded, but it will not have the Fish-eye effect.

The same is true for the HDR and Toy Camera effects—you can record a video, but it will look no different than one re-corded in AUTO mode. Similarly, several of the Scene mode settings have no effect for videos, in most cases because they involve settings that don't make sense for movies. These cat-egories are Smart Shutter, High-Speed Burst HQ, Handheld Night Scene, and Stitch Assist. However, you can still press the Movie button in any of those shooting modes, and the video will be recorded with standard settings.

Several of the settings from the Scene and Creative Filters modes, though, do have their intended effect when recording a video, namely, Portrait, Nostalgic, Miniature Effect, Mono-chrome, Super Vivid, Poster Effect, Color Accent, Color Swap, Underwater, Snow, and Fireworks. (In the case of Fireworks, colors are rendered more vividly than usual. Of course, the long shutter speed used for still photos with that setting is not applicable for shooting movies.)

Here is a summary of the situation for recording in shoot-ing modes other than Movie mode. If you just want to record a quick video clip with standard settings, you can leave the camera set on AUTO mode and fire away with the red button. If you want to record a video using any of the above-listed "special" settings, turn the mode dial to the Scene or Creative Filters slot and select the setting you want using the Function menu. The camera will record the video using that effect, if it is one that carries over to video-making. If you happen to choose one of the settings that does not carry over to video-making, don't worry; the video will not be made using that effect, but it will still be recorded as a plain video sequence.

If you happen to be shooting in Program, Aperture Priority, Shutter Priority, or Manual exposure mode, you can press the red button to start recording a video at any time. Some, but not all, of the settings in your current shooting mode will carry over to the video recording. The two most important settings that do carry over are white balance and My Colors. If you have the mode dial set to Movie Digest mode, you can still press the red Movie button to record a movie, and certain functions will be available, including My Colors, metering method, ND Filter, and most white balance settings, but not white balance correction.

Finally, a quick note about focus and zoom while shooting movies: You can use the normal autofocus or manual focus settings, including macro focus, and you can use the optical zoom if you want. But be careful using the zoom while recording a video, because the sound of the zoom lens mechanism will be recorded on the video's sound track. You cannot adjust manual focus while recording a movie, although you can set the focus distance manually before starting the recording. (The lens cannot be zoomed when shooting a movie with the Miniature Effect setting of Creative Filters mode or with the Super Slow Motion options.)

If you want to have more control over the camera's exposure settings while shooting your movie, that's the role of the Movie setting on the mode dial.

Shooting in Movie Mode

The steps outlined above will get you started recording video with the PowerShot S110 by pressing the red Movie button, no matter what shooting mode the camera is set for. Once you have got the hang of the basic steps for movie-making, though, you may want to experiment with some of the other settings that are available when you turn the mode dial to the Movie position. So, turn the dial to put the movie camera icon next to the white selector line, as shown in Figure 8-1, and I will discuss all of the settings that are available in that mode.

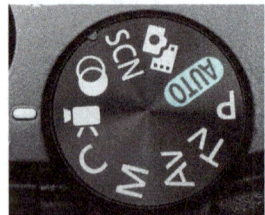

Fig. 8-1: Movie Mode

Function Menu

When you press the Func./Set button while the camera is set to Movie mode, you will see that there are 7 settings that you can make, arrayed up and down the left side of the screen, as shown in Figure 8-2.

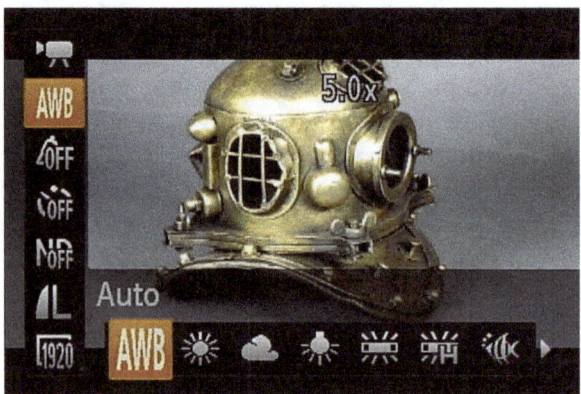

Fig. 8-2: Function Menu in Movie Mode

This is not as long a list of options as are available for still shooting; in Program mode, for example, there are 13 options on the Function menu. But the PowerShot S110 is well equipped to let you control the settings for your video sequences. I will discuss each of these options below, with special attention to the items that are not applicable to shooting still images.

Movie Mode

The first item you can select from the Function menu in Movie mode is the "mode" or general type of movie you can record. This choice can be a bit confusing, because there are several levels of choices involved in recording movies with the S110.

First, you need to decide whether to record a movie as opposed to a still image. That decision is made by pressing the red Movie button as opposed to the shutter button. Just as you can record a movie when the mode dial is set to a still-shooting mode such as AUTO, Program, or Aperture Priority, you can shoot a still image when the mode dial is set to the Movie mode. Just press the shutter button instead of the red Movie button, and the camera will record a still image using the menu settings that are in effect.

Second, you need to decide whether to set the mode dial to Movie mode or not. As discussed above, the mode dial can be set to any position when you record a movie; if you set it to Movie mode you have more options for movie recording than you do otherwise.

Third, you can use this first option on the Function menu in Movie mode to select from three types of movie to record: Standard, iFrame, or Super Slow Motion. I will discuss those choices shortly.

Finally, you can choose what format, or resolution, the movie should be recorded in. Those choices appear on the Function menu, in the very last item. The possibilities are 1920, 1280, and 640; I will discuss those later in this chapter.

319

For now, with that introduction, we are still discussing the first item on the Function menu in Movie mode—the movie "mode," as Canon calls it, or general movie type. As shown in Figure 8-3, there are three choices for this menu option, represented by three different movie-camera icons.

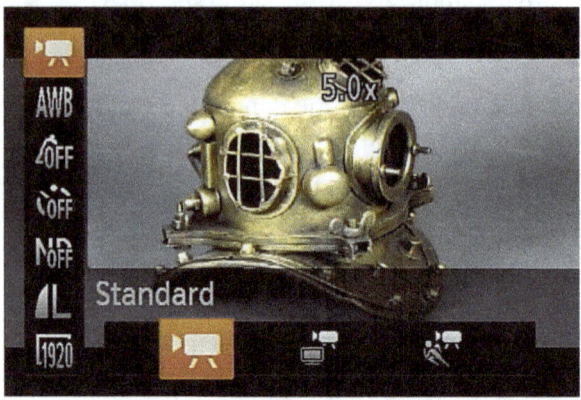

Fig. 8-3: Options for Movie Mode Setting

From left to right, the icons represent Standard mode, iFrame Movie, and Super Slow Motion Movie. In most cases, for everyday movie-making, you probably will want to choose the Standard variety of movie. That is the only selection that will produce a movie at normal speed that can be viewed and edited by the most common equipment and software.

The second choice, iFrame Movie, is provided for those photographers who are using Apple software. The iFrame video format is unique to Apple, and is not compatible with other formats. Unless you are familiar with the iFrame format and prefer it to other formats, you are probably better off not selecting this option.

The third choice for this menu option, Super Slow Motion Movie, is a useful and powerful feature that you likely will want to take advantage of on some occasions. With this selection, the camera records the video at a faster rate than usual, so the action will be slowed down dramatically when the footage is played back. To use this option, select the icon at the right, showing a movie camera and a running person. Then scroll all the way to the bottom of the Function menu, as shown in Figure 8-4, and select either 240 or 120 for the shooting frame rate—240 frames per second or 120 frames per second. (The normal frame rate for recording video in the United States is 30 frames per second.)

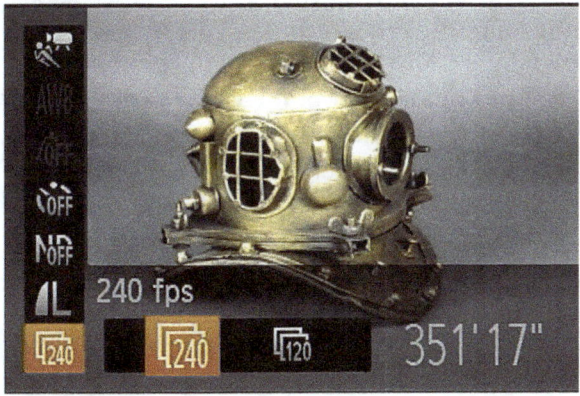

Fig. 8-4: Options for Super Slow Motion Movie Setting

If you choose 240, the video will be slowed down eight times when played back; if you choose 120, it will be slowed down four times. In either case, no sound is recorded, and the maximum time for recording is about 30 seconds. This means that the maximum time for playback is about four minutes with the 240 setting and about two minutes with the 120 setting. In both cases, the video will be in a relatively low-quality format with low resolution. You cannot zoom while recording, and the exposure and focus will be locked when the shooting starts. However, this video feature can be very useful for analyzing a sports action, slowing down the motion of a bird or other animal, or for creative applications.

White Balance

The next option on the Function menu for movie shooting, white balance, behaves just as it does for still images, except

321

that it does not include the ability to make fine adjustments of amber, blue, green, and magenta, as you can with still shooting. The white balance option is available for setting only when the Movie mode is Standard or iFrame—you can't set white balance if you are using the Super Slow Motion option.

My Colors

The My Colors settings are completely available when shooting movies, but only in Standard mode and iFrame mode, not Super Slow Motion. Just as with the more advanced still-shooting modes, you can use any of the various color effects, including Vivid, Sepia, and the others, and you can create a Custom Color selection by adjusting contrast, sharpness, saturation, red, green, blue, and skin tone to your own specifications.

Self-timer

The self-timer is available for movie shooting in any mode, even Super Slow Motion. You can set it to delay ten seconds, two seconds, or a custom time that you select from zero to 30 seconds, just as with shooting stills. Naturally enough, though, you cannot set the number of shots to be taken when the shutter is triggered.

Having the ability to use the self-timer is quite useful for video shooting. For example, if you want to analyze your golf swing, you can set the timer to a ten-second delay, then press the red Movie button to start a Super Slow Motion video recording as you move into place before the lens. Of course, you have to return to the camera to press the red button again to stop the recording at the appropriate time, unless you want to use the full 30 seconds of recording time that is available in that mode, after which the camera will stop recording on its own.

ND Filter

The ND Filter option can be used for recording any sort of video, including Super Slow Motion. This option is useful if you are filming in very bright conditions and the exposure system is unable to darken the footage sufficiently. Also, you might try activating the ND filter to force the camera to use a wider aperture in order to blur the background.

Image Size

This next option on the Function menu for shooting movies has nothing to do with movies. This item lets you select the image size to be used for any still shots you take while the camera is set to Movie mode. If you press the shutter release button while the camera is set to Movie mode, the camera will record a still image, just as in other shooting modes. It will use the settings you have made on the abbreviated Movie mode Function menu, including white balance, My Colors, and this selection for image size. You can select Large, Medium 1 or 2, or Small, but you cannot specify the compression amount or quality, which is fixed at Fine; Superfine is not available in this shooting mode. The Raw image format also is not available when the mode dial is set to Movie mode.

Movie Resolution

The final item on the Function menu for movies provides three choices for the image quality, or pixel resolution, of your videos that are recorded in Standard mode: The first is 1920 X 1080 pixels, which is sometimes called Full HD (high-definition). With this format, the video is recorded at 24 frames per second.

The next option, 1280 X 720, can be considered to be a "standard" HD setting. It, like the Full HD setting, is a widescreen format that fits well on modern HDTVs. Videos in this format are recorded at 30 frames per second. (The frame rates discussed here are for cameras sold in the United States; cameras in other markets may use other rates, such as 25 frames per second.)

The final format selection, 640 X 480 pixels, is sometimes called the "VGA" resolution, and is a full-screen standard-definition format shot at a rate of 30 frames per second.

Choosing one of these settings should be relatively easy, because there are not many considerations involved. If you want the highest quality, the clear choice is 1920. If quality is not a major issue, because the video is just to record something such as an inventory of possessions or of items being donated, then 640 is a good choice. The 1280 format offers excellent quality without taking up as much storage space as the 1920 format. All of the movies recorded with the PowerShot S110 use the .mov file format, which is compatible with a wide range of editing software and is not difficult to work with on a computer.

Shooting Menu

When you press the Menu button to enter the Shooting menu while the camera is set to Movie mode, you will notice that there are only 11 items available for selection, as opposed to the several screens of settings for Program mode and some other still-shooting modes.

I'll discuss all of these menu options below. I won't spend much time on the items that work in the same way as they do for still pictures.

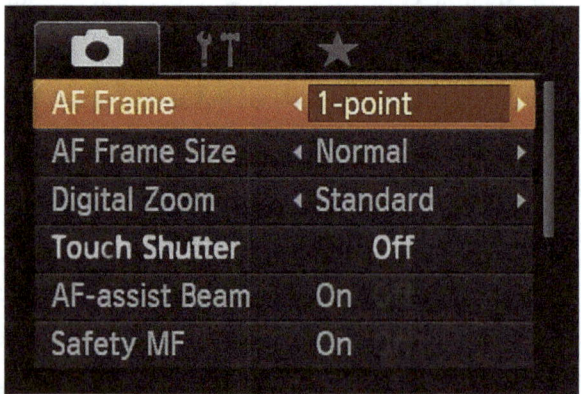

Fig. 8-5: *Shooting Menu in Movie Mode*

AF Frame

The AF Frame option, shown in Figure 8-5, lets you specify the autofocus frame to use for your video recording—Face AiAF or 1-point. These options are the same as for still shooting, but, with the 1-point setting, you cannot move the frame when the camera is in Movie mode; the 1-point frame is locked in the center of the image. Also, Touch AF is not available, so touching the screen will not direct the focus or activate the focus frame, as it does for still shooting. You can, however, change the size of the AF frame using the AF Frame Size option on the Shooting menu, discussed immediately below. The AF Frame option is available even for Super Slow Motion videos.

AF Frame Size

This second option on the Shooting menu in Movie mode is available for selection only when you have selected 1-point for the AF Frame type on the Shooting menu, as discussed above. In Movie mode, if you choose 1-point as opposed to Face AiAF, you can change the size of the autofocus frame to Small using this option on the Shooting menu. An example of the Small frame is shown in Figure 8-6.

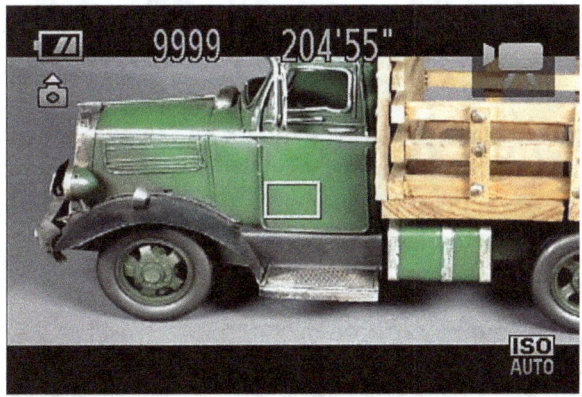

Fig. 8-6: Small AF Frame in Use in Movie Mode

This option might be useful if you are shooting video footage in which your main subject is quite small and you need

325

to make sure the focus on that small part of the image stays as sharp as possible.

Digital Zoom

Digital Zoom, the next item on the menu, works in a similar way for movies as for shooting still images. You can leave this option turned off or set it to Standard; there are no digital tele-converter settings as there are with the still-shooting modes. If you set Digital Zoom to Standard, you can zoom continuously while recording a video. The numbers showing the zoom factor on the screen will turn blue while the movie is being recorded as the zoom goes into the digital range beyond optical zoom, as shown in Figure 8-7.

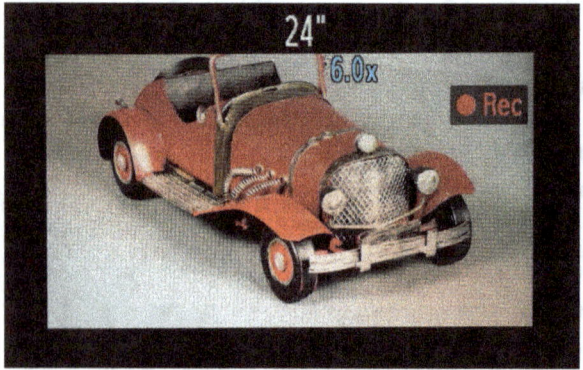

Fig. 8-7: Digital Zoom in Use in Movie Mode

Digital zoom is available with the Standard and iFrame movie modes, but not with Super Slow Motion. In fact, this menu option does not even appear on the menu if Super Slow Motion has been selected for the movie type.

Although I do not, as a rule, use digital zoom for still images, I find that it can be more useful when shooting videos, because the image quality may not be as much of a concern for videos; it may be more important to zoom in on a particular subject to emphasize it or isolate it for dramatic purposes. The ability to zoom in by a factor of 20 using digital zoom is an excellent feature to have at your fingertips for those occasions when it might be useful.

Touch Shutter

This menu option works in the same way as it does in other shooting modes, but it is effective only when you shoot a still image. In other words, when the mode dial is set to Movie mode, even if you have selected Super Slow Motion for the movie type, you can turn on the Touch Shutter feature. Then, if you touch the screen, the camera will take a picture. However, as noted above, there is no Touch AF feature available in Movie mode. You can touch the screen at any point, and the shutter will be triggered. Once you press the red Movie button to start recording a video, touching the screen with your finger will have no effect.

AF-Assist Beam

This menu option controls the use of the red lamp that helps the autofocus mechanism focus in dark areas. This feature works the same way in Movie mode as it does in other modes, but the lamp will light only when you are shooting still images. Once you have started recording a video, focus is adjusted automatically by the camera unless you have selected manual focus or used focus lock. Therefore, you cannot cause the camera to use its autofocus mechanism while a movie is being recorded; it does so on its own, and does not use the AF-Assist beam. (For Super Slow Motion movies, focus is set when the movie starts recording and is not adjusted further.)

Safety MF

This option, which lets you use the autofocus mechanism to fine-tune your manual focusing, works just as it does in other shooting modes, but it only functions for shooting still images or in adjusting focus before recording a movie. After you have made a rough attempt at setting the focus manually, you can half-press the shutter release button to cause the camera to make its best attempt to improve the focus automatically. Once you have pressed the red Movie button to start record-

327

ing a movie, the camera will adjust focus according to its own automation (unless manual focus is in effect).

Wind Filter

The wind filter option is one menu item that is of use only when recording movies. Its purpose is to reduce the hiss or other noise that can occur when recording in windy conditions. It's worth trying in those situations; it's best to disable it when there is no wind, because Canon warns that the recording could sound "unnatural" in that case.

Custom Display

This option works in much the same way as it does when the camera is recording still images—that is, it lets you select the items that appear on the two screens that result from pressing the Display button. The difference when the camera is in Movie mode is that the only options available are shooting information, grid lines, and the electronic level, as shown in Figure 8-8; the histogram option is not available in this situation.

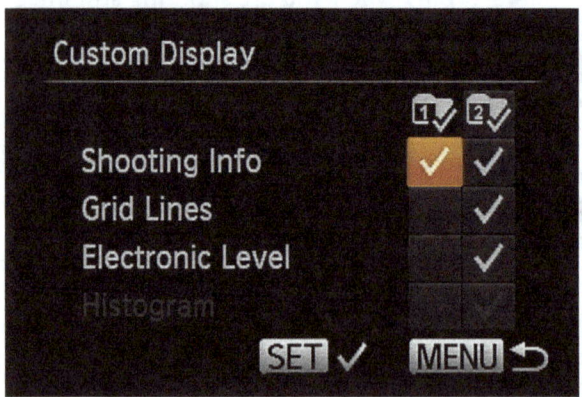

Fig. 8-8: *Custom Display Menu Option in Movie Mode*

However, the histogram is available for movies when they are displayed on the screen in playback mode, before they are actually playing. Press the Display button in playback mode to see a movie's detailed information and histogram.

IS Mode

With this option you can control the PowerShot S110's image stabilization system, just as you can when shooting still photos. However, in Movie mode, the menu only gives you two choices for IS Mode: either Continuous or Off. You can't select Shoot Only, which would not make sense for videos, because the IS system needs to keep operating continuously while recording movies. I recommend using the Continuous option whenever shooting movies unless you have the camera on a tripod; in that case, you should turn stabilization off.

Face ID Settings

This menu option works in the same way as it does in other shooting modes. You can turn the Face ID function on or off, add faces to the face registry, or edit face-detection information that was previously entered. However, the Face ID display does not operate while you are recording a video. The camera will detect faces while a video is being recorded, but it will not display names, even for registered faces.

Set Ring Function Button

Finally, Canon presents you with this menu option in Movie mode but with different options than in other shooting modes. When the mode dial is set for movie-making, this menu option lets you assign any one of the 19 possible settings to the Ring Function button, but discourages you by putting "negative" symbols (circles with lines through them) over 9 of the options, namely, those that do not function during video recording, such as ISO, continuous shooting, metering mode, and aspect ratio, as shown in Figure 8-9. If you go ahead and set one of these items anyway, it won't function during video recording, but if you later switch to a shooting mode in which it does function, the item will be active when you press the Ring Function button while the camera is in that mode.

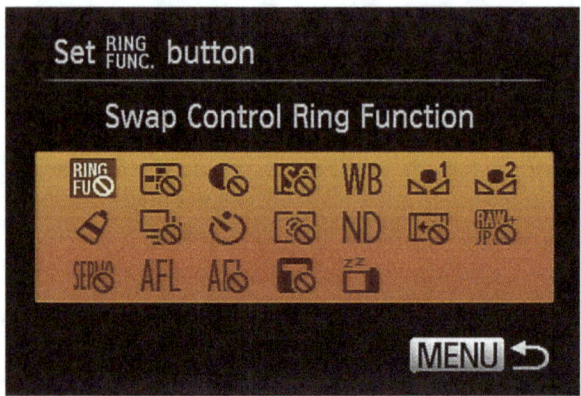

Fig. 8-9: Set Ring Function Button Option

I have discussed all of the Function menu and Shooting menu items that can be set for recording movies in Movie mode. There are still a few other items that can be set or adjusted, apart from the options on those menus. These items are discussed below.

Exposure Compensation and Exposure Lock

When you are shooting movies with the PowerShot S110, you don't have a lot of control over the exposure—the camera automatically adjusts the exposure for you. It does a good job of varying its settings as the lighting changes, so you can just rely on the camera's exposure automation in many instances. However, you do have a limited amount of exposure control available to you—before you actually start shooting.

Here are two exposure-related things you can do. First, you can use a limited amount of positive or negative exposure compensation if you believe the camera's automatic exposure will otherwise result in footage that is too bright or too dark. To do this, once the camera is in Movie mode, but before you have started recording, press the exposure compensation button (top direction button) and turn the control dial to the right or left to increase or decrease the exposure, relative to the automatic exposure the camera calculates. The exposure compensation scale that appears in the lower left of the screen in Movie mode, shown in Figure 8-10, is different from the one that appears when you're shooting still images.

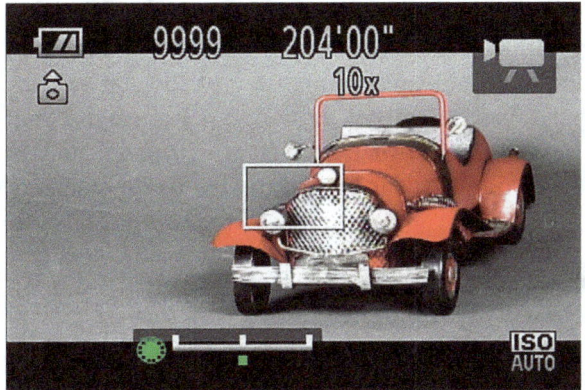

Fig. 8-10: Exposure Compensation Scale on Screen in Movie Mode

The Movie mode scale is shorter, and has no numerical markings. Use the control dial to move the green dot below the scale to the right for brighter exposure or to the left for darker exposure. When you press the Movie button to start recording the movie, the scale stays on the screen, but you cannot make any adjustments to it while the camera is recording.

Here again, as with ND Filter, this is a very useful option to have available for shooting your movies. Since you cannot adjust aperture, shutter speed, or ISO, it is helpful to have the ability to brighten or darken the scene with this feature when you are faced with a situation involving uneven or extreme lighting conditions.

Note that you cannot use the normal exposure compensation feature when shooting movies, even if you set it before starting to record the movie. For example, if you set a level of exposure compensation while the camera is in Program mode, and then press the red Movie button to start recording a video, the exposure compensation setting will have no effect. You have to have the camera set to the Movie mode to use any degree of

331

exposure compensation while shooting a movie.

Next, you can lock in a particular exposure so it stays set throughout the recording session. You might want to do this if you want the light and dark areas in your scene to appear naturally light and dark, rather than having the camera continuously adjust the exposure in an attempt to even out the lighting for all subjects that you record. Or, you might want to lock in a particular exposure for a creative reason, such as filming a "day for night" scene by making the daylight appear to be more like twilight.

Here are the steps to lock in exposure in this way. While the camera is in Movie mode, but before you have started recording, press the shutter button down halfway until you hear a beep, meaning the camera has evaluated the exposure and focus. Then release the shutter button and, within a second or two, press the up direction button. You will see the exposure compensation scale appear on the screen, looking exactly the same as shown in Figure 8-10. Now you can move the camera to any new location and the exposure will remain locked as you set it. You can also, as discussed above, adjust the exposure (before starting the video recording) by turning the control dial to move the green marker along the exposure compensation scale in either direction. When you are ready, press the red Movie button to start the movie recording with the locked exposure setting. You can unlock the exposure setting by pressing the up button again before you start recording.

Here again, as with exposure compensation, this function works for videos only when the camera is set to Movie mode. You can lock exposure using the same technique in some other shooting modes, such as Program, but that exposure lock will not have any effect while recording a video.

Control Ring

In Movie mode, the control ring around the lens can be used only for step zoom—that is, to zoom the lens to one of seven specific focal lengths: 24 mm, 28mm, 35mm, 50mm, 85mm, 100mm, or 120mm. You cannot set the ring to have any other function in this mode. The step zoom function does not operate while a movie is being recorded; you have to operate the control ring before pressing the red button to start recording. You can, however, as discussed earlier, zoom using the zoom lever during the recording.

Movie Playback

As with still images, you have the option of transferring your movies to your computer for editing and playback, or playing them back right in the camera, for displaying either on the camera's LCD or on a TV, when the camera is connected via the standard A/V cable or an optional HDMI cable.

If you play your movies in the camera, there are several options and controls available to you. First, as I discussed in Chapter 6, you can use the filtering feature to find your movies. To do this, while in playback mode, press the Menu button and select Image Search on the Playback menu. Scroll down to the fourth icon on the left side of the screen, for choosing movies or stills, as shown in Figure 8-11.

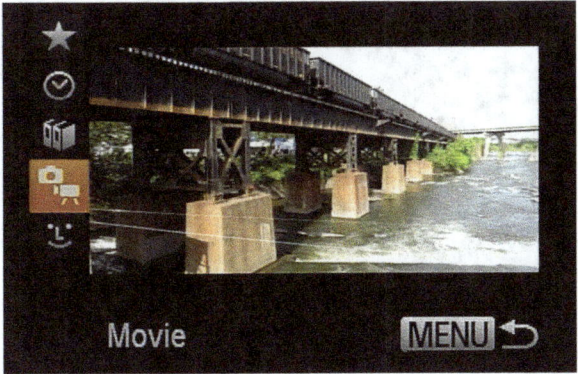

Fig. 8-11: Image Search Option to Find Movies

333

Use the right direction button, if necessary, to change the displayed category from Stills or Movie Digest to Movie, then turn the control dial to the right to start browsing through the movies that were found. The numbers in the upper right corner of the screen, as shown in Figure 8-12, will show how many movies are on the memory card, and which one of those is currently displayed.

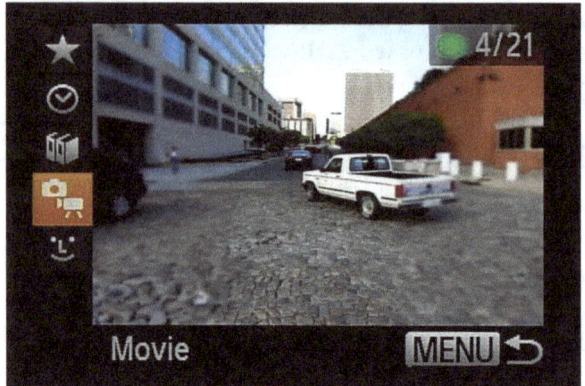

Fig. 8-12: Movies Selected for Viewing through Image Search

(That display, such as 4/21 as shown here, will disappear after a few seconds.) While the Movie category is displayed, continue to turn the control dial to scroll through the movies until you find the one you want to watch.

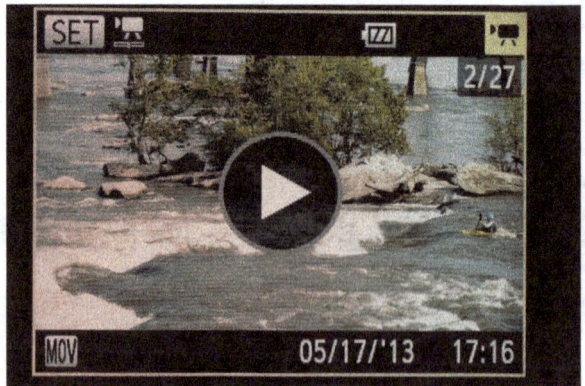

Fig. 8-13: Movie Displayed in Yellow Frame

334

Press the Func./Set button when that movie is on the screen, and its first frame will be displayed inside a yellow box, with a large Play icon in the center, as shown in Figure 8-13. You can now touch that icon with your finger to start the movie playing. If you do that, you can then pause the playback by touching the screen again. When the movie is paused, you will see an orange slider on the screen, as shown in Figure 8-14.

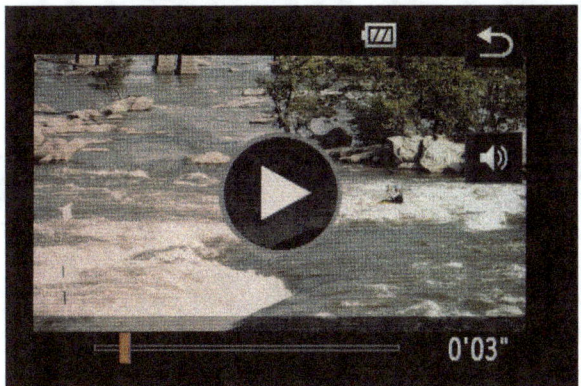

Fig. 8-14: Movie Paused with Orange Slider on Screen

You can move that slider with your finger to go forward or backward in the movie. You also can touch the speaker icon at the right of the screen and then touch the arrows that will appear along with a group of orange blocks, to raise or lower the volume. To stop the playback, press the Menu button.

The other way to control movie playback is to press the Func./Set button when the large Play icon on the screen. If you do this, a line of playback controls will appear at the bottom of the screen, as shown in Figure 8-15. From left to right, those icons represent Exit, Play, Slow Motion, Skip Backward, Previous Frame, Next Frame, Skip Forward, and Edit. Navigate through the line of icons using the left and right direction buttons or the control dial, and press the Func./Set button when the control you want to use is highlighted. The stack of orange bars at the far right indicates the volume control; you can change the volume by pressing the up and down direction buttons while

335

the icons are on the screen.

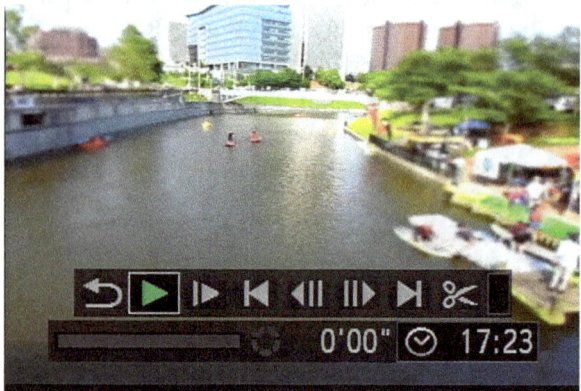

Fig. 8-15: Line of Movie Playback Controls

Several of these controls are self-explanatory, but a few need additional explanation.

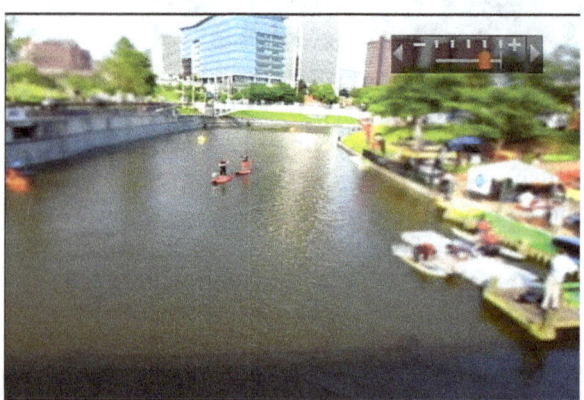

Fig. 8-16: Slow-Motion Playback Scale in Upper Right Corner

When you choose Slow Motion, you will see a scale at the upper right of the screen showing the speed of the playback, as shown in Figure 8-16; use the direction buttons or the control dial to change that speed. The Previous Frame control also acts as a Rewind control if you hold down the Func./Set button instead of just pressing it; the Skip Forward control acts the same

336

way in the other direction.

Finally, the last icon, Edit, marked by the scissors icon, can be used to mark the film for rough editing of a portion of the beginning or end of the film. After selecting the Edit icon, you will see a new panel of icons at the left side of the screen. From top to bottom, these are: Cut Beginning; Cut End; Play; Save; and Exit, as shown in Figure 8-17.

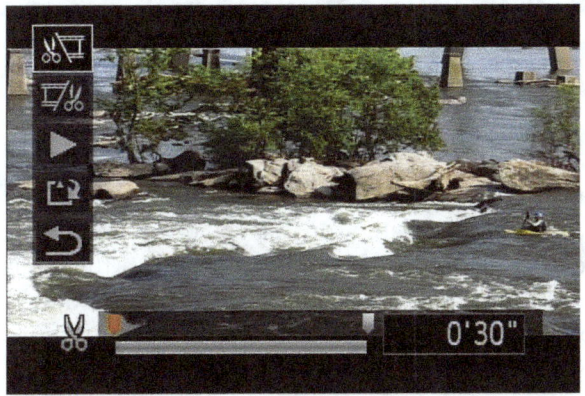

Fig. 8-17: Movie Edit Icons at Left of Screen

To carry out an edit, start by using the up and down direction buttons to highlight either of the top two icons, to trim either the start or the end of the video sequence. Then use the left and right direction buttons or the control dial to move the orange marker along the editing bar at the bottom of the screen to the point where you want to trim, either from the beginning or the end of the film. Watch for a white scissors icon to appear, as shown in Figure 8-18; when that icon appears beside the bar, you have reached a valid editing point. (If you don't stop at a scissors-marked point, the camera will use the nearest such point anyway.)

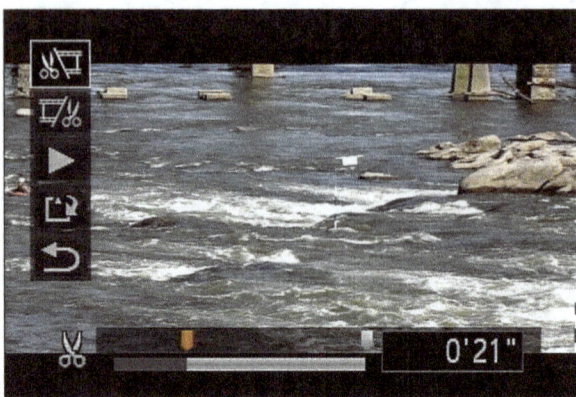

Fig. 8-18: Scissors Icon at Left Indicating Edit Point

Now you can use the down direction button to activate the Play option in the set of editing icons, so you can preview how the trimmed video will look. If necessary, you can then edit again. When you're satisfied, activate the Save icon. You are then prompted to select New File, Overwrite, or Cancel, as shown in Figure 8-19.

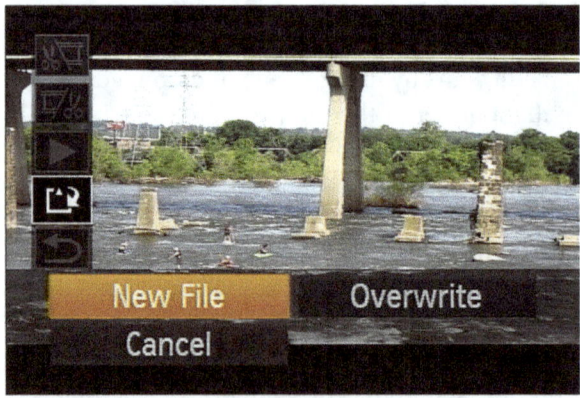

Fig. 8-19: Screen for Saving Movie After Edit

If you select Overwrite, the trimmed clip will overwrite and erase the original one; I recommend you select New File unless you are really certain you won't ever need the full clip again.

Certainly, this editing function is rudimentary and is no substitute for editing on a computer. If you're on a trip and have no other way to edit, though, this capability is much better than nothing.

Movie Digest Mode

Finally, there is one more movie-related shooting mode that needs to be discussed. This setting, which occupies its own place on the camera's mode dial, is an interesting feature of the PowerShot S110.

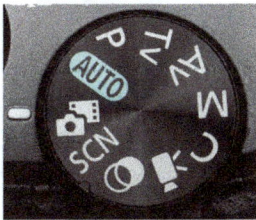

Fig. 8-20: Movie Digest Mode

The Movie Digest icon, shown in Figure 8-20, looks like a camera with a piece of film behind it. When you move the mode dial to this position, the camera sets itself up to record a very short video sequence each time you take a still picture. The camera accumulates all such video clips that are taken in this mode on any given date and assembles them into a single HD video sequence for that day that you can play back later to give you a video overview of the day's activities.

In effect, the Movie Digest mode sets the PowerShot S110 to shoot still images with the same settings as AUTO mode, but, when you press the shutter button, the camera first records a video sequence that is from two to four seconds long. This feature can be quite useful when you are on a trip with many stops or events during a given day. As you take pictures of various events and attractions, you are at the same time putting together a mini-documentary, somewhat like a television news story, that provides a video summary of the day's activities in chronological order, all ready to view at the end of the day.

If you happen to be talking while the clip is recording, your words are likely to be cut off in mid-sentence. However, the sound is not likely to be an important feature of these clips, and you may want to turn down the sound of your computer or TV set when playing back the digest clips.

Once some shots for a given day have been taken, you can view the movie digest from the Playback menu by selecting the Movie Digest Playback option and then choosing the date whose movie you want to view, as discussed in Chapter 6.

Chapter 9: Other Topics

Macro (Closeup) Shooting

Macro photography is the art or science of taking photographs when the subject is shown at actual size (1:1 ratio between size of subject and size of unenlarged image) or slightly magnified (greater than 1:1 ratio). So if you photograph a flower using macro techniques, the image on the camera's sensor will be about the same size as the actual flower. You can get wonderful detail in your images using macro photography, and you may discover things about the subject that you had not noticed before taking the photograph.

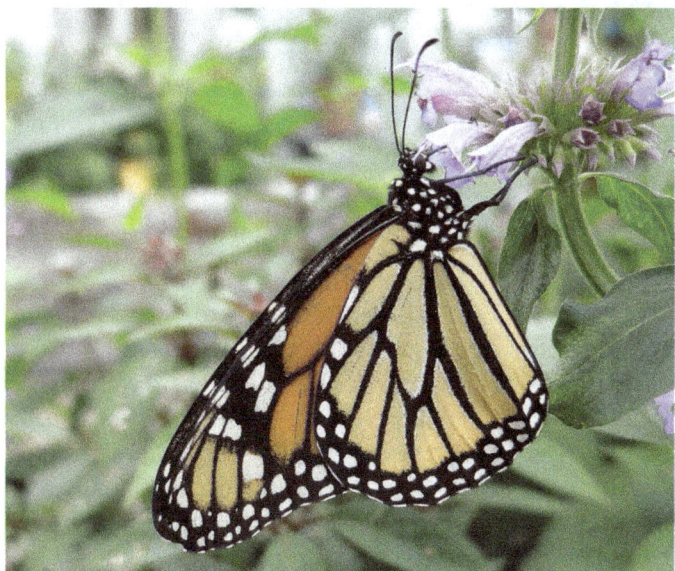

Fig. 9-1: Macro Example

The PowerShot S110, like many modern digital cameras, is quite capable of shooting macro photographs. For example, I took the image shown in Figure 9-1 at an indoor exhibition of butterflies using the High-Speed Burst HQ setting of Scene mode, with focus mode set to the macro range.

You set the autofocus system to macro focus as follows: Press the left direction button on the control dial to bring up the little menu of three icons, and press the left button again to move to the left-most choice, the flower icon, indicating macro autofocus mode, as shown in Figure 9-2.

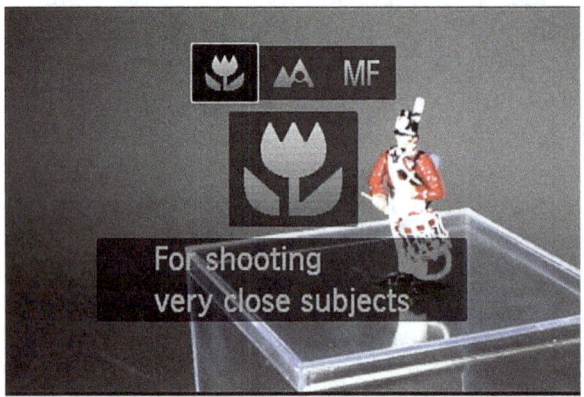

Fig. 9-2: Macro AF Icon Selected

You also can use the control dial, the touch screen, or the right direction button to move to this icon, but I find that pressing the left button repeatedly is the quickest way to do this.

With the PowerShot S110, setting the autofocus system to macro mode does not amount to a major change. In normal autofocus mode, the camera is able to focus as close as 2.0 inches (5 centimeters) from the subject, when the zoom lever is pushed all the way to the left for the wide-angle setting. In macro autofocus mode, the camera can focus a bit closer, to 1.2 inches (3 centimeters). With the lens zoomed in to the full extent of optical zoom, the camera can focus as close as 12 inches (30 cm) in either mode.

According to Canon's Camera User Guide, when the camera is in macro mode, it can only focus out to 20 inches (50 cm), whereas, in normal mode, it can focus out to infinity. In practice, the main difference between macro focus and normal focus that I have noticed is that, in macro mode, the camera will not focus at a distance when zoomed in for a telephoto shot. It appears to focus properly at any distance for a wide-angle shot, even in macro mode. However, because focus results may vary under different conditions, it is best to limit the use of macro autofocus mode to shots at a distance of no more than about 20 inches (50 cm) from the lens.

You might ask what the benefit is of using the macro setting at all, given that the camera can focus down to 2.0 inches (5 cm) even in the normal autofocus mode. The macro range of focusing as close as 1.2 inches (3 cm) does give you a slight advantage in close focusing, though not very much. It also appears that the camera may focus more reliably at close distances using the macro setting. But this does not mean that you can't focus at very close distances using the normal setting. I recommend that you try focusing at close range with the normal focus setting unless you encounter problems, and only then change to macro mode to see if that helps the camera achieve sharper focus.

You don't have to use either the macro autofocus setting or the normal autofocus setting to take macro shots; if you set the camera to manual focus by choosing the MF icon, you can also focus on objects very close to the lens. You do, however, lose the benefit of automatic focus, and it can be tricky finding the correct focus manually. If you have the Safety MF option turned on in the Shooting menu, though, you can check your focusing by pressing the shutter button down halfway after adjusting the focus manually as well as you can.

When shooting extreme closeups, you should use a tripod if at all possible given the subject matter and location, because the depth of field is very shallow at close distances and you need to keep the camera steady to take a usable photograph. It's also a good idea to take advantage of the two-second self-timer setting. If you take the picture using the self-timer, you will not be touching the camera when the shutter is activated, so the chance of camera shake is minimized. You should also leave the built-in flash retracted (set to Forced Off) so it can't fire. Flash from the built-in unit at such a close range would likely be of no use. If you need the extra lighting of a flash unit, you might want to consider using a special unit designed for close-up photography, such as a ring flash that is designed to provide even lighting surrounding the lens. Some photographers like to improvise solutions for closeup flash, such as using a piece of white plastic from a milk jug to diffuse the flash.

Using Raw Quality

I have discussed Raw images a few times in earlier chapters. Raw is a setting in the PowerShot S110's Function menu, as shown in Figure 9-3.

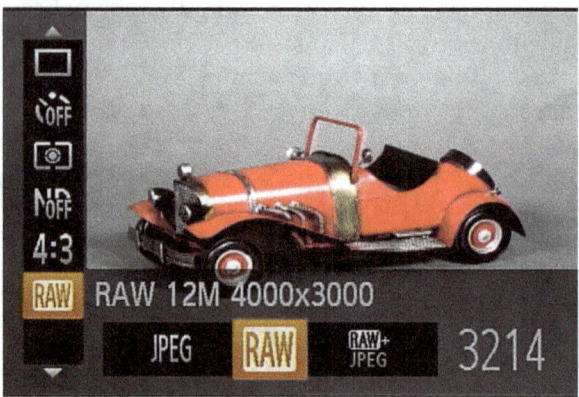

Fig. 9-3: Raw Selected for Image Type in Function Menu

The Raw format applies only to still images, not to motion pictures. When you set the image type to Raw, as opposed to JPEG, the camera records the image without any in-camera processing; essentially, it just takes in the "raw" data and records it.

344

There are both advantages and drawbacks to using Raw in this camera. First, the drawbacks. A Raw file takes up a lot of space on your memory card, and, if you copy it to your computer, a lot of space on your hard drive. Second, there are various functions of the PowerShot that won't work when you're using Raw. The functions that don't work with Raw mode include digital zoom, My Colors, i-Contrast, aspect ratio, Red-Eye Correction, Date Stamp, and certain options on the Playback menu, including Resize, Trimming, and DPOF (printing directly to a photo printer). Third, you may have problems working with Raw files on your computer, though those can be overcome.

The main advantage of using Raw is that Raw files give you an amazing amount of control and flexibility with your images. When you open up a Raw file (those from this camera have a .cr2 extension) in a compatible software program, the software gives you the opportunity to correct problems with exposure, white balance, color tints, and other settings.

Figure 9-4 shows an image as it is being opened in Adobe Camera Raw software, before being opened in Photoshop.

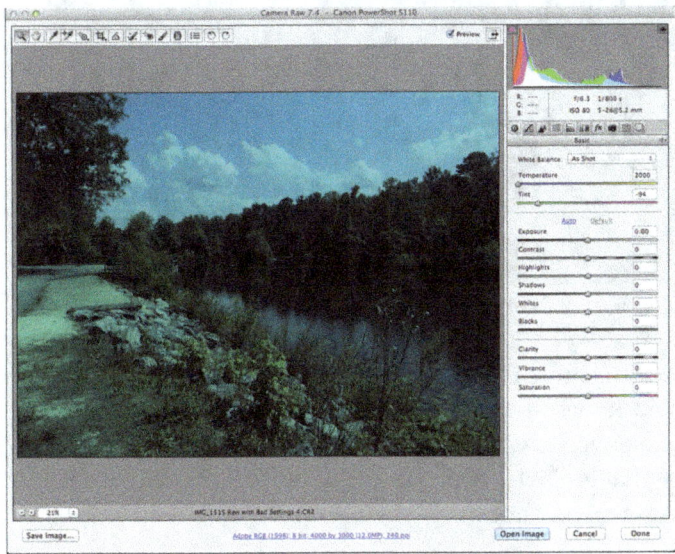

Fig. 9-4: Raw Image Being Opened in Adobe Camera Raw Software

If you had the aperture of the camera too narrow when you took the picture, and it looks badly underexposed, you can manipulate the Exposure slider in the software and recover the image to a proper exposure level. Similarly, you can adjust the white balance after the fact, and correct color tints. In effect, you get a second chance at making the correct settings, rather than being stuck with an unusable image because of unfortunate settings when you pushed the shutter button.

For example, Figure 9-5 shows a full view of the image from Figure 9-4. I took this image with the S110 using the Raw format and I purposely set the white balance to Tungsten, even though the picture was taken outdoors on a sunny day. I also purposely underexposed the shot by a considerable amount.

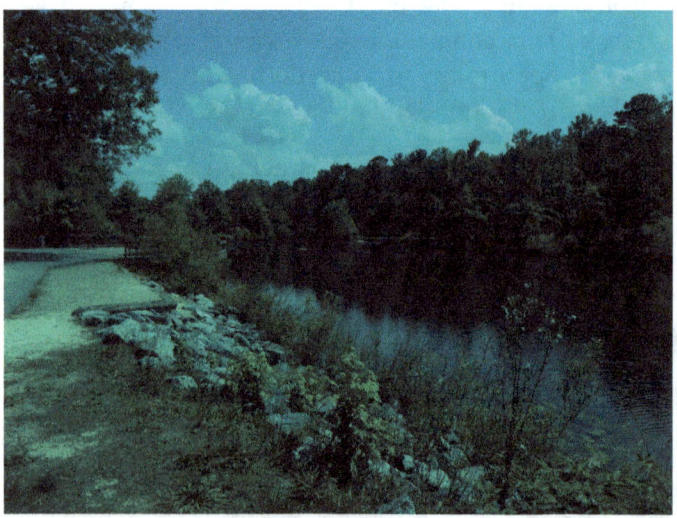

Fig. 9-5: Raw Image Taken with Improper Settings

Figure 9-6 shows the same image after I opened it up in Adobe Camera Raw software and adjusted the settings to correct the white balance and exposure. As you can see, the result was an image that looked just as it would have if I had used the correct settings when I shot it.

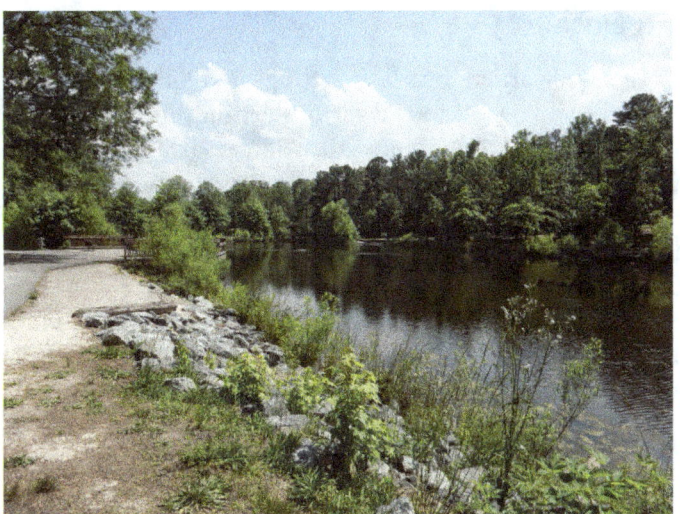

Fig. 9-6: Raw Image After Corrections in Raw Software

The drawbacks to using the Raw image type either are not too severe or they are counter-balanced by the great flexibility Raw gives you. The large size of the files may be an inconvenience, but the increasing size of hard drives and SD cards, with steadily dropping prices, makes file size much less of a concern than previously. I have heard some photographers grumble about the difficulties of having to process Raw files on the computer. That could be an issue if you don't regularly use a computer. I use my computer every day, so I don't notice. I have had problems with Raw files not loading when I didn't have the latest Camera Raw plug-in for Adobe Photoshop or Photoshop Elements, but with a little effort, you can download an updated plug-in and the software will then process and display your Raw images. The PowerShot S110 comes with Digital Photo Professional, a computer program for processing Raw files and converting them to JPEG or other formats that you can use for sending photos by e-mail and manipulating them with editing software.

The bottom line is you certainly don't have to use Raw, but you may be missing some opportunities if you avoid it.

Using Flash

As I discussed earlier, the Flash Settings item on the Shooting menu gives you access to the various settings for the built-in flash unit on the PowerShot S110. You can also get access to that sub-menu screen by pressing the Flash button (right direction button) followed quickly by the Menu button. Or, if you need access only to the basic setting of flash modes, including Auto, Forced On, Slow Synchro, and Forced Off (depending on the shooting mode), you can just press the Flash button to bring up a small menu with icons for the currently available flash modes, shown in Figure 9-7.

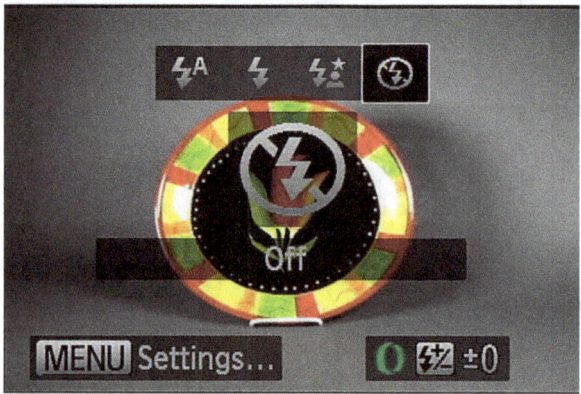

Fig. 9-7: Flash Mode Menu

Here are some general guidelines on the use of flash with this camera. What you decide about the use of flash depends to some extent on what shooting mode you select with the mode dial on top of the camera. In some shooting modes, you have no choice in the matter—the flash will be forced off and cannot be turned on. That is the case with Movie mode, the HDR setting of Creative Filters mode, and the High-Speed Burst HQ and Fireworks settings of Scene mode.

With all other shooting modes and settings, you can use the flash to some extent, though your choices are quite limited in some cases. If you are using AUTO mode, you can set the flash mode to Auto Flash or Forced Off. The camera may make its own decision to use Slow Synchro mode, though you cannot make that choice. With all of the Creative Filters settings except HDR, you can choose Auto Flash, Forced On, or Forced Off. The same is true for all of the Scene mode settings other than Fireworks and High-Speed Burst HQ, except that, with Handheld Night Scene, the camera may choose Slow Synchro, and with Stitch Assist you cannot use Auto Flash.

In Program mode, you can choose any of the flash mode settings; in other advanced shooting modes, the choices are more limited. In the Shutter Priority and Manual exposure modes, you can choose only Forced On or Forced Off; in Aperture Priority mode, you can choose Forced On, Slow Synchro, or Forced Off.

To consider the full range of flash options, let's assume you're shooting in Program mode. Now you have to decide whether to choose Auto Flash, Forced On, Slow Synchro, or Forced Off.

Let's start with Forced Off, probably the easiest choice to make. It's very useful to have this setting available, so you can be certain that the flash will not fire. Obviously, in certain environments it would be embarrassing or worse to have a flash go off, such as in a museum that allows cameras but not flash, or in a church or other religious setting. Also, you may prefer not to risk having the harsh lighting that often results from on-camera flash units, or you just may prefer to exercise your creative skills as a photographer to avoid the easy solution of lighting up the scene with flash.

A harder question to answer may be why you would want to use the Forced On setting, ensuring that the flash will fire, when you could use the Auto Flash setting and let the camera decide whether flash is needed. One case is when there is enough backlighting that the camera's exposure controls could be fooled into thinking the flash isn't needed. If, in your judgment, the subject will be too dark for that reason, you may want to force the flash to fire. Another such situation could be

349

an outdoor portrait for which you need fill-in flash to highlight your subject's face adequately. For example, for Figure 9-8, I took two photographs of a mannequin head outdoors on a partly cloudy day. I used Program mode, and all settings were identical except that, with the top image I did not use flash, and with the bottom one I used the Forced Flash setting.

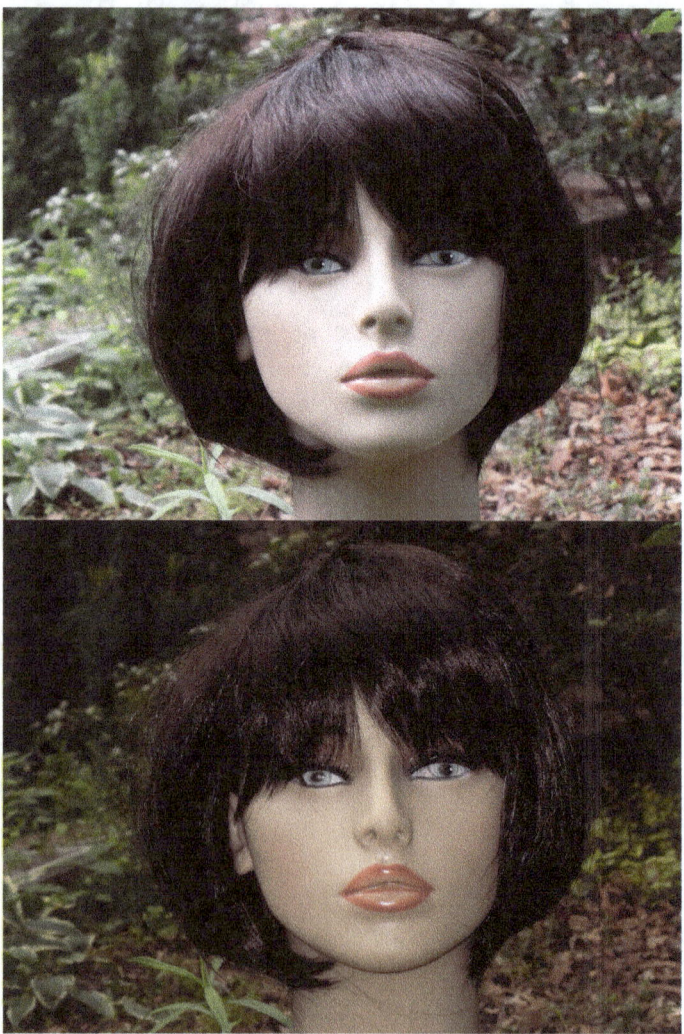

Fig. 9-8: Top Image No Flash - Bottom Image Fill Flash

350

As you can see, although flash was not needed in order to expose the image properly, the addition of flash made a fairly dramatic difference in the appearance of the mannequin. With flash, the head has a different coloration, there are different highlights on the lips and hair, and the shadow areas around the eyes are brightened, for example.

What about Slow Synchro? With this option, whose icon is shown in Figure 9-9, the camera sets a relatively slow shutter speed so that the ambient (natural) lighting will have time to register on the image along with the flash exposure.

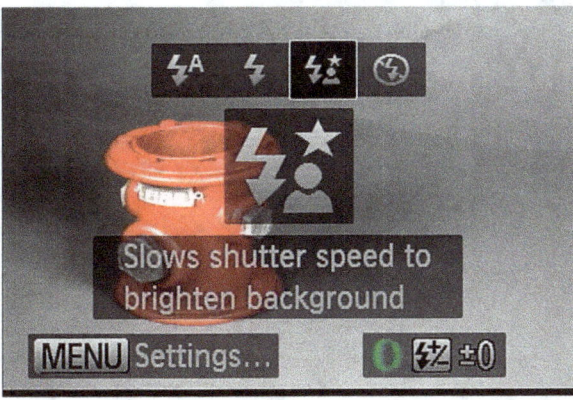

Fig. 9-9: Slow Synchro Icon Selected

In other words, if you're in a fairly dark environment and fire the flash normally, it will likely light up the subject (say a person), but because the exposure time is short, the surrounding scene may be black. If you use the Slow Synchro setting, the slower shutter speed allows the surrounding scene to be visible also.

The two example images shown here were taken by the S110 with identical room lighting and camera settings, except that Figure 9-10 was taken with the flash set to Forced On, resulting in an exposure of f/5.9 at 1/60 second, and Figure 9-11 was taken with the flash set to Slow Synchro, resulting in an exposure of f/5.9 for one full second. In the first image, the flash illuminated the doll in the foreground, but the background is dark. In the second image, the doll is lighted by the flash in the same way as in the first image, but this time the room beyond the doll is illuminated by ambient light, because of the much longer shutter speed.

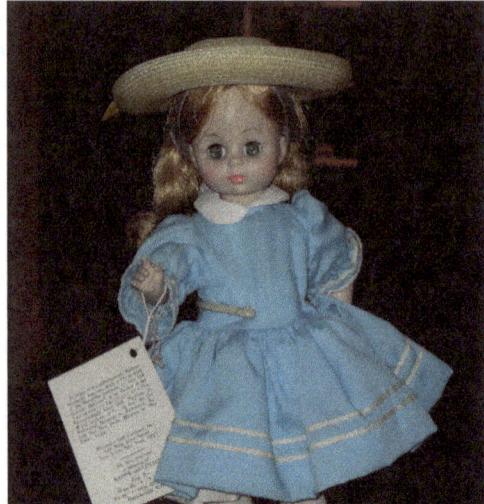

Fig. 9-10:   Fill Flash at 1/60 Second

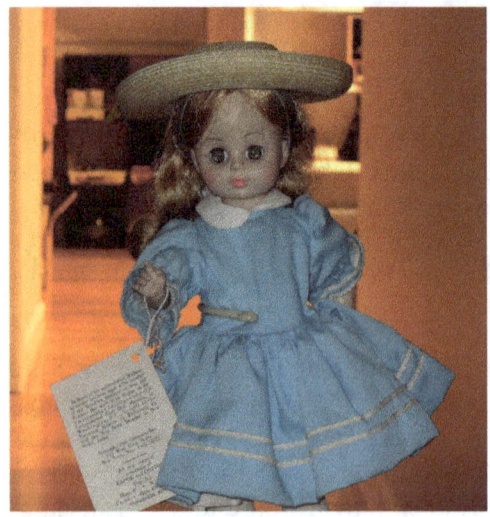

Fig. 9-11:   Slow Synchro at 1 Second

Finally, in the Program shooting mode you have the option of setting the Flash mode to Auto. Auto Flash gives the camera a chance to use its programming to determine the best setting. You might choose that route when you want to use some of the advantages of Program mode, such as the ability to use the Raw format or the My Colors settings, or to adjust the ISO, white balance, or metering method, but would like to let the camera decide when and if to use flash.

Other Flash Settings

Apart from the main flash modes, there are several other flash settings that you can take advantage of, all of which were discussed in Chapter 4 in connection with the Flash Settings item on the Shooting menu: Flash Mode (Auto or Manual), Flash Output (Minimum, Medium, or Maximum), Shutter Sync. (1st-curtain or 2nd-curtain), Red-Eye Correction (On or Off), Red-Eye Lamp (On or Off), and Safety FE (On or Off).

In addition to those settings, there is one other flash-related setting to discuss—FE lock, or Flash Exposure lock. This option is similar to AE lock (Auto Exposure lock), discussed earlier, which locks in a metered exposure so you can aim the camera at a different subject with the locked exposure settings. However, FE lock works when you will be using flash.

To use FE lock, set the camera to Program shooting mode and set the flash to Forced On, using the Flash button. Then, aim at your subject and press the shutter button down halfway to evaluate the exposure. While still holding down the shutter button, press the up direction button. The flash will fire so that the camera can evaluate the exposure with the flash, and you will see an asterisk (*) on the LCD screen, to the left of the shutter speed, as shown in Figure 9-12.

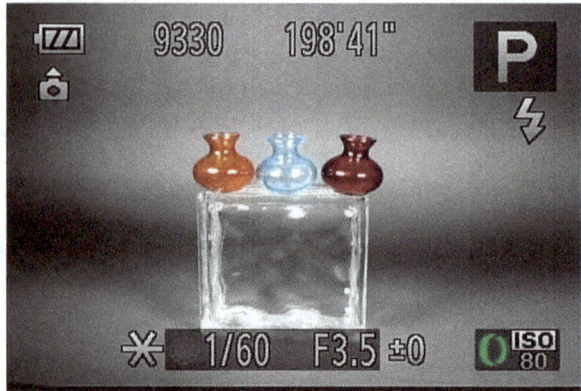

Fig. 9-12: Flash Exposure Lock in Effect

The exposure indicated on the LCD will now be locked in, and you can move the camera to another subject (or leave it aimed at the same subject) to take the picture using the locked-in exposure setting, with the flash firing. You can also activate FE lock by setting the Ring Function button to the AEL setting, as described in Chapter 5.

Infrared Photography

Infrared photography involves finding a way for the camera to record images that are illuminated by infrared light, which is invisible to the human eye because it occupies a place on the spectrum of light waves that is beyond our ability to see. In some circumstances, cameras, unlike our eyes, can record images using this type of light. The resulting photographs can be quite spectacular, producing scenes in which green foliage appears white and blue skies appear eerily dark.

Shooting infrared pictures in the times before digital photography involved selecting a particular infrared film and the appropriate filter to place on the lens. With the rise of digital imaging, you need to find a camera that is capable of "seeing" infrared light. Many cameras nowadays include internal filters that block infrared light. However, some cameras do not, or block it only to a relatively small extent. (You can do a quick

354

test of any digital camera by aiming it at the light-emitting end of an infrared remote control and taking a photograph while pressing a button on the remote; if the remote's light shows up as bright white, the camera can "see" infrared light at least to some extent.)

The PowerShot S110 is quite capable of taking infrared photographs. In order to unleash this capability, you need get a filter that blocks most visible light, but lets infrared light reach the camera's light sensor. (If you don't, the infrared light will be overwhelmed by the visible light, and you'll get an ordinary picture based on visible light.)

You can purchase an infrared filter and an adapter that lets you attach the filter securely to the camera. There is an adapter available from a company called Lensmate, which I discuss in Appendix A. The infrared filter I have seen most often recommended is the Hoya R72, and I have used that one as well as a similar one from Opteka. The filter is a very dark red and blocks most visible light, letting in mainly infrared light rays in the part of the spectrum that tends to yield interesting photographs. Figure 9-13 shows the Opteka 37mm R72 filter attached to the PowerShot S110 using the Lensmate adapter.

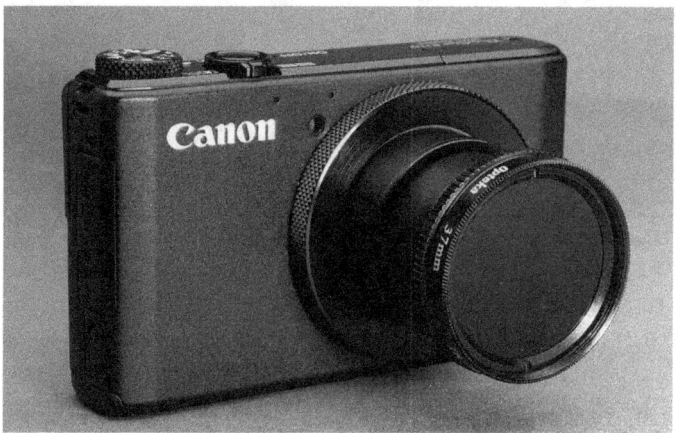

Fig. 9-13: Infrared Filter Attached to PowerShot S110 with Adapter

For the image shown here, I set a custom white balance, using brightly sunlit green foliage as the base. That is, I used the camera's white balance menu setting in the Function menu, and, using the screen for setting a custom white balance, I aimed the camera at the foliage and pressed the Ring Function button to lock in that setting.

For exposure, I set the camera to shoot in Aperture Priority mode and let it select the shutter speed, which was slightly long because of the dark filter, so I set the camera on a tripod. The PowerShot S110 exposed the image for 0.4 second at f/5.0, with an ISO setting of 1600. The image had a green tint, so I converted the image to black and white in Photoshop to give it a more conventional infrared appearance.

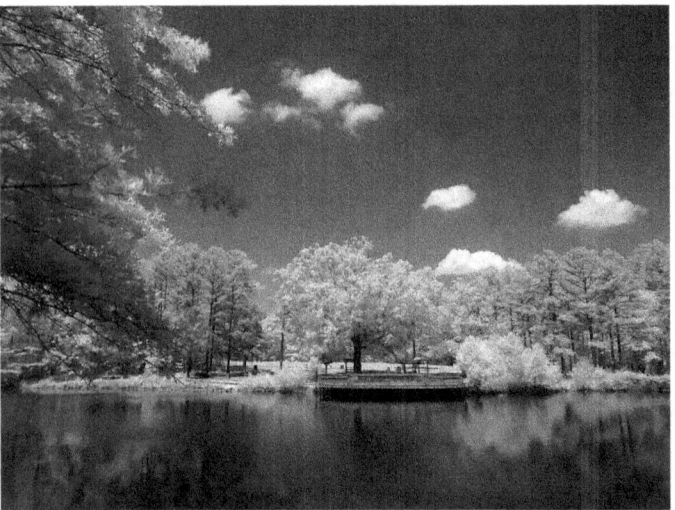

Fig. 9-14: Infrared Example Image

The results, seen in Figure 9-14, were essentially what I expected from infrared photography: a scene with tree leaves and grass that look almost white, and other unusual, but pleasing effects, including a darkened sky and contrasting white clouds. You can often get interesting results if you include a good amount of green grass and trees in the image, as well as blue sky and clouds.

Street Photography

One of the reasons many users prize the PowerShot S110 is because it is very well suited for street photography—that is, for shooting candid pictures in public settings, often without the subject being aware of your activity. The camera has several features that make it well-suited for this type of work—it is small, lightweight, and unobtrusive in appearance, so it can easily be held casually or hidden in the photographer's hand. Its 24mm equivalent wide-angle lens is excellent for taking in a broad field of view, for times when you shoot from the hip without framing the image carefully on the screen. Its f/2.0 lens lets in plenty of light, and it performs well at high ISO settings, so you can use a relatively fast shutter speed to avoid motion blur. You can make the camera almost completely silent by turning off the beeps and shutter sounds.

As far as the best settings are concerned, I'm going to give you some fairly broad guidelines as a starting point. The answer depends in part on your own personal style of shooting, such as whether you will talk to your subjects and get their agreement to being photographed before you start shooting, or whether you will fire away from across the street with a palmed camera and hope you are getting a usable image.

Here are a couple of approaches you can start with and modify as you see fit. One method that some photographers like is to shoot in Raw, and then use post-processing software such as Photoshop or Lightroom to convert your images to black and white, along with any other effects you are looking for, such as extra grain to achieve a gritty look. (Of course, you don't have to produce your street photography in black and white, but that is a common practice.) If you decide to shoot in Raw, you can't use settings such as My Colors or i-Contrast. You can, however, play around with your basic exposure settings. I recommend you shoot in Shutter Priority mode at a fairly fast shutter speed, say, 1/100 second or faster, to stop action on the

357

street and to avoid blur from camera movement. You can set ISO to Auto, or possibly use a high ISO setting, in the range of 800 or so, if you don't mind some visual noise. You may want to set the aspect ratio to 4:3 in order to use all available pixels and have options for cropping your images later.

In the alternative, you can set the image type to JPEG, at Large size and Superfine quality, to take advantage of the camera's image-processing capabilities. To get the gritty "street" look, try using the My Colors B/W setting, with ISO set somewhat high, in the range of 800 or above, to include some visual grain in the image while boosting sensitivity enough to stop action with a fast shutter speed.

Or, you might try turning the mode dial to the Creative Filters setting and using the Nostalgic scene type, with its intensity dialed all the way up to the maximum using the control dial to get a completely desaturated (black and white) image with some built-in grainy effect. Of course, when you're using a Creative Filters or Scene mode setting, you don't have as many other menu settings available, but if this mode gives you the effect you're looking for, it's worth trying.

Also, consider turning on continuous shooting so you'll get several images to choose from for each shutter press. You may want to use the High-Speed Burst HQ setting that is available in Scene mode, with its bursts of 10 shots at up to 10 frames per second.

When you're ready to start shooting, select manual focus and set the focus to roughly the distance you expect to shoot at, such as 6 feet (2 meters) on the MF scale. When you're ready to snap a picture, press the shutter button halfway to make a quick fine-tuning of the focus. (Make sure that Safety MF is turned on in the Shooting menu. I would also turn off MF-point Zoom, because the enlarged area on the screen could make it hard to compose the shot.) Some street photographers find this method to be faster and more efficient than relying on the autofocus system. For any of this sort of shooting, I suggest that you leave the lens zoomed back to its full wide-angle position, unless a specific situation comes up when you can hold the camera very steady and zoom in on a specific subject.

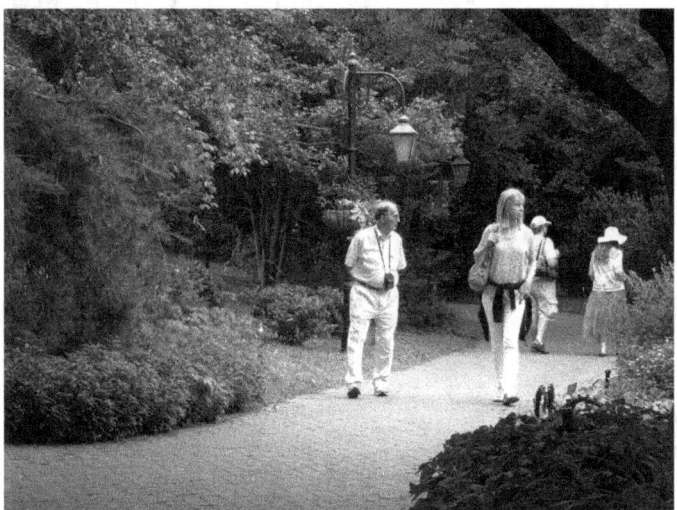

Fig. 9-15: Street Photography Example

For the photo shown in Figure 9-15, even though I was shooting images in a botanical garden filled with colorful subjects, I decided to use the My Colors B/W setting in Program mode to photograph some of the people browsing through the grounds. It seemed to me that the black and white option worked well for highlighting the contrast between the light clothing of the people and the dark areas of the trees and bushes.

Using the Wi-Fi Features of the S110

As I discussed in Chapter 1, you can transfer your images and videos wirelessly from the PowerShot S110 to your computer, tablet, or smartphone using an Eye-Fi card, which is a special type of SD card with a built-in transmitter. With the S110, though, Canon has added Wi-Fi features to the camera itself, thereby removing the need to spend extra money for a specialized memory card to transfer images over a wireless network.

I will not try to explain all aspects of the Wi-Fi features of the S110 in this book; the Canon Camera User Guide devotes 51 pages to the many details that are involved in setting up and using various types of wireless network connections between the camera and computers, smartphones, and other devices. You should consult that guide for the technical details.

In this discussion, I will provide an overview of the S110's Wi-Fi features and the steps involved in connecting the camera to a computer. I also will discuss briefly how to connect the camera to a smartphone to add GPS location data to your images.

Overview of Wi-Fi Features

The PowerShot S110 comes with a powerful set of wireless connection features built in. Once you have gone through the technical steps involved in setting up a connection, you can transfer images from the camera to various internet services, such as Facebook, YouTube, and Twitter, through a portal called the Canon Image Gateway. You also can connect the camera to a smartphone or tablet, such as an iPhone, iPad, or Android device, and send images to the device. If the phone or tablet includes Global Positioning System (GPS) features, you can geotag your images through the connection from the device. In other words, you can use the phone or other device to obtain satellite information about the geographical position of an image, and send the data to the camera so the information can be recorded with the image.

In addition, just as with an Eye-Fi card, you can set up a connection that lets you transfer your images wirelessly over a Wi-Fi network from the camera to a computer. I will discuss the steps involved in that process later in this chapter.

You also can connect the S110 to another Canon camera that has the ability to make this connection, and you can connect the camera to a printer that uses the PictBridge protocol and has Wi-Fi features, so you can print your images directly on that printer.

Connecting the Camera by Wi-Fi to a Computer

As I noted above, I am not going to discuss all of the S110's Wi-Fi capabilities in this book. Instead, I will describe the steps involved for one operation—connecting the camera to a computer so you can transfer images. I chose this procedure in part because I believe it is one of the most useful applications for the Wi-Fi features. If you can connect to your computer wirelessly, then you can transfer images quickly and without the need to take a memory card from the camera and put it in a card reader, or to connect the camera to the computer with a USB cable. You also avoid the expense of purchasing an Eye-Fi card or other memory card that has its own Wi-Fi features.

In my case, I use a Macintosh desktop computer. I will describe the steps that are used to connect this computer to the S110 and transfer some pictures.

First, you need to give the camera a nickname so it can be identified on the network. To do this, you put the S110 into playback mode, with any screen displayed other than the detailed screen with the histogram. (If that screen is displayed, the up button is used for toggling the RGB histogram, and that button is needed for the wireless network setup.)

Next, press the up button, and you will see the screen shown in Figure 9-16.

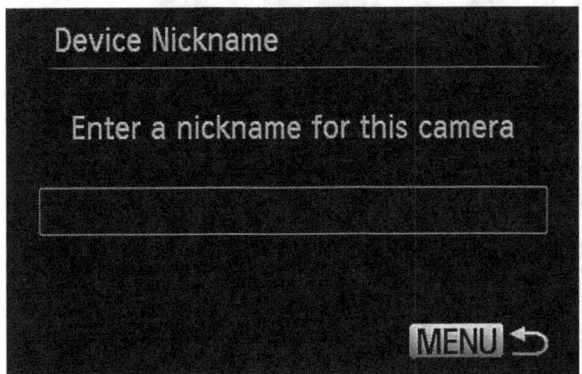

Fig. 9-16: Screen for Setting Device Nickname

If you have not previously given your S110 a nickname, this screen will prompt you to do so. You can enter a name of up to 16 characters using the touch-screen keyboard. Then press the Menu button and follow the prompts to proceed to the next screen, shown in Figure 9-17, where the camera will prompt you to select a device that it can connect to wirelessly.

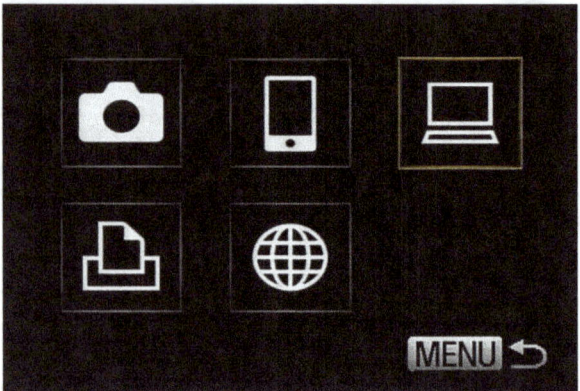

Fig. 9-17: Wi-Fi Device Selection Screen

On that screen, highlight the icon for a computer and press OK; the camera then searches for wireless access points within range, and shows a screen like the one in Figure 9-18, with a list of those networks.

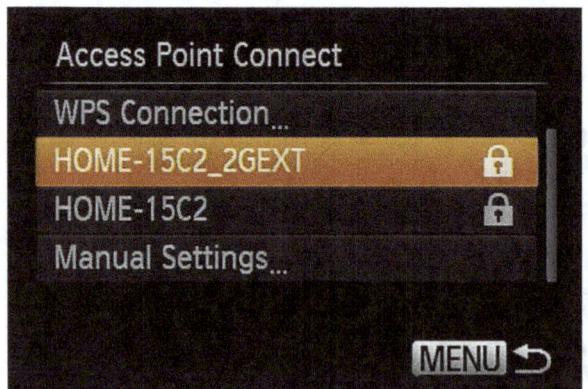

Fig. 9-18:   List of Wireless Access Points Available for Connection

In my case, I selected my network, and the camera prompted me as shown in Figure 9-19 to enter the password.

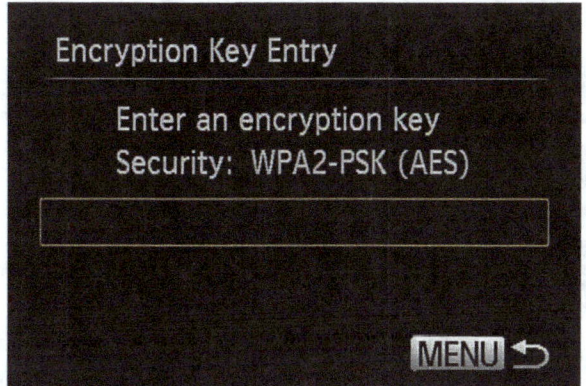

Fig. 9-19: Screen for Entering Wi-Fi Password

After a screen of configuration, where I chose Auto for Network Settings, the camera searched for and connected to my computer on the designated network; it then showed the name of my Mac Pro computer on the Select a Device screen, as shown in Figure 9-20.

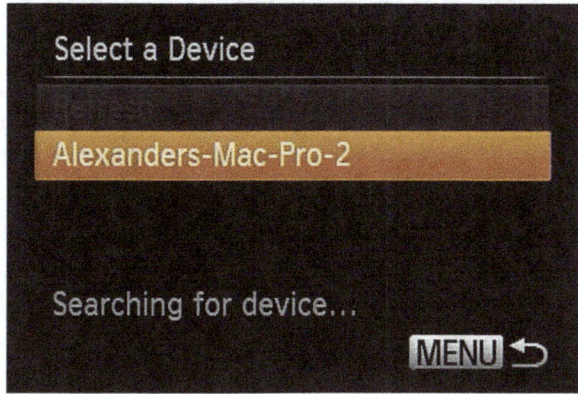

Fig. 9-20: Screen Shown After Camera Finds Computer on Network

On that screen, I touched the name of my computer to select it, and the computer then automatically opened the Canon

Camera Window application, as shown in Figure 9-21.

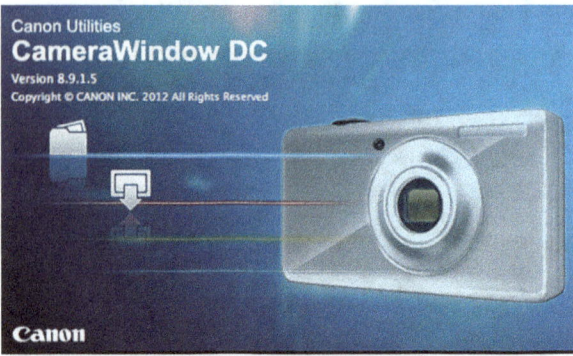

Fig. 9-21: Canon Camera Window Software Screen

When I clicked on its main screen, the program moved to the selection screen shown in Figure 9-22, where I could choose to upload images from the camera to the computer.

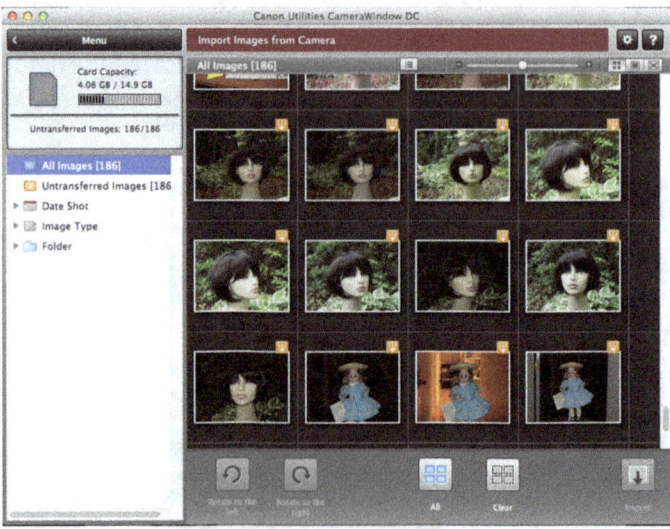

Fig. 9-22: Canon Camera Window Image Selection Screen

I eventually uploaded several images to my Macintosh wirelessly using this system. For whatever reason, perhaps some glitch in my network, the uploading process was very slow, taking several minutes to transfer just six JPEG images. However, the connection did work, and with some tweaking this system could become a very useful addition to your workflow.

Of course, you may find it more useful to connect your Power-Shot S110 to a smartphone, to connect to the internet to share images, or to print from the camera wirelessly to a printer, all of which are possible with the built-in Wi-Fi capabilities of the camera.

Adding GPS Location Data to Images

If you connect the camera to a smartphone that has GPS capability, you can use that connection to tag your photos with GPS data. For example, here are the steps to add GPS data to your images if you are using an iPhone. First, press the up button on the camera in playback mode to get access to the Wi-Fi screen, and select the smartphone icon. Choose Add a Device from that screen, and then choose Set Camera as Access Point. You then need to go to the Settings screen on the iPhone, select the Wi-Fi network that will be transmitted from the camera, and enter into the iPhone the password that is shown on the camera's screen.

Then, on the iPhone, you need to start up the Canon CameraWindow app, which can be downloaded for free. Once the camera is connected to the iPhone over the camera's Wi-Fi network, you will see a screen like that shown in Figure 9-23.

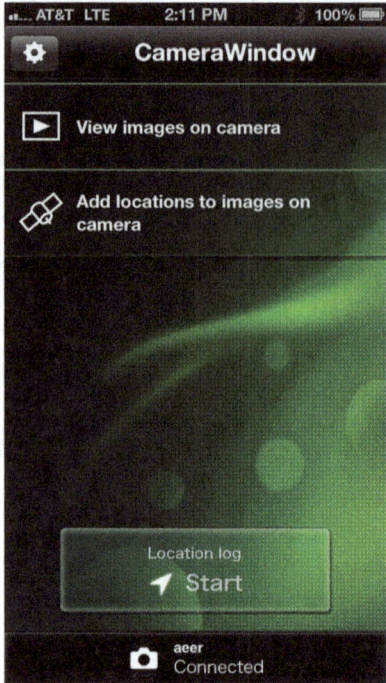

Fig. 9-23: CameraWindow App on iPhone

On that screen on the iPhone, select Location Log–Start. Then, as you take pictures with the PowerShot S110 while the app is activated, the iPhone will record the locations according to the times the pictures are taken.

Later, when you have finished taking pictures, go to the same screen while the two devices are connected, and select Add Locations to Images on Camera. The iPhone will then transmit its GPS location information for each image that was taken while the location log was being recorded. For any of those images, you can call up the location screen from the detailed display in playback mode. First, press the up button to call up the RGB histogram screen, then press that button again to call up the GPS screen, as seen in Figure 9-24.

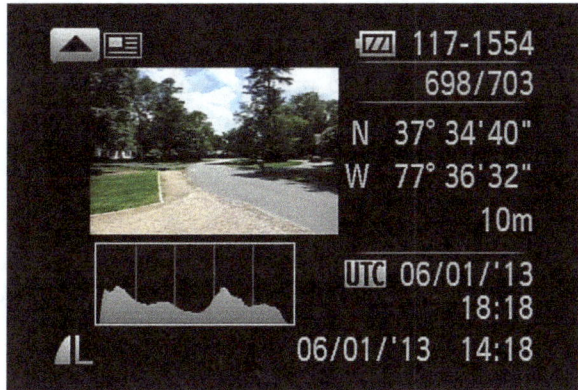

Fig. 9-24: GPS Location Information Screen

Connecting to a Television Set

The PowerShot S110 is quite capable of playing back its still images and videos on an external television set—either a standard-definition set or an HDTV. The camera does not come with any audio-video cable as standard equipment, so you have to purchase your own to connect to either type of set.

To connect to a standard TV, you need Canon's special audio-video cable or the equivalent, two versions of which are shown in Figure 9-25.

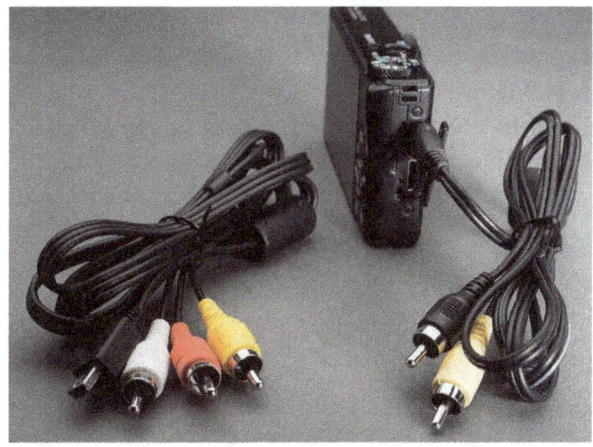

Fig. 9-25: Audio-Video Cables for Connecting Camera to TV

The monophonic cable, with just one channel of sound, shown at the right in this image, has part number AVC-DC400. If you prefer having two audio plugs to provide stereo sound, you can use model number AVC-DC400ST, shown at the left.

Either cable has Canon's special connector at one end and two or three composite, or RCA, connectors at the other end. The red and white RCA plugs are for stereophonic audio, left and right; the black plug is for monophonic audio; the yellow plugs are for composite video.

To connect the cable to the camera, you need to open the little door on the camera's right side (when held in shooting position) and plug the small Canon connector into the upper one of the two ports inside the door.

Then connect the appropriate plugs to the composite video and audio inputs of a television set. You may need to set the TV's input selector to Video 1, AUX, or some other setting so it will switch to the input from the camera.

Once the connections are set and the TV is turned on with the correct input selected, turn on the camera in playback mode, and you can play back any images or videos you have recorded. HD video will play back with no problems on a standard television set.

You also can purchase an optional HDMI cable to connect the camera to an HD television set. You can purchase Canon's official HTC-100 cable, or you can use any generic HDMI cable, as long as one end has a mini-HDMI male connector and the other end has a standard HDMI male connector, as shown in Figure 9-26.

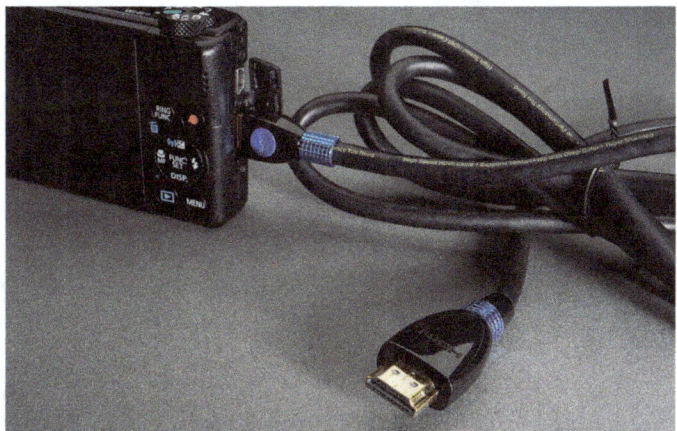

Fig. 9-26:   HDMI Cable for Connecting Camera to HDTV

Once you have connected the camera to a TV set, the camera operates very much the same way it does on its own. Of course, depending on the size and quality of the TV set, you will likely get a much larger image, possibly better quality (on an HD set), and certainly better sound.

When the camera is connected to a TV with the standard video cable, it not only can play back recorded images; it also can record. When it is hooked up to a TV while in recording mode, you can see on the TV screen the live image being seen by the camera. In that way, you can use the TV screen as a large monitor to help you compose your photographs and videos. (This capability is not available when the camera is connected to the TV by an HDMI cable.)

APPENDIX A: Accessories

When people buy a new camera, especially a fairly expensive model like the PowerShot S110, they often ask what accessories they should buy to go with it. I will cover some highlights, sticking mostly with items I have used personally. For example, I won't provide any details about the Canon waterproof case, model number WP-DC47, because I don't have any experience with that item.

Cases

There are many types of camera cases on the market. In selecting a case for my PowerShot S110, I looked at many different types. I came to the realization that, at least for me, there is no single "perfect" case for the S110. The type of case I use with this camera depends on what activity I am involved in, and what my purpose is for carrying the camera at a given time.

For example, when I am engaged in day-to-day non-photographic activities but want to have a good camera handy in case a photographic opportunity presents itself, I often put the S110 into a Lowepro Tahoe 30 case, shown in Figure A-1.

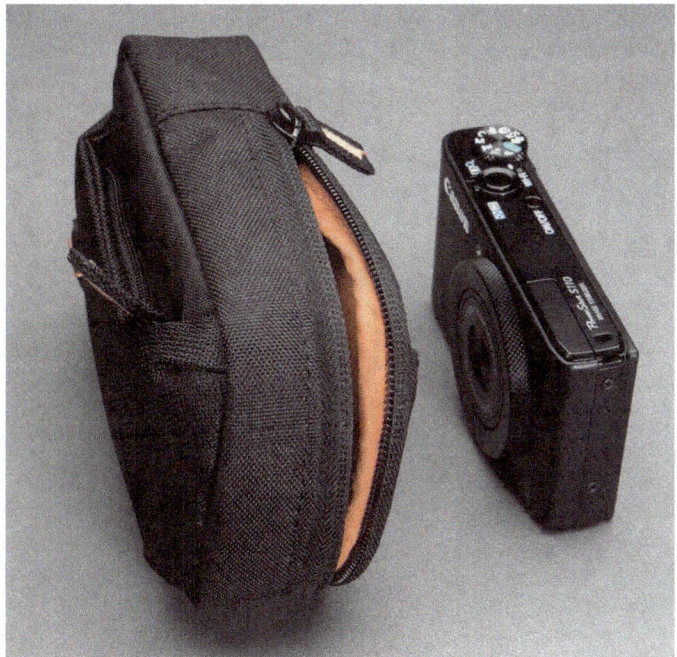

Fig. A-1: Lowepro Tahoe 30 Case with PowerShot S110

This soft black case is very compact, with just enough room to fit the camera comfortably inside and zip shut securely. There is not much room for extra batteries, memory cards, or other accessories, but that's the way I like it. After all, one of the great virtues of the S110 is its small size, so it doesn't make sense to stick the camera into a large, bulky case with a lot of additional items when you're just keeping the camera handy in case you see a good picture and want to grab it. (If you want an even smaller case that still provides a good fit, try the Lowepro Tahoe 10 or the Case Logic TBC-302.)

When I'm going on a trip that's specifically oriented to photography, I put the camera in a larger case, though I usually also leave it inside the Tahoe 30 case, at least at the outset, for extra protection.

371

I recently enjoyed a day trip using a waist pack made by Lowepro, the Inverse 100AW, shown in Figure A-2, which has room for the camera, some accessories, and a couple of small water bottles.

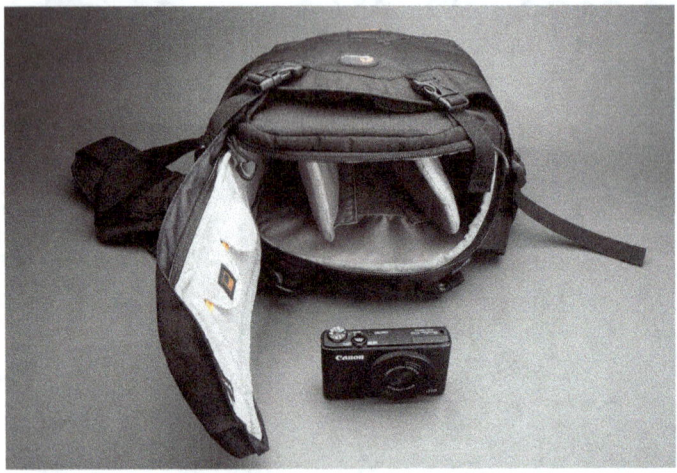

Fig. A-2: Lowepro Inverse 100AW Case with S110

Batteries

This is one item you should seriously consider purchasing either when you get the camera or right afterwards. I use the camera pretty heavily, and I find it runs through batteries quickly. You can't use disposable batteries, so if you're out taking pictures and the battery dies, you're out of luck unless you have a spare battery (or an AC adapter and a place to plug it in; see below). The model number of the official Canon battery is NB-5L. You don't necessarily have to buy a Canon-branded battery; there are other brands available that will do just as well. For example, some generic replacements for this model of battery are currently on sale at Amazon.com for less than $10.00, with many positive user ratings. I have used the SterlingTek replacement battery shown in Figure A-3, and it has worked well.

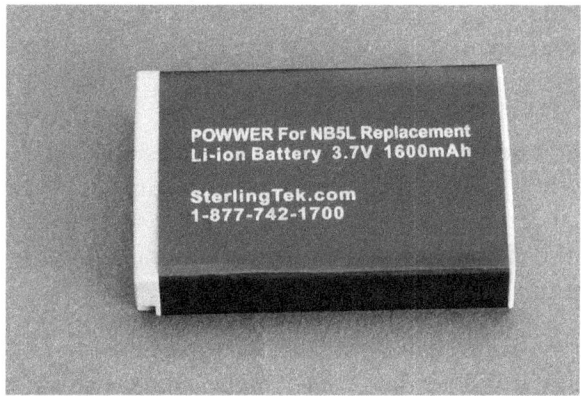

Fig. A-3: Generic Battery by SterlingTek

However, you need to use some caution and common sense; there probably are some "super-cheap" batteries that are not a good idea to use. I rely on the dealer's reputation to avoid shoddy merchandise in that sort of situation. I have had excellent online shopping experiences with B&H Photo-Video, 17th Street Photo, and Amazon.com, among others.

AC Adapter

The other alternative for supplying power to the S110 is the AC adapter kit, Canon model number ACK-DC30, shown in Figure A-4.

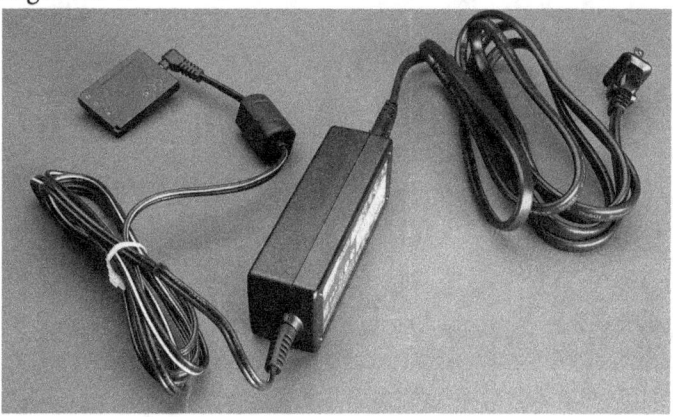

Fig. A-4: AC Adapter ACK-DC30

There is not too much to say about this accessory. It works well for what it does, in terms of providing a constant source of power to the camera. It consists of three parts: a standard-sized AC cord that you plug into a power brick and into an AC outlet; the fairly large power brick, which is attached to a long cable ending in a small connector that plugs into the camera; and an item called a DC coupler, which is exactly the size of the camera's battery, and fits into the camera's battery compartment in place of the battery.

The DC coupler has a small jack into which you plug the cord that comes from the power brick. Each of the two power cables is about 79 inches (2 meters) long, so the whole AC adapter assembly gives you about 13 feet (4 meters) of distance between the power outlet and the camera.

The one tricky aspect of connecting the adapter to the camera is that, once you have the DC coupler inserted into the battery compartment and have closed the door to that compartment, you have to open up a small flap in that door so you can insert the power cord's connector into the DC coupler's jack, as shown in Figure A-5.

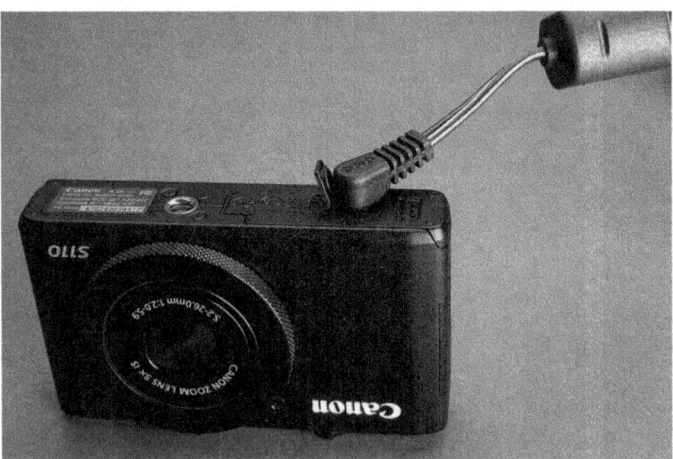

Fig. A-5:   Cord of AC Adapter Going into Camera

It's not obvious how to do this; what you have to do is pull up on a small rubber flap in the battery compartment door. That little flap stays up while the power connector is in the jack.

I should emphasize that providing power to the camera is all this adapter does. It does not act as a battery charger, either for batteries outside of the camera or for batteries while they are installed in the camera. It is strictly a power source for the camera. It may be useful if you are doing extensive indoor work in a studio or laboratory setting, to eliminate the trouble of constantly charging and replacing batteries. It also could be useful if you are recording a long series of movies in a setting where you have access to AC power. And, if you are connecting the camera to your computer in order to upload a large quantity of images or videos, it can be useful to have an endless source of power to complete that process.

However, the AC adapter's cables and power brick are considerably bulkier and heavier than the camera itself, so using the adapter is inconvenient. If you don't have a real need for this setup, I recommend you invest in one or more extra batteries, and perhaps even an extra battery charger, so you can always have a couple of charged batteries ready. In short, the AC adapter should not be considered a high-priority purchase for most photographers.

Add-on Filters and Lenses

There is no way to attach a filter or other add-on item, such as a closeup lens, directly to the lens of the PowerShot S110, as you can with DSLRs and other larger cameras whose lenses are threaded to accept filters and auxiliary lenses. With the S110, in order to add such accessory items, you need to get an adapter. There is no such adapter made by Canon, but enterprising inventors have stepped into the breach. You can obtain a very workable adapter from Lensmate, at lensmateonline.com.

The adapter consists of two parts, as shown in Figure A-6.

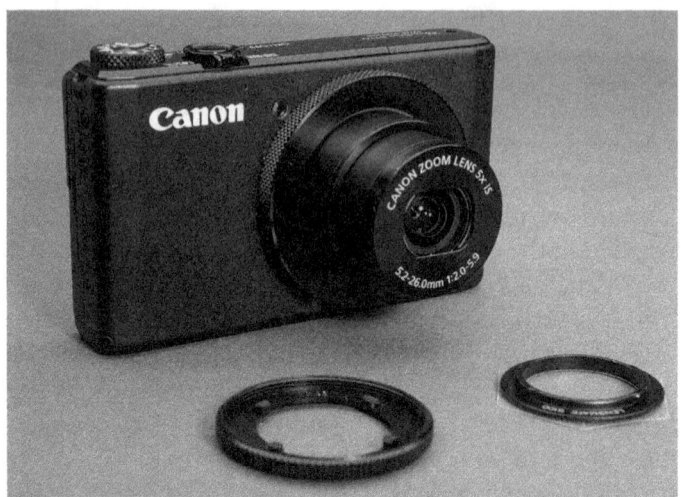

Fig. A-6: Lensmate Filter Adapter Before Installation

The first part, shown on the right in Figure A-6, is a very small plastic ring called the "receiver" that you glue onto the front of the lens barrel, as shown in Figure A-7.

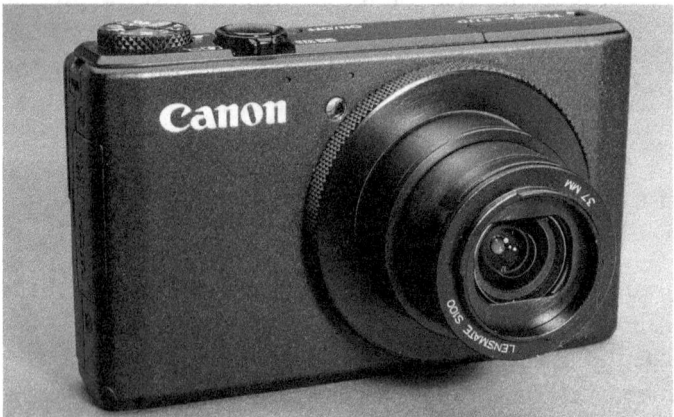

Fig. A-7: Lensmate Receiver Attached to Lens

This piece stays in place and does not interfere with the lens or the automatic lens cover. When you want to use a filter, you attach a larger piece, the "filter holder," which bayonets onto the receiver, as shown in Figure A-8.

376

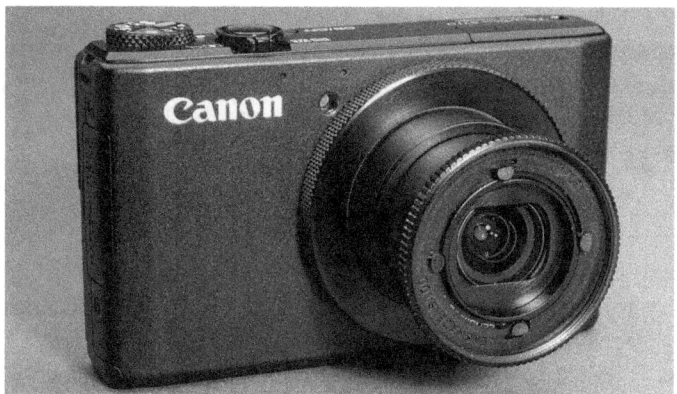

Fig. A-8: *Lensmate Filter Adapter Attached to Receiver*

Then you can screw any 37mm diameter filter or other item into the holder, such as the UV filter shown in Figure A-9.

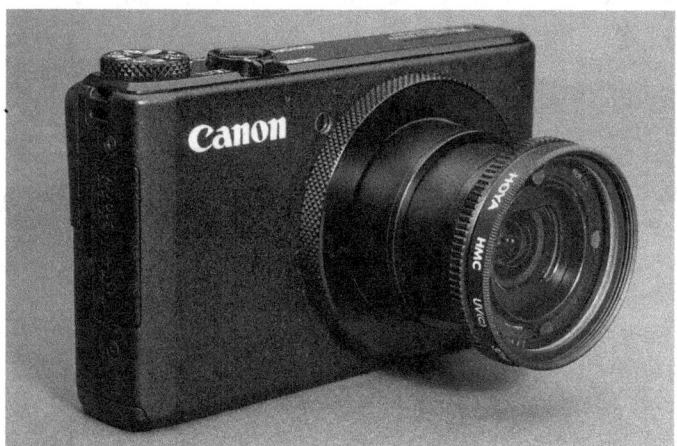

Fig. A-9: *UV Filter Screwed into Filter Adapter*

The receiver is readily removable if you later want to take it off the lens.

As you might expect, this system is not as sturdy as the natural screw-on capability of other cameras, because everything depends on a small plastic ring that is glued in place. So, don't expect to attach large items such as teleconverters or anything

377

heavier than a standard 37mm filter. Just having the ability to attach filters, however, enhances the usefulness of the camera considerably. You can use infrared filters, UV (ultraviolet) filters, polarizers, or any of a wide assortment of closeup lenses, among other items.

External Flash Units

Clearly, Canon did not consider the use of external flash units to be a high priority for users of the PowerShot S110, because the camera does not have an accessory flash shoe on top, as many other advanced compact cameras do. This decision by Canon makes perfect sense for this camera, because one of the virtues of the S110 is its very small size. It would defeat the purpose of designing such a compact camera to load it up with a bulky flash unit that would make the camera top-heavy. Also, it may well be concluded that this camera really does not need a very powerful flash, for a couple of reasons. First, it has a sensor that is very capable of taking excellent pictures in low light, with ISO settings reaching up to 12800.

Second, even apart from the S110's dim-light shooting prowess, for everyday snapshots that are not taken at long distances, the built-in flash should suffice. It works automatically with the camera's light-metering controls to expose the images well, and it is even capable of illuminating bursts of continuous exposures. It is limited by its low power, though. According to Canon, at the wide-angle focal length, the range of the built-in flash is about 23 feet (7 m), and, at the telephoto setting, about 7.5 feet (2.3 m), not very strong.

So, if you will often use the camera to take photos of groups of people in large spaces or otherwise need additional power from your flash, you may need to supplement the built-in unit. Fortunately, there are some options, including two units made by Canon that work with the PowerShot S110. These are the HF-DC1 and HF-DC2 High-Power Flash, similar small units that fit well with the camera in terms of looks and function.

378

These flash units both come with a bracket that attaches to the underside of the camera, using the tripod socket. The flash is then screwed into the bracket, right up against the camera. Either of these units operates as a "slave," meaning that its flash is triggered by the light from the camera's built-in flash. The HF-DC1, shown in Figure A-10, provides more power than the built-in flash (its guide number is 18, meaning its maximum range at ISO 100 is about 18 meters, or 59 feet), and communicates automatically with the camera in the same way that the built-in flash does.

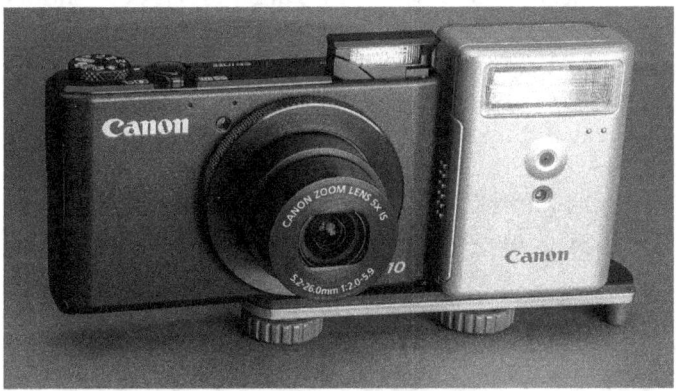

Fig.A-10: Canon HF-DC1 Flash with PowerShot S110

One limitation of the HF-DC1 is that it is a single unit with no rotating flash head, so that, if you mount it right next to the camera on its bracket, there is no possibility of bouncing the flash off of the ceiling or pointing it anywhere other than where the camera is pointing. However, because there is no direct connection between this flash unit and the camera, the flash can be mounted away from the camera, at any location within about 20 feet (6 meters). So, you can place the flash, with its bracket, on a separate tripod, or even hold it in your hand and aim it at the ceiling for a bounce effect.

One reported issue with this unit is that, if you are in a location where other photographers may be firing off flashes from PowerShot cameras, your flash may be triggered by those flashes.

In that event, you can set the HF-DC1 to Manual mode, in which case the flash will not fire unless you hold down the red Test button on the flash while pressing the shutter button on your camera. This system is designed to let you avoid having your flash accidentally triggered by those other flashes.

In my experience, I have had the best results with the HF-DC1 unit using it with the camera set to Manual exposure mode, and taking several test shots until I found the correct exposure. I also found that it worked well when the S110 was set to Aperture Priority mode. When the camera was set to Shutter Priority mode, the flash was too bright and overexposed the image unless I set the ISO to a low value, such as 80. I did not get great results with the camera set to Program or AUTO mode, because the flash tended to be too bright in those modes. However, this external flash does provide a capability for stronger illumination, as long as you are willing to tweak your settings to find the best exposure.

Figure A-11 shows the more recent model HF-DC2, which is very similar to the HF-DC1.

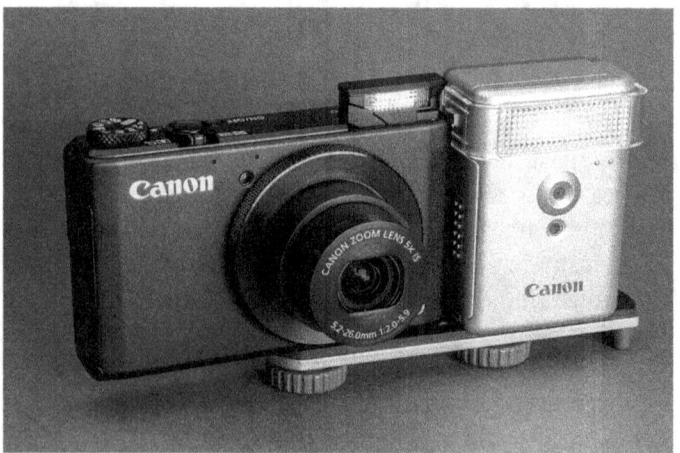

Fig. A-11: Canon HF-DC2 Flash with PowerShot S110

One difference is that the HF-DC2 comes with a diffusing

panel, shown here installed on the flash, for use when the lens is in its wide-angle position. With this unit, as with the HF-DC1, I had the best results with the camera set to Manual exposure mode or to Aperture Priority mode.

If you would like to consider other options for flash, there are some other possibilities. You can get a more powerful external flash unit, such as the Yongnuo Speedlite YN560, whose front and back are pictured in Figure A-12. This unit works well with the PowerShot S110.

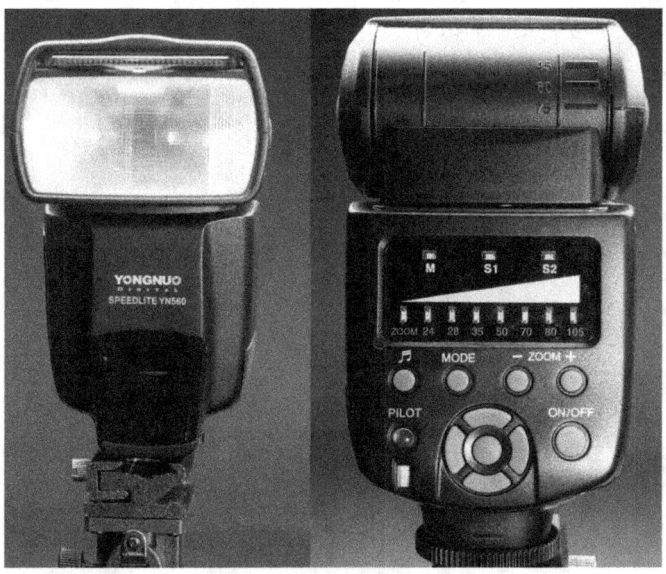

Fig. A-12:   Front and Back of the Yongnuo Speedlite YN560

The Yongnuo YN560 is designed to operate as a slave flash, and has a built-in optical slave capability. To use it with the PowerShot S110, there are two main options. First, you can set the flash to its mode S2. With that setting, the flash ignores the pre-flash that is fired by the PowerShot S110. Therefore, you can use the Yongnuo unit with the S110 set to its non-manual shooting modes, such as Program, Aperture Priority, or Shutter Priority. You probably will have to adjust your settings, and it may be difficult to achieve a good exposure, because the camera's metering system will not take account of the light from the external flash unit.

The technique I like to use is to set the Yongnuo unit to mode S1, in which it does not ignore a pre-flash. In that case, you need to set the PowerShot S110 to Manual exposure mode and set the shutter speed and aperture manually. Once you have found the best settings, you can take advantage of the powerful flash from the Yongnuo unit for enhanced flash images.

Finally, it is worth mentioning that, if you happen to have access to a more powerful studio flash unit, such as the Hensel Integra 500 Plus shown in Figure A-13, the PowerShot S110 is quite capable of triggering that sort of unit, when you turn on the optical slave setting of the flash.

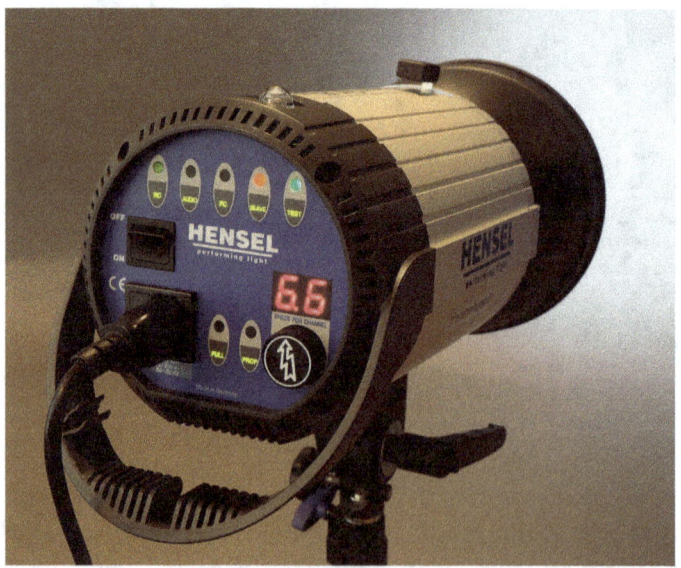

Fig. A-13: Hensel Integra 500 Plus Studio Flash

There again, you have to set the PowerShot to Manual exposure mode so the camera's built-in flash unit does not fire a pre-flash. (Actually, as discussed in Chapter 4, you also could set the PowerShot S110 to either Aperture Priority or Shutter

Priority mode and select Manual for the Flash Mode setting on the Shooting menu; in that case the camera does not fire a pre-flash, and it will trigger the external flash properly. However, the camera's metering system would not gauge the exposure properly, so Manual exposure is the better option to use.)

APPENDIX B: Quick Tips

In this section, I'm going to list some tips and facts that might be useful as reminders, especially to those who are new to digital cameras like the PowerShot S110. My goal is to give you small chunks of information that might help you in certain situations, or that might not be obvious to everyone. I have tried to put down bits of information that you might not remember from day to day, especially if you don't use the S110 constantly.

Use continuous shooting. I recommend that you consider turning continuous shooting on as a matter of routine, unless you are running out of storage space or battery power, or have a particular reason not to use it. In the days of film, burst shooting was expensive and inconvenient, because you had to keep changing film and you had to pay for film and processing. With digital cameras like the S110, it just gives you more options. Even with stationary portraits, you may get the perfect fleeting expression on your subject's face with the fourth or fifth shot. So, press the Func./Set button to call up the Function menu, scroll down to continuous shooting, and turn it on. Remember that continuous shooting is not available in AUTO shooting mode (except for Auto Drive, which is a different sort of setting) and in certain settings of Scene and Creative Filters modes, such as HDR, Handheld Night Scene, and Movie Digest. Also recall that you can shoot more rapidly if you set the camera to the High-Speed Burst HQ setting in Scene mode, but you then lose the ability to make some settings such as white balance, My Colors, and i-Contrast.

Avoid the Shooting menu. You can't completely avoid it, but you can speed up your access to needed settings by placing them on your My Menu list. In some cases, as with flash settings, you can press a button (the Flash button) to get access to the features you need. Also, set the Ring Function button to call up an often-used option. When you do use the Shooting menu, speed through it by using the control dial to move rapidly, and wrap around to reach items that are far from your current position. The touch screen also can speed your access to menu items. Use the Custom shooting mode to set up your most important group of settings. For example, right now I have the C shooting mode slot set up for my latest settings for street photography: Shooting mode = P; ISO = 800; JPEG Large Superfine; My Colors = B/W; lens at full wide-angle setting; Mute on; aspect ratio 4:3; continuous shooting on.

Watch for the Display button's and Menu button's extra functions. There are several options on the S110 that can be tweaked with extra settings by pressing the Display button or the Menu button. In those cases, the Display or Menu button icon will appear on the LCD next to a hint about what setting can be made by pressing the button, but it can be easy to overlook that icon on the small LCD. Here are some of the places to watch for these extra settings: white balance; image size and quality; exposure compensation; Smart Shutter; Color Accent; Color Swap; Miniature Effect; and manual focus.

Use macro shooting for subjects other than nature. Many photographers create beautiful images using the macro ability of the S110, shooting insects, flowers, and other natural items. But, with its focusing down to 1.2 inch (3 cm), its wide-angle lens, and its low-light performance, the S110 can serve you in many other ways with its macro shooting. If you need a quick copy of a shopping list, memo, driving directions, sales receipt, or cancelled check, it might make sense to set the S110's focus mode to macro, maybe boost the ISO to 800 or so, and snap a quick image of it. When you get to your destination, you can display it on the LCD and enlarge it using the zoom lever, then scroll around in the document with the direction buttons. The

S110 becomes a pocketable copy machine, if you need it to.

Don't forget the camera's audio capability. While I'm on the subject of possible business-related and other non-photographic uses of the camera, here is one to consider: Although the camera's audio features are not that strong, it does have a built-in stereo microphone that is quite capable of recording voices clearly. If you need an audio recorder to record a spoken memo or to keep a record of a meeting, set the S110 to Movie mode at the 640 resolution (to give more recording time and use less space on the memory card). Try to aim the voices at the two small holes for the stereo microphone, on the front of the camera just above the Canon logo.

Play your movies in iTunes, and on iPods, iPhones, and iPads. Because the S110's movie files are in the .mov format, which uses Apple Computer's QuickTime software, they are compatible with iTunes. So, it's very easy to play these movies on your computer, if you have downloaded Apple's free iTunes software. Just open a window on your computer to display the icon for a movie file (using Windows Explorer or Macintosh Finder), open iTunes on the same computer, and drag the .mov file from the Explorer or Finder window to the panel for the Library in iTunes. You can then play the movie from iTunes. If you want to play it on an iPod, iPhone, or iPad, you will need to take a few more steps: Select the video in iTunes, then select File from the iTunes menu, and, from that menu item, choose Create New Version, and select iPod or iPhone version or iPad or AppleTV version, as appropriate. Then you can sync iTunes with your device, and the movie will play very nicely on that device.

Explore the S110's creative potential. The PowerShot S110 is a very sophisticated camera, with several advanced features that give you the ability to explore experimental photographic techniques. Here are a few suggestions: Use Manual exposure mode with its shutter speeds as long as 15 seconds to take night-time shots with trails of lights from automobiles, storefronts, and other sources. Use shutter speeds as fast as 1/2000 second to freeze moving motorcycles, track runners, and other speedy subjects in mid-motion. Try "camera tossing," in which you toss the camera in the air, set to a multi-second shutter speed, to capture trails of light and color as the camera spins around. (But be sure to catch it on the way down!) Try panning or otherwise steadily moving the camera during a multi-second exposure. Use long exposures (on a tripod) to turn night into day. Take HDR images with partly blurred subjects, such as blowing flags.

Adjust the camera's color settings. The PowerShot S110 has several settings that can be fine-tuned with further color-related adjustments: white balance, several of the Creative Filters mode varieties (HDR, Nostalgic, Monochrome, Super Vivid, Poster Effect, Color Accent, and Color Swap), and the My Colors feature on the Function menu. Try different settings for each of these until you find color combinations that convey what you would like to express with your images. With white balance, you can achieve unusual effects by purposely setting a custom white balance while aiming at a colored surface rather than a white or gray one.

Take advantage of the Raw format. If you haven't previously used a camera that shoots Raw files, get to know the benefits of this capability and use them to improve your images. Install and use the Digital Photo Professional software that comes with the S110, or use other software, such as Adobe Photoshop or Photoshop Elements, to "develop" the Raw images. Learn how to fix problems with white balance, exposure, and other issues after the fact, using the flexibility of Raw shooting.

Use the neutral density (ND) filter for some shots. There are times when you want a slow shutter speed but, in bright light, you can't achieve it, because the aperture can only go as narrow as f/8. One solution is to use the built-in ND Filter setting on the Function menu to reduce the incoming light so you can use slower shutter speeds. You might want to do this to slow down the rush of a waterfall to a smooth, blended look, or to achieve a motion blur in a shot of a passing runner or walker.

Diffuse your flash. If you find the built-in flash produces light that's too harsh for macro or other shots, try using translucent plastic pieces from milk jugs, other food containers, or broken ping-pong balls as homemade flash diffusers. Just hold the plastic up between the flash and the subject. Another approach you can try when using fill flash outdoors is to use the flash exposure compensation setting on the Shooting menu to reduce the intensity of the flash by -2/3 EV.

Use the self-timer to avoid camera shake. The S110 has a self-timer capability that is very easy to use; just select it from the Function menu and choose your settings. This feature is not just for group portraits; you can use it whenever you'll be using a slow shutter speed and you need to avoid camera shake. It also can be useful when you're doing macro photography, digiscoping, or astrophotography (see next page). And don't forget that you can set the self-timer to take multiple shots, which can increase your chances of getting more great images.

Set zone focusing. If you're doing street photography or are in any other situation in which you want to set the camera on manual focus for a general distance or zone, here is a quick way to do so. Set the focus mode to normal autofocus, then aim the camera at a subject that is approximately the distance at which you want to be able to focus quickly. Once focus has been confirmed, press the left direction button and then select MF from the focus icons that appear on the screen, to select manual focus. Now you will have locked in the manual focus at your chosen distance, and you're ready to shoot any subject at that distance without the need to re-focus.

Experiment with astrophotography and digiscoping. In some of my books about other cameras, I discussed this topic in the main text, but for the PowerShot S110 I'm just including it here in the Quick Tips. That's because this camera is not all that well suited for connecting to a telescope for photographing planets and stars (astrophotography), or for connecting to a spotting scope for photographing wildlife (digiscoping).

Although, as discussed in Appendix A, you can obtain an adapter from Lensmate to attach lightweight items such as filters, the adapter is glued on to the lens barrel and not screwed on as with some other cameras, so it would not be a good idea to rely on that glued piece of plastic to hold the weight of the camera when it's attached to a scope's eyepiece. If you're very careful, it might work, but I don't recommend it.

You also can try taking pictures through a scope's eyepiece by just holding the camera up to the eyepiece. I have tried that approach, with only limited success, but if you're persistent and patient you may be able to get some usable results. I did manage to attach the PowerShot S110, but not very firmly, to a Celestron Regal 80F-ED spotting scope using the Lensmate filter adapter, and I took a few shots through the scope. Figure B-1 shows an image of geese on the other side of a pond. You can see the vignetting that darkened the edges of the image from shooting through the eyepiece and tube.

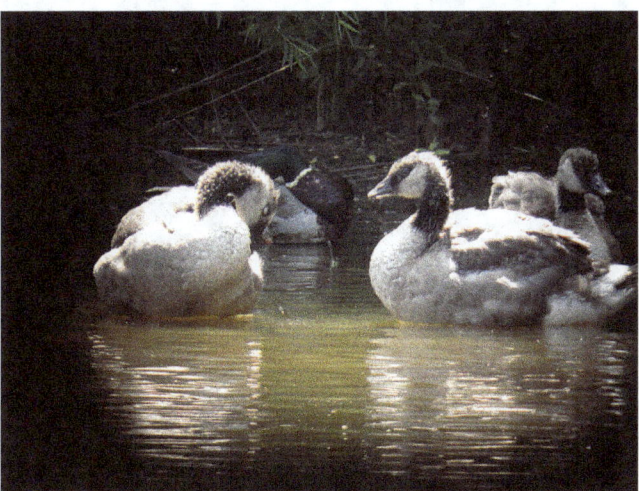

Fig. B-1: Image Taken with S110 Through Celestron Spotting Scope

Figure B-2 is a comparison shot taken with the camera's full optical zoom from the same location, to show how much the scene was magnified by shooting through the spotting scope.

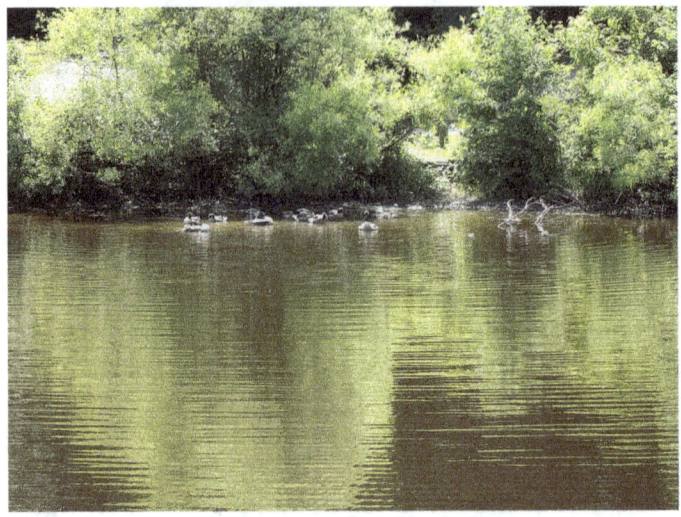

Fig. B-2: Comparison to Digiscoping Shot Taken at Full Optical Zoom

APPENDIX C: Resources for Further Information

Books

Avisit to a good bookstore or a search on Amazon.com will reveal the vast assortment of books about digital photography that is currently available. Rather than trying to compile a long bibliography, I will list a few especially useful books that I consulted while writing this guide.

H. Horenstein, *Digital Photography: A Basic Manual* (Little, Brown 2011)

C. George, *Mastering Digital Flash Photography* (Lark Books, 2008)

C. Harnischmacher, *Closeup Shooting* (Rocky Nook, 2007)

J. Paduano, *The Art of Infrared Photography* (4th ed., Amherst Media, 1998)

Web Sites

Since web sites come and go and change their addresses, it's impossible to compile a list of sites that discuss the PowerShot S110 that will be accurate far into the future. One way to find the latest sites is to use a good search engine such as Google or Bing and type in "Canon PowerShot S110." I just did so in Google and got more than 1.6 million results.

Another approach can be to go to Amazon.com, search for the camera, and read the users' reviews, though you have to be careful to weed out reviews by people who are disgruntled for reasons that don't have anything to do with the product itself. You can also visit a reputable dealer's site, such as that of B&H Photo Video, and read the users' reviews of the camera there. I will include below a list of some of the sites or links I have found useful, with the caveat that some of them may not be accessible by the time you read this.

Digital Photography Review

http://www.dpreview.com/forums/1010

This is the current web address for the "Canon PowerShot Talk" forum within the dpreview.com site. Dpreview.com is one of the most established and authoritative sites for reviews, discussion forums, technical information, and other resources concerning digital cameras.

Reviews of the PowerShot S110

The links below lead to reviews or previews of the PowerShot S110 by dpreview.com, photographyblog.com, cameralabs. com, and others.

http://gizmodo.com/5953242/canon-s110-review-the-best-camera-you-can-fit-in-your-pocket

http://www.dpreview.com/previews/canon-powershot-s110

http://www.cameralabs.com/reviews/Canon_PowerShot_S110/

http://reviews.cnet.co.uk/compact-digital-cameras/canon-powershot-s110-review-50010468/

http://reviews.cnet.com/digital-cameras/canon-power-shot-s110-black/4505-6501_7-35438017.html

http://www.photographyblog.com/reviews/canon_power-shot_s110_review/

http://www.pcmag.com/article2/0,2817,2411206,00.asp

http://www.steves-digicams.com/news/now_live_our_can-on_powershot_s110_camera_reivew.html#b

http://www.imaging-resource.com/PRODS/canon-s110/can-on-s110A.HTM/

http://www.ephotozine.com/article/canon-powershot-s110-review-20901

http://www.pocket-lint.com/review/72995-canon-power-shot-s110-high-end-compact-camera-review

The Official Canon Site

The United States arm of the Canon company provides re-sources on its web site, including the downloadable version of the user's manual for the PowerShot S110 and other technical information.

http://www.usa.canon.com/cusa/consumer/products/cam-eras/digital_cameras/powershot_s110/

Infrared Photography

This site provides some helpful information about infrared photography with digital cameras.

http://www.wrotniak.net/photo/infrared/

Lensmate

This is the site for Lensmate, a company that sells accesso-ries for the PowerShot S110 and other cameras, including an adapter for attaching filters.

http://www.lensmateonline.com/store/s90v2.php

CHDK: Experimental Tinkering

If you are of a deeply curious, scientific bent and don't mind digging into computer programming and other somewhat geeky pursuits, you can delve into, and change, the inner workings of your Canon compact camera with the information at this site. CHDK stands for "Canon Hack Development Kit." The activities discussed at this site require a good deal of detailed work with programming, and they conceivably could cause some damage to the camera; see the FAQ at the site before attempting any alterations to the camera's firmware.

http://chdk.wikia.com/CHDK

Cambridge in Colour

This site offers excellent tutorials on many subjects having to do with digital photography.

http://www.cambridgeincolour.com

Index

Symbols

A

D

T

Y

YouTube
  sending videos to 360

Z

Zone focusing 388
Zoom lever 218
  using to move between menus 164, 219